D1223280

JUDGING THE
FRENCH REFORMATION

JUDGING THE FRENCH REFORMATION

Heresy Trials by Sixteenth-Century Parlements

WILLIAM MONTER

HARVARD UNIVERSITY PRESS

Cambridge, Massachusetts,

and London, England

1999

Library of Congress Cataloging-in-Publication Data

Monter, E. William.
    Judging the French Reformation : heresy trials by sixteenth-
century parlements / William Monter.
        p.   cm.
    Includes bibliographical references and index.
    ISBN 0-674-48860-1 (alk. paper)
        1. Trials (Heresy)—France—History—16th century.
    2. Reformation—France.   I. Title.
    KJV129.H47M66   1999
    345.44′0288—dc21   99-19419

ACKNOWLEDGMENTS

It is a great pleasure to acknowledge the many forms of support I have received while undertaking this project. My greatest single debt is undoubtedly owed to Alfred Soman, the expatriate American who has single-handedly deciphered the heretofore-unreadable handwriting of the *plumitifs,* or prisoner interrogations, of the Paris Parlement. Soman has also revealed the peculiar richness of the almost-unbroken series of jailers' lists of entries and exits, starting in 1564, for the Parlement's prison. At the outset of this enterprise, Soman helped persuade me that it was possible to control all the information in the copious criminal-justice records of the Paris Parlement preserved at the Archives Nationales. His cooperation has been essential and unfailing throughout my sifting of Parisian documents, and his unparalleled mastery of Parisian parlementary evidence has enabled me to make useful comparisons with other French parlements.

Two other active scholars have provided invaluable assistance in exploring the heresy trials preserved in provincial parlementary archives. The pioneering work of Raymond Mentzer with the records left by the Parlement of Toulouse offers a model approach to Reformation-era heresy trials, all the more valuable since some of these records were damaged a few years ago. The works of Gabriel Audisio, peerless connoisseur of the Waldensians of Provence, include much indispensable information about the peculiar history of heresy trials in southeastern France. I have been able to follow their abundant leads and to retrace many of their steps in order to obtain information that can be profitably compared, for example, with Henry Patry's older collection of printed heresy *arrêts* from the Parlement of Bordeaux.

Throughout my scholar's tour through parlementary France, I have relied on the kindness of colleagues to smooth my path in various ways, providing both hospitality and labor-saving clues. The academic year

1992–93, subsidized by a Senior Fellowship from the National Endowment for the Humanities and spent in the suburbs of Paris, enabled me to sift the relevant sources from the Parlement of Paris at the Archives Nationales. Both the late Ellery Schalk and Josef Konvitz provided much practical assistance about the art of living and working in the Paris area. In 1994 a Guggenheim Fellowship made it possible to read through the relevant heresy *arrêts* from the parlements of Rouen, Aix, and Grenoble, while a fellowship from the Camargo Foundation at Cassis provided splendid living quarters for research time in Provence. Outside the capital, Jean-Pierre Dedieu introduced me to Bordeaux, and Bartolomé Bennassar helped at Toulouse. American colleagues have also rendered assistance: Philip Benedict told me how to explore the archives profitably at Rouen, while my former student Jim Farr did the same for Dijon. Jean Delumeau provided an unforgettable opportunity to summarize my Parisian findings before a distinguished audience at the Collège de France in 1994 (published in revised form in the *Bulletin de la Société pour l'histoire du Protestantisme francais* 142 [1996], 191–223).

A special thanks is due to my Chicago-area colleague George Huppert, who did much to persuade me that an ambitious project in sixteenth-century French history would be both feasible and pleasant; many years later, he provided a sympathetic reading of the manuscript. An even greater debt is owed to a friend of even longer standing, Alain Dufour of Geneva, who has tried patiently to correct some of my misrepresentations of France in the early 1560s. My wife, Rosellen, and younger daughter, Andrea, have supported the entire enterprise with unfailing patience and good cheer, confronting the challenges of shuttling daily life, work, and public school between two continents over several years. Rosellen also prepared the map of French parlementary districts and heresy executions. My late mother, Florence Monter, provided her own forms of encouragement throughout the waning years of her life; this work is dedicated to her.

CONTENTS

TABLES

MAP

JUDGING THE
FRENCH REFORMATION

Introduction

This book represents the first attempt to explore fully the prolonged legal clash between the largest state in Renaissance Europe and the sixteenth-century Protestant Reformation. It provides a fresh angle from which to study the French Reformation, by presenting the first complete account of governmental attempts to repress it through what was probably the best-run, and certainly the most prestigious, secular court system in Europe. For forty years after Luther first appeared on the international horizon in 1520, the French appellate courts made frequent, strenuous, and ultimately futile efforts to control the "Lutheran" movement. It is a fascinating story, resembling the proverbial collision between an irresistible force and an immovable object. In this instance, the self-confident legal guardians of French tradition, including religious tradition, encountered the most dynamic forms of the Protestant Reformation, and the high courts of Renaissance France unhesitatingly opposed these religious innovators. In the 1520s the largest and most prestigious tribunal, the Parlement of Paris, seemed far more eager than the French king to criminalize the new movement and to punish its adherents. By the early 1530s the major provincial parlements had followed suit. By 1540 the French monarchy had largely removed the prosecution of heresy from ecclesiastical courts and handed it to the parlements; heresy trials and executions escalated dramatically. But twenty years later the irresistible force had overcome the immovable object: French appellate courts abandoned the prosecution of Protestant heresy. The intensive prosecution of French heretics gradually diminished during the 1550s, before de facto decriminalization occured suddenly in mid-1560, through the intervention of Catherine de Médicis. Even during the multiple civil wars that soon followed, French courts never resumed heresy trials on any significant scale.

The tale that emerges from reading French judicial sources, showing the Protestants gradually eroding the stubborn traditionalism of their kingdom's legal system, exactly reverses the standard account of religious persecution. French Protestant authors, primarily in the famous martyrology by Jean Crespin in the mid-1550s and the semiofficial *Ecclesiastical History of the French Reformed Church* (first printed in 1580), maintained that repression of heresy increased in proportion to the numbers and organization of Protestant churches in Valois France. But these books—both produced in Geneva—told the story of repression backward. They erred through sheer ignorance. Because their authors worked outside France, their information was extremely haphazard and incomplete for the period before prominent French refugees (including Crespin and the principal author of the *Ecclesiastical History*) arrived in Calvin's Geneva at the end of the 1540s. But once Reformed churches, in constant contact with Geneva, operated in France, these Protestant chroniclers possessed excellent information. Knowing a great deal about the legal repression of Protestantism in the later 1550s, but relatively little about what had happened before 1550 apart from a few spectacular incidents, Crespin and the Genevans inadvertently reversed the story. In Reformation France the legal repression of "Lutheranism" varied inversely, not directly, with the growth of the Protestant movement. The ultimate judicial consequence of the full development of French Reformed churches by 1560 was not a holocaust, but the virtual breakdown of the French legal system.

Despite the significance of the topic, no one—not even in France—has ever tried to investigate the history of the French Reformation before the Wars of Religion by examining all of the myriad encounters between Protestants and judges in French parlements. My research design has been simple: I have attempted to locate every preserved bit of information about the heresy trials conducted by French parlements from 1523 to 1560, paying particular attention to any public executions for heresy mentioned in either printed or archival sources, and continuing with extensive sampling during the early religious wars of the following decade. In 1990 a well-intentioned scholar tried to explain to me why such a project would be impossible to accomplish. The records from the Parlement of Paris alone seemed too vast to be covered satisfactorily, since their criminal decisions survive in abundance after 1535, but always in haphazard order and with no usable indexes of any sort. Extending the investigation to cover the entire kingdom of France seemed an even more utopian goal, since between eight and ten parlements operated from 1536 until 1560, and none offered useful shortcuts to exploring its archives. A novice quickly understands why there are so few empirical investigations of sixteenth-century French criminal justice, and why no one has ever undertaken something as important as the legal treatment of Protestant heretics by French royal courts on a national level.

Nonetheless, with scholarly and financial help from many sources, I have completed my archival tour of parlementary France from Francis I to Francis II. Several visits from 1992 to 1998, totaling about two years of archival digging, yielded up the surviving evidence from various parts of France. In order to do judicial history at the national level in early modern France, one must begin in Paris, but one must never confuse Paris with France: the *ressort,* or judicial district, dependent upon the Parlement of Paris covered approximately half the kingdom. Following the tracks left by Raymond Mentzer (but handicapped by a recent outbreak of archival arson), I then explored records from Toulouse, the kingdom's second-largest parlement. Other provincial archives sometimes provided pleasant surprises, such as the nearly complete set of criminal judicial rulings, or *arrêts,* from the short-lived Parlement of Chambéry (1536–1559).

In order to compare the rulings from various French parlements with minimal distortion, I have concentrated on official sentences involving prisoners charged with some form of heresy, supplemented by published accounts from Crespin's martyrology and by the few but precious parlementary accounts of interrogations of prisoners charged with heresy. This approach sheds light on the various strategies employed by judges, but privileges only the part of their legal business that I believe to be crucial. I have paid little attention to the numerous provisional or "interlocutory" sentences, which reveal various procedural problems (such as unavailability of essential documents or of testimony from key witnesses, appeals to be transferred to a different jurisdiction, or decisions to torture a prisoner) that delayed the final outcome of a trial. Such decisions prove that someone had been imprisoned for heresy and that the case had been appealed to a parlement, but almost none of them enable us to determine the probable outcome.

I have also discriminated between suspects charged with heresy and those judged in person by these courts; investigating and condemning absentees was a very different matter from interrogating and sentencing live prisoners. Extremely rare in the 1540s, heresy trials of absentees became quite common in the later 1550s, when large numbers of them fill the pages of criminal *arrêts* from several parlements. For example, although Mentzer counted nearly eighty accused heretics at Toulouse in 1559, sixty of them never appeared before the Parlement; only two prisoners received any form of public punishment that year, while sixteen were released with warnings.[1] Rather than authentic trials, these episodes reveal the French legal system granting hunting licenses to interested subjects, enabling them to take legal possession of assets left behind by Protestants who had fled France. Official condemnations rarely included public punishments of effigies representing refugees, because they advertised the judiciary's inability to capture prominent heretics.

As far as possible, I have also tried to discriminate between prisoners charged with heresy and numerous cases of those indicted for related crimes, principally blasphemy and sacrilege. Thus, an official sentence for "execrable" blasphemy, as opposed to "heretical" blasphemy, offers fascinating clues about how seriously sixteenth-century judges regarded other kinds of *lèse-majesté divine,* or treason against God, but it should not count as an indictment for Protestantism. On the other hand, the adjective "sacramentarian" applied to official charges of blasphemy invariably connotes Protestantism. Fortunately, nearly all cases in which defendants received severe punishments for blasphemy can be sorted into one of these two categories. Similarly, cases of severe punishments for sacrilege sometimes seem ambiguous. Although responsible Protestant leaders condemned iconoclasm, I have included those few pre-1560 instances in which Protestants were executed for wanton destruction of relics or hosts. When several charges are combined in a final sentence, the judges normally listed the most serious charge first, and I have tried to follow their lead. Heresy was occasionally combined with other offenses, but before 1560 it usually stood alone, and it almost always took priority over other charges.

While expanding the subject of heresy trials from Paris to the rest of the French kingdom, I encountered some differences between the "style" (as sixteenth-century sources call it) of the Paris tribunal and those practiced elsewhere. For example, because the city of Marseille claimed the privilege of having all its citizens judged within its walls, the Parlement of Provence left Aix to sit there for one week every year, usually in March. The strangest local custom was followed by the Parlement of Normandy, which each year permitted the cathedral chapter of Rouen to pardon one condemned criminal at the feast of St. Romain.[2] The southern parts of France, hunting grounds of papal inquisitors since the thirteenth century, handled heresy trials a bit differently from northern tribunals until the mid-1530s, but not thereafter. Such local curiosities, however, do not outweigh the basic operational similarities among all French parlements in criminal matters, including cases of heresy.

Those similarities lay not where I originally expected to find them, in united obedience to royal legislation throughout the kingdom, but rather in the "arbitrary" methods used by each parlement to judge criminal cases. The history of sixteenth-century French heresy trials fits awkwardly with the history of sixteenth-century French heresy legislation, and learning what the judges did seems far more important than studying what the decrees urged them to do. The numerous royal edicts concerning the repression of heresy were rarely applied in uniform manner throughout the kingdom, and most of them proved completely ineffective; only the Edict of Fontainebleau (June 1540), which transferred laymen accused of heresy from church courts to parlements, significantly affected the entire kingdom. The really important uniformity lay in French criminal procedures, overhauled by the Edict of Villers-Cotterets in 1539 and applied throughout the kingdom in fundamentally identical fashion by judges trained in Roman law.

Records of French parlementary criminal *arrêts* are incomplete everywhere, but they are usually abundant enough to provide satisfactory general patterns of their activities. The two largest tribunals, Paris and Toulouse, have preserved about four-fifths of their criminal decisions between 1540 and 1560. Two of the smallest parlements, Chambéry and Grenoble, boast the most complete records. The criminal *arrêts* of three important provincial parlements (Rouen, Aix, and Bordeaux) have sizable lacunae between 1535 and 1560; however, enough evidence survives at all three places to permit plausible estimates of the dimensions and chronology of their antiheresy campaigns. For various reasons, no criminal *arrêts* from this period survive for the parlements of Dijon or Rennes. Only one slender volume of criminal decisions survives from the French Parlement of Turin (opened in 1539 and dissolved, together with

Chambéry, in 1559), and its *arrêts* on heresy cases were published long ago.[3] Outside Paris, only the Norman Parlement has preserved any *plumitifs*, the interrogations of prisoners, from the period of heresy trials.

To be described satisfactorily, the heresy trials of Reformation France must first be set in two very different comparative contexts: heresy must be seen in relation to other sixteenth-century crimes judged in France, and France must be seen in relation to other states of Reformation Europe. The first two chapters survey these topics.[4] The core of the book chronicles the major phases in the French parlements' campaigns against Protestantism and sketches the shifting relationships between the legal repression of heresy and the history of the French Reformation. Beginning with the first attempt by the Parlement of Paris in 1523 to depict a crazy hermit as a "Lutheran," in the story divides at four threshold dates: 1540 (Edict of Fontainebleau and escalating royal prosecution of heresy), 1549 (end of the special antiheresy branch of the Paris Parlement and early emigration to Geneva), 1555 (Crespin's martyrology and clandestine pastors in France), and 1560 (effective decriminalization of heresy after the Edict of Amboise). Thereafter a bewildering sequence of shifts in royal policy created a peculiar legal situation for Reformed Protestants, which endured with few interruptions throughout the French Wars of Religion. Although public worship was nearly always permitted under certain restrictions, Huguenots were prosecuted by judges for sedition and often lynched by Catholic mobs for their heresy. French parlements, previously central actors in campaigns against Protestantism, were now confined to marginal roles. My account ends in the 1590s with the near-collapse of French parlements, squeezed between the Holy League and the Salic law.

An analytic chapter probes the often abortive dialogues between parlementary judges and accused Protestants, which have been reported in grotesquely different ways (and words) by court clerks and by Protestant martyrologists. Under the conventions of arbitrary justice, the judges offered very few clues about their motives in assigning punishments, whereas martyrologists made the prisoners' motives utterly transparent, even under implausible circumstances. An appendix offers a list and map of every documented heresy execution ordered in the kingdom of France from 1523 through 1560. Afterward, remarkably few Huguenots were executed for the crime of heresy by French parlements.

1

Criminal Justice in Sixteenth-Century France

It is not necessary that every crime be punished. There would not be enough judges, nor enough executioners. So it ordinarily happens that, of ten crimes, only one ever gets punished by the judges; and usually only scum *[belistres]* get condemned.
                    —*Jean Bodin,* Démonomanie des sorciers *(1580)*

We are about to enter a system of criminal justice that the French themselves abandoned long ago, and have mostly forgotten. Both of its key concepts, "enormous" crimes and "arbitrary" justice, seem equally alien today; the first lacks meaning for modern readers, while the second is misleading. However, a thorough understanding of both concepts is essential to understand how heresy trials were conducted in Reformation France. The first category—*cas énormes,* in the lexicon of sixteenth-century jurists—provides its substance: this book attempts to describe how French royal courts judged the offense of heresy, certainly an "enormous" crime during the Protestant Reformation. The other concept, "arbitrary" legal decisions, provides the method through which sixteenth-century French criminal courts actually judged and punished prisoners, whether charged with "enormous" or with less spectacular offenses.

An efficient and fair-minded royal justice provided a fundamental prop supporting any sixteenth-century government. France, the largest monarchy in Christendom, had long drawn support and genuine popularity from the operations of its court system; it was a venerated French maxim that "the king is most royal when sitting in justice" on behalf of his subjects. The tradition of the king as the fountainhead of true justice had developed most impressively under Louis IX in the mid-thirteenth century. The image of this saintly monarch sitting beneath an oak tree near Vincennes, listening to complaints from his subjects and ordering his councillors to examine each case, became an enduring French legend.[1] In reality, Louis IX created the Parlement of Paris in 1263 to arbitrate legal problems throughout his domains. In order to combat heresy, he also supported the introduction of papal inquisitors in his recently conquered southern provinces of Languedoc. Moreover, he literally fought heresy by going on two crusades against muslim infidels. His grandson, the devout but very unsaintly Philip the Fair (1285–1314), was routinely addressed by his officials as *Rex christianissimus*, the "most Christian king." The term stuck.[2] The title "most Christian king" and the reputation of the king as the fountainhead of justice for his subjects reinforced each other for many centuries.

What kind of justice did the most Christian king of France offer in the sixteenth century, and how did his appointed judges administer it? The simplest and most logical way to begin answering such questions is to study operations at the very summit of French civil and criminal justice, the parlements. As their members proudly noted, these were "sovereign" courts whose final judgments could not be appealed; although the king always reserved his theoretical right to alter any decision or to pardon any convicted criminal, in practice these appellate judges were allowed to conduct business as they saw fit. Because French criminal procedures were based firmly on Roman law and uniform throughout the kingdom, the judges who sat in sixteenth-century French parlements had to be very well trained. Although judicial posts were sold in Renaissance France, sixteenth-century French parlements also required entrance examinations,[3] and promotions were often based on merit. The career of Jean de Selve furnishes a remarkable early example under Francis I: starting as a judge at the Parlement of Toulouse, he became president of the Norman Exchequer (direct ancestor of the Rouen Parlement), then First President of the Parlement of Bordeaux, and finished his career (after stints as vice-chancellor at Milan and ambassador to England) as First President of the Parlement of Paris.[4] Professional reputations could determine judicial careers; heredity, so crucial to judicial promotion by the end of the century, as yet counted for little. André Tiraqueau acquired enough fame through his juristic publications that he refused a seat in the Parlement of Bordeaux, waiting six years for a call to Paris.[5] At Toulouse, the law professor Jean de Boysonné's professional standing enabled him to overcome a public abjuration for heresy and to earn a seat in a parlement only seven years later.[6]

Not only was the parlementary judiciary of Valois France a meritocracy based on careful study of Roman law, but its members were fully interchangeable. A good example occurred after Henry II abolished the Parlement of Bordeaux in October 1548 for its vacillating behavior during a revolt. Punishment of the Bordeaux judges did not deprive the king's subjects living within their district, or *ressort,* of an appellate court. A substitute tribunal was created by drawing ten judges from the Parlement of Paris, eight from the Parlement of Toulouse, and six from the Parlement of Rouen.[7] Since they were not particularly eager to serve in a distant place, no tribunal actually reopened in Bordeaux until the end of August 1549. Only two Parisians, four Normans, and four Languedoc judges had reported for work, and they sat in Bordeaux for barely four months, until the old Parlement was restored on 7 January 1550. Like bishops, parlementary judges could be transferred from one location to another. Judges were often not natives of the region they served; when Francis I created a parlement to serve his newly conquered province of Savoy in 1536, he appointed only two Savoyards among its twelve judges.[8] One new judge, Pomponne de Bellièvre, was the son of the First President at Grenoble and eventually became chancellor of France; another (Boysonné) was a recently convicted heretic. As an italophile Renaissance monarch, Francis I cheerfully placed Italians on his appellate courts; the chief justice at Toulouse when Boysonné was condemned for heresy, formerly the second-ranking judge at Bordeaux, had been born in Milan.[9]

"Enormous" Crimes in Long-Term Perspective

In order to grasp the French legal response to the sixteenth-century heresy called "Lutheranism," we need to place it in the context of French criminal justice. Standing at the summit of the royal legal system, parlementary judges situated this new and dangerous offense in the context of other crimes that they regarded as peculiarly heinous and thus punished with maximum severity. Although "Lutheranism" was a novel offense, and the parlements' concern with cases of heresy—which seems a quintessentially religious offense—was unprecedented, they could judge and punish it by analogy to other crimes that bore a partial resemblance to it, working from the known toward the unknown.

Modern scholars have frequently observed that sixteenth-century secular justice did not try to distinguish clearly between the concepts of sin and crime. A parlementary ruling from 1554 talked about the "*sin* of sodomy" on one line, and in the next justified the final sentence on the ground of "the enormity and detestation of the said *crime* of sodomy."[10] Sixteenth-century jurists often used the concept of *cas énormes* to describe the most serious infractions that incorporated elements of both sin and crime. Although they rarely defined this term with any degree of precision, they assumed that everyone knew well enough what they meant. These were crimes peculiarly odious to the public interest, entailing a remarkable amount of scandal. Most fell into one of two categories. Some of them infringed religious values to an exceptional degree; using an analogy to high treason, jurists and judges described them as *lèse-majesté divine,* divine treason. This concept included offenses both of word and of deed. Treasonous speech against God and Christianity, for example, included not only the crime of heresy but also the most extreme and elaborate forms of blasphemy, usually qualified by French jurists as "execrable" (but without giving concrete examples of what had been said, because such words did not need to be written down and remembered). Treasonous deeds against God and the Christian religion involved the most extreme forms of sacrilege and iconoclasm, the theft and destruction of sacred relics, and especially of that holiest of objects, the Eucharist.

The nonreligious group of "enormous" crimes usually infringed some basic moral taboo. Most of them involved physical violence against members of one's immediate family: the murder of a spouse, infanticide, or incest. However, two other types of "enormous" crime reached beyond such a simple definition by intermingling religious and secular offenses. Witchcraft was performed with diabolical assistance and therefore bore some theological resemblance to heresy, but it also involved concrete damage to people or property. "Sodomy," a hybrid offense that included both homosexuality and bestiality, drew its name from the book of Genesis; its "enormity" came from the belief that both such forms of unnatural sexual intercourse offended the Creator as well as the public. Burning made sense as appropriate punishment for convicted arsonists, a few of whom were in fact executed by this method; arson was the only type of *cas énorme* with no religious or sexual dimension.

What criteria best enable us to fit such a heterogenous mixture of offenses under a single rubric? If we follow the practices of sixteenth-century justice rather than studying its theories, we will find two purely legal aspects shared by all types of *cas énormes,* but by no other groups of criminal offenses. First, these cases were always recorded as being prosecuted by public authorities rather than private plaintiffs. This detail was more than a legal formality, because it relieved the king's subjects of the trouble and cost of bringing such suits (of course, it also made it impossible for a plaintiff to claim damages). The old French term for criminal law was *droit privé,* private law, because most ordinary criminal suits—normally over such matters as thefts and physical assaults, or even homicides—were brought by private individuals; however, "enormous" offenses engaged the public interest and were therefore invariably brought by public officials. The second criterion distinguishing the *cas énormes* is very simple: those convicted were executed and their bodies burned (a few of them were burned to death). Capital punishment was widespread throughout sixteenth-century Europe; travelers entering towns were frequently greeted by skulls stuck on gates. This extreme severity in public punishments was a deliberate policy of governments and their court systems; jurists explained that maximum severity and maximum publicity provided necessary deterrents, intended to frighten potential wrongdoers in a society that had nothing resembling modern police forces. But such considerations do not explain why French courts, like most others throughout Europe, burned people who had been convicted of "enormous" crimes against God or humanity. They were punished in this manner because of very ancient notions about ritual purification occurring through fire.

How often were corpses of French prisoners burned during the sixteenth century, and for which offenses? The Norman Parlement of Rouen offers a useful pattern of punishments for "enormous" crimes during the earliest period when its criminal records become sufficiently abundant. (See Table 1.) Recorded burnings per decade correspond roughly to the amount of information available: by the 1590s, slightly fuller criminal-case records yield a few more burnings, and each sample suggests that four or five prisoners per year were punished in this manner. In these samples, among 101 executions for "enormous" crimes, only one man and one woman were ordered to be burned alive. Both cases occurred in the 1550s. One was an ecstatic prophet and cult leader who had come to Normandy from Flanders; the other had murdered her husband with the complicity of a priest.

By far the leading crime for which corpses were condemned to be

Table 1.   Burnings for "enormous" crimes at Rouen, 1550s–1590s

Offense	1550s	1570s	1590s
Heresy	12	0	0
Blasphemy	1	0	1
Sacrilege	3	0	2
Witchcraft	0	2	7
Infanticide	10	30	26
Homosexuality	1	1	0
Murdering spouse	1	0	0
Incest	0	1	2
Poisoning	0	1	0

Source: Surviving criminal *arrêts* in ADSM, 1B 3138–51 for the 1550s, 1B 3165–86 for the 1570s, and 1B 3216–35 and 5720–29 for the 1590s. I have added three burnings for heresy ordered in the Rouen *plumitifs* for 1552 and 1553 (ADSM, 1B 3004), from a period for which the *arrêts* are missing.

Note: Figures reflect the percentages of *arrêts* preserved: 62% for the 1550s, 75% for the 1570s, and 90% for the 1590s.

burned, accounting for two-thirds of the overall total, was infanticide. It was exclusively a woman's crime, and almost the only "enormous" crime for which women were convicted and burned. Both women burned for the crime of incest had also been convicted of infanticide, whereas only three women were burned as witches. After the 1556 royal edict was registered at Rouen, employing procedures that made legal proof of infanticide easier, convictions for this offense far outpaced those for all other "enormous" crimes together. However, the Parlement's criminal rulings do not fit modern notions about gender stereotyping. For example, although witchcraft was overwhelmingly a woman's crime, at Rouen six of the nine people in this sample who were hanged and burned for *sortilège* were men.[11] Poisoning has also been stereotyped as a woman's crime, but the lone burning in this sample involved a man.[12] On the other hand, although men were likelier than women to murder their spouse, the only person in our sample burned for this offense was a woman.[13]

Although the Parlement of Rouen ordered fewer than thirty men to have their corpses burned during these thirty years, they had been convicted of seven different categories of "enormous" crimes. Several crimes involving *lèse-majesté divine* were reserved for men: heresy, sacrilege, and blasphemy. In this sample, two aspects of extreme religious crimes emerge sharply. First, in the 1550s nearly half of all posthumous burnings resulted from heresy convictions, although this offense disappears completely from subsequent samples. This statistical correlation is as sharp and sudden as the mushrooming convictions for infanticide after 1556, but more mysterious. We know that the growing Protestant movement, which was extremely strong in Normandy, preoccupied the French monarchy around 1560. The French Wars of Religion broke out in 1562 and, with several interruptions, lasted until 1598. Yet, as religious conflicts intensified in Normandy, burnings for heresy disappeared from the arsenal of punishments used at Rouen. Subsequent chapters will explore this paradox in depth across the kingdom of France.

Meanwhile, throughout the sixteenth century and beyond, the Parlement of Rouen occasionally punished other forms of *lèse-majesté divine* with fire. Because they did not punish the vast majority of criminal cases that involved either blasphemy or sacrilege with burning, we need to examine exactly which forms of these offenses were being sanctioned in this manner. Let us first consider sacrilege, a relatively common charge among Norman criminal trials as early as the 1530s, when four registers provide ten such instances within two years.[14] All but one of the men charged with sacrilege were appealing death sentences, though only two had been condemned to be burned as well as hanged. Both condemnations involving burnings were upheld by the Parlement, but neither sentence tells us why this punishment was inflicted.[15] In the other eight cases, the charge of sacrilege clearly referred to the theft of some object inside a church. Three hangings were upheld; four sentences were reduced, three of them to service in the galleys; and one prisoner was returned for a new trial.

Later sixteenth-century evidence suggests that only very specific forms of extreme sacrilege, usually involving desecration of consecrated Hosts, induced French parlements to order a defendant's corpse burned. Jean Papon's collection of noteworthy decisions described a case of sacrilege "in the first degree" that deserved such a punishment: the defendant had stamped his foot upon a *custode* full of consecrated Hosts in order to break it into smaller pieces of gold and silver that could be resold to jewelers.[16] A case judged at Rouen in 1552 closely fits his description, while another defendant had simply stolen the Hosts.[17] One man hanged and burned for sacrilege in the 1590s had broken a *custode* and spilled the holy oil; the other seems to have been an obstinate Protestant who "unworthily took a Host in his hand, threw it on the ground, and wiped his tongue with the same hand," as well as "committing several other impieties and indignities against the Holy Catholic Church."[18]

The ordinary contours of the crime of blasphemy in Normandy during the 1530s seem as clear as those concerning sacrilege. By itself, blasphemy was never a capital crime, even though it was sometimes listed first among multiple charges against a prisoner. Its principal legal function seems to have been as an auxiliary accusation, permitting the judges to impose aggravated punishments upon men convicted of other offenses; for example, one of the two men hanged and burned for sacrilege was also convicted of blasphemy. In the 1530s a blasphemy conviction entailed a special and unique form of punishment: the hangman pierced the criminal's tongue with a hot iron. The Norman Parlement ordered this ritual performed six times during the ten months from September 1538 through July 1539, five times just before hanging someone.[19] The sixth man was charged with "scandalous speech" against the Virgin Mary and blasphemy against God; the Parlement cancelled his banishment, but upheld, in addition to piercing his tongue, the provision that he spend two hours on a scaffold in front of the main church of Caen, carrying a lighted taper and "asking, in a loud voice, forgiveness from God and the Virgin Mary."[20] Interestingly, the only time that the Rouen judges added piercing the tongue to a lower court's sentence, their prisoner was a nobleman charged with several violent crimes, and the prosecutor had appealed the original sentence as overly lenient.[21]

Parlementary explanations for capital punishment on charges of blasphemy seem extremely laconic. In 1552 a saddlemaker whose lower-court punishment (piercing the tongue, whipping, perpetual banishment from the kingdom) had been appealed as overly mild was hanged and burned for his "blasphemies and scandalous speech." Forty years later, the royalist Parlement sitting at Caen condemned a man from St.-Lô (a notorious Huguenot stronghold) for "repeated and execrable blasphemies tending toward impiety and atheism" against God, the Virgin Mary, the saints, and the apostles.[22] Understandably, the Rouen judges were reluctant to repeat in writing the oaths that they found peculiarly and exceptionally offensive; moreover, their punishments for "treasonous" speech against God sometimes included the provision that a record of the trial be burned together with the prisoner's corpse. One burned an official record in order to erase public memory of the crime, just as burning the corpse supposedly erased the culprit's physical remains.

In France the habit of punishing treason against God and other "enormous" crimes with burning endured for a remarkably long time. The French monarchy had acquired precocious firsthand experience in burning criminals as early as 1022, when the king and queen attended the first recorded heresy executions in Latin Europe. The traditions behind the coronation oath, in which the "most Christian" French monarchs swore to uproot heresy, were extremely long-lived. The condemnation and execution of François-Jean de La Barre on charges of impiety, blasphemy, and sacrilege in 1766 provides an unusually late instance of capital punishment for *lèse-majesté divine*.[23] The case against him and two other defendants began after a crucifix was found mutilated on a public road at Abbéville in August 1765; soon afterwards a second crucifix was found covered with excrement. It took only three days for the local royal prosecutor to notify the local appellate court and receive permission to open an investigation. Abundant testimony was soon gathered, completed by *monitoires* read from the pulpits of Abbéville's parish churches on three consecutive Sundays, obliging listeners to declare any relevant information about these outrages to the appropriate authorities on pain of both spiritual and temporal punishment. A week after the third *monitoire,* the octogenarian bishop of Amiens presided over an expiatory ceremony at Abbéville, kneeling bareheaded in front of the mutilated crucifix and pronouncing an *amende honorable,* a formal public apology, which he had written himself. A second official inquiry opened five days later.

Three of Abbéville's most privileged youths were implicated; La Barre, just turning twenty, was the oldest and the only nobleman. He was also the only outsider, having moved to Abbéville four years earlier to be raised by his aunt, an extremely worldly nonresident abbess, in her town house. The other principal suspect, d'Etallonde, was the sixteen-year-old son of the second-ranking judge of Abbéville's *présidial,* or regional court. Much gossip soon accumulated against the two older youths and a boy named Moisnel. By late September the court had issued arrest warrants against all three. The judge's son had fled, but La Barre and Moisnel were arrested four days later. At his first hearing, La Barre admitted many forms of impious behavior, but accused his absent friend of mutilating the crucifix; however, he had no alibi for the night the other crucifix was desecrated. His aunt had meanwhile removed and burned the shelf full of pornographic novels that La Barre called his "private shrine," but left behind his copy of Voltaire's *Portable Philosophical Dictionary,* which the judges promptly confiscated. The younger boy broke down at his second interrogation, accusing d'Etallonde of mutilating the crucifix and admitting singing blasphemous songs. After lengthy delays, the three defendants were sentenced at Abbéville in February 1766. The royal prosecutor recommended a death sentence with aggravation (cutting off the right hand) for the absent d'Etallonde, who was now living outside France; for La Barre, he recommended a public *amende honorable* for his blasphemous songs, impious books, and his sacrilegious behavior, followed by perpetual service in the galleys; young Moisnel, he thought, deserved a warning and a fine. The judges, however, went even further. First, they ordered d'Etallonde burned alive. La Barre was to be tortured beforehand to obtain additional information about his accomplices; he should then perform his public *amende,* after which the executioner would pierce his tongue with a hot iron before beheading him. Afterward La Barre's body and head were to be burned on a pyre, with his copy of Voltaire's book also thrown onto the flames. Moisnel was to watch La Barre's execution before receiving his official warning.

Since 1670, any sentence involving severe physical punishment was automatically appealed to the nearest parlement. The fate of La Barre and Moisnel was not decided until June, when, to the surprise of many observers (since La Barre's aunt was distantly related to a major figure in the Parlement), the Parlement of Paris confirmed the Abbéville sentence. Although the bishop of Amiens tried to have La Barre's life spared, Louis XV refused to issue a pardon. Referring to his futile recent attempt to stop the trial of his would-be assassin, the king reportedly remarked that someone charged with treason against God should not be treated more leniently than someone accused of treason against a monarch.

On 1 July 1766, after everyone had waited all day for a last-second pardon that never arrived, La Barre's torture and execution were carried out exactly as ordered, while officials burned a cardboard effigy of d'Etallonde. Before being tortured, La Barre admitted defiling the crucifix in the cemetery; under torture, he admitted that another youth (who was never arrested) had accompanied him. The public *amende* went off smoothly; the executioner, after symbolically passing his sword in front of La Barre's mouth, cut off his head cleanly at the first blow. At Abbéville, few mourned his passing. But a shocked Voltaire, upon learning what had happened to La Barre and to his book, ducked across the border into Switzerland for several months and began a counterattack, which however produced no concrete results until long afterward. Twenty-one years later, d'Etallonde, now a veteran officer in the Prussian army, was finally pardoned by Louis XVI. In 1794 the Jacobins posthumously rehabilitated La Barre's memory, venerating him as a "victim of superstition."

From our perspective, the most remarkable aspect of La Barre's trial and execution is how closely it resembles early sixteenth-century French legal practice. Remove La Barre's pornographic novels and his posthumous rehabilitation, replace Voltaire with Calvin, and the whole business begins to resemble the great sacrilege at Alençon in 1533, when a crucifix was found hanging upside down outside a church and a statue of the Virgin was left in a gutter. Local legal officials delayed formal prosecution of this spectacular crime long enough to let the principal suspects escape. Many months later they were imprisoned at Paris, and then transferred to Alençon (which lay just outside the district of the Parlement of Paris) to be tried by a special team of Parisian judges. A brief reign of terror then ensued; in six weeks, five men were burned. Judges in the high Enlightenment behaved only slightly more mercifully than their predecessors had in the high Renaissance when it came to punishing an "enormous" crime against God like defiling a crucifix. Under Louis XV, parlementary judges still burned corpses or effigies of such prisoners, and still ordered La Barre's tongue pierced for his blasphemy.[24]

Arbitrary Justice in Long-Term Perspective

When stipulating possible punishments for such offenses as blasphemy, royal edicts were extremely careful to leave an enormous amount of discretionary power to their judges. From St. Louis onward, French monarchs were aware that their subjects frequently blasphemed the name of God, and therefore they issued many decrees punishing this offense. When Francis I's mother ordered the old regulations reissued early in her 1525 regency, the First President of the Paris Parlement observed that because the extant edicts proposed contradictory punishments, "the judges of this kingdom will be in a dilemma about which one to observe, although they may not excuse themselves from punishing blasphemers"; President de Selve helpfully advised her to reissue only the most recent one, from 1499.[25] Scholars note that laws that are frequently repeated are rarely enforced, which was certainly the case with blasphemy. A helpful glimpse comes from a chronicler describing Francis I's visit to Toulouse in 1534; a few days after a new edict on the subject had been decreed, "a blasphemer experienced the danger in offending against laws *while they are still fresh:* he was burned alive."[26]

Despite all these laws, the practice of blaspheming in public persisted. When Louis XIV came to review the problem in 1666, he sounded much like Louis XII or even Louis IX. "We learn with displeasure," reads his preamble to this umpteenth set of regulations, "that, despite our prohibitions, to the scandal of the Church and to the ruin of the salvation of some of our subjects, this crime abounds almost everywhere in our kingdom, because of its impunity." Louis XIV proposed a series of punishments, beginning with an "arbitrary" fine based on the culprit's relative wealth and social position and escalating, after seven convictions, to removal of the blasphemer's tongue. Nevertheless, repeating one of his previous rulings, Louis XIV asserted that these punishments "do not include cases of enormous blasphemies [*les énormes blasphèmes*], which theologians associate with infidelity and infringe God's goodness and grandeur and his other attributes." For such extreme blasphemies, continued Louis XIV, "we wish that the said crimes be punished in greater degree than the others, at the discretion of the judges, according to their enormity."[27] For our purposes, the key provisions of Louis XIV's edict lie in its system of "arbitrary" fines at the bottom and its close association of "enormous" crimes with "arbitrary" punishments at its climax. Both extremes, the scale of fines and the possible capital punishments, were left entirely to the discretion of his judges.

Few crimes received such careful legislative attention as blasphemy. Sacrilege, for example, was one of several potentially "enormous" offenses that were never regulated at all by royal edicts. Neither was sodomy, nor witchcraft until 1682. The reason behind this situation, which seems so odd today, was that in early modern France, as jurists noted, "all punishments are arbitrary." In other words, even in those unusual situations in which specific royal legislation existed, it nearly always avoided prescribing fixed punishments for the crimes it condemned. Everything was left to judicial discretion, *à l'arbitrage des juges*. For us, the key word in that phrase is *arbitrage*. To an English speaker, the adjective "arbitrary" has become dissociated from the notion of arbitration. Sixteenth-century French criminal law, in proclaiming that all punishments were arbitrary, meant that they were to be arbitrated by judges. But what did that mean? Essentially, that judges were free to select from a wide menu of punishments, several of which might be appropriate for a particular offender. In every instance, the judges were expected to arbitrate their sentence according to the particular circumstances of the case, which might either aggravate or attenuate the most common sanctions in current use. Therefore, royal edicts avoided trying to impose fixed punishments, while even the shrewdest jurists were unable to bring much order to the doctrine of circumstances. The lone jurist even to attempt such a task in Renaissance France, the much-praised André Tiraqueau, had seventeen years of experience on the bench of the Paris Parlement when he finished his book *On Punishments* in 1559. Tiraqueau, who usually confined himself to civil law, basically did little more than list, with appropriate examples, sixty-four types of attenuating circumstances for judges to use when "tempering" or remitting sentences.[28]

French criminal law had not always practiced arbitrary sentencing. A lengthy and magisterial essay by Bernard Schnapper has sketched its long-term rise and fall in France, beginning with the medieval revival of Roman law and ending with its destruction by eighteenth-century *philosophes* and revolutionaries.[29] Before Montesquieu began in the 1720s to undermine the legal system for which he had worked, no negative connotation applied to the adjective "arbitrary" in front of the word "justice" or "punishment." On the contrary, judges in the age of Montaigne treasured their right to decide cases freely, unhampered by medieval guidelines stipulating precise punishments for each offense. Fitting the punishment to the crime became almost an art form: the art of judging, honed to a fine edge through careful study both of Roman laws and of human nature. The most extreme legal maxims of early modern Europe in favor of arbitrary punishments came from outside France. It was a Spaniard who first asserted that "all punishments are arbitrary"; a German who argued that judges could punish crimes that were not defined by any statute; and an Italian whose 700-page work on arbitrary judgments was printed in France in 1606.[30] But the French followed such practices as enthusiastically as anyone else. Sixteenth-century French *parlementaires* neither asked for nor received many royal laws to guide them when deciding criminal cases. During the Renaissance, the French aversion to proliferating laws can be seen as clearly in nonlawyers like Rabelais as in judges like Montaigne, both of whom mocked the Roman codifier Tribonian for making too many laws and thus limiting the judge's autonomy.[31] Montaigne went even further by suggesting that having no laws at all was preferable to having too many.

Under arbitrary justice, the criminal legislation of early modern France therefore remained minimal and stressed that punishments must be arbitrated *selon l'exigence du cas,* according to the merits of the case. What modern readers usually interpret as concrete prescriptions in royal edicts actually provided only approximate guidelines for royal judges. Royal legislation often began with the wistful preamble, "We wish that our ordinances and edicts be observed," implying that in reality they were usually ignored. The best studies of criminal justice in pre-Revolutionary France argue that much royal legislation really amounted to little more than ritual incantation. "Everything happened," says Arlette Lebigre, "as if, aware of his powerlessness to ensure order and security in his kingdom, the legislator compensated for his weaknesses with grandiloquent words."[32] Schnapper notes how little attention royal judges actually paid to royal edicts: "at bottom, except at the moment it was made and not throughout the entire kingdom, even the most imperative ordinance had no more validity than any other."[33] Reading royal decrees therefore tells us almost nothing about how criminal justice was actually administered in early modern France. As Louis XIV's chancellor told the senior president of the Parlement of Bordeaux in 1679, "The king is not accustomed to prescribe for his judges the punishments that they should ordain against those accused of any crime whatsoever."[34] However, because its major edicts have been conveniently assembled and can be easily understood, many scholars have mistakenly equated French royal legislation with French judicial practice.

If we wish to learn how Renaissance France actually administered criminal justice "arbitrarily," there is no alternative but to read through its preserved criminal decisions one by one. Two circumstances immediately confront us. First, virtually no records of sixteenth-century decisions have been preserved from lower-level royal or seigneurial courts;

for that matter, we have very few preserved decisions from French ecclesiastical courts. Only the decisions, or *arrêts,* of the sovereign appellate
courts, the parlements, survive in abundance. They have usually been
bound in huge volumes, arranged in approximate chronological order,
but without any kind of table or inventory. Examining them seriatim is a
labor-intensive task. Moreover, they are extremely laconic, often failing
to specify any reasons for a particular decision. Not surprisingly, one
can count on the fingers of one hand those scholars who have actually
worked through thousands of criminal-case rulings in order to create an
informed portrait of these "arbitrary" judges at work. Bernard Schnapper
has provided the first useful samples of applied criminal justice during
the sixteenth-century heyday of arbitrary punishments, while Alfred Soman has added some extremely valuable information about the Parlement of Paris, enabling us to set Schnapper's findings in a broader context. Both proceeded by analyzing short series of preserved criminal
decisions. Schnapper first sampled several years for the Parlement of
Bordeaux between 1511 and 1565, before taking two samples from the
much larger Parlement of Paris for the years 1536 and 1546.[35] Soman
crafted a two-year Parisian sample between those years and added later
samples from 1572 and 1610.[36] When combined, these samples provide
criminal decisions from two French parlements both before and after the
code of Villers-Cotterets was adopted in 1539, regulating basic French
criminal-court procedures until Louis XIV overhauled them in 1670.

Given the enormous latitude of judicial discretion, one might expect
to find a considerable variety of punishments imposed by parlementary
judges. Such is indeed the case. Schnapper's Paris sample from 1536
includes a classificatory scheme listing no fewer than thirty types of
sentences pronounced against 357 defendants. France's greatest court
found nine different ways to sentence a prisoner to be whipped, beginning with one done privately or by parents (6 instances) and escalating
up to three separate public whippings followed by perpetual banishment
from the entire kingdom (27 instances). They used seven different methods of inflicting capital punishment, ranging from simple beheading (2
instances) to burning alive (2 instances). The judges also found six
different ways to conclude cases without formally condemning the prisoner. Although nobody was absolved in 1536, 8 cases were thrown out of
court; 17 prisoners were released without being tortured, and 15 others
after successfully withstanding torture; 16 men received official pardons;

4 cases were transferred from criminal to civil suits; and 8 defendants were ordered to pay damages to their accusers. Parisian judges also ordered six different forms of nonphysical punishment, principally fines or the formal public apologies known as *amendes honorables* (25 cases). Ten years later the judges used seven ways not to condemn prisoners (some were now absolved), eight methods of nonphysical punishment, and fourteen modes of corporal punishment short of death sentences. They now practiced only six methods of executing prisoners, but the cruelest form of all (breaking on the wheel, used against 2 men in 1546) had been introduced in the intervening decade.[37]

Between these samples lay the new legal code of Villers-Cotterets, adopted in 1539. This landmark in the history of criminal procedure introduced several significant changes in French court practice. As many commentators have noted, the new code, lacking anything like a public police force, placed local criminal investigations in the hands of public prosecutors (*lieutenants criminels*). He gathered all preliminary information and depositions and turned them over to a local-level royal *conseillier,* or judge, who ordered arrests, verified testimony, interrogated prisoners, and cross-examined witnesses. The official codes, in 1539 and again in 1670, insisted that these officials act immediately whenever a crime had been committed, and threatened disciplinary actions against any official who failed to "work diligently at expediting all criminal cases, preliminary to and ahead of all other business." What the king desired was "good and swift" justice.[38] His investigating *lieutenants* and *conseilliers* did not simply act as public accusers; they could discharge suspects as well as indict them.

However, the 1539 rules stacked the deck against suspected criminals. For example, suspects could prove an alibi only after the judge authorized them to. Local royal officers were required to listen to all testimony against a suspect but were free to ignore any witnesses he might name in his defense. (Although witnesses for the prosecution could be punished for perjury, defense witnesses could not.) All pertinent testimony, including confrontations between witnesses and the prisoner, was written down and then submitted to the judges, who made their rulings on the basis of the written record alone; defendants could object to witnesses, but had to present their objections before being confronted with them. The 1539 code prescribed that suspects who were indicted be imprisoned immediately; it also made bail as difficult as possible, since in the absence of a public police force, a criminal defendant released on bail was rarely seen again in court. For us, perhaps its strangest provision stipulated that prisoners, after being confronted with their accusers, were required to answer questions put to them by the judge "with their mouth and without the counsel or advice of other persons." In other words, no defense lawyers were permitted in French criminal cases. These provisions were maintained in 1670 when the code of Villers-Cotterets was comprehensively overhauled, because permitting defense lawyers would merely benefit the rich, "who have the means to put many lawyers to work and pay them."[39]

The 1539 criminal code also helped defendants by greatly speeding up their appellate procedure. It abolished all intermediate jurisdictions between the court of first instance, whether seigneurial or royal, and the parlements, the courts of last appeal. In order to appeal any criminal conviction that involved physical punishment (whippings, torture, or death), one need only pronounce four words, "I appeal to Parlement," whereupon guards supposedly took the appellant directly (and at public expense) to the nearest parlementary prison, together with a written copy of his trial. After reading it, a panel of parlementary judges then interrogated the prisoner, seating him on a special three-legged stool known as a *sellette,* and immediately made their final ruling. These provisions of the Villers-Cotterets code tried to protect defendants in criminal cases against miscarriages of justice by expanding their opportunities for a swift judicial review through a recently enlarged network of parlements.

As one might expect, the volume of criminal cases heard by parlements increased noticeably after 1540. At Paris about 275 criminal defendants were judged each year around 1540. By 1572 this figure had doubled, although from then until 1610 it increased only slightly (6 percent).[40] Evidence from Bordeaux corroborates this picture; "criminal cases brought before the Parlement," Schnapper observes, "multiplied in a crushing manner around the mid-sixteenth century," tripling their pre-1540 averages by 1565.[41] The provisions for quick and easy appeal in the Villers-Cotterets code doubled the load of criminal cases heard by French parlements within a few decades. However, this sharp increase in parlementary business did not greatly increase the number of capital punishments. At both Paris and Bordeaux, the number of death sentences confirmed (or occasionally imposed) by the Parlement increased only moderately. At Paris, death sentences confirmed after appeal rose from sixty per annum around 1540 to about seventy by 1600;[42] at Bordeaux they increased from nearly thirty executions per year before Villers-Cotterets to about three dozen by 1565.[43] In their vast majority, the flood of criminal defendants invading French parlements after 1540 were not appealing death sentences.

Arbitrary punishments were adjusted through careful attention to attenuating or aggravating circumstances, verified by impartial judges after personal interrogation of each prisoner. Despite (or because of) the advantages enjoyed by the prosecution under the code of Villers-Cotterets, the parlements found cause to reduce sentences in about half of the appeals they heard.[44] These sovereign and arbitrary judges could also increase a lower court's punishment if they saw fit, or else transform it into something entirely different; the penal code of 1539 enabled royal officials to appeal *a minima* to a parlement, if they believed that a judge's sentence was overly lenient; and in a few cases both the prisoner and the *lieutenant criminel* appealed a lower-court ruling. Schnapper's samples show about fifty *a minima* appeals judged at Paris in 1536 and 1546, compared with more than a thousand appeals by prisoners. Among cases appealed *a minima,* fourteen sentences were upheld and twenty-four were increased, but thirteen punishments were actually reduced.[45] No better illustration could be imagined to show just how "arbitrarily" sixteenth-century French parlements actually judged accused criminals—without permitting them any form of defense counsel.

Judicial Torture in France

How did sixteenth-century French parlements, judging so many defendants charged with capital crimes, employ torture? It is well known that the revival of Roman law and inquisitorial procedure in Latin Christendom entailed a sharp increase in the use of judicial torture. Bartolus and his colleagues required that confessions made under torture be ratified by the prisoner "freely," outside the torture chamber and at least a day afterward, in order to become legally valid. Moreover, a prisoner who withstood torture successfully should be discharged without further punishment. Roman law neither prescribed any particular form of torture nor specified how many times it could be applied. In 1499 a royal ordinance had forbidden judges to employ torture more than once, unless pertinent new evidence had come to light. When the records of the Parlement of Paris become usable around 1540, only a small minority of its prisoners underwent torture—and fewer than 10 percent of them confessed to the crimes of which they stood accused, although this rate was undoubtedly higher among those who were returned to undergo torture at the place from which they came.[46] By 1600 the rate of confessions under torture had declined even further at Paris: a sample of 257 applications of torture now produced only 6 confessions. Even at Bordeaux, among prisoners whose sentences were determined primarily by their behavior under torture, over three-fifths were released.[47] During the sixteenth century the balance shifted from convicting the innocent through torture to releasing the guilty after torture.

Although sixteenth-century judges did not expect that torture would extract many truthful confessions from prisoners, French parlements maintained their right to employ torture right up to the Revolution—but rarely exercised it. When revising the criminal code in 1670, one expert complained that torture "had always seemed useless to him," but in the end it stayed, because judges had no other final method to determine guilt or innocence in cases in which the evidence remained inconclusive, especially when the charges involved "enormous" crimes.[48] However imperfect its use, judicial torture provided a way out of this impasse, with the additional advantage that in practice it usually gave defendants the benefit of the doubt. By the mid-sixteenth century, parlementary judges began defining new circumstances for the employment of torture. They now permitted its use on convicted prisoners, especially those guilty of an "enormous" crime, immediately before their public execution. This was known as "torture beforehand," *la question préalable,* which the hangman still inflicted on the unfortunate La Barre in 1766. Its principal purpose was to coerce a guilty person into making a full and final statement about his associates or accomplices; La Barre, for example, finally admitted his sacrilege in the cemetery and named a companion.[49] In the 1500s, as convictions through torture became increasingly rare, parlementary judges also developed the practice (technically forbidden by royal statute since 1499) of "torture with reservation of other proofs," which enabled them to condemn prisoners who withstood it to an "extraordinary" penalty somewhere below the legal maximum. Although this practice was not officially permitted until 1670, torture was already being administered at Paris "with reservation of proofs" about one time in four by the late 1530s, and this tactic was also known at Bordeaux by 1565.[50]

With torture no longer providing a relatively simple way to obtain legal proof of a prisoner's guilt, sixteenth-century French parlements had nothing on which to base their judgments except written trial records, which usually offered imperfect evidence against a defendant, supplemented by a brief firsthand questioning of the accused on the *sellette*. Jurists spoke of "half-proofs," of "presumptions" that were more or less "violent," and of other indices which that lead judges to hand out "extraordinary" sentences sanctioning crimes somewhere below the maximum level. In theory, full legal proof of a major crime was required for a sentence of capital punishment. At the opposite extreme, French judges almost never simply acquitted a prisoner: this situation occurred less than 3 percent of the time at Bordeaux and Paris.[51] However, they released one prisoner in four or five (about as many as they sentenced to death) in the 1540s, generally because of insufficient evidence. Usually, relying on the "presumptions" and partial proofs contained in trial records, they ordered such intermediate punishments as whippings or banishments, escalating up to their most severe condemnation below a death sentence, perpetual service in the galleys.

Both the concept of "enormous" crimes and the use of "arbitrary" punishments reached their peak during the sixteenth century, and both came under sustained attack from the eighteenth-century Enlightenment. Despite its manifest shortcomings, arbitrary justice evolved with glacial slowness between the early Renaissance and the high Enlightenment. With defense lawyers banned from criminal cases, only appellate judges could detect miscarriages of justice; but the only reforms ever envisaged were to make appeals to the parlements quick and easy after 1539, and automatic after 1670, whenever a lower court pronounced a major punishment. Because Roman law remained unchanged, French criminal practice retained such basic features as inquisitorial procedure, the doctrine of proofs "clearer than the noonday sun," the use of judicial torture, and the principle of arbitrary punishment, for many centuries with few substantive changes. The concept of treason against God, *lèse-majesté divine,* also endured for a long time, from well before the age of "Lutheranism" to the La Barre case.

During the eighteenth century the statutory legality of punishments

increased while the frequency of death sentences declined.[52] Montesquieu, a retired parlementary judge when he wrote *The Spirit of the Laws,*
popularized the slogan that judges were only "the mouth which pro-
nounces the words of the law." He fully recognized that France did not
yet have laws covering all criminal situations; therefore, in his "monarchical" system, "judges follow the law when it is precise and seek out its
spirit when it is not." But his reformism was soon overtaken by more
dogmatic *philosophes.* In the 1760s Cesare Beccaria argued against both
judicial torture and the death penalty, while Voltaire tackled the criminal rulings of the great French parlements head-on, first Toulouse with
Jean Calas and then Paris with La Barre. In the time of Philip the Fair,
Roman law had been prestigious; under Louis XV, Voltaire found it "barbarous." After La Barre's execution in 1766, a young royal attorney at
Guy Pape's Parlement of Grenoble proclaimed that arbitrary punishment
was "shameful." The French system of arbitrary punishments was finally
pushed into the dustbin of history by Beccaria's disciples and abolished,
together with the parlementary system, during the French Revolution.
One extreme followed another: judicial license was replaced with a
"paint-by-numbers" concept of sentencing, with every conceivable offense covered by legislation prescribing the exact punishment to be imposed. Replacing judicial torture with the judge's "intimate conviction"
as the final method for establishing guilt, the French have lived uncom-
fortably with their criminal legislation since the 1790s. But they have
never tried to bring back arbitrary punishments, let alone the practice of
burning people convicted of "enormous" crimes.

2

Heresy Trials in Reformation Europe

Never in the preceding fifteen centuries did any persecution continue
for so long a time without alleviation, never were there in so small a
space so many dark prisons, deadly tribunals, scaffolds, fiery stakes,
and other instruments of torture erected and used as were at that time
in Germany and the Netherlands.
　　—*T. J. van Braght,* The Bloody Theater or Martyrs' Mirror *(1660)*

When an Augustinian monk named Martin Luther first ran afoul of
church authorities in the Holy Roman Empire, they had much trouble
and no success trying to correct or to punish him. Everyone knows how
Luther attacked the doctrine of indulgences in 1517 and, soon thereafter,
the authority of the papacy. But few realize how personally unscathed he
was throughout this risky enterprise: for all his daring and stubbornness,
Luther never spent a day in prison, never was even put under house
arrest by either ecclesiastical or secular authorities. After being condemned *in absentia* at Rome and excommunicated by the papacy in 1520,
Luther was summoned to appear before the Diet of Worms early in the
next year. He made his famous "Here I stand" speech and once again
walked away untouched.[1] Though placed under the ban of the empire by
that same Diet, Luther occasionally traveled around the German empire
and died in bed twenty-five years later. Many people, Albrecht Dürer for
one, had fully expected to see him captured and burned at the stake in
1521; but neither the pope nor the emperor was ever able to punish him
for his actions or his writings across a period of nearly thirty years.
Luther committed heresy on a grand scale and got away with complete
personal safety.

How was this possible? When Luther was born, the Latin church had
been punishing heretics with fire for more than 450 years, and papal

inquisitors had been active in many parts of Christendom, including the Holy Roman Empire, for more than two centuries. But Luther benefited from two pieces of good luck. First, he happened to attack papal authority at a time when the prestige of its disciplinary arm, the papal Inquisition, was near its all-time nadir in the German empire; it had put no heretics on trial since before Luther was born.[2] Worse still, the papal Inquisition in the empire had just been rudely buffeted by the noisy young German humanist movement for its ignorance and obscurantism in attempting (but failing) to censure the Hebrew grammar published in 1506 by Johannes Reuchlin. This controversy provided the German humanists with their first great propaganda triumph at the expense of the Dominican inquisitor Johannes Pfefferkorn. Leo X finally transferred Reuchlin's case to Rome and imposed perpetual silence on both sides. When Luther's doctrinal challenges suddenly emerged just a few years later, virtually nobody in the empire took the local papally appointed inquisitors very seriously.

The second fortuitous circumstance that benefited Luther was the papacy's great need for the goodwill of Luther's prince, Elector Frederick of Saxony, precisely when the Luther controversy began in earnest in 1518. No other German prince enjoyed so much political autonomy during the troubled period of determining Maximilian's successor as emperor in 1518–19, and very few matched him in judgment or courage. As a result, Luther had only one serious brush with papal authority. It occurred at Augsburg in the autumn of 1518, after the Elector of Saxony persuaded a papal legate to transfer Luther's case from Rome to a "neutral" site. Luther, accompanied by two of the Elector's lawyers, met Cardinal Cajetan in Augsburg after the imperial Diet had ended. At their second meeting, Luther brought along a notary to emphasize he would not retract his position unless refuted from scripture. After three meetings and some delays, Luther fled from Augsburg at night, leaving behind a notarized appeal, drafted by the two lawyers, to the pope "better informed." Safely back in Wittenberg, Luther drafted another notarized appeal in late November 1518 to a future general Council while having the proceedings of his Augsburg hearings published. By Christmas 1518 the Elector informed the legate that Luther would never be handed over to Rome. Subsequent negotiations by the young Saxon notary sent from Rome, Karl von Miltitz, got Luther's case transferred to the archbishop of Salzburg; the Elector later had it transferred to the archbishop-elector of

Trier, who finally conducted two polite interviews with Luther during the Diet of Worms.

Meanwhile, after the famous debate with Johann Eck at Leipzig in 1519, Luther's Roman trial was pushed to a speedy conclusion once Eck himself arrived in Rome in May 1520; the famous bull *Exsurge Domine* was published one month later. With the imperial succession now settled, another nuncio, Girolamo Aleandro, equipped with inquisitorial powers and with Eck alongside as papal protonotary, represented the papacy at the next Diet. By now, getting the bull against Luther published throughout the empire and the heretic effectively condemned had become his major business. With unexpectedly vigorous help from the new emperor, Aleandro partially succeeded. The Diet itself debated the issue for a week before inviting Luther to appear under an imperial safe-conduct. When he appeared, Luther's remarks irritated Charles V enormously. The young emperor stayed awake writing a declaration, which was read next morning (first in Charles's native French, then in German) to the electors, the nuncio, and other assembled dignitaries. Charles concluded:

> After the impudent reply which Luther gave yesterday . . . I declare that I regret having delayed for so long the proceedings against this Luther and his false doctrine. I have now resolved never again, under any circumstances, to hear him. He is to be escorted home immediately . . . with due regard for the stipulations of his safe-conduct . . . I am resolved to act and proceed against him as a notorious heretic. I ask you to declare yourselves in this affair as good Christians, and to keep the promise you made to me.[3]

The princes responded by approving the lengthy Edict of Worms, drafted three weeks later and signed in late May 1521, outlawing Luther and attempting to destroy his and his followers' writings. But not even the emperor's arms were long enough to reach Luther. Within a year Charles V was in Spain, and Luther was back in Wittenberg. In a few years, several imperial free cities and a few other princes began converting to Lutheranism. The Edict of Worms remained on the books, but its only practical effect was to bar Luther from ever again attending an imperial Diet. Protestantism began with an unenforceable papal bull and an equally unenforceable imperial edict.

Determined to enforce the imperial Edict of Worms rigorously in his most ancient patrimony, Charles attempted to impose a Spanish-style general inquisitor on the Low Countries in 1522. But the brief career of the Brabant councillor Franz Van der Hulst as director-general of the war against Luther quickly revealed two flaws in this plan. First, Charles's authority in the Low Countries was purely temporal, and Lutheranism was undoubtedly a religious offense; so Van der Hulst, much to the annoyance of Charles and his regent, proceeded to obtain parallel powers from Pope Adrian VI, who was both a Dutchman and a former inquisitor-general of Spain. Second, Van der Hulst's ominous monopoly stirred up a hornets' nest of opposition. The province of Holland soon found a serious legal error in Van der Hulst's commission, accused him of deliberate fraud, and ruined his career in a matter of months. Charles withdrew his commission; Adrian VI conveniently died, and his successor quickly withdrew the papal commission. The only serious attempt to introduce a centrally directed state inquisition in the Low Countries ended almost before it began.[4] However, Van der Hulst's career lasted just long enough to produce the first Lutheran martyrs in Europe. Three Augustinians were taken from the Antwerp convent to a castle near Brussels and convicted; in July 1523 two of them were burned (the other recanted, and his life was spared). Through the rest of the decade local authorities in various centers of the Low Countries arrested, convicted, and sometimes executed other Lutherans. The victims were relatively few—barely a dozen died—but they sufficed to turn the Erasmian Low Countries into the leading producer of early Lutheran martyrs in Europe. At the same time, the prominence of its printing industry transformed the Low Countries into the originator of Protestant martyrologies: several anonymous pamphlets praised the courage and the beliefs of those who were executed for heresy.[5]

Condemnation of Luther, however, was international. By the end of 1521 his writings had been condemned by the Sorbonne, refuted in print by Henry VIII of England, and anathematized by the Spanish Inquisition. Despite all this furor, however, remarkably little legal action was undertaken against Luther's followers in the 1520s. Outside the empire, they seemed few in number and relatively harmless. A handful of them were burned for heresy. After the first Brussels executions of 1523, other "Lutherans" soon followed elsewhere—at widely scattered sites in the empire, at Paris, and even as far away as Scotland by 1528.[6] Inside the empire, however, Luther's early followers generally escaped any form of legal prosecution, because they were so remarkably well positioned. From their base at Luther's university at Wittenberg, they held political control over a key territory (electoral Saxony) and soon acquired cultural hegemony over German public opinion through their quasi-monopoly of the printing industry in the empire.[7] But while Lutheranism made slow, steady political gains in German cities and principalities in the mid-1520s, the issue of prosecuting heresy suddenly acquired enormous urgency from an unanticipated source.

The Tyrolean Hutterites of Austria

Empty condemnations of Luther provide a false start for the history of religious persecution in Reformation Europe. However, the rise of Anabaptism in the immediate aftermath of the great German peasant rebellions of 1524–25 quickly led to massive and unprecedented acts of repression. Relatively few known Anabaptists participated directly in the numerous risings affecting much of southern Germany, Austria, and Switzerland, spilling as far west as Lorraine.[8] The most prominent Anabaptist leader to inspire and help lead the revolt was Luther's nemesis Thomas Müntzer; he was captured and put to death on 27 May 1525, after his Thuringian peasants and miners had been crushed by the young Landgrave of Hesse, soon to emerge as a Protestant leader. Two days later, in a small and deeply conservative Swiss canton, the first pacifist Anabaptist was put to death by Catholic authorities. Zwingli's Zurich, where Anabaptism had increasingly bothered both the civil authorities and their distinguished evangelical preacher since 1523, decreed in March 1526 that anyone who rebaptized another person would be drowned; on 5 January 1527 they began to enforce his law.

The greatest persecution of Anabaptists also began in 1527, in a land where the final dangerous episode of the German peasants' war had ended only a few months before. Michael Gaismair, a charismatic leader of the Tyrolean rebels who had terrified Ferdinand I's government for much of 1525 and 1526, continued to harass them from his refuge in Italy, surviving numerous attempted assassinations over the next six years.[9] Gaismair was no Anabaptist, but he had imported Zwinglian preachers into Tyrol in 1525 and remained an ally of Zwingli while living in Venetian territory. He shared a communitarian economic vision with his fellow Tyrolean and near-contemporary Jacob Hutter, a spiritual revolutionary who began putting his Anabaptist vision into practice in distant Moravia. Gaismair's armed invasion of Tyrol in 1526 coincided with the first Anabaptist missions in the province's high Alps. By 1527 Archduke Ferdinand had become obsessed with exterminating both forms of resistance, each of which, he realized, defied both feudal authority and the established church.

Under these circumstances, Anabaptism was persecuted in Ferdinand's Austrian lands with unparalleled throughness and savagery. During the next few years his government tried to extirpate Anabaptism throughout his hereditary Austrian provinces by every means imaginable. From 1527 through 1529 Archduke Ferdinand took his first decisive steps toward secularizing the crime of heresy. His decrees were widely distributed and well enough enforced to provoke the first major persecution of heretics in Reformation Europe. Ferdinand's first major step came on 20 August 1527, when his government promulgated a decree drafted by Zwingli's old opponent, the episcopal vicar of Constance, Johann Faber. The obligation of each loyal Austrian subject to denounce suspected Anabaptists to the secular authorities was to be read from every parish pulpit in Austria twice a year, at Easter and at Christmas, for ten years. Two thousand copies were immediately distributed to the appropriate provincial authorities. This edict declared that anyone who denied the basic Christian doctrines or the sacraments would be punished as a heretic "in body and life."[10] It threatened death by burning, the traditional penalty for stubborn or relapsed heretics. Indeed, Ferdinand's officials had already burned the well-known Anabaptist preacher Michael Sattler, who had been caught in the Black Forest and taken to the nearest Austrian court for trial in May 1527. Four of Sattler's followers who had been captured with him were beheaded; Sattler's wife was drowned.

Meanwhile the archduke devised another new idea to complement his 1527 edict and extirpate Anabaptism in his Austrian domains. Early in 1528 his officials in Vienna had extracted a confession from another prominent Anabaptist leader, Balthasar Hubmaier, who had composed rebel manifestos during the Peasants' War.[11] Ferdinand thereupon announced that four special "commissioners for extirpating the sect of Anabaptists" would be appointed for different regions of his lands, each of them armed with powers of summary justice. Two days later came orders for a general visitation against the "damnable heresies" throughout the province of Lower Austria.[12] The arbitrary actions of Dietrich von Hartisch, the special provost charged with this mission, overrode the traditional Austrian courts. Because of possible "rebellion, uprising, and bloodshed," Ferdinand permitted von Hartisch to deal with stubborn Anabaptists "without the solemnity of the law." He had Ferdinand's full confidence, reinforced by a detailed governmental order of July 1528, insisting on trying Anabaptists with all possible speed. Von Hartisch complied: in one village, the commissioner had eighteen Anabaptists hanged or beheaded in one day. His summary procedures irritated ecclesiastical as well as secular officials. For example, according to the bishop of Passau, Ferdinand's orders literally forcing local priests to absolve recanting Anabaptists "violated all justice and fairness."[13] Evidence from Styria, the one province in which the official register of the 1528 "Visitation and Inquisition" survives, suggests that other commissioners behaved less arbitrarily than von Hartisch.[14]

Ferdinand's Austrian domains continued to suffer numerous prosecutions after von Hartisch had completed his bloody mission. Hutterite martyrologies recorded huge groups of martyrs at Linz, the capital of Upper Austria, in 1529, and in the independent archbishopric of Salzburg in 1528; smaller groups perished in Styria in 1529 and in Carinthia by 1531. Although Anabaptist sources claim that almost 350 of their early martyrs died in other parts of Austria and Salzburg, official sources record barely a hundred deaths outside Tyrol.[15] The only other imperial territory to execute many Anabaptists before 1530 was the neighboring duchy of Bavaria. A "Lutheran" had been burned at Munich early in 1527, before Austrian officials caught Sattler. Eight Anabaptists followed him in the Bavarian capital in 1528; others died elsewhere in Bavaria next year. (The first Anabaptist preacher executed in Tyrol, in January 1528, was refused extradition to Bavaria).[16] Other Anabaptists were executed in some of the smaller free cities of Swabia and in parts of Franconia from 1527 through 1529; a few others died by the order of Protestant city cantons in Switzerland.

Capping the edifice of legal persecution throughout the empire was a decree emanating from the Diet of Speyer in 1529, best known as the point where "Protestantism" originated through a joint protest of Lutheran princes and cities against the anti-Lutheran laws. On April 9 the Diet approved a new imperial law decreeing that all rebaptized men and women who refused to recant or who had relapsed were to be put to death, without requiring any form of ecclesiastical inquisition; those who expressed repentance could be pardoned.[17] The 1529 edict was confirmed in 1544, with an important procedural change: everywhere in the empire, even where customary law dictated otherwise, authorities were given the right to arrest Anabaptists without prior denunciations—"a measure," notes C.-P. Clasen, "also used in the prosecution of witches."[18] When one reflects how completely void of effect had been the 1521 Edict of Worms condemning Luther and how few "Lutherans" had been punished in the intervening years, it is ironic how quickly and how often this 1529 imperial mandate, condemning all forms of Anabaptism as direct threats to states as well as to the church, was put into practice by punishing them with death. Fully 80 percent of Clasen's 845 documented executions of Anabaptists in the empire (exclusive of the Low Countries) occurred from 1527 through 1533, most of them after the new law had been proclaimed in April 1529. Overall, about two-thirds of the heretics executed in the empire before 1533 were Austrian Anabaptists. A plurality of these executions occurred in Tyrol, the only region where Anabaptism flourished without previous exposure to other forms of Protestantism and the only region where it survived such intensive persecution.[19]

Tyrol, which produced not only the rebel Gaismair but also the most successful Austrian Anabaptist leader, Jacob Hutter, suffered far more from 1528 through 1533 than any other part of Austria, or indeed any other province in Christendom. A collection of government documents concerning the Tyrolean repression includes almost 750 items from the summer of 1527 to Christmas 1531, most of them from 1528 or 1529.[20] Records from the early Hutterites basically confirm the impression left by evidence from the Tyrolean government at Innsbruck. The Moravian Hutterites, many of whom came from Tyrol, recalled slightly over 350 Tyrolean martyrs when they drew up their first general list about 1542; official sources suggest close to 250 deaths of Tyrolean Anabaptists from 1528 through 1533, many of them occurring in different parts of Tyrol in 1529.[21] During the early Reformation, no similar-sized region of Europe even remotely approached these figures for heresy prosecution and executions. From the most remote valleys in the Tyrolean Alps to the silver-mining towns near the River Inn, Ferdinand I and his officials conducted the greatest heresy persecution seen anywhere in Europe since the Albigensian crusade.

This persecution can best be understood from the perspective of Ferdinand's Tyrolean officials, caught in a squeeze between their ruler's unwavering determination to eliminate a dangerous threat to his authority and their subjects' continuing unwillingness to oppress people whom they believed to be harmless. By early 1528, answering Ferdinand's order to accelerate punishment of Anabaptists, Tyrolean officials explained that they had already punished foreigners for this offense in seven important towns; but they complained vehemently that Ferdinand's edicts infringed Tyrolean traditions and liberties. Their juries, whose consent was necessary for carying out executions, claimed they could not understand or accept Ferdinand's recent decree. Tyrolean officials also criticized the edict's lack of mercy toward repentant Anabaptists. Ferdinand's court therefore issued new mandates early in 1528, giving Tyrolean Anabaptists a grace period in which to recant, trying to accommodate authoritarian wishes and Alpine customs.[22] One month after this grace period had expired, Tyrolean officials sadly reported that one-third of those who had used it were already backsliders.[23]

Nowhere was the new 1529 edict applied so thoroughly as in Tyrol. Mass executions began here on 12 May 1529 at Rattenburg on the Inn; eighteen people died "without any disturbance," reported local officials, although "so many people had never been executed at one time."[24] They continued throughout the year at frequent intervals. In February 1530, worried by spectacular recent disclosures at Linz about Anabaptist communism, crypto-Catharism, and lack of law enforcement, Ferdinand tried to intensify persecution in Tyrol; he asked provincial authorities to choose between sending mounted patrols to conduct surprise raids and summary executions in Alpine valleys, and sending two high officials to tour every village to alert the public to these dangers and require them to hand all Anabaptists to the authorities.[25] The response from Innsbruck was extremely instructive. For various reasons, Tyrolean officials rejected both alternatives. Using cavalry was both impractical and illegal, as they had told him two years ago; official propaganda in the villages, they said, would be counterproductive because it would reinforce Swiss claims that Austrian officials were merely tools of the Spaniards, "the most evil people in the world," who punished people merely for their religious opinions.[26] At the same time, Tyrolean officials insisted that they had been remarkably zealous in uprooting Anabaptism, despite local reluctance to implement Ferdinand's edicts (at this moment they knew that, high in the Alps, a judge's barn had been burned, seditious writings had appeared in public, and banished Anabaptists had brazenly returned to their farms).[27] They informed their lord that "for two years, seldom has a day passed without Anabaptist business being discussed in our council, and we have sentenced about two hundred men and women to death for it in this County of Tyrol." Many more had been banished, they added, and their property had been confiscated.[28] They had paid cash bounties to informers to catch Anabaptist preachers; they had required all Tyrolean priests and judges to read Ferdinand's 1529 mandate in every parish; and they had made liberal use of torture—an experience that convinced them, if not Ferdinand, that Anabaptists were nonviolent.

By 1530 Tyrolean authorities spoke of Anabaptist meetings as "synagogues," a term also used for witches' sabbaths.[29] Over the next few years they continued to be haunted by phobias about clandestine rural groups plotting various forms of disobedience and perhaps rebellion (in defense of their paranoia, they had captured a talkative Anabaptist follower of Gaismair from Cologne, whom they finally burned in 1533). In 1538 they still instructed local officials to ask suspects "whether there isn't some secret practice going on under the appearance of your sect, that you are really trying to raise some new rebellion [*bundschuh*] among ordinary people."[30] They had some successes against both rebels and preachers: Gaismair was finally assassinated in Italy in 1532, and they captured their greatest Anabaptist enemy, Jacob Hutter, late in 1535. Hutter was taken to Innsbruck and executed after considerable torture. His wife, imprisoned in the Alps, escaped later in 1536, symbolizing the ways in which Hutter's system outlived him and illustrating the easy acceptance his followers continued to enjoy among ordinary Tyroleans.[31] The next Anabaptist preachers captured by the Tyrolean government proved more slippery than stubborn: one of them pretended to recant and then tried to escape.[32] Hutterite missionaries continued to work in the Tyrol for over fifty years afterward; Austrian authorities managed to capture and execute a few of them.

Violent and Pacifist Anabaptism in the Low Countries

Charles V's prosecution of Anabaptism in the Low Countries differed from his brother's Austrian system in two main respects. First, Charles had spent more than a decade implementing measures against Lutheranism in his native land before he and his advisers became aware of any Anabaptist menace there. Second, he had to confront an even greater degree of resistance to central authority in this highly decentralized, populous, and prosperous federation of provinces than Ferdinand encountered in his Austrian lands. Provincial autonomy had ruined Charles's attempt to introduce a general Inquisition in the Low Countries in the 1520s. He attempted to remedy this situation by simultaneously stiffening the penalties against heresy and handing its enforcement to local secular authorities. Charles's first major decree (*plakkaat*) of October 1529 prescribed the death penalty for unrepentant Lutherans. In 1531, at a meeting of the States-General of the Low Countries, Charles reissued this decree with minor modifications, still directing it against "Lutherans" and their writings; he had as yet no inkling of what the Anabaptists were doing in his northern provinces.[33] His legislation increased the prosecution of Protestants by removing it from the jurisdiction of the relatively gentle and slow-moving ecclesiastical judges.

One can see its effects by comparing the two earliest mentions of "Lutherans" in a diary from Mons, capital of the province of Hainaut. In May 1525 it reported that

> an act of justice was done in Mons by officers of the Bishop of Cambrai . . . as judges of ten people accused of being Lutherans, eight men and two women. With them was a monk, Inquisitor of the Faith for the diocese of Cambrai, who, after their trials had been seen and judged, as such cases deserve, pronounced their condemnations in the market of Mons and at two churches, publicly according to their deserts. Namely, some of them got seven years, others four, others three or two, in prison on bread and water; then, their time having expired, they would carry some wax candles to their respective parish churches. Then some of them were publicly given yellow cloth crosses to wear on their right arms, and others got yellow cloth caps with crosses of red cloth sewn on them, which they were to wear on their heads so that they could be recognized as people who had abused and lived contrary to the church of the Christian faith. Afterward they were taken to the castle of Selles to perform the penances that had been enjoined on them by their definitive sentence, where the Great Bailiff of Hainaut was present. And the mysteries were certainly great and very handsome to make this condemnation, because it was done to give an example to others. May God in his grace see that they are well converted, because there was

very little appearance that they would do so, judging by the attitude they displayed.[34]

As the diarist suspected, this theatrical performance did not extinguish "Lutheranism" in Hainaut. Eight years later he encountered another, very different method of punishing Protestants:

> The lord of Esmeriez arrested a servant of the previous lord of Esmeriez who had been his barber, and charged him with being a Lutheran. He had him taken to Mons for his trial, which was done on Wednesday, May 28, 1533, and on that same day he was taken from the castle of Mons and led to Pons-sur-Sambre, to be executed and burned the following Thursday, where the lord of Esmeriez was present in person, because it was the first act of criminal justice which he had done.

No ecclesiastical officials appeared during the barber's trial and execution; the local seigneur stood at the center of the spectacle. The diarist closed this entry by observing that "at Nivelles someone had been similarly put to death for such reasons, and at Lille several who belonged to this Lutheranism."[35] The barber became the first victim in Hainaut of Charles V's policy of fully secularizing the crime of heresy throughout his ancestral provinces; many others soon followed.

The intensified assault on Lutheranism after the edicts of 1529 and 1531 had only a brief and minimal impact in the Low Countries, compared with the frantic responses by some officials in northern provinces to counter the political and even military menace posed by some early forms of Anabaptism. During the Reformation only one other group, the Dutch Mennonites, suffered punishment on anything like the scale of the Tyrolean Hutterites. The latter had given great trouble to Archduke Ferdinand, while the northern Anabaptists disturbed his older brother Charles V. Both brothers adopted unusually drastic measures in their unsuccessful efforts to extirpate these religious radicals and social subversives. In both instances, their laws against Anabaptism eliminated church courts in order to produce appropriately swift and severe punishments. The major assault against the Netherlands Anabaptists got underway during the mid-1530s, just as the intensive "cleansing" of the Tyrolean Anabaptists finally began to slacken. The explanation is not far to seek. If the famous episode of the Anabaptist "New Jerusalem" at the city of Münster in 1533–34 had very little effect in stimulating persecution in other parts of the empire, it had enormous resonance in the Low Countries, especially in the province of Holland. Besides sending many of these revolutionaries upriver to Münster, Holland had also provided its two charismatic leaders, Jan Matthys of Haarlem and Jan van Leyden.

Throughout the early 1530s, local and provincial authorities in the Low Countries seem to have been a step or two behind the Anabaptists. They knew little about the responses to Melchior Hoffmann's apocalyptic sermons spreading south and west from Frisia after 1529, taking deep root in Holland and Utrecht and reaching as far as Antwerp, which prudently expelled its Melchiorites in 1534. Although they used a few informants, Hapsburg officials were constantly reacting to unforeseen Anabaptist projects. They seemed overwhelmed by the massive emigration to Münster, and one town in Holland (Monnikendam) became so predominantly Anabaptist that provincial authorities dared not set foot in it for years. In 1535 local authorities in rural Frisia and at Amsterdam seemed totally unprepared for Anabaptist military assaults. Not until June 1535, after both risings had been suppressed and immediately before the fall of Münster, did the regency at Brussels issue a general edict against the Anabaptist menace.[36]

By then a frantic bloodbath was already under way in Holland and Frisia. Holland—home of Erasmus and soon the self-proclaimed birthplace of religious toleration in western Europe—now became the most intensive center of heresy executions anywhere in Christendom, with almost three hundred known instances in the 1530s;[37] when the regent's council questioned the provincial council of Holland about its leniency toward some accused heretics in 1537, the latter confidently and correctly responded that it had already executed many more heretics than any other province.[38] The carnage in Holland during the decade after 1534 probably exceeded even that in Tyrol during the decade after 1527. Prosecution of Anabaptists had begun earlier: in 1531 Amsterdam authorities caught ten Melchiorites, who were soon beheaded at The Hague, the first cluster of Protestant heretics executed in the Low Countries. That year Menno Simons, still a parish priest, saw a Melchiorite die at the capital of Friesland.[39] During the peak of the agitation and emigration to Münster, few radical Anabaptists were troubled by authorities. But after one group staged an abortive coup at Amsterdam in April 1534, repression accelerated: fifteen men were captured and executed at Amsterdam, and still others at The Hague.[40] However, as events in Münster moved toward their climax early in 1535, Dutch Anabaptists staged two bloody risings and triggered unprecedented reprisals. In Friesland, hundreds of them stormed the Oldeklooster convent late in March 1535, holding it for a week until the government drove them out. During the following month, dozens of Anabaptists caught near the battlefield were executed at Leeuwarden, including forty-two women who were drowned.[41] Meanwhile the rebel leader escaped and went to Amsterdam.

When seven men and five women ran naked through Amsterdam's streets in February 1535 in order to proclaim the "naked truth," they escaped punishment. But after forty armed men, led by the Oldeklooster commander, successfully stormed Amsterdam's town hall on May 10 and held it overnight, killing a leading magistrate, the authorities struck back hard. Almost half of the forty-five Anabaptist "rebels" executed at Amsterdam from May 14 through June 1 were women, including a few who were hanged.[42] So long as Münster remained unconquered under its plebeian Dutch "king," public authorities throughout the northern half of the Low Countries remained terrified by what their volatile subjects might try next. However, they would destroy those who tried to overthrow them. During April and May 1535, authorities in Frisia and Amsterdam carried out over a hundred death sentences. Because most of these captured apocalyptic "rebels" were women, the Brussels government advised authorities in both places to avoid public executions.

Under the strain of the Münster experience, the hunt for Anabaptists intensified after 1535 throughout the Dutch- and Flemish-speaking provinces. The regency government of Mary of Hungary directed its efforts against the remnants of Melchiorite revolutionaries. However, local officials soon discovered a rich variety of non-Melchiorite Anabaptists, most of them (at least after the fall of Münster) professing pacifism, including a few adepts of the Manichaean artisan from Antwerp, Loys Pruystinck, and many followers of the elusive prophet David Joris. Officials in Artois also caught a veteran adventurer who had survived Münster, Jan van Batenburg. Arrested in 1537 before he could flee to France, Batenburg, who specialized in robbing churches, was tortured and executed at Brussels; lists of his associates were sent to Groningen and Amsterdam.[43] Ultimately, most of the people they discovered proved to be followers of a former Frisian parish priest, Menno Simons. He became sufficiently important for the Frisian government to put a price on his head in 1542. Menno lived quietly in Groningen, a remote corner of the Habsburg provinces that never attempted to enforce any of the numerous decrees against heresy.[44] Like Luther, Menno Simons died in bed after decades of outlawry; unlike Luther, he could only watch helplessly when his wife was caught, tortured, and martyred at Leeuwarden in 1549.

Confronted with related but distinct species of Anabaptists and spurred by the news from Münster, officials in Dutch- and Flemish-speaking parts of the Low Countries increased persecution after the spring of 1535. In the Frisian capital, fifteen more Anabaptists were publicly executed from 1536 through 1539; thirteen others died at Amsterdam from July 1535 through December 1539.[45] Groups of Anabaptists perished at several locations across the northern provinces. In Brabant and Flanders, twenty of them died in cosmopolitan Antwerp between 1535 and 1539; its old commercial rivals, Bruges and Ghent, executed fourteen others.[46] Overall, public officials put at least four hundred Anabaptists to death from 1534 through 1540 across the Dutch- and Flemish-speaking regions.[47] This figure surpasses the official estimate for Anabaptists executed in Ferdinand's Austrian lands from 1527 through 1533, and exactly follows it chronologically.

The regency of Charles V's sister, the widowed Queen Mary of Hungary, lasted until the emperor's abdication in 1555. In the 1540s the repression of Protestant heresies dropped off considerably after the panic years following Münster; the Low Countries now averaged just over twenty public executions for heresy per year, one-third as many as during the late 1530s. Miscellaneous heretics continued to be tracked down and sometimes executed in all major cities and most provinces of the Low Countries. Deaths occurred in many smaller towns; in Flanders, for example, heresy executions took place in fifteen different localities in the fifteen years after 1539.[48] Francophone regions first began to rival the three major provinces of Holland, Brabant, and Flanders in the later 1540s. Nearly half of the Walloon executions occurred at Tournai, a city acquired from the French in 1521 and incorporated into the Low Countries as a separate province.

Charles V issued yet another cycle of increasingly severe edicts against heresy from 1544 through 1550; but, as Guido Marnef notes (and his observation holds true for many parts of Reformation Europe), "edicts against heresy were only operational to the extent that local authorities implemented them."[49] In the 1550s, with ever-stiffer edicts and the exceptionally diligent and dedicated Peter Titelmans serving as inquisitor for Flanders, the pace of heresy prosecutions and executions slowly increased across several provinces of the Low Countries. In the Dutch- and Frisian-speaking regions, virtually everyone executed for heresy was an Anabaptist, but most of them were now followers of Menno Simons; almost half of the known 1540–1554 heresy executions in the Low Countries can be traced in Mennonite martyrologies. Meanwhile, a new element had been added to the Protestant mix in the Low Countries; Calvinism produced its first Low Countries martyr at Tournai in February 1545: Pierre Brully, Calvin's successor as pastor of the French church at Strasbourg.[50] Sent to Tournai in order to preach against the chief local "libertine," Brully was soon captured, tortured, and burned. However, the next year Tournai's Calvinists got a measure of revenge. After capturing the local libertine chief, the magistrates bought a copy of Calvin's treatise against him (a prohibited book) at Lille in order to help condemn and finally execute him. Calvinism flourished at Tournai afterward, accounting for most of those arrested for heresy, and spread across other French-speaking areas of the Low Countries. By mid-century it had reached Flemish regions: a Calvinist schoolteacher was executed at Ghent in 1549, and five Flemish-speaking Calvinists died at Bruges in 1552 and 1553.[51]

The European Apogee, 1555–1564

Many signs indicate that, overall, heresy trials and public executions of various kinds of Protestants peaked throughout Europe in the years after 1555. The totals for these years clearly surpassed those from the great slaughter of various types of Anabaptists, first in the Austrian lands and then in the Low Countries, from 1525 through 1540. Table 2, containing relatively small margins of error, enables us to measure the differing rhythms of heresy trials across western and central Europe during the age of the Protestant Reformation.

Several features converge to help explain the sharp upsurge in heresy executions after 1555. This decade began with the election of a former head of the Roman Inquisition as Pope Paul IV and Mary Tudor's commitment to purge England of heresy, if necessary through ruthless persecution. It saw the apogee of confessionalization in much of Christian Europe, beginning with the first despatch of missionary pastors from Calvin's Geneva and concluding with the decrees of the Council of Trent

Table 2.   Heresy executions in Europe, 1525–1564 (annual averages in parentheses)

Country	1525–1539	1540–1554	1555–1559	1560–1564
German Empire	680 (42)	30 (2)	8 (1.6)	10 (2)
Switzerland	48 (3)	22 (1.5)	5 (1)	5 (1)
Low Countries	600 (40)	320 (21)	160 (32)	225 (45)
France	50 (4)	280 (18)	80 (16)	12 (2.5)
England and Scotland	32 (2)	20 (1.3)	300 (60)	0
Spain and Portugal	5	8	35 (7)	100 (20)
Italy and Sicily	0	12 (0.8)	15 (3)	5 (1)
Totals (annual averages)	91	45	120	72

Sources: C.-P. Clasen, *Anabaptism: A Social History, 1525–1618* (Ithaca, 1972), pp. 370–438; Alastair Duke, *Reformation and Revolt in the Low Countries* (London, 1990), p. 99; A. G. Dickens, *The English Reformation* (London, 1964), pp. 264–272; Jasper Ridley, *Thomas Cranmer* (Oxford, 1962), p. 253n.; William Monter, *Frontiers of Heresy* (Cambridge, 1990), pp. 37–39, 233–240; Paul Grendler, *The Roman Inquisition and the Venetian Press, 1540–1605* (Princeton, 1977), p. 57; and Domenico Orano, *Liberi pensatori bruciati a Roma (sec. XVI–XVIII)* (Rome, 1904). For France, see the Appendix.

and the adoption of the Thirty-nine Articles of the Church of England. It saw the outbreak of the French Wars of Religion, which became far longer and bloodier than the previous struggles of the Lutheran Schmalkaldic League against Charles V after 1547. The decade also witnessed the publication of various Protestant martyrologies: Jean Crespin's version underwent several revisions and updatings after 1554; the Antwerp pastor Adrian van Haemstede published a Dutch collection in 1559; and John Foxe, after producing a smaller Latin version during his exile on the continent, brought out his great English collection in 1564.

Perhaps the most surprising aspect of European heresy executions after 1555 is the statistically infinitesimal role played by the papacy and its Roman Inquisition, which had been created in 1542 for the express purpose of combatting Protestantism in Italy.[52] Even under the ruthless Pope Paul IV, who boasted that he would bring faggots to help burn his own father if he were declared to be a heretic, the Roman Inquisition executed fewer heretics than many towns in the Low Countries. Neither Protestant martyrologies nor official Catholic sources record any "Lutherans" executed by the Roman Inquisition until 1546, and that victim was a Spaniard.[53] Only a handful of heretics were executed in Italy by the Roman Inquisition before Paul IV's pontificate; the Spanish Inquisition in Sicily remained the most active agency of anti-Protestant repression in Italy until 1555.[54] The new Roman Inquisition was underequipped to deal with the problem of Protestant heresy, even in a land where Protestantism had few opportunities to proselytize and never exhibited a seditious edge. Unlike the older Spanish and Portuguese models, both run as branches of the state bureaucracy by royally appointed officials, the papacy's version of a permanent Holy Office appears to have been understaffed, inadequately housed, and underpaid.[55] Although the remnants of Protestant activity in Italy had been snuffed out by 1600, the Roman Inquisition never terrorized dissidents through massive public executions of heretics; even at its most brutal, during the decade after 1565, it executed fewer than four Protestants per year. The relative feebleness of the papacy's physical attacks on Protestant heretics underlines what we have already seen of Rome's failure to control or even deflect Luther and of the ineffectiveness of ecclesiastical justice in the Low Countries in the 1520s. From top to bottom, from pope to bishop, church courts and canon law simply could not cope with the early Reformation.

The sharp rise in public executions for heresy in the decade after 1555 cannot therefore be attributed to the excessive zeal of the aged Caraffa pope or the Roman Inquisition. The obvious place to look is in the large and sprawling collection of lands owing allegiance to Charles V's son and principal heir, Philip II of Spain. The statistical picture of heresy executions across Reformation Europe fits the itinerary of this prince like a glove: after 1554, wherever Philip went, vast numbers of Protestants were being executed. At first one finds him in England as royal consort; soon thereafter one finds him in the Low Countries; by 1559 he had returned to Spain. The Protestant "Black Legend" feeds on such correlations, forgetting the prince's official title of *El Prudente*. Moreover, in none of these three different states did Philip exercise sovereign power directly. All three had women rulers when the persecution of Protestants either erupted or, in the Low Countries, escalated. In England, Philip and his Spanish advisers were excluded from domestic policymaking decisions throughout the reign of Mary I; moreover, there is ample evidence that they were deeply worried by the excesses of the Marian persecutions. In the Low Countries, which had been governed by female regents for more than fifty years, Philip installed another Habsburg princess in 1555. As had already happened in England, prosecution of Protestants in the Low Countries peaked in the early 1560s, after Philip had left the region. However, the persecution of *Luteranos* in Spain peaked just as Philip was returning in 1559. It remained high over the next half-dozen years, although many fewer Protestants died in Philip II's Spain than in either Marian England or Margaret of Parma's Low Countries. Even in Spain, the sudden, dramatic increase in prosecution of Protestants in 1559 had been prepared and begun under the regency government of his widowed sister, Juana of Portugal. Much was done in Philip's name in all three places, but only in Castile after 1560 did *El Prudente* take control of daily administration, and there it was largely a matter of following through on well-established policies.

English Exceptionalism

The kingdom of England must have seemed a very strange place to Philip and his Spanish advisers, who spent a relatively short time there during Mary Tudor's reign. The island's recent religious history had been remarkably chaotic. In the previous thirty years, its official religion had moved from traditional Catholic, to schismatic, to radical Protestant, and had now returned abruptly to traditional Catholicism. With respect to the prosecution of heretics, England was also a strange place. An abundance of medieval heretics, especially John Wycliffe and his Lollard followers, had induced the English to entrust the prosecution of heretics entirely to secular officials: a parliamentary statute of 1401 bore the ominous and accurate title *De Haeretico Comburendo* (On burning heretics). Whereas heresy executions had ceased in the German empire by 1460, Lollards were still being executed in various parts of England as late as 1520.

Lutheranism appeared in England during the 1520s, complicating the picture. Although Henry VIII's humanist chancellor, Thomas More, spoke of the need to punish heretics both old and new with proper severity, the first known Lutheran to be executed in the British Isles died in Scotland in 1528. After 1530 a handful of English Lutheran martyrs followed, both before and after Henry VIII's Parliament passed the Act of Supremacy in 1534, cutting England's ties with Rome. During the Münster scare in 1535, Henry VIII's government also discovered some Dutch

Anabaptist refugees in the land. They proceeded to burn fourteen of them, discouraging further immigration for a time. A dozen more Lutherans and a few more Anabaptists followed them during the last decade of Henry's long reign.[56] For a schismatic kingdom, proclaiming itself Catholic while repudiating papal authority, England saw a modest number of heresy prosecutions and executions. Over a dozen of these post-1534 trials and executions, involving both Anabaptists and more mainstream Protestants, required some intervention by Henry VIII's primate, the archbishop of Canterbury. Thomas Cranmer, himself a convinced Lutheran with a German wife, was unable to act upon his personal religious beliefs until after Henry's death, by which time he had evolved from a Lutheran to a Zwinglian.[57]

From Mary Tudor's viewpoint, however, the essential fact about English heresy executions since 1534 was that, unlike anywhere else in Europe, the majority of English victims were Roman Catholics. Like the Lollards before 1520 and the Lutherans or Anabaptists of the 1530s, these English "papists" were put to death under English statutory law; the Act of Supremacy carried a provision entailing capital punishment for those convicted of speaking "treasonous words" against the new religious settlements. No Protestant state, and no European ruler except this Anglo-Catholic "Defender of the Faith" ever threatened to behead his subjects for defending the pope's claim to be head of the church. Moreover, Henry VIII's government actually carried out this threat on troublemakers great and small, including his former chancellor and advocate of heresy prosecutions, Thomas More. Geoffrey Elton, the only historian to investigate this problem meticulously, concluded that during the time Thomas Cromwell pushed through his schismatic and at times crypto-Lutheran religious settlement, "sixty-three people died a traitor's death for words against the [royal] supremacy, which is quite enough for a period of five and a half years"; ten more, nine of them Carthusian monks, died in prison while awaiting trial on such charges.[58] Meanwhile, thousands more participated in plots and armed risings against Henry's religious reforms during the five years after 1534, and more than 250 of them were executed for the crimes of treason or conspiracy. Before "Bloody Mary" came to the throne, Cromwell's government had created hundreds of Catholic martyrs, among whom the most prominent ultimately became saints. Throughout the sixteenth century, both before and after Mary Tudor's five-year reign, England remained the only European state to produce hundreds of Catholic martyrs, including many monks slaughtered without trial by Elizabethan troops in Ireland.

It is against this background that one must view the famous Marian persecutions of the period 1555–1558.[59] While memories were still fresh, the returning exile John Foxe worked diligently at compiling a complete list of those who died as heretics during Mary's reign. He very nearly succeeded: the names in his *Acts and Monuments* include all but a handful of the Protestant martyrs known to subsequent scholars. We know much about them as a group, thanks largely to Foxe. They clustered heavily in southeastern England, precisely the area where subsequent scholarship has uncovered the earliest and strongest signs of Protestant sympathies. Only one person was burned in any of the northern counties, where popular support for Protestantism remained weakest. Socially, they clustered at the lower end of the scale. Although the Marian martyrs included a few prominent people, including five bishops, most were of very modest origins, and often illiterate. They included a sizable group of women, about fifty in all, mostly poor widows—a feature that resembles the Anabaptist martyrs rather than those from "mainstream" Protestantism. Although we know tantalizingly little about the precise religious beliefs for which they were executed, it seems probable that most of them, from Archbishop Cranmer down, had become what continental Catholic authorities called "sacramentarians." Except for gender distribution, they seem quite close to both the religious and the social patterns discernible among the comparably-sized group of Frenchmen executed for heresy in the 1540s and early 1550s. Meanwhile, hundreds of England's most notorious Protestants, mostly from relatively prosperous and educated backgrounds, fled the realm as soon as Mary I began to reign. The persecutions ceased slightly before Queen Mary's death, the prominent exiles returned, and Foxe soon set to work.

Calvinsts and Mennonites in the Low Countries

After Philip II replaced his father as sovereign in the Low Countries in 1555 and installed Margaret of Parma as regent, heresy prosecutions rose until 1564. During this decade, annual averages for public executions nearly doubled over those from the final fifteen years of Mary of Hungary's regency. Once again, Philip bore only indirect responsibility for this accelerating persecution, since he was busy managing a war with

France until 1559, and heresy persecutions increased markedly in the Low Countries after he left for Spain. Their distribution within the Low Countries was now quite different. Holland, which had dominated heresy repression in the 1530s, now contributed only a handful of executions, and none of them came from Amsterdam, which had put more heretics to death than any other city in Christendom from 1534 through 1554.[60] However, the reduced persecution of heretics in Holland and other northern provinces in the decade after Charles's abdication was offset by redoubled prosecutions in Flanders, which averaged about 160 trials and sixteen executions for heresy per year during this decade. In Brabant, the great city of Antwerp—which raised noisy and effective protests whenever the Brussels government tried to move against its Spanish Marrano merchants—outdid itself in prosecuting Anabaptists. Notwithstanding its vehement protests against the introduction of any outside Inquisition, Antwerp became the epicenter of religious repression in the Low Countries during the first decade of Philip II's reign, executing more than ten heretics per year. The Walloon regions added about eight heresy executions per year.

Most Low Countries heresy executions after 1555 can be traced in Mennonite or Calvinist martyrologies, whose entries include almost three-fourths of those put to death for heresy from 1555 to 1564. Never before or afterward was the correlation this high. Some of these Netherlands martyrs were included in the *History and Death of Pious Martyrs who have Shed their Blood for the Truths of the Gospel from the Time of Christ Jesus until* A.D. *1559,* published in Emden by the most ecumenical-minded pastor in Antwerp's Calvinist church, Adrian van Haemstede. Sympathetic to the Mennonites whom he saw dying in such numbers, van Haemstede was the first Protestant martyrologist to include members of more than one confession in his account, as well as the first author to compose such a work in the Low Countries.[61] The vast majority of these victims were Mennonites, who were soon commemorated in rhyming song with amazing precision by their own brethren through an anonymous work, *The Sacrifice unto the Lord,* first published in 1562.

By 1560 Calvinism had permeated most urban centers in the French-speaking regions, and it was also flourishing in metropolitan Antwerp. Combatting this development became a major concern of the regency government; although only three heretics died at Brussels during Philip II's first decade, all three were Calvinists. Although they created the first martyrology from the Low Countries, Calvinists contributed relatively few martyrs to these totals. Even at such strongholds as Tournai or Lille, Calvinists accounted for only half of the heresy executions from 1555 through 1564. The disproportion between Anabaptist and Calvinist martyrs was greatest at Van Haemstede's Antwerp, where municipal authorities executed ninety-two Anabaptists and only eight Calvinists during this decade. Under Inquisitor Peter Titelmans' watchful eye, the main Flemish cities, Ghent and Bruges, executed seventy-two Anabaptists and only two Calvinists from 1555 through 1564.

This superabundance of Anabaptist martyrs—nearly fifteen for every Calvinist martyr in the greatest cities of Brabant and Flanders—obviously does not reflect the respective numbers of each underground church. Such a huge disproportion between the fates of two clandestine Protestant congregations, which by 1560 were approximately the same size in Antwerp (each had several hundred members in a city of eighty thousand), suggests a strong class bias behind its heresy trials.[62] Although both groups drew from the city's large artisan class (Antwerp's first Calvinist pastor was a shoemaker), Anabaptists tended to be recent immigrants who recruited down the social scale, while Calvinists recruited upward into the merchant and professional classes. Many officials of Antwerp's Calvinist congregation were merchants, and several of their pastors had some formal academic training. The higher social standing of the Calvinists, who were also longer-term urban residents, protected them from the relentless prosecution unleashed by Antwerp's authorities upon the rootless and proletarian Mennonites. Assumptions about the social biases in urban heresy trials of the Low Countries are reinforced by evidence from the Francophone city of Tournai, which displays a pattern as clear as Antwerp's: one-third of the working-class people tried for heresy were executed, but only 6 percent of the priests and other upper-class heresy defendants.[63]

Heresy trials in the Low Countries affected regions, as well as social classes, to widely different degrees. Although numerous heresy trials took place in all major urban centers, their distribution among the predominantly rural provinces of this federation varied greatly. Whereas Friesland executed a hundred Anabaptists under Charles V and another dozen under Philip II, the neighboring province of Groningen, where Menno Simons lived undisturbed, never prosecuted anyone for heresy. It relied on its remoteness from Brussels and its special legal privileges as a recently acquired territory, ignoring the edicts and advice sent by the central government; even after 1564 neither the duke of Alva nor the Dutch Reformed Church could persuade them to harass their Anabaptists.[64] For very different reasons, the equally remote but much larger province of Luxemburg never prosecuted heretics. This time the explanation lies less in Luxemburg's well-developed provincial particularism than in its extremely rural and mountainous geography. Without good roads, manufacturing, or sizable towns, Luxemburg simply never produced any heretics worth prosecuting. The only Reformation they encountered in the sixteenth century was the Tridentine variety, and it too encountered difficulties there.[65] Another essentially rural province, Namur, a bit closer to the major Walloon towns, had arrested about fifty heretics and executed eleven of them by 1565. However, provincial authorities here spent much more time and effort investigating witchcraft, putting almost 150 suspected witches on trial and burning at least 40 of them during those same years.[66] The urban-rural dichotomy, provincial traditions, and the phenomenon of class justice in the major commercial and governmental centers of the Low Countries all help explain the remarkably different patterns of prosecution inflicted on Anabaptists and Calvinists in various places after 1555.

The Spanish Variant

Philip II left the Low Countries permanently in 1559, partly because serious manifestations of Lutheranism had recently appeared in the heart of Castile; he returned there in time to supervise its extermination, which Juana had already begun. Here he succeeded. The brief history of Spanish Protestantism (quite different from the history of Protestantism in Spain) offers the best evidence anywhere in Reformation Europe that a movement of religious dissidence could be stamped out if met promptly and with ruthless energy. The almost simultaneous discovery of evangelical groups at Seville and in the Castilian capital of Valladolid in 1557 had been followed up carefully. Three well-publicized *autos-da-fé* in 1559, the last one attended by Philip II, launched a seven-year cycle of feverish anti-Protestant activity by the Spanish Inquisition. The period 1559–1565 was the only moment in its long existence when Spain's Holy Office worried more about Protestants than about Judaizers or Moriscos. Unlike its prolonged struggles with Iberians of non-Christian ancestry, this time the Spanish Inquisition suceeded in completely eradicating a Christian heresy.

Three significant features distinguish the Spanish Inquisition's persecutions of *Luteranos* in the early years of Philip II's reign from parallel events in England or the Low Countries.[67] First, from a sociological point of view, the native Spanish *Luteranos* who ran afoul of the Spanish Inquisition were almost the exact reverse of the sacramentarian heretics burned in Marian England or Margaret of Parma's Low Countries. The nascent Protestant movement in Spain had sufficient upper-class leadership, but very few lower-class followers. Consequently, the Spanish Holy Office, which prided itself on sparing no one because of social standing, began this prosecution at Valladolid by burning a former *corregidor* of the city of Toro. In 1559 it also executed both clerics and laity from prominent families at both Valladolid and Seville. It was operating at this moment with special powers granted by Pope Paul IV, enabling it to execute even penitent first offenders for heresy. Therefore, Spain in 1559 was in the unique position of punishing upper-class heretics more severely than plebeians. The inquisitors also treated upper-class women with remarkable severity: over 40 percent of the fifty-seven Spanish *Luteranos* executed during this period were patrician women. At the other end of the process, the last important Spanish Protestant executed by the Inquisition was Don Gaspar de Centelles, a great landowner in Sardinia and Valencia and former courtier of Charles V, who died at an *auto-da-fé* in Valencia in 1564.

The second peculiar aspect of the Spanish Inquisition's major assault on the kingdom's "Lutherans" after 1559 is that it took a completely different form in the crown of Aragon than in Castile. In the Aragonese tribunals, at least three dozen "Lutherans" died at *autos-da-fé* in the 1560s. All but three of them were immigrant artisans from France. As the official report of Barcelona's municipality noted when recording its public *auto* of 1566,

> There were about forty people and some effigies, nearly all of them Lutherans . . . three men and seven effigies were burned, along with the bones and clothes of five others who had already died; some of the books of the Lutherans were also burned . . . According to what was said, the Lutherans were all French. May God, in his infinite goodness and mercy, be praised for keeping this province in his hand, and spare everyone afflicted by such an evil pestilence.[68]

In the crown of Castile, only the tribunal of Toledo behaved similarly, prosecuting many French immigrants but few native Castilians in the early 1560s. A vast social gulf separated Spanish patricians from French "guest workers," but they occasionally died side by side at public *autos-da-fé* in the 1560s. What is missing from this picture is the Spanish analogue to the archetypical Protestant martyr elsewhere in western Europe, namely the native-born craftsman.

A third peculiarity distinguishes the Spanish Inquisition's sudden persecution of its Protestants in 1559: its immediate international publicity. Unlike the situation in the Low Countries, where a Calvinist pastor quietly collected information for his martyrology and smuggled his manuscript to Emden to be printed in 1559, the propaganda about the first great *auto-da-fé* at Valladolid in May 1559, attended by the regent Juana and Philip's son Don Carlos, was quickly disseminated abroad by Catholic sources. Although the Spanish Inquisition never authorized the Spanish publication of any official sentences from an *auto-da-fé* until the famous episode of the Basque witches in 1610, reasonably accurate pamphlet versions of the sentences from the May 1559 Valladolid *auto* appeared almost immediately in Italian at both Venice and Bologna.[69] Since official representatives of the papacy and the Venetian Republic had attended the ceremony, they presumably acquired authentic copies of the sentences and encouraged their dissemination in Italy. Because German Protestants lived in Venice and its nearby university at Padua, these pamphlets immediately found their way into the Holy Roman Empire, where they were promptly reissued in anonymous and "Lutheranized" form (for example, the famous Dominican Melchior Cano, who preached the official sermon at this Valladolid *auto,* became "Melchior Hund"). From Germany the pamphlets found their way to the Low Countries, whose Protestant propagandists quickly made them into grist for their anti-Spanish "Black Legend" by adding gory engravings of the (purely imaginary) tortures suffered by these Spanish *Luteranos.*[70]

By 1565 more than three thousand Protestants had been executed for the crime of heresy throughout Reformation Europe. The overwhelming majority had been put to death by secular authorities, originally because many Anabaptists were perceived as politically and socially subversive. The connections, whether real or imaginary, between Gaismair and the Tyrolean Hutterites and soon afterward between Jan of Leiden and the Dutch Anabaptists, had momentous legal consequences: over a thousand Anabaptists perished in Austria and the Low Countries from 1528 through 1540. When the immediate aftereffects of the Peasants'

War and the tragedy of Münster wore off, heresy prosecutions ebbed. Across most of Latin Christendom, the least active phase of heresy prosecutions occurred from 1540 through 1554, before executions again escalated dramatically during the years preceding the outbreak of religious warfare in France and the Netherlands.

In Europe's largest state, the kingdom of France, the prosecution of Protestant heresy followed a very different chronological pattern. Most French heresy trials and executions were concentrated during the decade after 1544, a time when Habsburg governments had slackened their early drive to eliminate religious deviance by fire and sword. In all, France witnessed almost 450 heresy deaths from 1523 through 1560, about one-seventh of the European total, ranking far behind the Low Countries but ahead of other European states. However, considering its great size and population, the French kingdom executed proportionately fewer heretics than Tudor England or Habsburg Austria, and vastly fewer than the Habsburg Netherlands, which had barely one-sixth the population of France but put three times as many Protestants to death before 1565. The French experience of heresy trials during the Protestant Reformation also included two unusual features—the complete absence of any Anabaptist peril, and the surprising initiative of the court system itself in instigating persecution—which cannot be appreciated unless they are set within the general context of sixteenth-century European Christendom.

3

Parlementary Initiatives and Public Scandals, 1523–1539

In matters of faith, the court, which is the sovereign consistory of the most Christian prince, has customarily claimed and may now claim jurisdiction by both law and reason.

—*Pierre Lizet (1525)*

France was the only major state in Christendom where the early drive to repress the new heresy of Lutheranism came from the court system itself rather than from the crown. As we have seen, Charles V responded vehemently to Luther's challenge with the Edict of Worms and soon made an ill-fated attempt to adapt the Spanish Inquisition to his domains in the Low Countries. Later in the 1520s, his younger brother, Ferdinand, responded to the linked challenges of peasant revolt and Anabaptism with extermination campaigns of unprecedented savagery in his Austrian possessions. In England, the monarch quickly took personal responsibility for refuting Luther's errors, and his chancellor Thomas More undertook a vigorous repression by the early 1530s. But in the largest Christian kingdom, ruled by a "most Christian" king whose coronation oath included a special clause requiring him to combat heresy, the monarch remained conspicuously absent from the first attempts to punish "Lutherans." Under Francis I, a ruler well known for his absolutism, it was the judicial system itself, principally the oldest and most prestigious appellate court in western Europe, the Parlement of Paris, which quickly seized the initiative in this matter. Until 1540 Francis gave only sporadic encouragement to his appellate courts in their pursuit of Protestant heretics; his most significant piece of early legislation was actually a conditional pardon for non-"sacramentarian" heretics in 1535.

Since France's coronation oath required him, as "most Christian king," to uproot heresy, Francis clearly felt a duty to uphold this provision and repeatedly expressed his opposition to heresy. On the other hand, by the mid-1520s political necessity required him to maintain friendship not only with heretical Swiss cantons and Lutheran princes in the Holy Roman Empire, but even with the most dangerous infidel known to Renaissance Europe, the Ottoman sultan. Francis I's domestic and foreign policies flagrantly contradicted each other in this respect over the last twenty years of his long reign (1515–1547). Normally, however, foreign policy considerations did not interfere with his opposition to domestic heresy; Francis simply told his allies not to meddle with his internal affairs, just as he avoided meddling in theirs.

If Francis I's attitudes toward the Reformation movement seem inconsistent, his attachment to the fashionable values of the Renaissance was as solid and predictable as his daily attendance at Mass. He decorated his kingdom with such durable assets as the sumptuous castle of Fontainebleau and the prestigious Collège de France, enduring symbols of the art and humanism of his day. Two extremely influential voices at court constantly encouraged Francis' patronage of humanism. An internationally famous humanist, Guillaume Budé, served as his principal private secretary. Even more influential was his only sibling, a sister two years older than he; Marguerite d'Angoulême not only shared his admiration for humanism but even created significant works of literature herself. Because he admired humanism while hating heresy, Francis I generally believed that these two did not mix, that humanists—even those who wanted to use biblical scholarship in order to reform the church, like Erasmus or Lefèvre d'Etaples—were not heretics.

However, two of the oldest and most important institutions of his kingdom saw things very differently in the 1520s. Both the Faculty of Theology of the University of Paris, under the leadership of Noel Béda (its syndic from 1520 to 1533), and the Parlement of Paris, whose future First President Pierre Lizet (1529–1550) was emerging as chief royal prosecutor of heresy, viewed Christian and biblical humanism as a necessary prelude to the Protestant movement. Unlike the king, they believed that "Erasmus laid the egg which Luther hatched." Together they mounted an early and vigorous campaign against the dangers of "Lutheranism." Since Béda's theological faculty and Lizet's appellate court agreed on this major issue, during most of Francis' reign they avoided much of the mutual suspicion that normally troubled their relationship. By 1523 the oldest and most prestigious appellate court in Christendom, proud of its ability to judge freely and arbitrarily, had allied itself against the novelties of "Lutheranism" with the oldest theological faculty in Christendom, to which Luther himself had appealed in 1519.[1] However, Francis I often showed little patience with either theologians or jurists. He displayed a "strongly authoritarian disposition from the outset of his reign,"[2] and seldom was this king more firmly "absolutist" than when dealing with the royal judiciary. A deeply conservative institutional united front of Sorbonne and Parlement therefore encountered an authoritarian and unpredictable monarch, whose views about heresy and Christian humanism clashed violently with theirs.

In the absence of any effective ecclesiastical inquisition in northern France, the Parlement of Paris and its emergent antiheresy spokesman played the major role in the repression of the early Protestant movement. Although modern scholarship has produced abundant work of high quality on all major figures of French humanism (especially on the king's sister, Marguerite) and on the proto-Reformers (especially her protégé Guillaume Briçonnet, bishop of Meaux), we know extremely little about the leader of conservative repression, Pierre Lizet.[3] While he probably owed his unexpected promotion to First President to his political connections, and his eventual fall to court factions, Lizet's honesty and professional dedication were acknowledged by even his worst enemies. We possess one important clue to his intellectual preferences, which tells us a good deal about the man leading the early prosecution of "Lutherans" in France: Lizet's personal library, inventoried after his death in 1554.[4] It was unusual because of its size (more than five hundred titles, far larger than the holdings of his colleagues), but even more for its contents. Lizet owned comprehensive collections about both jurisprudence (318 titles) and theology, including almost everything pertaining to Roman law, canon law, or patristics.[5] But he owned virtually nothing of recent vintage in either theology or law, although he published both a textbook on legal procedure and a lengthy refutation of Protestant errors after his forced retirement from the bench.[6] Remarkably, this bibliophilic head of the French court system owned no collections of French royal edicts. The lacunae of Pierre Lizet's library speak to us at least as eloquently as its riches. The head of the French legal system never consulted personal collections of French royal legislation. It is difficult to imagine more striking confirmation of the argument that arbitrary justice, as practiced in Renaissance France, bore little relationship to French royal edicts.

Hunting "Lutherans" at Paris, 1523–1529

On 6 June 1523 Pierre Lizet, a royal attorney for the Parlement of Paris, first approached the Paris Faculty of Theology for assistance in repressing heresy.[7] The Parlement of Paris had just launched the first major investigation into the spread of the new heresy of "Lutheranism," defined and condemned by the Faculty of Theology in 1521, in the heart of France. The problem was centered on the diocese of Meaux, only fifty kilometers east of Paris. Its reforming bishop, Guillaume Briçonnet, had encouraged sermons based only on biblical texts and patronized Christian humanist scholarship under the leadership of Lefèvre d'Etaples. But "Lutheranism" was also present in Paris, where the Parlement had arrested a humanist nobleman and *conseillier-clerc* named Louis de Berquin, seizing his library and manuscripts, which included translations of Luther. In the summer of 1523, Francis intervened one day too late to prevent Berquin's works from being condemned by the Faculty of Theology and their author from being imprisoned on a charge of heresy; but he soon quashed Berquin's indictment by evoking the case to his privy council, and promptly releasing him.

It was precisely then, on 8 August 1523, that the Parlement of Paris decreed its first public execution of a French "Lutheran." They condemned a hermit from Normandy named Jean Vallière under their existing power to repress gross blasphemy. They created a public spectacle which combined his execution at Paris' pig market with the public burning of Berquin's condemned Lutheran books and writings at the square in front of Notre-Dame cathedral, and they made some attempt to depict the eccentric hermit as a "Lutheran." Of the three contemporary Paris' chroniclers who report Vallière's death, one specified that he was "burned alive in his hermit's dress"; another tells us that he performed an *amende honorable* at Notre-Dame before his execution, stressing that he was "ignorant" and had not been ordained. However, our third source, a lawyer at the Parlement, links the two ceremonies at Notre-Dame, the bonfire of Berquin's books, and the *amende honorable* of "this poor, ignorant man, calling himself a hermit." The lawyer described the specific nature of Vallière's blasphemy—he had claimed publicly that Jesus was merely the son of Joseph—and then asserted that "the said hermit had been induced in part to preach thus by the books of Luther," insinuating that Berquin believed the same thing but lacked the courage to say so in public.[8] Luther himself, had he known about the case, would have brought plenty of wood for Vallière's bonfire, though not for Berquin's books. The fine art of guilt by association was etched sharply into the first known public execution of a "Lutheran" in France. Berquin they could not have (not yet, anyway); but the judges could burn his writings together with a real heretic, joining them together under the label "Lutheran."

Two other aspects of this episode also deserve mention. First, the ceremony of 8 August 1523 united two of the essential features of a Spanish-style "act of faith," namely the public repentance of a confessed heretic (who, one chronicler was informed by a priest, "died as a good Christian") combined with the burning of heretical materials and the death of the heretic, in unconsecrated and indeed shameful ground well removed from the site of his abjuration. Second, Vallière was executed largely because he had preached his blasphemous errors. Contrast his case with that of a monastic hermit named Guibert, who lived near Meaux. Banished for Lutheranism by his ecclesiastical judges because he had replaced the Mass with gospel readings, Guibert appealed to Parlement; Lizet proposed in November 1523 that he merely be confined in a Benedictine monastery.[9]

After these first skirmishes, further scandals at Meaux around Christmas 1524 (papal bulls were defaced and prayers lacerated on the door of the cathedral) provided fresh pretexts for the Parlement of Paris to resume its campaigns against the humanist heresies of Briçonnet's preachers. After the king's capture in February 1525 and prolonged captivity in Italy and Spain, they renewed their attack against such old enemies as Berquin. Seldom were the judges presented with an opportunity to act without effective royal constraint, and they took full advantage of the exceptional circumstances provided by Francis' long absence from France. In March 1525 the Parlement's senior president raised the problem of heresy, "which is great and rampant in the kingdom and has been much discussed, and not without reason, because there are people who accept Luther's doctrines." He complained that previously, whenever heresy had been discussed in their court, "great personages [doubtless referring to the king's sister] have obstructed our taking cognizance of it."[10] But times had now changed.

During the regency of Francis I's mother in 1525–1526, acting in alliance with the Sorbonne, the Parlement of Paris intervened extensively in heresy cases. First President Jean de Selve expressed the court's conventional wisdom with respect to heresy in March 1525: "its correction belongs to the Church, and the execution to laymen." It also sounded serious about enforcement, threatening to put on trial any judges who were "found to be negligent in the pursuit and punishment of blasphemers."[11] The Parlement's major innovation during Francis' captivity was to propose a special mixed tribunal to try cases of heresy, composed of two of its own judges and two members of the Paris Faculty of Theology, known as the *juges delegués*. Quickly approved by both the regent and the papacy in the spring of 1525, this special tribunal functioned for about two years.[12] We hear of about two dozen defendants, mostly laymen and clerics from Briçonnet's diocese of Meaux, tried during this period, usually because the Parlement gave the delegated judges procedural instructions or reviewed their decisions. Echoes of their condemnations appear in three contemporary Parisian chronicles, kept by a cleric, a lawyer, and an unidentified layman. For instance, all three reported the dramatic *amende honorable* at Notre-Dame just before Christmas 1525 by a cleric from Meaux; his heretical translations were burned in his presence, and he was afterward confined to a monastery on bread and water.[13]

The Parlement and the theology faculty had already frightened Bishop Briçonnet in 1523; now, with the king out of the picture, they managed to silence him and destroy his program of Christian humanist reform at Meaux.[14] Adding insult to injury, they even made Briçonnet pay the handsome sum of two hundred livres in order to subsidize the prosecution of his protégés.[15] Although some of the Parlement's initiatives during the king's captivity were quashed after his return, the precedent of forcing local bishops to pay for the prosecution of accused Protestants in their dioceses became standard practice during the great heresy hunt of the 1540s. Making bishops financially reponsible for prosecuting heretics in lay courts sat very well with the Gallican traditions of Renaissance France. It effectively solved one major difficulty in prodding the cumbersome legal machinery of both church and state into action against something defined as a clear and present danger, but against which private accusers rarely came forward to inaugurate a long and expensive legal process.

The most ambitious initiative of the delegated judges was to rearrest Berquin, their most obnoxious parlementary colleague, during the winter of 1525–26.[16] Ignoring an order from the still-absent king to release Berquin, Parlement reported that their prisoner "appeared to be very contumacious" by denying that the special tribunal had the power to try him. After discussing his case, the Parlement increased its proposed punishments against clerics or laymen who spoke or wrote against transubstantiation or possessed prohibited books. A Parisian cleric attended Berquin's public sentencing in March 1526 "concerning the heresies of Luther" and carefully named all the judges present; but a layman, reporting the same event, stressed instead how Berquin was ultimately saved through the king's intervention.[17] The king's return to France had indeed spared Berquin a second time. In early April Francis asked the chief justice to provide fuller information about Berquin's "alleged errors"; after much further maneuvering and protesting, the judges were forced to release him in November. Early in 1527, under pressure from the French crown, Pope Clement VII revoked his commission to the delegated judges. A few months later Francis I finally quashed them, together with several other recent parlementary innovations, at a *lit de justice*.

During Francis' absence, two religious offenders were executed at Paris in February 1526, although neither can be classified as a Lutheran. Two chroniclers report a spectacular case of sacrilege, in which a young boatman and his companion stole a monstrance and destroyed the Hosts in it; after an expiatory procession, the boatman (whose companion had escaped) was drawn through the streets on a sled and burned at the Place de Grève during Mardi Gras.[18] Three days later, all three chroniclers apparently witnessed the last moments of an apprentice attorney from La Rochelle, strangled and burned at Place Maubert after two public apologies for his atrocious blasphemies; a copy of his trial was thrown into the flames. Two observers stressed his exemplary degree of repentance; one noted that his trial had lasted only fifteen days and that his father had offered a large bribe to spare his life.[19] Later that year, after King Francis had returned, a relapsed Lutheran named Jacques Pavanes was burned in the Place de Grève. A student from Picardy who held a benefice but was not yet ordained, Pavanes had performed the well-attended formal abjuration at Christmas 1525 and been sentenced to seven years' imprison-

ment. Apparently he provoked his custodians by revoking his revoca-
tions, and this time the king demanded severe punishment. All three
chroniclers stress his public blasphemies against the Eucharist. They also
agree that this prisoner refused to make any public apology and "died
obstinate in his error," refusing to confess to the accompanying priest.[20]

These three deaths, each one exemplary, illustrate what things were
punished with utmost severity and how public punishments, decreed by
the most famous tribunal in Christendom, actually worked. Blasphemy
long antedated Luther; the young attorney's bad luck lay in being caught
at the wrong time, during Francis' captivity, when the delegated judges
wanted to demonstrate their seriousness of purpose. Sacrilege was another old problem, exacerbated in this instance by wanton misuse of
the Eucharist; it provided an opportunity for a participatory catharsis
through the public procession (on a major holy day) coinciding with the
culprit's death. But the third religious execution of 1526 provided the
first instance of a true Protestant martyr at Paris—an example carefully
commemorated by the famous martyrologist Jean Crespin.

After the king's return, both clerical and lay chroniclers reported public executions for blasphemy and another sacrilege at Paris in the next
few years. The defendants included highly prominent and privileged
people. In March 1527 a clerical protonotary from Anjou, who held
several benefices and had served at the papal court, was burned for "great
blasphemy against Our Lord and his glorious mother" after a very short
trial; he refused to perform his public apology.[21] In June 1528 a dramatic
act of iconoclasm occurred at Paris, when a statue of the Virgin and Child
was destroyed. The occasion enabled parlementary spokesmen to lament
the evils of the age and particularly the continuing spread of Lutheranism, on which the incident was immediately blamed. At the ensuing
plenary session of Parlement, where official reactions from the king, the
chancellor, the municiality, the bishop, and the university were recorded,
Pierre Lizet, as royal attorney, made the main speech. His remarks eloquently summarized the Parlement's instinctive suspicion of religious
novelties, above all if they provoked any form of public disorder.

Lizet began with a ringing defense of religious images as instruments
for inculcating obedience and reverence both to God and to civil authority. He next discussed the increase of "execrable blasphemies" during the
past decade, involving public mockery of the saints and even of the
Eucharist. Lizet added that "several secret meetings [*conventicules*] had

been held, at which numberless errors and heretical propositions have been discussed, such that public order has been and continues to be disturbed; and whatever punishments the court of Parlement has been able to make with repeated orders and unwavering royal support, the evil has not been extinguished." The recent sacrilege demonstrated as much. All these scandals, blasphemies, and irreverences, Lizet insisted, "proceed from this pestiferous and contagious Lutheran sect, which is indubitably the source of all these scandals and evils, because the Lutherans, as one can see by their writings, have detested not only the images placed in churches but even the prayers made to saints: the origin and source of all these blasphemies and scandals is the impudent and turpid lake of the Lutheran sect." Citing St. Ambrose, he compared heresy to a hydra: "in order to chop off these heads and major scandals proceeding from the monstrous Lutheran hydra, there is no other remedy than to destroy it entirely and uproot it completely from this kingdom."[22] The Parlement immediately approved a magnificent expiatory procession, and the king paid for a new and finer statue, but such demonstrations certainly did not exterminate heresy. Although the king offered a huge reward, the culprits were never found.

Although these iconoclastic "Lutherans" remained beyond its reach, the Paris Parlement carried out three other capital punishments for heresy and "execrable" blasphemy during the next year. Bracketing the third and final trial of their colleague Louis de Berquin in April 1529 were two other executions. In December 1528 a boatman from Meaux was arrested for heresy by Bishop Briçonnet and taken to Paris, where he was burned alive for saying that the Virgin Mary had no more power than an image that he held in his hand and then broke.[23] In August 1529 the married son of a Paris cloth merchant was burned alive for blasphemy against God, the Virgin, and several saints, with a copy of his trial thrown onto the flames. Although his local judge in Paris had condemned him only to an *amende honorable,* the prisoner appealed to Parlement, which promptly increased his sentence to capital punishment.[24]

Berquin's death for heresy in April 1529 is a well-known tale. Since there were no more *juges delegués,* his last trial was conducted by a special tribunal of twelve laymen appointed by the pope at the king's request. Although the papal nuncio revoked their powers, they nevertheless convicted Berquin and sentenced him to life imprisonment. Berquin then made the same kind of tactical mistake that Bishop Briçonnet had done in 1525, namely appealing his case to Parlement at a time when the king was out of reach. Briçonnet's blunder ruined his program of humanist reform at Meaux, cost him much money, and set an important financial precedent; but Berquin's mistake cost him his life in front of a huge audience, which one source estimated at twenty thousand. Three years earlier, the Parlement of Paris had wasted more than eight months trying in vain to pass sentence on him because of King Francis' opposition, finally watching helplessly as he was forcibly removed from their prison by the king's soldiers. This time they acted with blinding speed, rejecting Berquin's appeal, increasing his punishment from imprisonment to death as a relapsed heretic, and carrying out his execution, all within forty-eight hours. Thus the French Reformation acquired a prominent martyr. Although the king's sister viewed the outcome as little more than a lynching, a parlementary lawyer and diarist justified the court's action; "admitting that [Berquin] was learned in literature," he said, "nevertheless he abused his knowledge evilly."[25]

Repressing Public Scandals, 1532–1534

French parlementary campaigns against "Lutheranism" expanded both geographically and quantitatively in the early 1530s, as the appellate courts attempted to repress serious public scandals implicating sizable groups of malcontents. Still relying on their own initiatives, with minimal encouragement from the crown, parlementary campaigns against the new heresies now spread beyond Paris, reaching the kingdom's second oldest and second largest parlement at Toulouse.[26] Two episodes reveal these mechanisms at work. Various scandals at Toulouse in the winter of 1531–32 led to the first massive French parlementary action against suspected "Lutherans." Then, an unusually provocative act of sacrilege in the summer of 1533 at Marguerite's personal apanage of Alençon, located just outside the legal boundaries of Lizet's tribunal, was brutally punished the following year by a special committee of the Paris Parlement. In dealing with such problems, French parlements developed novel tactics of repression. Suspects, including many who fled in order to avoid arrest, were now being investigated en masse; special commissions were organized in order to investigate collective heretical acts committed in public.

The Toulouse Parlement prosecuted more than fifty "Lutherans" in

1532.[27] The public scandals that provoked this investigation began after three Augustinians preached "Lutheran" sermons in the city in 1531. The Augustinians quickly disappeared, but provocative heretical behavior soon erupted at the municipal university. At a major banquet on Twelfth Night in 1532 the festivities were dominated by speeches featuring evangelical scholarship instead of serious drinking; the "Lutherans" at the University of Toulouse thus went public almost two years sooner than their counterparts at the University of Paris. Despite the relative moderation of its Italian-born First President, the Parlement of Languedoc immediately investigated Evangelical intellectuals throughout the university community. On 31 March 1532 warrants were issued against more than fifty suspected radicals. Thirty-two of them, including both French and Italian law professors and the anti-Trinitarian Spanish student Michael Servetus, managed to escape. They were condemned in absentia for holding a variety of "Lutheran" articles, including justification by faith and reliance on scriptural authority alone in religious matters. Two dozen others were imprisoned and soon punished at two significant ceremonies, both attended by huge crowds. First, Jean de Boysonné, a highly regarded professor of Roman law, performed an elaborate public abjuration on a special scaffold set up outside the cathedral of St. Etienne, dressed in a shabby gray robe and with shaven head, while an episcopal inquisitor addressed the audience.[28] The humiliated professor was further condemned to pay a huge fine of 1,000 livres and left immediately for Italy, although he and one of his fugitive colleagues were subsequently pardoned by Francis I.

The Parlement of Toulouse also took the unusual step of investigating the legal title of Languedoc's recently appointed provincial inquisitor, whom they accused of protecting heretics; in fact he had disappeared from Toulouse simultaneously with dozens of accused "Lutherans." The Parlement proceeded to threaten both the archbishop of Toulouse and subordinate secular courts if they failed to cooperate with their special commissioners against heresy. Four judges, then six, then eight, including one of the Parlement's presidents, joined the archbishop's judge in sentencing heretics.[29] A law graduate and university instructor, who had presided over the notorious banquet, was defrocked and burned in May, slandering his judges in Latin with his dying words.[30] To complete the ceremony, twenty-one other members of the university performed public abjurations, and a priest was condemned to perpetual imprisonment.

The compromised inquisitor, a close friend of the executed law instructor, was prosecuted by a special tribunal of "subdelegated" judges; in the end, he escaped formal punishment but was forced to resign in disgrace.[31]

Soon afterward a young humanist named Etienne Dolet arrived at the University of Toulouse and criticized the judges for their excessive harshness in executing Caturce. He made friends with the returned Boysonné, got himself briefly imprisoned for other reasons, and left for Lyon. Rabelais's *Pantagruel* refused to study at Toulouse because "he saw that they sautéed their regents alive like herrings." Despite his public condemnation for heresy, Boysonné retained enough prestige and influence to be appointed to the recently created Parlement of Chambéry in 1539, where he served quietly for the next dozen years.[32] The most notorious fugitive of all, Servetus, eventually moved to a quiet town near Lyon and successfully obtained French naturalization in 1548 under a pseudonym.[33] Nascent Protestantism had been extinguished at the University of Toulouse. The *Histoire Ecclésiastique* sketched the subsequent careers of three protégés of Marguerite's who had been involved in the early Reformation movement at Toulouse: one became a bishop and cardinal; a monk named De Nuptiis moved to Bourges (another possession of Marguerite's) "and never did anything worthwhile afterward," while his younger companion in flight subsequently "did a great deal worse."[34]

Although Pierre Lizet became chief justice of the Parlement of Paris a few months after Berquin's death in 1529, sources indicate no sudden increase in activity against heresy. We know that Lizet tricked and arrested one suspect early in 1530 without notifying his colleagues beforehand,[35] while that summer the Parlement "made punishment of some residents of Meaux who held to the error of Luther" and others from a Paris suburb who had denied the existence of purgatory or the power of saints.[36] But there are no records of important heresy trials at Paris in the early 1530s. Many matters occupied the king and his Parlement, including the antipapal divorce case of Henry VIII of England and Francis' alliance with the new political league of Germany's Lutheran princes and cities. Nothing goaded the king or his Paris judges into vigorous action against suspected heretics until 1533, a year filled with multiple provocations both by Reformers and by Sorbonne conservatives. The final episode, a blatantly Lutheran public address by the new rector of the University of Paris in November 1533, provoked, among other consequences, John Calvin's flight. An angry king ordered the bishop of Paris to delegate two parlementary judges as his vicars to try heresy cases, although he stopped short of restoring the system of delegated judges.[37]

Capital punishments for heresy resumed at Paris in 1534. That spring we hear of a physician burned alive "on account of the huge blasphemies he had said." Like a few of his predecessors, he refused to repent and suffered what the martyrologist Jean Crespin insisted was a newly invented form of cruelty: his tongue was cut out before his execution.[38] Three months later a former Dominican, who had not only preached secretly in Switzerland and Lyon (where he had been caught) but had also got married, heard Parlement deny his appeal from his death sentence. Alexander Canus, alias Laurent de la Croix, was formally defrocked at Paris by the archbishop of Lyon; showing inadequate signs of repentance during the ceremony of degradation, he too was burned alive.[39] In August 1534, more than five years after Berquin's case, another high-profile religious radical, "le magnifique" Laurent Meigret, underwent his second trial for heresy. Meigret was extremely well connected: one brother had been a paymaster for the king's Swiss mercenaries, and another was a judge in the Paris Parlement. Like Berquin, he was tried by a special court, which similarly stopped short of imposing a death penalty. Nonetheless, the process of his humiliation is edifying. Meigret had to perform no fewer than three public abjurations: first in front of the civil court of Parlement, then in front of the court that tried him, and finally in front of a large crowd at Notre-Dame, because he stood convicted of eating meat during Lent and regularly on Fridays and Saturdays. His property was confiscated, and he was banished from France for five years. Immediately afterward he turned up in Geneva, where he soon became a good friend of Calvin's and for the next dozen years opened every letter Francis sent to his Swiss ambassadors.[40]

In 1534 the Parisian judges struck their most significant blow against the king's sister. After successfully prosecuting Marguerite's friend Briçonnet in the mid-1520s, Lizet and his colleagues now moved against her principal personal possession, the capital of her dowry apanage, which was located just outside their huge judicial district. Like Meaux, the Norman city of Alençon had long had a reputation as a trouble spot. Marguerite had sent one of Briçonnet's heretical preachers there soon after he had been condemned during the first cycle of repression in 1523–24. Worse still, a parish priest in her duchy of Alençon had been put on trial by the Dominican inquisitor of Normandy in 1531. The archbishop of Rouen ordered an opinion on his case from the Paris theology faculty, which condemned a long list of his heretical propositions in February 1532. After further procedural delays in Normandy, he was finally condemned to be defrocked, then strangled and burned at Rouen in December 1533—the first known Protestant, though not the first heretic, sentenced to death by the Parlement of Normandy.[41]

Meanwhile, an even more serious incident had erupted in Alençon itself.[42] In June 1533 pranksters stole statues of the Virgin and St. Claude from an urban chapel on the eve of a major festival and hanged them in public. The investigation of this spectacular sacrilege was undertaken by the Paris Parlement, although it had no legal right to do so. A special Parisian parlementary commission began work only three weeks after the sacrilege, following the Paris theologians' intervention in the lengthy heresy trial of the nearby priest. After the arrest of two principal suspects in the capital, the Paris Parlement, in a remarkable judicial tour de force, outmaneuvered a deeply embarrassed Marguerite, winning the absent king's permission to take full control of the case and compelling her unconditional cooperation.[43] In September 1534 a seven-judge committee from the Parlement of Paris entered Normandy in order to punish these "enormous and execrable blasphemies and scandals." The first special parlementary commission devoted to the problem of heresy and the only one ever sent beyond the vast boundaries of the Paris district, they spent a fortnight in Alençon judging seven prisoners (including the two it brought from Paris), arresting others, and condemning many fugitives.[44] They executed both men brought from Paris and two men being held in Alençon; they also extradited a layman from the local bishop's court at Séez and arranged his execution two days after he reached Alençon. Three other prisoners, who had attended private heretical sermons, made public apologies and received whippings; one of these was also banished. The Paris judges issued more than thirty arrest warrants, which were promptly obeyed only by three women (whom they promptly released) and a priest (whom they transferred to his local episcopal court). They also condemned four fugitives to death and three others to banishment; however, at least three of them still held official positions in and around Alençon many years later.[45]

The "Sacramentarians" of 1534

By October 1534 the repression of "Lutheranism" by French royal courts had spread beyond the Parlement of Paris. Clusters of heretics had recently been condemned to the flames in both Normandy and Provence. A handful of dissident intellectuals had been condemned and executed with great pomp by authority of royal parlements at Toulouse, Rouen, and Paris; other prominent men, like Boysonné at Toulouse or Meigret at Lyon, had been publicly humiliated and forced into exile or silence. Dozens more had been investigated; most of them had simply fled, a few still managed to retain some protection at court, and a handful had become sufficiently intimidated to discard their evangelistic opinions, retreating into feigned or genuine conformism. Meanwhile, the public audacity of French Protestants had also escalated. In 1533, for example, we hear of a statue of the Virgin hanged in a town in Normandy, of armed attacks by peasants on inquisitorial officials prosecuting heretics in a Provençal village, and of a "Lutheran" public address by the rector of the University of Paris. But nothing prepared the parlementary judges or the king for the shock they received in the autumn of 1534.

The "Affair of the Placards," which erupted both in Paris and at the king's current residence at Amboise on 18 October, is justly considered one of the principal events both in the reign of Francis I and in the history of the French Reformation. Its general outlines have been told often and well.[46] Here we must emphasize a few of its significant features in order to place this pivotal event satisfactorily within the history of the legal repression of Protestantism by French secular justice under Francis I. Pivotal it most certainly was, above all in two ways. First, the scale of legal repression across the next several months at Paris was unsurpassed. The two dozen people who died at Paris within seven months after the placards appeared on 18 October 1534 constituted the largest total ever executed for heresy in one French city within such a brief period.[47] Second, the Affair of the Placards redefined the crimes associated with "Lutheranism" by introducing a new and peculiarly virulent strain of Protestant heresy into the legal vocabulary used by French royal judges. During the winter of 1534–35, "sacramentarians" became the chief culprits in the Paris persecutions, and the term became embedded in French legal discourse about Protestant heresy throughout the following decades.

Both the contents of the placard and the circumstances of its appearance do much to explain these extreme reactions to it. First, its physical distribution was remarkable. Printed outside the kingdom by Protestant refugees, smuggled across France and displayed simultaneously at many public places in the capital, some provincial towns, and even at a royal residence on 18 October, the placards represented on one level (seldom stressed by Protestant historians) a remarkably well-organized conspiracy by the most radical wing of French religious reformers. In a kingdom without indigenous Anabaptists—who had at this very moment taken over the imperial city of Münster and had just staged a military coup against Amsterdam—the Affair of the Placards constituted the most aggressive provocation imaginable against the Sorbonne theologians and their allies in the royal judiciary.

Reading the single-page tract enables one to see why the term "sacramentarian" came into existence. Titled "Truthful articles about the horrible, great and unbearable (*importables*) abuses of the papal Mass," it contained a preamble and four paragraphs, shrinking Zwingli's symbolic eucharistic theology to the dimensions of a sixteenth-century sound bite. The Mass is not and cannot possibly be a sacrifice; Christ cannot possibly be physically present in a consecrated Host; the Mass is an invention of the papacy and contradicts the gospel. Dogmas reduced to propaganda slogans could be scanned and assimilated in a minute. Moreover, the placard delivered its message through a vocabulary that seems remarkably provocative, even when measured against the invective of Luther or Rabelais. Transubstantiation was "execrable blasphemy" and a form of "public idolatry," the "doctrine of devils"; priests who consecrated Hosts were "miserable sacrificers," "false antichrists," and "enemies of God." Its implications were explosive, and Paris immediately exploded—but in exactly the opposite way to that intended by the broadsheet's politically naive author and distributors.

Hysterical frenzy broke out against the foreigners, particularly Germans, who were assumed to have organized this conspiracy; a Flemish merchant was lynched. However, parlementary authorities immediately took control of the situation. Within twenty-four hours after the placards appeared, the Parlement of Paris ordered a general procession to take place a few days later, as the king had done six years earlier after an act of iconoclasm, in order to atone for this public insult to the Christian religion. At the same time, the judges also offered a huge reward for evidence that would convict people who had arranged their distribution, including those who had knowingly sheltered the conspirators. This time, unlike the iconoclasm episode, the offer of rewards worked; almost fifty years later, the nickname of the key informer who broke open this conspiracy was still recalled by the semiofficial history of the French Reformation.[48] The Parlement's jail soon filled to capacity with suspects.

Barely three weeks later (an interval that included the Parlement's ordinary annual vacation in early November), it began to sentence the first conspirators. The first *sacramentaire,* a shoemaker known as "the paralytic," was burned at Paris' principal cemetery on 13 November, dying unrepentant. Next day a wealthy merchant followed him, burned alive at the Paris market. During the following week, a weaver was executed at the pig market, a bookseller at Place Maubert, a mason (who had been tried previously for heresy) on Rue St. Antoine. Two young apprentices died during the first week of December at the Rue du Temple and the Pont St.-Michel. This geographic pattern suggests that the Paris Parlement had each man executed as close as possible to the scene of his particular crime, at a location near which he had posted a placard. The judges ended their year's work with an edifying spectacle on Christmas Eve, when a printer from Poitou who showed some signs of repentance performed an *amende honorable* at Notre-Dame before he was hanged and his corpse burned at Place Maubert.

The king, who had remained away from Paris all this time, expressed great satisfaction with the Parlement's handling of the situation. He appointed a committee of twelve judges to dispose of the remaining suspects before entering his capital in January 1535. Shortly after Francis' arrival, however, a few copies of yet another brief treatise against the doctrine of transubstantiation were found, "wherewith the Kynge was highly offended."[49] The episode provoked a second wave of persecution and a remarkable special procession in honor of the Eucharist on 21 January. Every notable in Paris marched: courtiers, judges, professors, clergy, city officials, guildsmen. Large numbers of relics rarely seen outside churches were displayed in public, including the crown of thorns from the Parlement's church of Sainte-Chapelle. At the very center of this vast procession came its featured exhibit, the Holy Eucharist, carried by the bishop of Paris under a canopy borne by the king's three sons and a duke. Behind the sacrament marched King Francis, bareheaded, dressed in black and holding a lighted candle. It was the most spectacular event of its kind ever staged in sixteenth-century Paris, accompanied by tolling of church bells and both vocal and instrumental music, punctuated by stops where the Host was placed on temporary altars. Just as a major modern festival and parade often ends with fireworks, so the day of the great eucharistic procession concluded with the burnings of six prominent "sacramentarian" heretics, culled from prisoners remaining in the Parlement's jail, who were executed in two symmetrical groups. Three clerics and officials, including a royal tax collector based in Brittany and a junior law-court clerk, died on the Rue St. Honoré; three "mechanics," including a rich grocer, died at the Paris market. King Francis did not watch the executions himself, but left the city as soon as the victims had performed their public abjurations.

A radical schoolmistress, who refused to teach her pupils the Ave Maria and ate meat on Fridays and Saturdays, was apparently judged unsuitable to be sacrificed in conjunction with the great procession; she was instead burned at the Paris slaughterhouse two days later. Her death preceded a general proclamation the following day, condemning no fewer than seventy-three fugitives charged with heresy.[50] They included such famous names as Clément Marot and such usual suspects as Pierre Caroli, first tried for heresy ten years before, subsequently parish priest at scandal-ridden Alençon, and presently living in Switzerland, where he would soon quarrel with Calvin. Five days afterward the Parlement decreed that those who knowingly concealed heretics would incur the same penalties as heretics themselves, and promised informers one-fourth of the property confiscated from convicted heretics. The hunt continued.

A notable monetary element and hints of xenophobia permeate the next cluster of Parisian heresy prosecutions during the 1535 Lenten season. Two very wealthy merchants, one born in the Low Countries and the other in Italy, were strangled and burned for heresy in February; two prominent Parisian goldsmiths narrowly escaped execution. Half a dozen well-off married women, including the widow of the Tournai merchant, had their property confiscated and were banished. The long arms of the judges also reached a few more of the original offenders. A student from Dauphiné, ordered by his teacher to affix the placards, was burned, although his teacher was never caught; a minor courtier who had put a placard in the king's residence at Amboise was finally caught and burned. The Parlement's prosecutions continued beyond Easter. Three more Protestants, two artisans (one from the Low Countries) and an attorney, were burned on 5 May, while another artisan got off with a public abjuration and a fine the next day. A lawyer at the Paris Châtelet made his public abjuration on 11 May.[51] Within seven months after the first appearance of the placards in Paris, the Parlement had ordered almost two dozen executions of "sacramentarians" in the capital.

The Parlement of Rouen also experienced repercussions from these notorious events. After a second priest had been defrocked and burned at Christmastime 1534,[52] "sacramentarian" pamphlets were discovered within the Norman Parlement's magnificent new gothic palace in January 1535. After a frantic chase, Norman officials finally caught the wandering propagandist calling himself "he who is permitted by the law" ("le permis en la loy") at Dieppe, just before he boarded a ship to England. This man, whose real name was Guillaume Huchon, had probably distributed one of the notorious placards at the royal castle of Blois. Taken to the king together with a copy of his trial, Huchon was then returned to Rouen under armed escort. Late in the summer of 1535, after delaying his execution by unsuccessfully claiming benefit of clergy, he was burned at Rouen.[53] However, the Rouen Parlement evidently did not pursue less notorious Protestants with equal diligence. Later in 1535 it also heard appeals from two heretics condemned to death at Caen, one by a royal court and the other by an episcopal court; both men were returned to their original judges for further testimony.[54] Although Normandy abounded with "Lutheran" heretics in the 1530s, and despite Francis I's sharp warning to the Norman Parlement at Christmas 1538 to use greater severity toward accused heretics, we know of no further confirmed executions for heresy by this court for many years.[55]

Meanwhile, diplomatic pressure on the king helped persuade him to issue a conditional pardon for imprisoned or fugitive heretics. A Parisian chronicler asserts that the pope sent the king a letter in June, rebuking him for his "execrable and horrible justice . . . on the Lutherans." In July Francis I issued the Edict of Coucy, ordering the release of prisoners charged with heresy, permitting exiles to return to France, and offering royal pardons to both groups. However, he specifically excluded *sacramentaires* and *placardaires,* and all returnees had to abjure publicly within six months on pain of being hanged. A British Protestant author has pointed out that, rather than being a pardon pure and simple, this edict also contained "the first regulation to introduce the death penalty for the propagation of heresy by any spoken or written means."[56] As the criminal *arrêts* of the Paris Parlement (first preserved from the court year starting in November 1535) confirm, a few people, those who like Clément Marot sought royal patronage or those who wanted their property and offices restored, took advantage of the king's pardon.[57] A handful of accused heretics were also released outright under its terms.[58] But most accused heretics either did not or could not benefit from it.

The Parlement of Paris, of course, had never needed any royal edicts in order to justify condemning either "Lutheran" or "sacramentarian" heretics to death before July 1535. It conducted business in much the same way after the pardon of Coucy as before. The next executions for heresy at Paris occurred in late September 1535, when two apprentice ribbonmakers were burned after they had returned from Germany and Flanders carrying Lutheran literature in their baggage.[59] Just before Christmas 1535, Lizet and his colleagues upheld a death sentence issued by a royal court at Sainte-Menehould for "execrable blasphemies, erroneous speech and words against the holy sacrament of the altar"; they simply ordered the defendant hanged and then burned, rather than burned alive.[60] A few months later they confirmed the sentence of the Paris *bailli* condemning François LeGros to be hanged and burned together with a copy of his trial after performing an *amende honorable* at Notre-Dame, on account of his "execrable blasphemies" spoken against the Virgin Mary while he was in jail; the Parlement merely omitted the *bailli*'s decision to have LeGros's tongue cut out after his public apology. Near the end of the court year, they upheld a sentence by the court of the abbess of Faremoustier ordering Jean Lamoignan hanged for blasphemies. Their ruling reveals that Lamoignan remarked that he "had eaten the gentleman" (*avoir mangé le bonhomme*) after taking communion, an expression that sounds more like Rabelais than Zwingli but that nevertheless marked him as an unpardonable freethinker.[61] The Paris Parlement refrained from judging three ordained clerics accused of heresy, all of whom were immediately transferred to the "judges delegated by our holy father the Pope," whom they urged "to proceed to their judgment . . . as soon as possible" at Christmas 1535, meanwhile ordering the bishops of their respective dioceses to pay all court costs.[62] The system of forcing bishops to pay most of the cost of heresy trials, developed a decade earlier with the short-lived *juges delegués*, had now become an essential feature of such procedures.

During the year after the Edict of Coucy, the Paris Parlement judged relatively few cases of heresy and heretical blasphemy. Even including the registration of pardons and the three death sentences, one finds fewer than ten rulings. One of the most revealing involved a nobleman, first accused of heresy and other crimes in March 1532 and tried by a special court in January 1534. In the summer of 1536 he petitioned the Parlement to be released from prison under terms of the recent royal pardon. The judges agreed to pardon him for the crime of heresy, on condition that he make the usual public abjuration; two court officers took him to the episcopal vicar and the Paris inquisitor for the ceremony. But the judges also ordered him returned immediately to prison on other charges and made him pay for summoning defense witnesses. However, three weeks later he was released on bond of 1,000 livres "in order to serve the king in his wars."[63] During the 1535–36 judicial year, the Parlement of Paris judged more cases of sacrilege than of heresy and punished the former more rigorously: they pronounced six death sentences for sacrilege and mutilated two men's ears.

Parlements and Inquisitors in the Midi, 1532–1539

During the 1530s, as the Paris Parlement investigated episodes of heretical behavior at Briçonnet's diocese of Meaux or Marguerite's possessions at Alençon and pursued miscreants in the great cities of Paris and Lyon, the problem of "Lutheranism" also disturbed two parlements in the Midi. Since Languedoc had been the cradle of the medieval Inquisition, it is not surprising to find papal inquisitors (who seem marginal in the early court trials of northern France) standing near the center of events in both instances. However, their roles were amazingly diverse. In Provence we find a ruthless persecutor, who first introduced violent tortures into the interrogations of suspected "Lutherans." In Languedoc we find a political appointee of the king's sister, an Erasmian reformer who attempted to obstruct any investigations into Lutheranism. For utterly different reasons, both of them ran into serious trouble from their respective parlements in 1532 and 1533, a time when both parlements confirmed their first death sentences against Protestant heretics.

Even after the scandal of 1532, the king's sister continued to control the appointments of Languedoc's inquisitor, thereby maintaining for several years a situation in which the provincial parlement prosecuted accused heretics despite the lack of cooperation from such evangelically inclined inquisitors. When an inquisitor was charged with heresy, as happened in 1532, his case, like Berquin's, was simply evoked to the royal privy council and quietly dropped. Ultimately, this unstable situation exploded, with far-reaching consequences.

In Provence, both the inquisitors and the Parlement confronted an utterly different situation from that in Languedoc.[64] The active inquisitor here was a hard-bitten Dominican veteran named Jean de Roma, who had been invited to the diocese of Apt late in 1530 with a mandate to "pursue blasphemers, concubines, heretics, usurers, and witches." Unexpectedly, he soon found many traces of Waldensianism among the peasants of this diocese. By the spring of 1532, while the Parlement of Toulouse wrested control of heresy prosecutions from its reluctant inquisitor, de Roma obtained the support of the provincial governor in order to extend his investigation into other parts of Provence, because his prisoners had implicated many Waldensians living outside the diocese of Apt. In June 1532 the Parlement of Aix ordered all local officials to cooperate fully with Inquisitor de Roma, who had complained that some heretics had armed themselves in order to resist him.

In the winter of 1532–33 de Roma and his assistants conducted a reign of terror against the numerous Waldensian peasants who had settled in deserted districts of the Luberon hills during the late fifteenth century. Dozens were arrested. Their prize catch, in November 1532, was a young Waldensian preacher, or *barbe,* named Pierre Griot, whom de Roma interrogated carefully and from whom he elicited much information.[65] Exploiting his discovery of Waldensianism in Provence, Jean de Roma eventually compiled a list of 150 suspects scattered across a dozen villages, and estimated that as many as 6,000 Waldensian heretics had been living undisturbed in Provence. With support from the governor, who repeated his orders to support the inquisitor in October 1532, and from the Parlement of Provence, he and his assistants began tracking them down.

Some suspects were tortured with unusual brutality, using methods de Roma had developed long ago in the duchy of Savoy. When subsequently forced to defend his actions before secular judges, the inquisitor explained how and why he tortured suspects. His justifications deserve close attention, because this was the first known instance in France where any form of torture had been employed against suspected heretics after the Reformation. After insisting that he had tortured only 4 of his 150 suspected heretics, those who blasphemed by calling the Virgin a whore or else denied Christ's real presence in the Eucharist, de Roma continued:[66]

> I believe that one will say that I have done well to condemn them to torture, but one might object that I should torture them otherwise than by fire, because I had heated their feet. I would answer first and say that the the form of torture and punishment appropriate for heretics is by fire. Secondly, I have seen it used in Savoy against witches [*masques*], invokers of devils; I am not the first who has done so, and I have used it in lesser crimes than the crime of heresy.

Terrified and infuriated peasants sent messengers to the king, describing in gruesome detail how de Roma and his assistants put grease into prisoners' boots and then roasted their feet over a fire; this is what he meant by "heating their feet." They complained that the inquisitor did not torture them in order to get them to confess to heresy; virtually all these Waldensians, including the young *barbe*, expressed a willingness to abjure their errors, but de Roma usually refused to accept their abjurations. The Waldensians' mission to the king charged that they were being tortured only in order to reveal where their assets were hidden, since the property of convicted heretics was forfeited. If Inquisitor de Roma had learned how to torture suspects by investigating witches in Savoy more than thirty years ago, the Waldenisans had learned about the same time that the king of France and his justices could protect them against the excesses of papal inquisitors and local secular judges. Specifically, the Waldensians in Provence remembered very well how royal commissioners had overturned many of their relatives' convictions in Dauphiné in the first years of the sixteenth century.[67]

Both campaigns, those of de Roma and of the Waldensians of Provence, came to a head early in 1533. The inquisitor struck first. In February five men and two women whom he had condemned to death for heresy (not including the *barbe* Griot) appealed to the Parlement of Aix, but their convictions were immediately upheld. Two men and a woman were ordered burned at Aix; the corpse of one who had died in prison was to be exhumed and publically executed at Aix "for the damnation of his memory and example"; the other three were returned to be executed in their home villages.[68] This episode set several precedents. It marked the first time since Luther's appearance that any French royal court had ordered a group of people executed for heresy. It also marked the first time in Reformation France that a heretic's corpse had been publically executed, and the first time that women had been executed for heresy.

But the Waldensians struck back powerfully shortly thereafter and brought down their inquisitorial persecutor, resisting him first with weapons and then trumping him through royal intervention.[69] In March 1533 the Parlement of Provence ordered several arrests in a Waldensian village after an armed attack on the inquisitor's assistants. Only two weeks later, however, both the archbishop of Aix and the Parlement received angry royal letters prohibiting any further activities by Inquisitor de Roma and ordering a special commission to investigate him and report within three months. Two days later, the Parlement of Provence suspended de Roma's activities, ordered all his trials sent to them immediately, and summoned him to Aix for questioning. The Waldensian emissaries had reached both the king and his Swiss and German allies with their tales of de Roma's rapacity and atrocities, and each had responded. The disgraced inquisitor prepared an elaborate defense, including a sixty-four-page treatise on the heresies of these Waldensians. He told the Parlement that he was ready to cease his activities in Provence, "although I fear no one." De Roma retired to Avignon, where he died of the plague a few months later. His discoveries about the extent of Waldensian heresy in Provence outlived him, although his ruthless methods of interrogation apparently ended with him.

While the hard-bitten Jean de Roma was alerting the Parlement of Provence to the extent of their Waldensian danger, a very different sort of inquisitor was provoking totally different problems for the Parlement of Languedoc. The second "liberal" Dominican inquisitor of Languedoc and Guyenne, Louis de Rochette, had been appointed after Marguerite's previous choice had resigned in disgrace. We know something about de Rochette's activity as inquisitor of Languedoc and Guyenne. During 1536, for example, he imposed small fines (one as high as five livres) against nine residents of Languedoc whom his office tried for heresy;[70] in March and April 1537, he investigated some "Lutherans" at Agen in Guyenne, ultimately imposing a formal apology on a local notable and handing two schoolteachers to the Parlement of Bordeaux, which gave them predictably light sentences.[71] Together with a judge commissioned by the Parlement of Bordeaux, de Rochette apparently ordered the arrest of other suspects, including Jerome Vindocin, who later became the first Protestant executed for heresy in Guyenne. However, well before Vindocin's death, Inquisitor de Rochette, like his predecessor, was himself indicted for heresy by the Parlement of Toulouse. This time Marguerite of Navarre did not intervene, perhaps because the judges moved almost as rapidly as their Parisian counterparts had when Berquin fell into their clutches one time too many.[72] Within two weeks after hearing its first report on his case, the Parlement stripped de Rochette from office; four days later it sentenced him to death and carried out his execution immediately.[73]

Nor was this the end of the vendetta against Marguerite's inquisitorial appointees for Languedoc. Two weeks after de Rochette died, his conservative Dominican rival, whose petition described his predecessor as his legal enemy *(partie adverse),* was officially confirmed by the Parlement. Vidal de Becanis, the new inquisitor, made a special trip to the royal court in order to secure definitive control of this office. Once installed, de Becanis promptly launched an investigation of his predecessor's deputy, another "unreformed" Dominican doubtless tinged with humanist sympathies. In May 1539 a joint committee representing the archbishop and the Parlement condemned Antoine Ricardi to be defrocked and handed to the secular arm as a "protector of heretics and also a sodomite." He had confessed (probably under torture); because he had been convicted of the "enormous crime" of sodomy, the Parlement immediately had him burned in the same public square where his supervisor had died eight months before.[74] Meanwhile, the hard-line Inquisitor de Becanis enjoyed the fruits of his office for many years, collecting his annual salary of 150 livres from the crown into the reign of Henry II.[75]

After the royal pardon of 1535 had officially ended the assault on *sacramentaires* and their placards, parlements throughout France resumed the business of prosecuting "Lutheran" heretics. Because the quantity of surviving criminal *arrêts* from appellate courts remains meager, one can only sketch parlementary repression of heresy across the French kingdom in the late 1530s.[76] Nonetheless, it is clear that the important regional parlements of Normandy, Provence, and Languedoc continued to deal with exactly the same problems of Protestant opinions and behavior throughout the 1530s. Crespin's martyrology informs us that in 1536 the

Parlement of Dauphiné also ordered its first known execution for Protestant heresy, and that early in 1539 the Parlement of Bordeaux approved its first heresy execution. Each prisoner was a mobile intellectual, the first a Waldensian friend of Farel's and the other a monk turned schoolteacher who had lived briefly in Farel's Geneva.[77] Meanwhile new criminal courts were being created in the parlements of Burgundy, Savoy, and Piedmont; we know that the first two had also upheld death sentences for heresy by 1540. A pattern of prosecuting Protestant heresy through occasional public executions had spread across most of Francis I's kingdom by 1540.

It may be more than coincidental that the few months for which we possess the minutes of Parisian criminal *arrêts* during these years (May 1535 and April 1538) constitute moments of intensive investigation of heretical activities.[78] We can thus watch President Lizet and his colleagues interrogating suspected heretics on the *sellette* both before and after torture in April 1538. We learn the exact details and order of voting on the final two of the three death sentences which they passed, those against the bookseller Jean de la Garde on 15 April and against Jean Salmon on 27 April. The first sentence, passed against the student Etienne Sabray on 12 April, includes an elaborate set of instructions on what questions he must be asked during the torture session preceding his death; basically, the judges wanted his memories of conversations about the Eucharist with de la Garde (and Sabray apparently confessed just enough to guarantee the latter's death sentence).[79] The printer whose arrest in early March apparently began the whole affair was sentenced only in June. Although he had sold four sacramentarian books to de la Garde, he had been a cooperative witness and was himself no *sacramentaire*. After presenting a formal supplication to the court, the printer escaped alive in mid-June. But he had to perform an *amende honorable* while watching some of his books burn, undergo a whipping at the pillory with a noose around his neck, had his property confiscated, and was perpetually banished from France.[80] A few other death sentences for heresy were probably confirmed by the Parlement of Paris in the later 1530s under Lizet's leadership, but we lack their original *arrêts*.

The Parlement of Aix, led by the famous jurist Barthelemy de Chassenée, similarly preserves records of a few heresy executions by following up Inquisitor de Roma's investigations of Waldensians in Provence after he left in 1533. Early in 1535, almost exactly two years after approving seven of de Roma's capital sentences, the Parlement of Aix approved death sentences for heresy against five men and a woman ordered by the local archepiscopal court. Half of them were to be executed in their home villages "in the most seemly locations close to the public roads"; transportation costs for the latter were to be paid by their local lords, "promptly and without dissimulation or negligence."[81] Afterward one finds no evidence of further executions for heresy in Provence until February 1539, when a priest was defrocked by the archbishop and burned at Aix by order of the Parlement for having "falsely, detestably and execrably blasphemed and misspoken against the Holy Eucharist, the blessed Virgin Mary, the saints of paradise, and the constitutions of the Church, and to have tried to make a new and damnable sect and make sedition and seduction in the lands of our Most Christian King and lord." An eyewitness reported that he showed *grande contrission,* made an edifying speech on the scaffold, and was strangled rather than being burned alive, as the Parlement had originally intended.[82]

Besides Paris and Aix, the only French parlement that continued to prosecute heresy with genuine determination during the late 1530s was Toulouse, which also had to bypass inquisitors appointed by the grace of Marguerite of Navarre. We hear of two obstinate "sacramentarian" heretics burned at Nîmes in autumn 1537, tried by an episcopal court with the approval of the Parlement; these events provoked Swiss intervention with the king on behalf of "several who were taken and [are] in danger of being burned."[83] As we have seen, both the inquisitor himself and his deputy were also burned by order of this court in 1538 and 1539. These remarkable scandals in Languedoc had significant legislative consequences. Between the trials of Inquisitor de Rochette and his deputy, the king answered a request by the royal prosecutor at the Toulouse Parlement, encouraging them to continue to prosecute heretics vigorously and to punish them in exemplary fashion.[84] The judges of Languedoc and their new inquisitor scarcely needed royal encouragement; they had just condemned a layman to death for heresy at Carcassonne, and they would execute a priest from Montauban shortly after the death of the former deputy inquisitor. When Francis I significantly widened the scope of secular judges in heresy trials in late June 1539, he was reacting to the disturbing news from Languedoc.

Dismantling the overly liberal Languedoc Inquisition preferred by Marguerite of Navarre became the final achievement initiated by French parlements in pursuit of Protestant heretics. But their record of successes is a lengthy one. Since the days when Lizet and Béda joined forces in 1523 to combat the networks of court protection sheltering the most audacious champions of Christian humanism, French parlements had compiled an impressive list of accomplishments. By 1525 they had driven Bishop Briçonnet into retreat and dispersed the preachers and scholars he had gathered at Meaux. Their obstreperous clerical colleague Berquin, long protected by the king's sister, had been executed in 1529. At Toulouse, the other principal parlement had demolished the local Christian humanist movement in 1532, either cowing it into conformity like Boysonné or forcing it into exile like Servetus. A similar experience at the University of Paris drove into exile the greatest French Protestant of all, Jean Calvin. The Parlement of Paris decisively outmaneuvered Marguerite of Navarre and compelled her cooperation in its invasion of her fief at Alençon in 1534. When the "sacramentarian" extremists among French Protestants staged an extremely well-organized coup shortly thereafter, Lizet's court had reacted immediately with remarkable vigor, offering large cash rewards in order to crack this conspiracy, making good use of informers, and then punishing the principal culprits with a brutal show of force. Meanwhile, their colleagues in the Midi humbled one veteran inquisitor for using illegal methods, drove another (de Badet) into resigning, and executed a third for heresy, followed by his deputy.

French parlements accomplished these results certainly not against the will of an absolute monarch—that would have been impossible—but despite Francis' reluctance to prosecute prominent evangelicals and his unwillingness to take any major legislative initiatives against Protestantism. Since Lizet's urging in 1528 to destroy the hydra-headed monster called "Lutheranism," French judges had made many conscientious efforts in that direction. *Parlementaires* understood perfectly well that printed literature provided the major vehicle for spreading Protestant propaganda. In collaboration with the Faculty of Theology of the University of Paris, the Paris Parlement therefore created procedures for censorship of printing, which worked reasonably well in the capital,[85] although they were manifestly ineffective at the kingdom's second printing center (Lyon), located at the eastern limit of the Paris Parlement's large judicial district.

These early heresy prosecutions had dispersed the once-flourishing

French Reformation movement of the early 1520s into holes and corners, frightening many waverers into obedience and driving the most committed Protestants into exile. The social and intellectual profiles of the early French "Lutheran" sympathizers help us understand why parlementary repression, even without direction from the French monarchy, could succeed as well as it did. To oversimplify, one can say that most early French "Lutherans" lacked both social standing and coherent doctrines. The social profile of these early French dissenters, carefully studied by scholars since the days of Henri Hauser, strongly suggests their general insignificance and harmlessness.[86] Before the enlarged French version of Calvin's *Institutes* appeared in 1541, most experts, whether Catholics like Imbart de la Tour or agnostics like Lucien Febvre, agree that their doctrines remained fluid and inchoate.[87]

Most clerical and lay "Lutheran" sympathizers were very obscure people. The earliest French Protestant martyr, executed for sacrilege with savage cruelty at Metz soon after the duke of Lorraine had crushed the rebellious peasants in 1525, was an artisan from Meaux, fleeing east after the failure of Bishop Briçonnet's ill-fated experiment in applied Christian humanism. The first two "Lutheran" martyrs executed at Paris in the 1520s, a clerical student and an artisan, were both associated with Meaux. The artisans of Meaux, university students at Paris and Toulouse, renegade monks and priests preaching in French towns, plus a few schoolteachers, accounted for the overwhelming majority of the "usual suspects" who turned up in the judiciary's nets in the 1520s and 1530s. About many of them we know nothing at all; for example, even the most meticulous Swiss Protestant schlarship has been unable to learn anything about nearly half of the heretics condemned in absentia at Paris in January 1535,[88] while the students condemned at Toulouse in 1532 seem even more anonymous. The occasional prestigious defendant, like Louis de Berquin or the "magnificent" Meigret, seems anomalous, like the handful of women accused of heresy in these early records; the first Frenchwoman executed as a sacramentarian belonged to the "dangerous class" of schoolteachers. Most potential suspects could be sucessfully frightened by a few well-chosen examples of "Lutherans" being put to death, or punished in such a way as to ruin their professional careers.

Doctrinal ambiguity reinforced the social vulnerability of early French Protestants. All experts agree that in the 1520s and 1530s, French "Protestantism" included a great variety of religious beliefs and opinions—understandably so, at a time when Catholic orthodoxy also lacked clear boundaries. In order to grasp the effect of parlementary prosecution across this wide spectrum of French religious dissidents, we need only notice the profiles of some intellectuals affected by the intensive Parisian investigations of 1533–1535, later sketched by the quasi-official *Ecclesiastical History of the French Reformed Church* in 1580.[89] Of the three seditious preachers investigated by the Sorbonne and the Parlement in 1533, the most famous, Gerard Roussel, remained aloof from both conservative and Protestant camps while retaining the patronage of Marguerite of Navarre; another, like Farel in 1523, fled to Switzerland; the third "saved his body and lost his soul," dying as a cathedral canon at Besançon. Similarly, it sketched the destinies of three promising young laymen who discreetly left Paris shortly after the affair of the placards: one, like de Nuptiis, moved to Bourges and later helped form a clandestine Protestant congregation; another ended as a successful lawyer in the Paris Parlement; the young Jacques Amyot, future translator of Plutarch, also fled to Bourges, but ultimately became tutor to the young Charles IX and died a bishop.[90] The early French Protestant sympathizers were not simply physically dispersed wanderers, like Calvin himself after 1534; they were also morally dispersed.

4

Royal Escalation and the Crisis of Nicodemism, 1540–1548

We enjoin that the judgment and expedition of [heresy] cases be
preferred ahead of all other criminal cases.
        —*Edict of Fontainebleau (1540), article 3*

France was the last major northern European state to transfer the crime
of heresy to secular courts. The Archduke Ferdinand had led the way in
Austria in 1527; his older brother, Charles, introduced a workable form
of secularization in the Low Countries with his 1529 placards; and after
1534, Henry VIII and his Parliament enabled English lay courts to punish heretical speech. Inspired by his judges at Toulouse, who had not
only punished heresy more firmly than ecclesiastical courts but had
even burned both an inquisitor and his deputy for favoring heresy, Francis I finally promulgated an edict in June 1539 intended to speed up the
procedures for punishing Protestants. While placing full financial responsibility for prosecuting heresy on church courts, the decree permitted lay courts, from parlements down to local tribunals, to proceed "in-
differently and concurrently" with church courts.[1] These new rules
caused much confusion; rather than speeding the pace of heresy trials,
procedural conflicts now threatened to slow them. In any event, parlementary judges were preoccupied at that moment with implementing
the major procedural reforms just decreed in the famous ordinances of
Villers-Cotterets, still regarded by legal scholars as the most important
act of Francis I's reign.[2] Ten months later, probably prodded by parlementary judges at Aix, the king and his chancellor decisively shifted the
burden of judging heresy cases to secular courts.

    The ten articles of the Edict of Fontainebleau constitute Francis I's most important legislation about heresy.[3] The king of France had finally positioned himself alongside his Habsburg and Tudor rivals in stripping most of the jurisdiction over heresy cases from ecclesiastical judges. Its second provision, "in order to reduce delays," ordered all royal courts to investigate heresy charges "immediately, dropping all other matters," and told them to proceed up to a final sentence or a condemnation to torture. They could proceed "not only against laymen, but also against clerics," unless fully ordained and therefore needing to be formally defrocked. Its next provision ordered all royal courts "to send all such trials and prisoners immediately and without delay to our sovereign courts [parlements], in order to be judged promptly with full diligence." Objections about a prisoner's privileges based on benefit of clergy, nobility, or the right of sanctuary were to be overridden. The parlements were to judge all such cases in their ordinary criminal chambers, delegating their clerical members *(conseilliers-clercs)* to help judge heretics in holy orders. "We enjoin," concluded the article, "that the judgment and expedition of such cases be preferred ahead of all other criminal cases." Other provisions attempted to remove means of legal obstruction or favoritism among royal judges at all levels, and threatened slackers with loss of office. Its eighth article included a memorable exhortation from the king: "because such errors and false doctrines contain in themselves the crime of human and divine *lèse-majesté,* sedition, and disturbance of our state," all his subjects should collaborate in denouncing heretics, "just as everyone must run to extinguish a fire." Francis was ordering every secular judge into an all-out campaign against heresy, pushing aside the slow-moving and merciful church courts, in favor of his parlements.

The Gradual Acceleration of Heresy Trials, 1540–1544

During the first few years after the Edict of Fontainebleau went into effect, our source materials, especially those from the Parlement of Paris, seem fuller. Several conclusions emerge from this abundant evidence. Because no major public scandals disturbed the rhythms of prosecution, there was no sudden increase in recorded heresy trials during the early 1540s. However, the system of public controls against the spread of heresy acquired two new or greatly improved aspects. The censorship of heretical writings by the Paris Faculty of Theology was tightened, and an index of prohibited books was finally printed in 1544. The same faculty had also defined an orthodox credo in 1543, which the parlements promptly imposed on all public officials.[4]

Within five years, the 1540 Edict of Fontainebleau had imposed an increasing burden of heresy cases on French parlements, especially Paris. Death sentences for heresy, however, increased only gradually. In the late 1520s the Parlement of Paris executed about one heretic per year. A decade later, French parlements sentenced about four or five heretics to death each year. By the time Francis I promulgated the Edict of Fontainebleau, public burnings of heretics had already spread across his kingdom; from 1535 through 1539, every provincial parlement except Dijon carried out heresy executions. From 1540 through 1544, these averages doubled, to nine recorded executions per year. However, for a kingdom as large as France, this seems a modest total; Thomas Cromwell's England, for example, with only one-fourth the population of France, averaged more than ten executions per year for "treasonous speech" in the late 1530s.

However, a closer look at the Parlement of Paris, whose district covered half the kingdom, reveals that the judges' caseloads of heresy trials—if not executions—increased steadily after 1540. By separating years into months, and eliminating cases of blasphemy or sacrilege with no Protestant overtones, we can measure this growth. (See Table 3.) Four years after Fontainebleau, the Parlement of Paris was judging eight cases of heresy each month, over twice as many as two years before. At a time when this court judged about three hundred criminal defendants each year, heresy cases had hitherto constituted a relatively small share of the court's load, except at occasional moments of crisis like the aftermath of the placards.[5] By 1544, with nearly a hundred heresy defendants passing through their prisons every year, a significant new burden had been added to their general responsibilities. Every fourth criminal case was now a trial for heresy. It was a sign of the times that the Parlement of Paris created a special register of "trial sacks, accusations, preparatory testimony, and other pieces of evidence against prisoners" in March 1543—and frequently noted in its margins those prisoners charged with heresy.[6]

When Francis I transferred most heresy trials to secular courts, particularly his parlements, he expected them to try cases more rapidly and to inflict more severe punishments than church courts had hitherto done. But these expectations were only partially met during the next

Table 3.   Heresy cases at Paris Parlement, 1540–1544

Year (no. of months preserved)	Death	Other punishment	Released	Cases per month
1540 (12)	3	7	2	1.0
1541 (6)	1	6	4	1.8
1542 (12)	5	18	16	3.3
1543 (12)	3	27	32	5.2
1544 (8)	9	26	28	7.9

Sources: Extant criminal *arrêts* in AN, X2a 89–97, supplemented for two months of the six-month lacuna in 1544 by the *minutes* in X2b 6–7; no *minutes* survive from the six-month lacuna in 1541.

few years. From November 1539 until June 1542, the Parlement of Paris judged seventeen cases of men sentenced to death for heresy and two men sentenced to death for non-Protestant forms of heretical blasphemy.[7] They upheld only nine heresy executions and one of the two executions for blasphemy. This 50 percent ratio roughly matches the Parlement's rate of death sentences confirmed for the most frequent capital crime, homicide. Lizet's court was establishing norms and routines for coping with a growing problem.

Why did they overturn half of the death sentences for heresy in the early 1540s? As we have seen, "arbitrary" justice paid very careful attention to relevant circumstances when making its judgments. Sometimes we can see what circumstances the appellate judges took into account. Late in 1540 the seneschal, or senior royal judge, of Anjou had condemned Nicolas Conart to perform a public apology at Angers and be burned for "crime of heresy and false propositions." Soon after the prisoner had arrived in Paris to make his appeal, the Parlement commissioned a medical report on him. After receiving it, they "enjoined that the prisoner be put in the house of one of his relatives, if any can be found, or else in some other place to be securely held . . . so that he can cause no further inconvenience."[8] Insanity was of course a defense well established in Roman law. So was extreme youth. In the summer of 1543, the *bailli* of Auxerre had tried Simon d'Asnières for "erroneous, scandalous and heretical speech" against God and the saints. The Paris Parlement, noting that the defendant was sixteen years old, ordered, "because of his youth," that he disavow (*soy desdire*) his speech and be whipped by the master of his school, "and this only as a form of discipline in the presence of his father and of the four witnesses against him." The judges stressed that this prisoner incurred no "note of infamy" from his punishment, but they also warned his father "to have him instructed in good manners and Catholic doctrine."[9]

Surprisingly, Simon d'Asnières was not the youngest prisoner to be judged for heresy by the Paris Parlement during these years. Two years after he had sentenced Conart to death, the same judge in Anjou tried René Prevost for "insolences and scandals" at the parish church of St. Jean de Mannevoz.[10] The Parlement noted that the defendant was a "young boy between ten and twelve years of age," but agreed there was solid evidence against him. They accordingly decreed that young Prevost perform a full *amende honorable* in that parish church, but added important stage directions: "all the little children of that place shall be summoned . . . each having a wax candle in his hands, fully lit and burning, while the said prisoner cries out in a loud voice, 'Pity' [*Misericorde*], asking God's mercy and pardon for the offenses he had made against His honor, and against the Holy Sacraments of our Holy Mother Church." Afterward came a procession, a High Mass, and a sermon by a doctor of theology, "exhorting fathers and mothers to nourish and indoctrinate their children well in the faith of God, to live in it, and to bear honor and reverence to God and to the saints in paradise." Young Prevost would then be whipped and taken to a Franciscan convent near Angers, where he was to be "enclosed and shut up" in some part of the convent for ten years. His parents were required to provide the friars with eighty livres per year "beyond his clothing" for his upkeep, and he could be whipped "at the discretion of the convent's guardian" during his stay there. For good measure, the judges ordered Prevost whipped two or three times in the Parlement's jail. In an age as famous for paternalism as for its religious differences, René Prevost was too young to lose his life, but for a preadolescent he certainly received the full measure of the law.

Of course, it also helped to have the king's pardon, although this was extremely difficult to obtain for people accused of heresy, and pardons did not guarantee immunity from further harassment. The most famous instance from these years is surely that of Etienne Dolet, a humanist printer in Lyon who was frequently in trouble for owning and publishing forbidden texts. Dolet's complicated legal problems are well known.[11]

After being conviced of heresy by the court of the archbishop of Lyon in October 1542, Dolet appealed to the Paris Parlement. Before his case was decided, he had managed to obtain a letter of pardon from the king in June 1543. However, the Paris Parlement found that it misrepresented Dolet's previous pardon for a homicide committed in 1536, and refused to register it; Dolet then pried supplementary letters of clarification (*ampliation*) from court officials in August. Only after receiving a formal royal order did the Parlement finally register Dolet's pardon in October, sending him to the court of the bishop of Paris for a formal abjuration and ordering some of his offensive books burned. Dolet did not remain at liberty for long. He was rearrested at Lyon a few months later for dealing in forbidden heretical books, but broke jail in January 1544. President Lizet quickly complied with the inquisitor's request to burn fifteen illegal publications in Dolet's possession, including two French Bibles and Calvin's *Institutes*, and an intensive manhunt was launched. Nine months later, the royal courier (*messager ordinaire*) from Lyon finally caught Dolet at Troyes in Champagne, after vainly searching in Germany, Geneva, Franche-Comté, and even Languedoc. He immediately sent a special messenger to Parlement to announce Dolet's capture, and hired a twenty-man escort to bring him to Paris. We do not know why the appellate court required almost two full years to sentence Dolet to death and burn him at Paris; but their final decision carefully stipulated that payments be made both to the heirs of the painter killed by Dolet in 1536 and to the man who had recaptured him in 1544. Royal pardons for such high-profile heretics certainly did not prevent further prosecutions.

Two lawyers acused of heresy found better ways than this humanist to escape from the clutches of the Parlement of Paris. Before Dolet negotiated his royal pardon in 1543, and three days after ruling on the twelve-year-old René Prevost, the Parlement finally concluded the trial of Jean Burgeat, an attorney from Vassy in Champagne. In the summer of 1542 the Parlement made a procedural ruling during his trial by his local bishop and royal *bailli* for "heretical, erroneous, and scandalous speech against our holy Catholic faith." In March 1543 they convicted Burgeat, despite his letter of pardon from the pope and his formal abjuration after receiving it, and despite a second pardon he had received when the Emperor Charles V had visited Paris in 1540. Burgeat had been charged with heretical speech after his abjuration and various pardons; the Paris judges, obviously unimpressed by this pettifogger, ordered him hanged and his corpse burned at Vassy.[12] But his case had not yet ended. Five weeks later the Paris Parlement opened an investigation of how Burgeat had managed to escape from prison at Vassy while awaiting execution. As late as March 1544, the jailer and the captain of the royal castle at Vassy were still being questioned about Burgeat's escape, but there is no evidence that he was ever recaptured.[13]

Another jurist, who narrowly avoided a death sentence for heresy early in 1544, also managed to escape some years later, and this time we know what happened to him. Giles Bobusse was the first heresy defendant listed when the special compilation was ordered in March 1543. But we do not learn the Parlement's decisions about him until the summer of 1544, when they mentioned his previous abjuration. With Lizet presiding and another well-known heretic-hunter, Claude DesAsses, as rapporteur, it is somewhat surprising that the court merely ordered him to be tortured, rather than executed as a recidivist. But, by ten of twelve votes, they did; the rapporteur wanted to return the case to the inquisitor of Paris, while one judge voted for death. If Bobusse survived torture, he would be condemned to an *amende honorable* at Notre-Dame, watch his heretical books burned in his presence, put into the pillory three times, and confined to a monastery for the rest of his days.[14] For two years we hear no more about him. But he obviously survived, because in December 1546 the Celestine convent in Paris complained that it had been charged with Bobusse's upkeep for a very long time; the Parlement thereupon ordered the prisoner transferred to the Franciscan convent at Chartres. In October 1548 the Parlement received another petition from Bobusse, licentiate of laws, who had "endured many torments, miseries, and calamities," still confined in the Celestine convent in Paris: this decrepit prisoner, who claimed to be eighty years old, asked to end his few remaining days in a monastery somewhere in his native diocese of Chartres, at the expense and surveillance of the local bishop. The royal *bailli* was ordered to find some suitable place for him, and it ordered the bishop to pay an annual pension of thirty-two livres for his upkeep.[15] Within thirty months, an undoubtedly rejuvenated Giles Bobusse turns up in the records of Geneva's Bourse Française: for at least twelve years he and his wife ran a subsidized boardinghouse in Geneva, welcoming Frenchmen fleeing from Henri II's persecution.[16]

All the appellate courts of Francis I's kingdom, except Turin in occupied Piedmont, had swung into action against "Lutheranism," and all had approved at least one public execution for this offense by 1541. Even the recently upgraded Burgundian provincial Parlement at Dijon, which had to send a few of its judges to Rouen in order to copy some criminal precedents from a slightly older cousin when it established its criminal chamber in the late 1530s, joined the hunt. In spring 1540 the Dijon court investigated an exceptionally scandalous case of sacrilege at Autun: a ciborium had been destroyed, and the Hosts within it had been "scattered into fragments that had been spread around and sown in the ground in front of the church door." Within a month, two *sacramentaires* were hanged and their corpses burned at Autun; the Parlement also ordered a special procession at Dijon "on account of the great heresies which are presently in the lands of Germany and Geneva, not very far distant from this city."[17]

Grenoble, another small parlement supervising a distant and mountainous province, convicted a *sacramentaire* in 1541 after careful questioning and ordered him executed at Romans. This court tried eight other prisoners for heresy in 1541, two of whom it tortured. Four of them performed public abjurations at Grenoble or Montelimar, but it released the other four, one of whom paid a fine for conversing with suspected heretics.[18] Heresy trials accounted for most of the Grenoble tribunal's criminal cases in 1541, but it obviously could not sustain this level of activity. During the presidency of Claude de Bellièvre (1541–1555) the Parlement of Dauphiné apparently never ordered another execution for heresy. However, its judges did conduct the trial of a humanist poet named Charles de Sainte-Marthe, whom the semiofficial history of the French Reformed churches later described as "full of levity rather than genuine zeal; in his case, there was more smoke than fire."[19] After being investigated for heresy at Poitiers in October 1537 and then absolved by papal officials at Avignon in July 1539, Sainte-Marthe was rearrested in Dauphiné during the summer of 1541. He spent almost two years in prison before receiving a stiff sentence: after performing *amendes honorables* at both Grenoble and Romans, he was banished permanently from Dauphiné.[20] Afterward Sainte-Marthe resurfaced as a judge in Marguerite's duchy of Alençon, composing a funeral eulogy for his patroness in 1549 and concealing the activities of local Protestants.

The province of Normandy had a peculiar record on heresy trials in the early 1540s. On the one hand, the Parlement of Rouen upheld no known death sentences for heresy for almost a decade after August

1535.[21] Francis' anger at the Norman judges in the late 1530s clearly had not goaded them into vigorous action against heresy. But there is much information that Protestant beliefs were increasing rapidly at this time, especially in parts of lower Normandy.[22] Our strongest, and perhaps also strangest, evidence is that two Norman noblemen were put to death for heresy by other French parlements in 1542. In July the Parlement of Paris ordered the *seigneur* of Fonteuil tortured and executed for "blasphemous and heretical speech" against God, the Eucharist, and other sacraments; in October the Parlement of Bordeaux executed a Norman esquire for "seditious blasphemy."[23] Apart from Louis de Berquin, they were the only known noblemen executed for heresy during the reign of Francis I. Meanwhile, however, relatively few heretics were being prosecuted by Normandy's own Parlement.

Across the Midi, things were different. Three-fourths of all death sentences for heresy approved by French provincial parlements during the five years after the Edict of Fontainebleau came from the three southern courts at Bordeaux, Toulouse, and Aix. The Parlement of Guyenne swung into vigorous action in 1542, approving five executions for heresy. They judged at least fourteen other accused heretics that year, many of them prominent people: priests, schoolteachers, clerks of court, a physician from Holland, plus at least three other university graduates and a local noblewoman, in addition to the unfortunate nobleman from Normandy. Nine of them were freed (although one had been tortured, and the noblewoman was also fined); of the five who made public amends, three also suffered various physical punishments.[24] Like their counterparts at Grenoble in 1541, the Bordeaux judges did not long sustain the intensity of this campaign, but they served notice that they had finally begun to follow the king's wishes in this respect. The Bordeaux Parlement also kept a prominent German humanist imprisoned for a remarkably long time before succumbing to foreign diplomatic pressure and the king's sister. Andreas Melanchthon, the nephew of Luther's famous colleague, originally arrested by the bishop of Agen, came under the Parlement's jurisdiction in June 1542. Marguerite of Navarre visited him in prison in March 1544, but Melanchthon was apparently not released for another year.[25]

After destroying Queen Marguerite's inquisitors in the late 1530s, the Parlement of Toulouse maintained intermittent pressure against heretics; it even experimented with making obstinate "Lutherans" into useful implements of royal policy by sending a few of them to the galleys instead of the stake. In the early 1540s this court ordered "Lutherans" executed at two episcopal towns along the Rhone, including the small city of Viviers on their northeastern border; they also upheld an inquisitor's ruling to execute a heretic at Béziers on the Mediterranean littoral.[26] The Parlement of Toulouse also contended with two public scandals involving heretical sermons preached in front of sizable assemblies; one incident occurred at Beaucaire, near the papal palace at Avignon. The Parlement ordered two of the Beaucaire group burned, one of them at Toulouse. Two others performed *amendes honorables* on a scaffold in front of the local cathedral after Mass, followed by a procession and a bonfire of a "defamatory libel in the form of a song" accompanied by effigies of five men who had escaped from the prison of the regional seneschal; afterward both prisoners were whipped and sent to the galleys.[27] At Ganges, north of Montpellier, where local notables had arranged a heretical sermon in 1541, the Parlement ordered another collective "act of faith" at the village church. It featured another procession, with a special sermon denouncing the "schismatic, false, heretical, and scandalous propositions preached by Brother Nicolas Militis against the Catholic faith, the law of the gospel, and apostolic traditions" to complement the *amendes honorables* spoken by six men and a woman. Two former village consuls were banished from Ganges for five years, a notary was sent to the galleys, and the defendants were collectively assessed an enormous fine of 2,000 livres, which regional authorities were still trying vainly to collect more than two years later.[28]

The Parlement of Aix, which had condemned more heretics to death in the 1530s than any other provincial parlement, maintained its vigilance. Worried by the long lists of heretics denounced by two exceptionally garrulous prisoners in 1539, it launched a vigorous offensive in the spring of 1540 against "all the Lutherans in Provence," sending a list of suspects to the king and his chancellor, devoting their midsummer recess to attacking the problem, and raising money in advance by assessing levies on seven prelates whose dioceses lay wholly or partly within their district.[29] In all probability this special mission to the royal court persuaded the king and Chancellor Poyet to issue the famous Edict of Fontainebleau. These careful preparations resulted in a sizable harvest of heretics arrested and tried at several towns across Provence during the summer of 1540. The court released more than two dozen prisoners who posted sizable bonds, and banished a few. Three heretics were burned at Aix that autumn, including a man from the Alpine diocese of Embrun, on the farthest northern frontier of their district; he had been caught with a heretical book titled *Great Pardons and Indulgences*. The other two were Waldensians. One, born in Piedmont, had been tried twice previously (first by Jean de Roma), but had been caught with heretical books and letters in his possession after his abjuration. His death provoked a riot shortly thereafter. "A large assembly of 100 to 120 men, armed with arquebuses, halberds, swords, and other weapons, ruined the mill [which he had owned jointly with his brother], beat up and threatened the miller and anybody else who interfered with the property of those of their sect."[30]

The day they signed their third death sentence of 1540 for heresy, the judges of Aix also issued the first collective arrest warrant ever decreed against the inhabitants of an entire village, the notorious *arrêt de Mérindol.* In its original form, it indicted the village *bayle,* or headmen, four of his clansmen, four pairs of husbands and wives, an immigrant schoolteacher, "a bookseller named Pomeri and his wife, a former nun from Nîmes," and four other men. All of them were to be burned alive or else in effigy, and their property was to be confiscated. More sinister and unprecedented were two provisions affecting every resident of Mérindol: all family members and servants were to be banished from the kingdom, and every house and farm building in the village razed. This remarkable edict, condemning all household dependents in one village and all homesteads, was composed by a court whose First President, Barthelemy de Chassenée, had once published a learned treatise about the trial and punishment of insects.[31] Assigning collective punishments was clearly one of Chassenée's legal specialties.

For four years, the Parlement and the Waldensians of Provence engaged in elaborate maneuvers in order to determine whether or not this remarkably draconian *arrêt* would be enforced. As they had done when confronted with Inquisitor de Roma, the Waldensians sent emissaries to their friends at court. Once again they had some measure of success. The king at first ordered the *arrêt* to be carried out; but within two months, Guillaume du Bellay—former governor of Piedmont, veteran negotiator with German Lutheran princes, and brother of the bishop of Paris—had persuaded Francis I to suspend its execution and grant the Waldensians a pardon instead. Each May, for three consecutive years, the king sent new conditional pardons for the Waldensians to Aix. Even after du Bellay's death, the king ordered a high-ranking official and a theologian to visit Provence in order to ensure that justice was being done to the Waldensians. Meanwhile, the Parlement of Provence continued to prosecute "Lutherans." During the prolonged game of cat-and-mouse with the Waldensians, it ordered more public executions, including that of one man named in the *arrêt* of Mérindol.[32] Finally, at the end of 1544, Francis I changed his mind and prepared to help the Parlement of Provence enforce its decrees against the Waldensians.

The Anti-Waldensian Crusade of 1545

The special horrors of religious persecution in the mid-1540s cannot be conveyed through statistics of legal public executions. The illegal executions were far worse, particularly those perpetrated in April 1545 against the Waldensians of the Luberon hills with the collaboration of the Parlement of Aix. When Francis I finally ordered their famous *arrêt* of Mérindol enforced early in 1545, he knew quite well what its consequences would be. By then, the operation had expanded from a judicial assault on a single village into an international military collaboration between the French monarch and the papacy.[33] The papal vice-legates at Avignon had been urging such a policy for some time, because the Waldensians had settled on both sides of the Provençal frontier; some were legally subjects of the king, some of the pope. The latter group were the more troublesome, since they had fortified one of their villages, Cabrières d'Avignon, and staged raids from this stronghold into both territories. They dared do no such thing on the French side of the border, because the king had much more effective agents of local government than the pope, and many more soldiers. In fact the papal government at Avignon was so militarily underequipped that, when joint military action actually happened in 1545, they had to borrow a few cannon from the French king and buy cannonballs for them (the unused surplus was carefully returned afterward for a refund).

An unusual combination of circumstances enabled Francis I and the vice-legate to stage their joint anti-Waldensian crusade in the spring of 1545. A truce in Italy had just freed a corps of veteran troops for a campaign against England; they were being shipped along the Mediterranean coast and could be used against the heretics of Provence and the papal enclave around Avignon, provided everything was done quickly. Vastly more effective than the local militias of either government, supported by artillery, they were ideal for staging a blitzkrieg against Waldensian peasants. At that moment the royal governor of Provence was outside the kingdom on diplomatic business. His deputized replacement, Jean Maynier d'Oppède, was Chassanée's successor as First President of the Parlement of Provence. Thus the judicial and political command of Provence were vested in the same person, who moreover happened to be a vassal of the pope (Oppède, the heart of his landed possessions, lay in papal territory) and therefore the ideal leader for a joint royal-papal venture. After intense lobbying, Francis I decided to seize this opportunity to crush his Waldensian subjects and to score points with Rome, just as the long-awaited Council of Trent prepared to open with no French prelates in attendance.

Militarily, the whole operation was completely successful. Wearing his judicial robes, Maynier d'Oppède swung his Parlement into legal action against the heretics of Mérindol at an unprecedented Sunday meeting in the port city of Marseilles. Wearing the helmet of the acting governor and military commander-in-chief of Provence, Maynier d'Oppède then welcomed his borrowed veterans, ordered out the local militia, and led his army inland. The papal government at Avignon simultaneously ordered out its militia. Six days later, after French soldiers and militia had sacked Mérindol and several other villages, they joined the papal militia and, under Maynier d'Oppède's command, besieged the fortified Waldensian village of Cabrières d'Avignon in papal territory. Here they met resistance; a few of Maynier's forces were killed. His men faced a barrage of insults from behind the walls: "idolaters, worshippers of stones, papists, boots and slippers of the pope," reported the subsequent official account composed by the Parlement of Aix.[34] But cannonballs outweighed insults. After eighteen hours of bombardment, Cabrières fell. By 21 April Maynier could disband both militias and take the veterans back to Marseilles as mopping-up operations began.

The most remarkable of these clean-up tasks was performed by three judges of the Parlement of Aix, accompanied by a clerk and a *huissier,* who had served as its official commissioners for executing the *arrêt* of Mérindol. They had to explain to posterity why the execution of a peculiar decree condemning one village had created chaos throughout an entire region after the sacking and looting of half a dozen other villages, none of which had been mentioned in the original indictment. They had to explain what they were doing at Cabrières d'Avignon, outside the boundaries of France, where this week-long crusade ended. Here, after boasting about the capture of the heretics' military leader and a preacher, they concluded sanctimoniously that "we place the execution done at Cabrières, which was the asylum of all the aforesaid Lutherans and Waldensians, under the account of divine justice."[35] But the preceding legal problems, which clearly fell under the heading of human justice, remained—and soon got worse.

Their official report, probably composed about a month after these events at the first hint of complaints from a few outraged landlords, therefore stressed the various pretexts under which other villages were brought into the same net with Mérindol. Some of their explanations resemble fig leaves adorning a nude. The lord of Villelaure and La Roque hastened to tell the commissioners that his subjects (who had put their valuables in his castle for safety) were rebels and heretics; the judges issued him what amounted to a hunting license to despoil them. The parish priest of Cabrières d'Aigues, where the landlord tried to protect her peasants, told the commissioners that most of his parishioners were holding the local "good Catholics" imprisoned in his church and were fortifying themselves against the soldiers. A local official at Cadenet complained to them that the villagers of Lourmarin, whose overlord was tearfully trying to mediate between her vassals and the Parlement's commissioners, had refused to contribute their share of provisions for the soldiers' passage. Armed with such testimony, the royal prosecutor solemnly requested the three commissioners to decree, "for obedience to the king and public example, the said Waldensians in the said places of Lourmarin, La Roque, Villelaure, Cabrières [d'Aigues], La Motte [d'Aigues], and other adherents, as obstructing the execution of this arrêt, [be declared] rebels and disobedient to the king and his justice and obstinate in their sects and heresies, and be punished as enemies of the king, just like the others of Mérindol." Three days after setting out on this expedition, having sent exactly six suspected heretics back to Aix to be judged, the commissioners solemnly registered this general extension, which took place as a kind of legal intermezzo during a council of war, presided over by Maynier d'Oppède.[36] Three small words ("and other adherents") made it an extremely general extension of a specific warrant seeking nineteen people who could not be caught even with the help of an army. The confusion of Maynier d'Oppède's dual roles, as presiding judge and as commander-in-chief, makes this legal subterfuge extremely unconvincing.

However, the official report was even more noteworthy for what it omitted than for what it included. Although the commissioners recorded the capture of six suspects whom they sent back to Aix, they omitted the one suspect who was captured at Mérindol itself, a young servant of the *bayle*. The incident deserves attention as being the closest approximation to a heresy trial conducted during this crusade; the clerk who accompanied the three commissioners even made a brief official report (*procès-verbal*) of the episode. When asked to repeat his prayers, the young man (whose native village escaped damage during this expedition) made some mistakes on both the Pater Noster and the Ave Maria and was therefore labelled a "Lutheran," which he vehemently denied. According to the *procès-verbal,* the Parlement's prosecutor, who had conducted this interrogation, demanded the death penalty. The prisoner was thereupon shot to death by a five-man firing squad at Maynier's orders. (This incident provides perhaps the earliest known European example of an ideological execution conducted by a firing squad.) Much later, when the three commissioners were questioned about this incident, they agreed that it happened, although Maynier denied having ordered a summary execution. Each of the three commissioners offered a different excuse why he had been either unwilling or unable to judge the prisoner. One lamely argued that the prisoner should be taken to Aix, but was overruled and then heard the shots; another claimed his balky mule prevented him from participating directly in the interrogation; the third denied he was present. Maynier d'Oppède, in his capacity as acting governor, had his own clerk draw up a different *procès-verbal* claiming that the execution had been ordered "after due deliberation with the three commissioners."[37] From a strictly legal point of view, this episode encapsulates the contradictions between Maynier d'Oppède's judicial and military roles. The moral unraveling of the Parlement of Aix, in both head and members, emerges all too clearly from this pathetic paper trail.

Other oversights and silences abound in the commissioners' report. They noted the capture of two prominent leaders in papal territory at Cabrières d'Avignon, but ignored their failure to capture the defendants named in the original *arrêt* of Mérindol. The judges also correctly suspected, from several bits of unconfirmed testimony, that the village sheltered a heretical preacher named "Perery." Along with many of his flock, Jean Perreri had "fled in his shirt" and turned up a month later in Geneva, begging for aid. He soon found another assignment in a safer Waldensian village in French-occupied Piedmont. Eighteen years after his precipitous flight, Perreri returned to his original base as the Protestant minister at Mérindol.[38] It would be difficult to imagine a better symbol of the long-term failure of the 1545 crusade.

The commissioners' official report is also silent about the cleverest tactical success of the crusade. This was the decision, evidently made in advance of the soldiers' deployment, to place all able-bodied men captured by the expedition on the royal galleys at Marseilles "in lieu of prison." Sentencing a few condemned heretics to the galleys, as we have seen, had already been done at Toulouse in the early 1540s. Putting hundreds of captives, all of whom could be classified as suspected heretics, in preventive detention on the galleys constituted a creative practical solution to a serious tactical problem. A subsequent investigation, based on official records from all galleys stationed at Marseilles that year, showed that no fewer than 666 prisoners were sent to this floating "jail" in ten different groups between April 15 and May 29. About two hundred of them died from disease and malnutrition; 330 others were released within a few months; the remainder were condemned to perform a kind of unpaid penance for their misdeeds as rebels and/or heretics.[39] Never before and never again—not even during the Wars of Religion— was anything comparable ever undertaken on this scale. Using the galleys solved the problem of how to dispose of and sort large quantities of prisoners of war. It was certainly more fastidious than the cold-blooded massacre of all male prisoners captured after the surrender of the Waldensian fortress, that act of "divine justice" to which the three commissioners referred.

The commissioners' report is also silent about the greatest tactical failure of the crusade, namely how to dispose of the huge numbers of women and children trapped by the soldiers and the militias. The only episode uglier than the slaughter of the disarmed men at Cabrières d'Avignon on 20 April was the accompanying incineration of hundreds of women and children in the village church. No one claimed that the people burned in their sanctuary were dangerous rebels; but these victims died in papal territory, and French justice cared nothing about atrocities committed by French officials across the border. However, another smaller-scale atrocity was committed against two dozen women and children on French soil one day later. They had taken refuge in a cave, pursued by a militia commander. After firing several shots in an unsuccessful attempt to dislodge them, he ordered them smoked out after sealing up the mouth of the cave. This story was often dismissed as apocryphal, until two archeologists explored this cave in 1971. Its narrow opening still held the metal supports that had once helped to seal it, along with the bones of more than twenty women and children who had died there in the sixteenth century.[40] Such atrocities occurred because women and children, who accounted for the majority of the two thousand victims of this crusade, could not be imprisoned on galleys as presumed rebels. Another solution was to sell such captives into slavery. Like the tale of the cave, which similarly emerged during the subsequent investigation of the affair, the enslavement of some captured Waldensian children and their subsequent sale (in papal territory) can be confirmed from surviving notarial evidence.[41]

Besides failing to deal with captive families, French authorities proved unable to follow up their decisive military strike of April 1545. Most of their biggest targets escaped their dragnet despite the surprise attack. They eventually located one defendant named in the *arrêt* of Mérindol and soon executed him at Aix. But the local preacher had escaped, along with the other officially wanted people. To be sure, the crusaders took many prisoners and handed them over to the Parlement for punishment. The court's legal records for 1545 are remarkably rich. It reportedly tried 255 people for heresy that year, and may have executed as many as sixteen of them; surviving records enable us to trace over a hundred trials and nine executions, including the one from the original *arrêt*.[42] But most of those actually tried, and most of those executed for heresy by the Parlement of Aix in 1545, had not been captured during that bloody week in April. The royal prosecutor who later investigated the affair enumerated exactly seven men from Mérindol condemned to the galleys and one executed; he pointed out that most prisoners captured during the raid were simply released, while most of those who were tried for heresy got off with relatively minor punishments.[43]

Without a permanent professional military force to enforce its decrees, the Parlement of Aix was unable to expel the Waldensians from Provence. Historians of the French Reformation have observed that artisans, or even professionals, were infinitely more mobile than peasants and thus more likely to emigrate in order to avoid religious persecution. The Parlement's harassment of the Waldensians of Provence, and of Mérindol in particular, offers a reverse illustration. Heretical peasants were not easily uprooted. "We are Israelites chased from our lands," they told one witness, adding that they expected to recover them once the troops vanished. These "Israelites" had resources. Most of their landlords, though unsympathetic to their religious beliefs, valued and supported such tenants. Few local Catholics rushed to purchase their lands or other confiscated assets. Ever since Jean de Roma's armed assistants roamed through the Luberon region, experience had shown how quickly the Waldensians resorted to threats and collective violence in order to protect their property. They really had nowhere else to go; Waldensians had to be either exterminated or converted. (In 1545 they were actually in the process of being converted, but not to Catholicism; instead of a *barbe,* Mérindol already possessed a heretical minister who escaped to Geneva rather than Piedmont.)

Maynier d'Oppède's troops destroyed a sizable share of the region's Waldensian population, more through famine than through actual killings (an official inquest four years later counted 1,840 deaths in Provence alone, omitting the massacres across the border);[44] they razed every building in Mérindol and many elsewhere (that same inquest counted 763 structures destroyed in twenty-four locations); they demolished the heretics' fortified stronghold beyond the French frontier, and prevented it from being repopulated by anyone except good Catholics; but they could not eliminate Waldensianism in Provence. French authorities could not even prevent the resettlement of Mérindol by some of the same Maynards against whom the Parlement had been breathing fire since 1540. An episcopal judge from Cavaillon learned from one witness in December 1549 that "Philippe Maynard, son of the old *bayle,* works regularly on Sundays and holidays, as do some others of those originally condemned, especially the Maynards; that the local preacher is married; that several of those formerly condemned had returned." Another witness, who had been allowed to resettle at Mérindol by Maynier d'Oppède, confirmed that "the old settlers had also come back and lived worse than before, without an altar and without the sacraments, working on holidays and singing heretical songs."[45] When Jean Perreri finally returned to Mérindol in 1563, he was greeted by some of the Maynards he had known almost twenty years before, still farming the same lands despite the death sentences from the Parlement and the crusaders of 1545. For that matter, Gabriel Audisio found several families named Meynard listed in the telephone directory with addresses in Mérindol.[46] Parlementary judges were ultimately helpless against such immobilism.

Francis I's Heresy Commissioners of 1545

The crusade of April was the most spectacular development approved by Francis I as he escalated his campaign against "Lutheranism" in 1545. His other innovations attempted to make heresy-hunting more effective and efficient within the huge district subject to the Parlement of Paris. Their *ressort* covered half of Francis' kingdom and presumably contained half the "Lutherans" in France. The essential problem was administrative: how could one tribunal, however well staffed with competent judges under its zealous First President, Lizet, adequately supervise the repression of heresy across so much territory? One solution was to send special commissioners to prosecute heresy in places where the problem was known to be acute but where local judges seemed inactive or corrupt, or both. If it was more efficient to deputize some incorruptible local investigator based in the region, it was ultimately more effective though more expensive to send a reliable Parisian judge out on mission. In one way, this policy dated back to the special mission that the Parlement of Paris had sent to Alençon in 1534. But by the mid-1540s the Parlement's special commissioners had to work for many months instead of a few weeks, and several of them were soon operating simultaneously.

Such developments emerged in the western regions of the huge Parisian district. Specially deputized local prosecutors were first used in the west during the summer of 1544, when the deputy *seneschal* of Anjou was despatched to Chinon specifically in order to prosecute heretics. He promptly encountered obstruction from the local deputy *bailli* of Touraine, eventually submitting a bill for seventy-seven days of work at Chinon trying several accused heretics.[47] The deputy royal prosecutor at Fontenay-le-Comte, who had been conducting heresy trials against several people from La Rochelle since October 1544, complained in March that his arrest warrants were unenforceable. The Parlement of Paris immediately commissioned a successor, Jean Ranfray, and ordered the warrants enforced. But after Ranfray complained that a judge had imprisoned a court bailiff (*sergeant*) who was trying to arrest a heresy suspect,

President Lizet took the unprecedented step of summoning the royal lieutenant of La Rochelle, Claude d'Angleur, his deputy royal prosecutor Hugues Poutard, and their *sergeant* Robert Foucault, to Paris. They were accused of criminal obstruction of justice and ordered imprisoned.[48]

Thus began a peculiar episode, as instructive in its way as the simultaneous crusade in Provence for demonstrating the practical limitations to the legal prosecution of heretics. D'Angleur and Poutard packed their bags and set out for Paris, which they reached by 20 June, but *sergeant* Foucault chose to disappear. Meanwhile commissioner Ranfray swung into action at Fontenay: in mid-June the Parlement upheld the execution of a defendant who had originally been condemned in September 1544.[49] In August the Parlement sent one of its *huissiers* all the way to La Rochelle to take testimony on the case "in order that there be no fear that [the defendants] could talk to or intimidate witnesses, given the distance of the place"; in exchange, both officials were released from prison on bond but ordered to remain in Paris. In late November, d'Angleur and Poutard presented their official defense to the Parlement, producing the "diligences that they maintained they had done in the pursuit of heretics in their district" and raising objections against two of their principal accusers.

Meanwhile the campaign against heresy fared no better in La Rochelle during their absence. On 1 October 1545 the special commissioner trying suspected Rochelais heretics at Fontenay-le-Comte complained that the royal governor of La Rochelle refused to confiscate the property of those condemned for heresy at Fontenay, alleging "popular rebellions and commotions" in his city; worse yet, many principal Rochelais suspects had withdrawn to fortified residences outside the walls. The Paris Parlement deputized two leading gentry to seize suspects and bring them to Fontenay. But other problems persisted. Commissioner Ranfray complained on 1 February 1546 that the magistrates (*échevins*) of La Rochelle still refused to hand over *sergeant* Foucault, whom President Lizet immediately ordered sent to Fontenay-le-Comte. Meanwhile we hear nothing about the Rochelais officials in Paris until January 1546, when the Parlement determined that they still owed 130 livres for their prison expenses since June 1545. Finally, on 16 February, d'Angleur and Poutard asked to return to La Rochelle, pointing out that "English and other sea pirates arrive there every day." The Parlement, "considering that they have been royal officials for a long time," granted their request, enjoining them "to investigate Lutherans and other religious offenders" with proper diligence. On the following day they posted bond and departed.[50]

Commissioner Ranfray finally got his hands on *sergeant* Foucault, tried him for heresy, and shipped him to Paris. In November 1546 President Lizet ordered him to be tortured concerning his blasphemies against the Eucharist; if Foucault confessed, he was to be hanged and his corpse burned at Fontenay. But the court bailiff, like Giles Bobusse and most others in this dilemma, survived torture. He received stiff punishment: a public abjuration at the principal church of Fontenay-le-Comte, a whipping, and perpetual banishment from the kingdom of France. However, because of Francis I's death, Robert Foucault's "perpetual" banishment actually lasted less than eighteen months. In March 1548 he obtained a royal pardon from Henry II, and four months later it was duly registered by the Parlement of Paris.[51] Like Lieutenant d'Angleur and his deputy, he was presumably reinstated at La Rochelle. The subsequent careers of these royal officials is instructive. Claude d'Angleur became the president of the new appellate court (*présidial*) created at La Rochelle in 1552 and ultimately emerged as the most distinguished member of the Reformed church of La Rochelle.[52] In December 1553 we find Hugues Poutard, now promoted to royal prosecutor at La Rochelle, accused of partiality by a priest.[53] In other words, royal officials who were notoriously lax toward heretics were as difficult to remove as Waldensian peasants in Provence. They too survived persecution, returned home, and eventually helped to create Reformed churches in their communities around 1560.

If Francis I could not remove royal officials who protected heretics or were themselves heretics, and if President Lizet could not frighten them into performing their public duty by imprisoning them in Paris, they could at least deputize roving commissioners from among the many qualified Parisian judges in order to prosecute heretics at various trouble spots across this huge district. During the summer of 1545, in the aftermath of the anti-Waldensian crusade, such commissions multiplied. In late July the king ordered three Parisian judges, including Guillaume Bourgoing, to investigate "the heretics and Lutherans . . . in the lands of Anjou, Touraine, Poitou, La Rochelle, Berry, Bourbonnais, and the *bailliage* of St. Pierre le Moûtier." The Parlement immediately despatched a *huissier* to court in order to obtain the necessary letters to carry out this huge assignment.[54] Although it is not certain that the other two men ever left Paris, within a month Bourgoing announced that he was ready to depart for Bourges in order to hunt "suspects of heresy and blasphemy" in Nivernais, La Charité-sur-Loire, Cosne-sur-Loire, Gien, the duchy of Berry, and several other places.[55]

Bourgoing's commission created a heavy paper trail among the *arrêts* of the Paris Parlement. He traveled deep into central France, moving from the upper Loire into Berry and Nivernais, even reaching Auvergne at Riom, touching several places specified in his instructions and some that were not. He apparently began his mission at the Parlement's temporary sessions (*Grands Jours*) held at Moulins in October 1545; by December he had also put a lawyer on trial at Chateauroux. During January 1546 he persecuted six defendants at Chateaudun. In mid-March came six more heresy prisoners at Nevers, followed by two others from Moulins. One heresy defendant at Nevers was a bookseller specializing in almanacs and prognostications.[56] All these defendants were either released or given relatively minor punishments; even the almanac-seller, whose stock included a suspicious little book titled *The Christian Man's Family Teachings*, got off with a warning, although his other titles were shipped to the Faculty of Theology for inspection and the *Instruction* was burned. The parade of Bourgoing's defendants included a large number of cases heard at Paris in May: a surgeon practicing at Montluçon, a group of five men and four women from the Nivernais (all released), an innkeeper at St. Pierre le Moûtier, a lawyer from Nevers, the deputy royal *bailli* from Bourbon and his noble wife, and two prominent widows from Bourbon. In June came a resident of Corbigny and a nobleman at Nevers. Another case was ready for trial in August, but by then Bourgoing was returning to Paris. This paper trail finally ends in October 1546, when the Paris Parlement approved the expense money Bourgoing had paid to several witnesses testifying against suspects accused of heresy in La Marche. A nobleman had charged for the expenses of two horses; an upholsterer had come from sixteen leagues away in order to testify; nine other witnesses, including a priest, received a total of thirty-eight livres in travel expenses.[57] It was extremely unusual for the state to pay travel expenses for prosecution witnesses, but heresy trials were a special priority, and the region in question lay in the remote southwestern corner of Bourgoing's assigned territory.

One would be misled by the language of the Parlement's *arrêts* in thinking that everyone tried by Bourgoing on this mission escaped with minor punishments. Apparently such special commissioners were listed as official prosecutors only in cases in which defendants did not suffer confiscation of their property. Convictions that resulted in more severe punishments, including confiscation, ordinarily appear in parlementary records as being prosecuted by local royal courts. It is therefore probable that two death sentences for heresy upheld by the Paris Parlement against men from Nevers in December 1545 and St. Pierre le Moûtier in August 1546 should be considered as by-products of Bourgoing's mission, along with many other appeals of heresy cases judged by the Paris Parlement at this time originating in regions visited by Bourgoing. One should also include the two men hanged and burned at Varennes in the Bourbonnais in May 1546 for "having burned the holy relics in the reliquary" of their parish church.[58]

At the opposite extreme from Bourgoing's year-long travels across much of central France stands a sedentary type of Parisian heresy commissioner who confined himself to a single city. In 1545–46 our clearest example of this kind is Nicolas Sanguin, who concentrated his efforts on the city of Meaux, still a very active center of heresy twenty years after Bishop Briçonnet had ended his controversial reforms. Although the paper trail left directly by this commissioner is much thinner, his achievements probably surpassed those of Bourgoing. Sanguin apparently got started shortly after a Jacobin named Noel Dubois, "captured clandestinely" at Paris in April 1545, provided considerable information about heretical circles at Meaux under torture a few weeks later. (Dubois was one of the very few heresy prisoners who provided much useful information to investigators under torture, which explains why he remained alive until December.)[59] By October commissioner Sanguin was officially at work. He pried some information from a cooperative barrel-maker of Meaux named Le Page, who had been arrested for making disparaging remarks about St. Hubert and for having hidden some heretical books about five years earlier, "when someone named Le Moine was executed for heresy at Meaux." After Le Page had been sent to Meaux for confrontations with other suspects, he was finally discharged in April 1546 with appropriate warnings.[60]

While Dubois and Le Page were talking, Sanguin was quietly following up their leads. During the spring and summer of 1546, when Bourgoing's prisoners clogged their dockets, the Paris Parlement judged only one insignificant heresy case from Sanguin's district.[61] But he had laid the groundwork for the greatest single police raid against heresy in Francis' long reign. In September 1546 commissioner Sanguin, accompanied by two royal officials, arrested the entire Protestant congregation of Meaux—more than sixty men and women—while they were worshiping at a private home. This coup was utterly different from the previous year's crusade in Provence: nobody was injured, the officiating clergyman was caught along with his audience, and sixty prisoners were led off on a fifty-kilometer march to the jail of the Paris Parlement, where they were tried with exemplary rapidity during its official annual vacation season. This is not the place to analyze the considerable consequences of Sanguin's raid. We should also remember that the Paris Parlement executed heretics from Meaux both shortly before Noel Dubois was captured and shortly after Sanguin's coup in September 1546; this town posed an ongoing problem.[62] The important point is that none of the Parlement's other special commissioners ever approached Sanguin's achievement.

At the opposite extreme from such active and skillful special commissioners stands the hapless but instructive example of Thibault Huart, sometime heresy commissioner at Blois. We first encounter him among the Parlement's *arrêts* in April 1545, when the duke of Vendôme asked the Parlement to extend Huart's special commission from the king to investigate heretics in his lands, although its official deadline had expired. The judges granted Huart a one-month extension. However, the local notables of Blois evidently opposed Huart and repeatedly petitioned the Parlement about his misdeeds. In August 1545 commissioner Huart was summoned to appear before the Paris Parlement, and in December we find him briefly imprisoned in the Parlement's jail. The squabbles continued. In May 1546 municipal officials at Blois accused Huart of bribery during his questioning of more than a hundred witnesses against a single defendant.[63] In order to clean up this mess, the Parlement sent one of its own judges, Etienne Fleury, to Blois. The Paris Parlement condemned some heretics from Blois in October 1546, including one whom they sentenced to death.[64] At the end of 1546, Fleury was in turn replaced by Antoine Le Coq, who inherited several suspects imprisoned at Montoire by his predecessor; the four priests imprisoned with them were transferred to their local bishop at the expense of the Duke of Vendôme, who owned Montoire [65] Blois and the duchy of Vendôme continued to draw special heresy commissioners for several years; although none experienced Thibault Huart's problems, none produced impressive results or demonstrated Bourgoing's energy and endurance.

The Zenith of French Heresy Prosecution, 1545–1548

Aided by such events as the crusade against the Waldensians of Provence and the creation of itinerant commissioners against heresy, French heresy prosecutions peaked in the final years of Francis I's long reign. As we have seen, this was a moment when the prosecution of Anabaptists and other Protestants had slackened in the Holy Roman Empire and the Low Countries; the mid-1540s were the only time when the kingdom of France punished Protestants more intensively and severely than any other part of Latin Christendom. Recorded executions of French heretics tripled, increasing from nine per year in the first half of the 1540s to twenty-eight per year between 1545 and 1549. (These annual averages then dropped to sixteen per year between 1550 and 1554.) Moreover, contrary to conventional wisdom, more heretics were executed in France during the final phase of Francis I's reign than during the early years of Henry II. From January 1545 until Francis' death at the end of March 1547, surviving evidence shows an average of three people burned for heresy each month across France; in the first part of his son's reign, before the heresy prisoners were removed from the Paris Parlement at the end of 1549, just over two capital punishments for heresy have been recorded per month throughout the kingdom. The glamor that still surrounds Francis I as patron of Chambord, Fontainebleau, and the Collège de France; his lifelong affection for a talented sister who admired all sorts of humanists; everything makes it difficult to believe that the debonair founder of the Valois dynasty also deserves to be remembered as the most savage persecutor of religious dissenters in modern French history. His uninspiring son, whose reign witnessed an enormous increase in the number of French Protestants and the quality of their leadership, has always seemed a far more logical candidate for the role of great royal persecutor. Beginning with the semiofficial *Ecclesiastical History of the French Reformed Churches* in 1580, French Reformation experts have agreed that "the fires were lit more than ever" under Henry II.[66] He established the infamous special heresy tribunal, the Chambre Ardente of the Parlement of Paris, soon after beginning his reign, and decreed France's most draconian laws against Protestantism in the 1550s. Moreover, the greatest modern Protestant and Catholic scholars who have investigated the repression of heresy in Reformation France agree that persecution peaked under Henry II.[67]

However, the well-preserved criminal decisions of the Parlement of Paris for the judicial year beginning in November 1546, covering the final five months of Francis I's life and the first seven months of his son's reign, show that the Parlement ordered thirteen death sentences for heresy during the former period but only one during the latter.[68] Perhaps even more revealing is the fate of a bookseller named Vincent la Vaquerie and his employee Andrieu Basoche, arrested at Reims carrying a quantity of heretical books. Early in March, the Parlement of Paris ordered la Vaquerie to be tortured and returned his trial to the *bailli* of Vermandois together with the prisoner. If the bookseller admitted anything important under torture, he should be burned; otherwise, he was to be given a sentence of perpetual service in the galleys. Reims was relatively distant from Paris, and courts worked slowly. Not until late August, after they had been tortured, do we meet la Vaquerie and Basoche again. This time, ignoring their sentence made while Francis I still lived, the Parisian judges merely ordered la Vaquerie to perform an *amende honorable* at the cathedral of Reims, watch his stock of heretical books burn, and leave the kingdom for three years; his assistant was simply given a warning and dismissed.[69] Seldom does one encounter a sharper short-term contrast in the records of such a prestigious tribunal. And that contrast opposes an aging monarch, whipping his principal judges into a frantic assault on the bodies of accused heretics, with his easygoing successor, opening his reign by relaxing his father's furious antiheretical campaign. Granted, Henry II would take up his father's heresy-hunting mantle soon enough and wore it often during his twelve-year reign. But he never equaled the excesses of his father's final years.

In the peak years of the mid- and late 1540s, the extent of legal activity against "Lutheran" and sacramentarian heretics, which was so intense in President Lizet's Paris district, remained very uneven across the other half of the French kingdom. At one extreme, the Alpine-region parlements rarely prosecuted "Lutherans." Both Grenoble and Turin held several Waldensian communities within their boundaries; but, given the recent experience with the Waldensians of Provence, neither court displayed much inclination to pursue such notorious heretics diligently. The Parlement of Dauphiné, under its humanist president, Claude de

Bellièvre, exhibited little eagerness to pursue heretics of any kind. In 1546 his court offered a long and thoughtful preamble to its "Provision against the 'Lutherans,'" in which Grenoble's judges deplored that butcher shops remained open during Lent throughout Dauphiné, icono-clasm was rampant, and there was much loose talk about the Eucharist. All these acts, they reasoned, "tended (a brutal thing and one that should be kept silent) toward atheism and exemption from all obedience that they owe to their natural princes." The court then threatened dire ac-tions against royal judges who showed "great turpidity . . . having seen and known of heretics and [who] had not done their duty in pursuing them with exemplary punishment"; but its bark was far worse than its bite. One need only examine the trials of Louise Privatelle, whose case was first evoked to Parlement in May 1547 after she had appealed from the court of the bishop of Valence and had also broken jail.[70] Two months later, after a further appeal from her archbishop's tribunal, the Parlement ordered Privatelle imprisoned for ten years in the jail of the bishop of Valence after making a formal abjuration, and threatened her with burn-ing alive if she relapsed. A few years later we encounter her again, duly classified as a relapsed heretic by the episcopal judge of Valence and handed to the secular arm for execution. Her case was again evoked to Parlement in April 1550; but although Grenoble's preserved *arrêts* show no visible lacunae for this period, we hear nothing more about her. Moreover, "in the Parlement's registers, the years 1551–1555 mark a cessation of persecution" against heretics.[71]

Other provincial parlements seemed more zealous in pursuit of here-tics. Imbart de la Tour's remark that some provincial parlements attacked heresy with "renewed energy" in 1546 certainly applies best to Toulouse. In 1546 the Parlement of Languedoc ordered six heretics executed and sent four more to the galleys; another suspect died in their prison.[72] During the next eighteen months this parlement ordered seven more "Lutherans" executed; it also upheld the execution of a man originally charged with sodomy, but then executed as a heretic after his convic-tion by the Inquisitor of Carcassonne.[73] Meanwhile the Parlement of Rouen also took stronger action against "Lutherans." On two occasions in 1547–48 the Rouen judges overturned lower court rulings and im-posed death sentences against "sacramentarians" from lower Normandy. Their special commissioner had objected to a local royal court's lenient sentence against a heretic for his "scandalous and blasphemous speech and blasphemies" against the saints and the Eucharist. The prisoner was taken to Rouen, where he was soon strangled and burned, while the royal judge from St.-Lô was summoned to Rouen to explain his conduct. A former monk, defrocked for heresy in September 1547 by the bishop of Bayeux, nevertheless escaped execution at Caen; in May 1548 the Parlement ordered the culprit hanged and burned, together with "certain small paper notebooks" of his filled with "heretical, schismatic, and contumacious propositions."[74] Rouen's recent zeal helps explain why Henry II named some of its judges to serve as replacements in rebellious Bordeaux in 1548, alongside those from Paris and Toulouse.

Calvin's Assault on Nicodemism

Perhaps the most significant story of the French Protestant movement in the mid-1540s, an age when it remained confined to isolated individuals or at most a few small and clandestine gatherings, concerns John Calvin's uphill campaign against dissimulation by Protestant sympathizers, people whom he called "Nicodemites." The mid-1540s were the last period in which most French Protestants remained both doctrinally and physically dispersed. With the wisdom of hindsight, we can see that Calvin's French version of his *Institutes* in 1541 mattered more than the simultaneous growth of official censorship or Catholic loyalty oaths; it provided clear doctrinal leadership to a previously inchoate movement. Here and there across France one glimpses small groups of evangelicals, slowly becoming acquainted with Calvin's works, meeting clandestinely to read and discuss the Bible. But for practical purposes, it remained a diffuse movement that had not yet grown into churches. The semiofficial history of the French Reformed church admitted in 1580 that the group arrested at Meaux in 1546 constituted the "first organization of a Church in France."[75] And we know about them only because they were all caught and put on trial. Much the same thing could be said about the small Angers community led by Marot's friend Germain Colin, which was decimated shortly after 1540,[76] or about the 1548 group at Langres led by the mysterious "Seraphim d'Argelles." A movement so dispersed, so disorganized, and so energetically tracked by royal judges in many parts of France had no real alternative defense other than the camouflage of external conformity to Catholic rituals.

Nicodemism, by its very nature, has left very few traces in historical records. Only a handful of its prominent French practitioners can be observed in the 1540s. Probably the most prominent of all was Marguerite of Navarre, who spent nearly all of her last decade far from Paris and the French court, much of it in the sovereign principality of Béarn.[77] After her death in 1549, Marguerite was commemorated by the poet Charles de Sainte-Marthe, whom she had installed in her old duchy of Alençon after two condemnations for heresy. She had remained loyal to her favorite cleric, Gérard Roussel, a Béarnese bishop since 1536, who died almost when she did. One of Roussel's pupils, caught at a Protestant assembly in Paris in 1557, was asked why Roussel continued to celebrate Mass at Oloron; "in order to keep his job," came the answer. At Angers, Colin watched his friends die, composed a poem describing his trial and asking the king's pardon, then died in poverty a few years later. At Paris, the briefly famous parish priest François Landry, whom the Sorbonne compelled to perform a spectacular public abjuration in the spring of 1543, lived fourteen more years in total obscurity; we hear of a pathetic meeting in the mid-1550s between Landry and the young zealot Antoine Chandieu, who assured the old priest that no one who behaved as he had could be saved.[78]

Calvin encouraged his French listeners, through a series of anti-Nicodemite treatises in the early 1540s, not to think in terms of self-preservation. For him, the issue was clear: a Christian either displayed his convictions where he lived, and thereby ran the risk of persecution, or else emigrated to a place where the gospel was truly preached, as Calvin had done himself. Addressing such rational and prudent evangelicals in his *Apology to the Nicodemites,* first printed in 1544, Calvin asked his readers, "if the Apostles had had this fantasy [of participating in idolatrous ceremonies to avoid physical danger], I ask you where would we be today?" Would they not, he continued, be ashamed to accuse the apostles of imprudence? "Could they," he asked with biting irony, "with their very great discretion and such circumspect wisdom, boast of ever having set up a church of ten people in some village? Whereas," he concluded, "the whole world was once gained by simple preaching of the Gospel." When considering the alternatives to risking punishment and even death for the gospel, Calvin's answer was equally simple, if unpalatable: emigration. "The departure of a man," he insisted, "sometimes preaches more effectively than he could do through his mouth."[79] This was not the only hard doctrine Calvin preached—consider predestination. His diatribe against Nicodemism was not widely distributed, and we have only a few signs of Frenchmen moving to Geneva by the mid-1540s. It required the great antiheresy campaigns of the mid- and late 1540s to persuade well-placed French Protestant sympathizers to leave their kingdom in order to save their souls from idolatry.

A handful of highly talented and well-placed Frenchmen heard Calvin's message and, after considerable and prolonged internal struggles, eventually accepted his conclusions. It seems particularly instructive to examine the dilemmas of three prominent men, all born around 1520, all persuaded of the essential correctness of the evangelical Reformation by the mid-1540s, but each extremely reluctant to sacrifice his professional and financial future for the sake of the gospel. Late in 1545 all three—a royal official from Picardy, a Burgundian nobleman seeking fame as a humanist, and a patrician lawyer banished from Artois for heresy—met in Paris, where the nobleman informed his two closest friends about his secret promise of marriage to a relatively poor orphan. All three had relocated in Calvin's Geneva three years later. The simultaneous, parallel, and prolonged Nicodemite hesitations of Theodore de Bèze, Jean Crespin, and Laurent de Normandie illustrate the practical problems facing the French Reformation "under the cross" during the major persecutions of the mid-1540s.

The most critical part of their struggles often involved financial worries; if Calvin required his listeners to flee from idolatry, he did not insist on apostolic poverty. Bèze later admitted that his engagement was kept secret "partly in order to avoid giving scandal to anyone and partly because I was not yet freed from the damned money that I drew from my ecclesiastical benefices"; Crespin's oldest hometown friend wrote from Paris in December 1545 that Crespin was "trying to recover both his wife and her dowry" before moving to Geneva.[80] We know little about how de Normandie resolved his financial problems; but by 1548 Bèze had sold his major benefice, de Normandie had similarly sold his office of royal lieutenant in Noyon, and Crespin had fully recovered his wife's dowry, probably augmented after her father's death. All three reached Calvin's Geneva almost simultaneously at the end of October 1548, fleeing "superstition" and preparing to refashion their professional lives. Beza, who had just published his poems in Paris, turned to study theology; the public official de Normandie remade himself into the largest wholesale distributor of Calvinist propaganda in France; and the Netherlands lawyer Crespin became a Swiss printer and, soon, author. Without Calvin's anti-Nicodemite propaganda—and without the great wave of French heresy prosecutions, the most intensive anywhere in Europe during the mid-1540s—the early brain drain to Geneva could never have happened.

5

The Limits of Prosecution and the Challenge of Geneva, 1549–1554

Hangmen, burn the saints; your efforts are vain.
Those you wish to extinguish are reborn from their ashes.
—*Simon Goulart (1597)*

Reinterpreting the early part of Henry II's reign as beginning the decline of French heresy prosecution, rather than marking its apogee, rearranges our conventional picture of the French Reformation. First, it reveals unexpected relationships between royal intentions and their judicial consequences. In the early years of Henry II's reign, specific legislation refined the mechanisms for punishing heresy through the Parisian Parlement's Chambre Ardente. In 1551, Henry II issued the first truly comprehesive set of French decrees against heresy, the well-known Edict of Chateaubriand. Yet the Chambre Ardente did not maintain existing levels of antiheretical activity at Paris, let alone increase them, and the Edict of Chateaubriand would prove as futile to apply as the numerous royal edicts against blasphemy. Increasingly severe royal legislation did not increase heresy indictments, nor, given the conventions of "arbitrary" justice, did it affect the severity with which French parlements judged defendants accused of "Lutheranism." Measured against the abundant surviving evidence from parlements across France, these developments illustrate not the zenith of punishments for heresy, but rather the effective limits of judicial prosecution for this particular offense.

Meanwhile, early in Henry II's reign, Calvin finally began to win his struggle against evangelical "Nicodemites." French Protestant emigration to Calvin's Geneva had become noticeable to Pierre Lizet and his

116

parlementary colleagues by 1549; it did not involve large numbers, but rather a few significant individuals. The first trickle of prominent French religious refugees moved to Geneva before being indicted or even officially investigated. They did not forsake all for the gospel and flee precipitously: the most prominent royal official among them had adequate time to sell his office; similarly, the most promising intellectual had managed to sell his ecclesiastical benefice, as Calvin had done. For our purposes, the main religious issues during the first half of Henry II's reign concern the triangular relationships among an increasingly severe royal policy against Protestantism, an intransigent Calvinist position opposing hypocrisy and "idolatry" among Protestant sympathizers, and French parlements, often unable and occasionally unwilling to enforce the crown's edicts against heresy. Seen in this light, the year 1549 offers two especially revealing details. That spring, the Republic of Geneva opened a special register for recent immigrants, the *Livre des habitants,* ostensibly in order to permit them to sell wine.[1] That autumn, the king permitted the Parlement of Paris to empty its prison of heresy suspects. Two signs that the tide had begun to turn.

Anticlimaxes: The Chambre Ardente and the Waldensian Revision

Henry II's reign opened with two loud but contradictory signals about the new ruler's intentions toward French "Lutherans." One of his very first acts was to listen to complaints from prominent landlords in Provence, and in May 1547 he arrested both commanders of the April 1545 crusade against Mérindol and other Waldensian villages. The First President of the Parlement of Aix, Maynier d'Oppède, and Captain Polin were to be tried for exceeding their instructions by a special court at Melun, comprised of twenty-one judges drawn from various parlements and called the Queen's Chamber. (The naming of this tribunal in honor of Catherine de Médicis provides our first bit of indirect evidence about the new queen's opposition to religious persecution.) When this tribunal was on the point of discharging both men on the grounds that they had merely carried out their duty of enforcing perfectly legal orders to punish rebels, it was suddenly dissolved. Pressure from two popes to liberate their loyal vassal Maynier d'Oppède was offset by pressure from the king's German Lutheran allies to punish the men responsible for the atrocities of 1545. Instead of releasing his prisoners, Henry II ordered their trial transferred to the Paris Parlement in March 1550.[2]

While he was setting up the special court of Queen's Chamber, Henry II also ordered the Parlement of Paris, when it began its judicial year in November 1547, to devote a special section to the pursuit of heretics. We do not know exactly when the Chambre Ardente actually began operating; its decisions were recorded in a separate cluster only between May and October 1548.[3] At the end of August, President Lizet had to order one of its judges, Nicolas Martineau, to stay at his post during the ordinary autumn vacation period, and twelve days later the king reinforced this ruling with an official decree. The problem may well have arisen because of the recent capture of a large group of heretics at Langres, four of whom President Lizet soon ordered transported to Paris.[4] The Parlement's criminal *arrêts* are missing during the first half of the following judicial year; however, their subsequent language and organization offer no evidence that any special division was still operating by the spring of 1549. The notorious "Burning Chamber" may well have lasted only one year, about the same insitutional lifetime as the long-forgotten "Queen's Chamber." Neither experiment can be judged a success.

By November 1549, five months after watching heretics burn during his Joyous Entry into Paris, Henry II had not only dissolved his special court at Melun but also promulgated a new ruling that effectively removed all defendants charged with heresy from the jail of the Paris Parlement. Shortly after the Christmas holiday of 1549, almost seventy prisoners were redistributed to several episcopal courts scattered across the vast district regulated by the Paris court: five went to Amiens, three to Poitiers, three to Soissons, four to Meaux, eight to Orléans, three to Sens, six to Troyes, three to Châlons, three to Noyon, one to Le Mans, four to Tours, a whole convoy of ten to Chartres, two all the way to Clermont in Auvergne, two to Lyon, one to Nevers, four to Bourges, one to Angers, and two were moved across town to the prison of the bishop of Paris. In addition, four prisoners were released with admonitions, and another was released unconditionally. Perhaps most remarkable of all was the fate of Jean Lefevre, arrested for heresy at Paris early in 1549. He had confesssed under torture in March, but President Lizet ordered his sentence postponed until another suspect named Brioude could be arrested; a week later an abbot in Languedoc informed the Paris Parlement that Lefevre's letters of ordination were forgeries. Since Brioude was never found, Lefevre was still sitting in the Parlement's jail on 1 February 1550. Even he benefited from the general climate of amnesty; Lizet signed a ruling that Lefevre was to perform an *amende honorable* at Notre-Dame, be whipped three times, and then banished from France. But unlike any other recent prisoner, he was not executed after confessing his heresy under torture.[5]

Why did Henry II order Parisian heresy prisoners returned to ecclesiastical courts at the end of 1549? As Imbart de la Tour noted, this ruling reversed ten years of intensive royal efforts, dating from the Edict of Fontainebleau, to improve the prosecution of heresy by removing prisoners from church courts. Strangely, neither President Lizet nor his colleagues protested against this sudden change, although in Lizet's case it threatened the work of a quarter-century during which he had signed nearly a hundred death warrants against heretics. Imbart de la Tour thought that royal diplomacy—renewing France's alliance with Germany's Lutheran princes after the decisive defeat of their Schmalkaldic League by Charles V—explained the king's actions.[6] But diplomacy cannot explain the supine acceptance of this new policy by the ultra-Gallican Parlement of Paris, who upheld their traditions only in stipulating that the costs of transporting all these prisoners would be borne by the bishops to whose courts they were sent. It is easier to guess why Henry II acted as he did than to understand why Lizet and his colleagues, ever ready to delay registration of unpleasant orders and send delegations to remonstrate with their monarch about his poor judgement, raised no protest. Great courts do not willingly abandon jurisdiction over a significant issue.

One possible explanantion why the Paris Parlement rid itself of responsibility for prosecuting heresy at the end of 1549 without an audible murmur of complaint lies in the cumulative strain that the great heresy hunt had imposed on its personnel and resources. When Francis I promulgated the Edict of Fontainebleau, neither he nor his chancellor (a veteran judge of the Paris Parlement) foresaw any need to increase the capacities of French parlements. Although their load of heresy cases increased every year thereafter, it seems probable that this additional burden remained bearable, at least until Francis I decided to send out roving heresy commissioners in 1545. The huge jump in cases from cities and regions in which these special commissioners had worked crowded the Parlement's dockets during the remainder of Francis' reign. After an initial pause in 1547, this situation persisted under his son. Even omitting the huge number of cases produced at Meaux in 1546 and those from Langres in 1548, the Parlement of Paris was judging at least ten accused heretics each month from 1545 through 1549, and sentencing about three of them to death every two months. They had maintained this pace for five years. In practical terms, this meant that well over one-fourth of the Parlement's criminal defendants had been charged with heresy. During the only year in this period for which the Parlement's overall criminal decisions have been tabulated, heresy cases accounted for almost 40 percent of its total.[7] The Parlement's size, its number of sitting judges, was not increased; the experiment of the Chambre Ardente merely redistributed its existing resources by requiring some judges to specialize in hearing only one type of case. Small wonder that this innovation was not received enthusiastically by judges like Nicolas Martineau. Nor was the size of the Parlement's jail increased. It had been designed to hold about 150 prisoners under ordinary conditions; therefore, the prisoners released to episcopal courts at the beginning of 1550 represented close to half of its regular capacity.

For five consecutive years, the great heresy hunt begun in the mid-1540s had strained the resources of the Paris Parlement to their limits. Accused heretics crowded their jail and their workloads. Moreover, some of these cases presented serious professional difficulties. Heretics were not easily or comfortably judged by men who had mastered every nuance of Roman Law but were untrained in theology. Meanwhile, the northern half of the kingdom produced its annual crop of felons appealing their convictions for various forms of theft, homicide, and a wide variety of other potentially capital crimes ranging from fraud to bestiality. Such criminals had provided the Parlement's staple occupation for centuries before anyone heard of "Lutherans." So for many of President Lizet's Parisian colleagues, the king's decision at the end of 1549 to hand accused heretics back to ecclesiastical courts was probably greeted with a sigh of relief: for five years these amateur theologians had toiled overtime to combat heresy, while treating accused individual heretics as fairly as possible, and now they could return to their ordinary business.

Or could they? In March 1550, its jail now empty of accused heretics, the Parlement of Paris learned that the king expected them to judge their colleagues from the Parlement of Provence, accused of abusing their authority by causing the deaths of eighteen hundred people in a futile attempt to capture twenty heretics in some remote village. The case had huge implications. In theory, all parlements were created equal, and there was no legal way for one of them to claim jurisdiction over another. If the sovereignty issue did not raise enough legal difficulties, one need only consider that the principal defendant had acted in the dual capacity of chief justice of a provincial parlement and acting governor of the same province. Perhaps trickiest of all was the problem of how to prosecute a judge for carrying out his own court's orders to exterminate a group of notorious heretics, without seeming to favor heretics overtly. Given such dilemmas, further compounded by the distance between Paris and Provence, which made the gathering of usable information extremely difficult, it is not surprising that some men avoided the dubious honor of serving as special royal prosecutor, or that the man who finally accepted, Jean Aubéry, took more than a year to prepare his case. What does seem surprising is that Maynier d'Oppède was never liberated on bail throughout these slow preparations, despite considerable pressure from papal representatives.

In mid-September 1551 the First President of the Parlement of Provence, three of his colleagues who had made up its official committee to supervise the implementation of the famous *arrêt* of Mérindol, the chief royal prosecutor who had accompanied them, and the commander of the expeditionary force that had sacked parts of the Luberon region were finally put on trial before the Grande Chambre of the Paris Parlement.[8] Special prosecutor Aubéry held forth for seven consecutive days, developing arguments laid out in the accusatory plea *(plaidoyer)* that his grandson published almost a century later. Aubéry began with Jean de Roma in order to depict the judicial background before stressing the purely legal flaws in the famous *arrêt* itself, which necessarily entailed severe punishments against many dependent persons who had committed no heresy. He dwelt on the confusion and occasional conflict between Maynier's dual roles as chief justice and acting governor. He rather unconvincingly denied that Francis I had actually given an official order to exterminate the village of Mérindol; more persuasively, he claimed that the addition of other ruined villages to the original 1540 indictment of Mérindol was based on testimony that was trivial, fraudulent, or both. He gave detailed summaries of the human damage wrought by the 1545 crusade, with precise information about how many French subjects were killed, including those who had been "imprisoned" on the galleys, and how few people had been tried for heresy, let alone punished, as a direct result of this expedition.

Aubéry was followed for two days by a lawyer for the plaintiff whose villages had been sacked on flimsy legal excuses. The defense included separate lawyers for each defendant, plus one who represented the corporate interests of the Parlement of Aix, another who represented the Estates of Provence, and even one who represented the papal government at Avignon. Maynier d'Oppède's lawyer took ten mornings to present his client's case; not content with claiming that Maynier deserved rewards instead of imprisonment, he took the offensive by concluding that the court should order the original plaintiff to perform an *amende honorable*. Essentially, lawyer Robert argued that his client was simply carrying out royal orders to punish people who were armed rebels in addition to being heretics. The Parlement's lawyer argued that no sovereign appellate court could pass judgment on another under any circumstances. Other lawyers, including the famous Christophe de Thou, then defended their respective clients; the papal lawyer was ultimately prevented from addressing the court by royal intervention. A full month after he had opened the king's case, special prosecutor Aubéry returned for three days of rebuttals. The remainder of October was devoted to further rebuttals by everone else's lawyers. The Paris Parlement then made its procedural ruling. In February 1552 the king liberated Captain Polin. Not until November 1553 were President Maynier d'Oppède and his three colleagues finally cleared of all wrongdoing by the king and restored to office. The only defendant to suffer physically was the former royal prosecutor of Aix, Guillaume Guérin, whom the Paris Parlement finally ordered hanged in 1554 for forgery of official documents—although they specified that his frauds were not directly connected to the 1545 crusade.[9]

Protestants expressed bitter disappointment with the official results of Aubéry's prosecution of Maynier and his associates. However, the Parlement of Aix had to endure an enormous insult to its collective prestige, one that still rankled two centuries later. Its presiding judge had been imprisoned for six years simply for enforcing one of its rulings, and its chief prosecutor had been hanged by order of a court with no right to judge him. Among other consequences, the collective trauma of the great Paris trial, regardless of its formal outcome, temporarily softened this court's attitudes toward defendants charged with Protestantism. From the time of Jean de Roma until Maynier d'Oppède's arrest in 1547, the Parlement of Provence had surpassed all other provincial tribunals in its eagerness to punish both "Lutheran" and Waldensian heretics. But after its chastened First President finally returned to Aix early in 1554, the Parlement of Provence rarely summoned the nerve to implement further heresy executions.

French Parlements Discover Geneva

During its last years under First President Lizet, the Parlement of Paris provides our earliest official French awareness of Calvin's efforts to draw his fellow countrymen to Geneva, evidence strewn through its huge *registre d'arrêts criminels* between mid-November 1548 and late April 1549.[10] Shortly after their annual session began, the royal prosecutor warned the court that episcopal officials at Noyon had arrested two laymen charged with "sacramentarian blasphemy" but were unable to transfer them to secular courts. Part of the reason was that the local lieutenant, a lynchpin of such prosecution machinery, had fled the kingdom; President Lizet therefore signed an order to "take evidence secretly and diligently" against the missing official, Laurent de Normandie (who was also the mayor of Noyon), "who one says is presently in Geneva," and to find out how long he had been "infected by that sect."[11] The report from Noyon, begun in late October and continued in December, confirmed their worst suspicions. In early February de Normandie, his servant, his clerk Lancelot de Montigny, and four other local men were ordered arrested and their property confiscated; de Normandie's wife was summoned to Paris, and a warrant was issued against a foreigner, "someone named Monsr. Crespin, from the province of Artois or maybe Hainaut, a man short of stature, with a red beard and a pale and thin face."[12] However, the Paris Parlement could capture only de Normandie's wife and a few unimportant suspects.[13] Meanwhile, de Normandie and his clerk were living alongside Noyon's most famous son, Jean Calvin, who is never mentioned in these documents.

On 2 January 1549 President Lizet decided to recapture a slippery cleric, Thibault Brosses, recently caught at Clermont-Ferrand: "infected with Lutheranism and having frequented familiarly with heretics in Geneva for several days and having received some books from them," he had escaped. Two months later he was rearrested at Tours but had in the meantime obtained a royal pardon.[14] A more dangerous person, Denis Raguenier, headed a group of four absentees from Sens condemned together in late January.[15] Although his whereabouts are never mentioned, we know that Raguenier soon surfaced in Geneva, where he began copying Calvin's sermons in August 1549 and became the first French refugee to be regularly subsidized by Geneva's Bourse Française.[16] On the other hand, there is no trace in these *arrêts* of the sudden disappearance of a highly visible and prominent Parisian, the son of Francis I's internationally famous humanist secretary; Jean Budé signed Geneva's *Livre des habitants* in June 1549 and soon became permanent secretary of the fund that subsidized Raguenier.

A few other prominent refugees to Geneva can be found in these *arrêts*. In April the Parlement ordered the arrest and confiscation of the property of *Maître* "Deode de Besze," prior of Longjumeau. It added two of his associates, including the humanist printer "Norard" Badius, who had recently published Theodore de Bèze's poems.[17] Since Bèze had sold his benefice before quitting France, an outraged President Lizet signed a general warning against "those unhappy men tainted with the Lutheran sect" who "had left the dwellings and habitations of this kingdom, [committing simony as well as heresy] . . . and had transported themselves to the city of Geneva, receptacle of the enemies of the Christian faith." Royal prosecutors were ordered to publish *monitoires*, general requests for information, in order to discover such reprobates.[18] This is the first piece of specifically anti-Genevan legislation emanating from French authorities. Ironically, it came in the same month that the Republic of Geneva took *its* first official step to regulate the growing numbers of religious refugees arriving from France: the young republic opened a special "Register and Roll of foreigners" who had come to Geneva "solely from the desire and good affection which they have to live under the holy evangelical religion, which is purely announced here, and live according to its holy Reformation."[19] Reciprocal and interconnected bits of legislation, each testifying in its own way to Calvin's increasing success at persuading his adherents to vote with their feet.

If Lizet's attempt to punish simoniacs among the French clerics escaping from the kingdom proved futile (no further cases of this type can be found in the Parisian records during the next few years), Geneva's *Livre des habitants* suggests Calvin's ability to attract distinguished

Frenchmen to his evangelical mecca around 1550. The first dozen pages of its printed edition, including inscriptions between April 1549 and August 1551, begin with two noblemen from the diocese of Sens. They include, in addition to Laurent de Normandie, his clerk and four of their fellow townsmen, such names as Didier Rousseau, the ancestor of Jean-Jacques; Philippe de Corguilleray, the Burgundian nobleman who later led the Genevan contingent to France's ill-fated Brazilian colony in 1556;[20] the second son and the widow of France's most famous court humanist, "noble Jean Budé, native of Paris, son of *Messire* Guillaume Budé, councillor and Master of Requests of the household of the king of France"; Bèze's Parisian printer, Conrad Badius; two renowned jurists from Bourges, Léon and Germain Colladon; Guillaume Trie, a wealthy merchant from Lyon, whom Calvin would use to denounce Servetus to French authorities in 1553; the "honorable" royal printer, Robert Estienne, who signed the *Livre des habitants* six months after his business agent Thomas Courteau; an erudite physician from Lyon, Philibert Sarrasin; an outstanding pedagogue from Nîmes, Claude Baduel, "professor of good letters"; and, last but not least, the mysterious lawyer from the Low Countries who had worked in Paris, "Monsr. Crespin." Such men became the backbone of Calvin's Geneva, supplanting the people who had previously run Calvin's propaganda campaign in France as it intensified its activities during the 1550s.

Among the less famous of these early registered refugees, one also finds men associated with French heresy executions, both in the future and in the past. In July 1549 a man named Philibert Hamelin signed, describing himself as a bookseller born at Tours; he was actually a renegade cleric who would be imprisoned twice for heresy by the Parlement of Bordeaux, and finally executed in 1557 for running a clandestine Protestant congregation on a small island off the coast of Saintonge.[21] In a different vein, three brothers from the tiny Alpine diocese of Embrun signed the *Livre des habitants* in June 1550 and became Genevan citizens five years later. Their father had been executed for heresy by order of the Parlement of Provence in 1540, and their older brother had been hanged and burned for sacrilege a year later, while one of them had been whipped and banished for the same reason in 1541.[22]

After 1550, relations between the Paris Parlement and Geneva consisted mainly in clashes of propaganda. On the one hand, the Parlement's involvement with heresy trials declined abruptly after January 1550.

While it conducted its famous trial of Maynier D'Oppède and his associates, the Parlement of Paris sharply curtailed—indeed, it almost abandoned—its involvement in heresy trials. After emptying its prison in January 1550, its heresy caseloads dropped abruptly from judging more than ten defendants per month during 1545–1549 to fewer than one per month in 1550–1551,[23] gradually increasing thereafter to about four defendants per month by 1554. It executed one heretic for sacrilege in December 1550; he had been caught while trying to damage a statue of the Virgin Mary in the cathedral of Notre-Dame. This man was indeed judged expeditiously: he was handed directly to the Parlement by the cathedral canons who captured him, admitted his intentions under torture, and was burned within four days of his arrest.[24] Except under such unusual circumstances, the Paris Parlement rarely intervened in heresy cases, apart from trials resulting from the activities of a few veteran special commissioners. In April 1551 the king ordered Antoine le Coq to Blois for his second tour of duty, accompanied by two of his colleagues. Over the next year this commission sent twenty-three prisoners to Paris for judgment. But eighteen of them were simply released with warnings, four were ordered to perform public apologies in their parish churches, and only one even paid a sizable fine.[25]

While the Paris Parlement slackened its actions against accused heretics, the propaganda campaigns escalated on both sides. In 1550 the Genevans reprinted a satirical imitation of French parlementary decrees against Protestants, titled *Royal Decrees and Regulations from the Supreme Most High and Sovereign Court of the Kingdom of Heaven*; instead of prohibiting vernacular Bibles, it proposed to require people to read them.[26] The doughty Norman priest Artus Desiré quickly counterattacked with the first pamphlet specifically targeting Geneva: *The Struggles of the Faithful Papist and Roman Pilgrim against the Apostate Priapist, Drawn to the Synagogue of Geneva, That Babylonian House of Lutherans*.[27] Its word-play opposed the Reformers' pejorative "papist" with the even more pejorative "priapist," thus already suggesting the sexual debauchery stressed by Alain Dufour as a central feature of the negative myth about Geneva.[28] After 1551 the French refugees installed in Geneva refurbished and expanded the Calvinist campaign of printed propaganda into France, with the well-heeled Laurent de Normandie remaking himself from magistrate into a major distributor and his fellow lawyer Crespin becoming a celebrated printer, while such previously established Parisian printers as Estienne and Badius churned out uncensored editions during the next few years. Meanwhile, Pierre Lizet's involuntary retirement as head of the Paris Parlement in 1550 as the result of a court intrigue also forced a career change on their most dangerous enemy. Comfortably installed at the head of an abbey just outside Paris, Lizet occupied his retirement by composing a legal handbook, but primarily remade himself into a religious polemicist, publishing two enormous volumes of anti-"Lutheran" polemic in 1551. The most effective answer to it came from Bèze, in the form of a satiric pamphlet purporting to be a report by Lizet's agent, sent on mission to Geneva. "Master Benedict Passavant" (who descends directly from both Rabelais and the *Letters of Obscure Men*) satirized Lizet's arguments, his prose, and even his large red nose.[29]

During this interval of escalating propaganda and diminishing prosecution, Henry II intervened in June 1551 by issuing his most comprehensive body of legislation against heresy, the Edict of Chateaubriand. The published preamble to its forty-seven articles (signed by the ambitious royal prosecutor, Pierre Séguier, who soon became a president of the Paris Parlement) used Roman history to stress that religious schisms were invariably catastrophic for political stability. This edict reviewed and confirmed previous decrees ordering the death penalty for unrepentant heretics. It attempted to ensure the religious orthodoxy of highly placed royal officials and lowly schoolteachers. Many of its provisions dealt with dangers posed by propaganda coming from Geneva; careful prescriptions attempted to control printers, booksellers, and even the many itinerant peddlers who carried prohibited literature on their backs. This piece of legislation indeed constituted an important landmark, which specifically recognized the multiple dangers posed by Geneva to the stability of the French kingdom. Subsequent Protestant historians believed that its most dangerous provision was the authority given to the new presidial courts to pronounce capital punishments for heresy without the possibility of appealing to parlements.[30] Nevertheless, for the most part its practical effect was remarkably small. Far from reducing the amount of heretical Genevan propaganda entering France, it only stimulated de Normandie and other refugees to redouble their efforts to spread clandestine literature throughout the kingdom. The Edict of Chateaubriand utterly failed to reduce emigraton from France to Geneva. Tellingly, it did not even spur any visible increase in the number of heresy trials and executions throughout France.

As parlements across France ratified the Edict of Chateaubriand, one finds increasing awareness of the Genevan danger. In August 1551 the Parlement of Toulouse ordered a convicted heretic from Pontoise to be tortured before his execution in order to learn "if he had been sent from Geneva in order to sow errors."[31] In July 1552, after a scandal involving the kidnapping of a nun, they executed a heretical tanner from the Bourbonnais, identified as "living in Geneva for ten years," and arrested his companion, a native Genevan.[32] Meanwhile, the earliest preserved *plumitifs,* or interrogations of prisoners, at the Norman Parlement of Rouen enable us to identify a pair of Genevan couriers captured in 1552 and 1553. One, apparently a native Frenchman, had come from Geneva and was heading for England;[33] the other was caught carrying letters from Normandy to Geneva.[34] They were not the first Genevan couriers in French parlementary records; in 1548 the Parlement of Aix had interrogated a man carrying letters from former residents of Provence "now residing in the city of Geneva" to their local relatives.[35] But after the Edict of Chateaubriand, both couriers caught in Normandy were executed as heretics.

Other prisoners charged with heresy at Rouen were now questioned closely about any possible contacts they might have had with Geneva. A barber, who had traveled to places as distant as London and Naples, admitted that he had spent three months in Geneva. Although he correctly identified Calvin as the principal preacher there, he insisted to the judges that he had not followed their customs ("n'a point usé de leur manière à faire"), much less taken communion; instead, he had traveled into France to hear Mass at the nearest available place. One finds no sign of a negative myth, however. The barber recalled that the Genevans "paid him well while he was there" and insisted that "there are no bordellos in Geneva." Another prisoner, a middle-aged shopkeeper whom they questioned the next day, indignantly told his judges that he had never even heard of the place, much less seen it.[36]

One episode in particular reveals a growing judicial involvement with Calvin's Geneva. In the spring of 1552 Cardinal Bourbon asked the Paris Parlement to send a special heresy commissioner to Noyon (which was his possession) to investigate the mutilation of a crucifix. A veteran judge, Louis Gayant, undertook the mission and spent almost a year in Noyon. Although he never did catch the perpetrators of this sacrilege, Gayant eventually convicted five local heretics. One of them was condemned to death; another, who had moved to Geneva three years earlier and had left his family there, was sentenced to life in the galleys.[37] However, Gayant also possessed abundant information, dating back several years, about prominent citizens who had fled abroad, including Laurent de Normandie. The Parlement therefore approved Gayant's recommendation that ten men and seven women be declared guilty of *lèse-majesté* for moving to Geneva, "a suspect city, the receptacle for suspects of the crime of heresy," thereby making "voluntary desertion of the faith." Although none of them had any connection with this iconoclastic deed, the effigies of these ten men (but none of the women) were to be burned in front of the parish church to which the defaced crucifix was taken. Their official sentences were to be written out "in large script" on a table in front of the belfry of Noyon's main church "in perpetual memory of the crime" and the infamy of those "infected with the Lutheran sect."[38] The deed marked one of the judges' most innovative attempts at guilt by association since the mingling of Berquin's books and Vallière's *amende honorable* thirty years before. Moreover, Noyon's most famous heretic became irritated when news of Gayant's decree reached him in Geneva; Calvin expressed indignation that a minor Genevan preacher had been mentioned in this solemn document, while he himself had been overlooked.[39]

Paris Recessional and Provincial Resurgence, 1550–1554

Apart from a few special missions like Gayant's journey to Noyon, the Paris Parlement avoided most opportunities to intervene in heresy cases after 1550. Their reluctance shows up most clearly, and had its most significant consequences, when they were confronted early in 1553 with an appeal from five Protestant students, coming from various parts of France, who had been condemned to death at Lyon. The incident deserves special consideration for both its statements and its silences, as they appear in the Parlement's criminal records. On 17 February the judges told the vicar of Cardinal Tournon (the archbishop of Lyon) "that he had to send them from the jails of Lyon four or five prisoners accused of heresy and blasphemy, who were appealing *comme d'abus*." The vicar responded "that a hundred armed men would not be sufficient to bring them in safely," because "they would be in danger of being rescued along the way." It was obvious both to the cardinal's spokesman and to the judges that Tournon would have to pay the cost of their transportation, including an armed escort. The Parlement's spokesman pointed out that they were unable to judge an *appel comme d'abus* against an ecclesiastical court "without hearing the prisoners explain [in person] the reasons for their appeal." The court was simply enunciating one of the legal cornerstones of its famous Gallicanism, a set of policies that both preceded and followed the age of the Reformation. In order to break this impasse, the cardinal's vicar (who represented the most influential man in France at the time) revealed that one of his companions was carrying written memoranda from the prisoners who were his clients, and suggested that the court summon him instead. The whole entry is unsigned, and the court then recessed.[40]

We can guess what decisions they made that evening. The following day, the court reopened the case of the five students sitting in the archbishop of Lyon's prison, all of whom are now named. *Maître* Guillaume Boucherat, their lawyer, appeared, accompanied by his deputy, Pierre Falaise. The latter apparently spoke first, explaining that he was carrying a bag given to him by the prisoners six weeks ago; the court promptly ordered him to hand it to them. Meanwhile, the official minutes now tell us that one of the Parlement's four notaries had been sent to court to sound out the crown's advice on this matter; he was also instructed to ask if they wanted a copy of the defendants' writings in order to send to the king's ambassador in Switzerland. The notary reported "that the king wishes and commands to ignore their appeal [*passer oultre à l'appel d'abus*]." Fortified by information provided with such exemplary cooperation by the prisoners' lawyer and by the report about the king's orders on this case, the Parlement's minutes then concluded with their official decision. Like any other formal ruling, it began by summarizing the decision of the court that had originally tried them. The five students, now further identified by their home towns in Languedoc, Guyenne, Gascony, Angoumois, and Limousin, said the archbishop's judge, had been treated with benignity (thus there had been no *abus* from which to appeal) but had displayed "great pertinacity and willful obstination . . . to resist and repulse" all attempts to convert them. They were therefore declared "heretics, pernicious and pertinacious schismatics, and as such removed and handed to the secular arm." Then came the Parlement's own ruling. Specifying that they had heard the defendants' lawyers (naming Boucherat and Falaise) and read the petitioners' signed *mémoires* (which were actually statements of their theological positions), the court then denied their appeal, declaring it *non recepvable*. Lizet's successor as First President, Claude le Maistre, signed the decree.[41]

The significance of the Paris Parlement's behavior in this case is that its procedures and its decision contradicted two of its oldest and most cherished traditions. Laymen had manipulated the *appel comme d'abus* as a weapon that almost automatically nullified decisions of French church courts; the Parlement might well deny an appeal *comme d'abus* from a cleric, but very rarely from a layman. Even stranger was the Parlement's bland acceptance of the excuse of the archbishop's vicar for refusing to send the five students to Paris; although such an escape had occurred recently, he was probably less afraid of their being rescued than of having to pay the cost of a round trip with a suitable escort. If Gallicanism and the *appel comme d'abus* were one of the major hallmarks of the Parlement of Paris' jurisprudence, its insistence on hearing all appellants in person at Paris was a procedural cornerstone whose importance cannot be exaggerated. Yet both fundamental aspects were flouted here. In a purely judicial way, the episode is as strange as the *arrêt* of Mérindol, although it cost fewer people their lives.

The case of the "Lyon five" was no accident. Two episodes in the following months demonstrate the continuing desire of the Parisian court to shun responsibility for judging accused heretics. Only a few weeks after his judges followed royal advice and refused to hear the five students in person, Henry II failed to reestablish the Chambre Ardente through an edict creating a "second criminal chamber for judgment of trials for heretical blasphemy and of Lutherans." The announcement stirred debate but no action. Two days later the Parlement obediently registered the new edict, but immediately sent a delegation to complain to the king, who apparently withdrew it.[42] Three months later the Paris Parlement quickly dismissed another *appel comme d'abus* from a merchant who had been condemned to death by the judge of the archbishop of Lyon, supported by an Inquisitor and confirmed by the local seneschal.[43] The common feature of all three episodes is the Parlement's visible desire to minimize its institutional involvement. Unless their own commissioners had conducted the investigations or the canons of Notre-Dame handed over some iconoclast caught in the act, they seemed unwilling to judge heretics in the early 1550s.

When he handed the Parisian heresy prisoners back to ecclesiastical justice at the end of 1549, Henry II never expected that the slow-moving and relatively gentle episcopal courts would be able to deal adequately with the problem of heresy. Early in 1552 the king created sixty-two new presidial courts with considerable powers, including the right to pronounce and execute death sentences without the right of appeal to regional parlements; they shared jurisdiction over heresy suspects with church courts, just like the parlements. Unfortunately for historians, virtually all early records from these new courts, which had theoretically decentralized heresy prosecutions throughout the kingdom, have disappeared. We simply have no idea how individual presidial courts handled the crime of heresy, except for the details of a few martyrdoms described by Crespin, who also printed the official sentence of one such execution.[44] These glimpses suggest that a few presidial courts functioned autonomously in regions near the edges of the two largest parlementary districts, Paris and Toulouse. The executions reported by Crespin came from the most remote corners of the huge Parisian district, at such places as Bourg-en-Bresse (between Paris and Chambéry) and Limoges (between Paris and Bordeaux), or from Nîmes, a traditional rival of Toulouse. In all probability, most presidial courts pronounced no death sentences for heresy. At La Rochelle, on the western edge of the vast Parisian district, a veteran judge, imprisoned at Paris in 1545 for obstructing the prosecution of heretics, headed the new presidial court; one can easily imagine his behavior on the bench.

Lyon, France's second-largest city, located on the eastern frontier of the Parisian district, offers the most significant case of effective local autonomy in handling heresy prosecutions during the early 1550s. The religious problem at Lyon came to the Paris Parlement's notice in August 1551, with reports of a "great assembly of people, men and women, upwards of five hundred people" gathering to hear "a preacher reading the Gospels to them in the manner of Geneva, with the said men and women having books of Holy Scripture in French and other prohibited books."[45] In the aftermath of such a spectacular public scandal, local authorities arrested a few principal suspects. One was defrocked and burned at Lyon in October. Another was condemned to death, but appealed to the Parlement of Paris—and was rescued in January 1552 before he reached his destination. Between May 1553 and August 1554, Crespin's martyrology provides information about twelve heresy executions at Lyon, including six who had appealed to the Paris Parlement. Even the man who had previously escaped, Richard Lefevre, was soon rearrested in Dauphiné. The Parlement of Grenoble, despite receiving a copy of Lefevre's original sentence, avoided executing this recidivist and finally extradited him to Lyon.[46] The province of Dauphiné seemed incapable of prosecuting heretics in the early 1550s; its governor, the duke of Guise, complained in 1551 that a seneschal (who he correctly suspected was himself a Protestant) had enabled a Franciscan monk, already arrested for heresy, to escape.[47]

While Paris minimized its involvement with heresy cases in the early 1550s, some French provincial parlements increased theirs. During the second half of the 1540s, provincial parlements had averaged about eight public executions per year for heresy. In 1550 six different parlements recorded public executions for heresy, a record never equaled.[48] From 1550 to 1554 they averaged more than ten known heresy executions per year, distributed everywhere except Grenoble. (Provincial averages then fell by half during the next five years.) Major regional parlements now recorded several burnings of heretics. At Bordeaux Henry II abolished the Parlement in October 1548 because of its complicity in a serious provincial rebellion, and restored it only in January 1550.[49] The replacement judges he named to serve in Guyenne were drawn from the parlements of Paris, Toulouse, and Rouen; they included a seasoned Parisian heresy commissioner, Guillaume Bourgoing. Although these interim judges pronounced three death sentences for heresy during their five months of activity, the restored Parlement of Guyenne decreed only five known heresy executions across the next five years.[50] They were the colleagues whom Montaigne would soon join.

Early in 1550 the Rouen Parlement staged the final public spectacle ordered by a French parlement that resembles an *auto-da-fé*. It featured a flamboyant Flemish prophet who called himself "the Angel of God"; in all, eleven people had been captured.[51] After an attempted jailbreak at Rouen, the court finally ordered Jean Filleul, *l'ange de Dieu,* to be burned alive (*brulé vif* is carefully underlined in their official sentence) together with his writings, while one of his principal followers was hanged and his corpse burned. Four other men and Filleul's wife performed *amendes honorables* at the cathedral of Rouen. Three of the men were whipped and banished afterward; two men and two women were released. The local man who had arranged the attempted jailbreak was hanged; four of his accomplices were whipped, while a servant who had stolen Filleul's manuscript to give to a prisoner was also whipped after making a formal apology in court. A month afterwards, one of the prisoners received a second whipping for his "scandalous speech" protesting their treatment of Filleul. This episode was the most dramatic antiheresy spectacle staged by any French provincial parlement in these years, but its victims were "libertines" rather than followers of Calvin.

In the new French parlements created for Savoy and Piedmont, provinces captured from the duke of Savoy in 1536, Protestantism was being prosecuted somewhat more vigorously by 1550. The Parlement of Turin had ignored its Waldensians during the 1540s, partly because their French governor was sympathetic toward them. After an Italian replaced him, they began to investigate and punish more heretics. Their lone surviving register of criminal *arrêts* reveals that a defrocked Franciscan was executed as a relapsed "adherent of the Lutheran sect" late in 1550. He was followed by four witches whom they ordered burned nine months later; however, the Parlement of Turin ordered no further known heresy executions until 1555.[52] The Parlement of Chambéry, located much closer to the heretical capital of Geneva, burned two French artisans as *sacramentaires* in 1550; one, originally sentenced to the galleys, made heretical remarks while attending his companion's execution and was condemned to death three days later.[53]

But there were limits to Chambéry's zeal in the early 1550s, best illustrated by the history of Germain Colladon.[54] Colladon's father, a prominent jurist from Bourges, registered as a Genevan resident early in 1551. Young Colladon and Michel Protin, merchants doing business out of Lyon, were arrested on heresy charges at Bourg-en-Bresse (part of the district of the Parlement of Chambéry) in October 1550, having been caught with correspondence addressed to known heretics. Their cases reached Chambéry in March 1551, when the Parlement, carefully following the revised procedural code of November 1549, required the archbishop of Lyon to deputize two of Chambéry's *conseilliers-clercs* in order to conduct their trial. Six months later they reached a verdict: both defendants were convicted of "human and divine *lèse-majesté*" involving both heresy and sedition, and were sentenced to perpetual service in the royal galleys. The case seems clear—but a small clue in the Chambéry records suggests hesitation, a worried letter from the duke of Guise confirms these suspicions, and two entries in Genevan records reveal an unexpected outcome. Although the Parlement of Chambéry had endorsed the galley sentences on 18 September, it avoided pronouncing them in public until 27 October, probably in order to permit unofficial negotiations with young Colladon's distinguished relatives in nearby Geneva.[55] Colladon probably paid some kind of unrecorded ransom or pardon, and neither he nor his associate ever saw the inside of a French galley. Instead, we find a "Michel, escaped from the galleys, who had been a prisoner with Colladon" given assistance by Geneva's relief agency for religious refugees in 1552; one year later, young Colladon married the daughter of a wealthy Lyon merchant in Geneva.[56] Soon thereafter, the Parlement of Chambéry was unable to capture a prominent local surgeon accused of heresy; they arrested his wife and two of his friends, but could only burn him in effigy in 1553, as he, like young Colladon and his companion, remained safely in Geneva.[57]

The Provincial Apogee: Toulouse, 1554

Most of the rise in provincial heresy executions after 1549 came from France's largest provincial Parlement. After the Paris Parlement emptied its prison of accused heretics at the beginning of 1550, Toulouse became France's leading tribunal in prosecuting heretics during the next five years. A comparison between France's first and second parlements best reveals the remarkable changes in their relative eagerness to prosecute "Lutherans" during this decade. (See Table 4.) From 1550 through 1554, almost 40 percent of all French Protestants known to have been publicly executed for heresy had been condemned by the Parlement of Toulouse. After Lizet's retirement, the most zealous enemies of "Lutheranism" among French *parlementaires* sat in Toulouse, that capital of thirteenth-century papal inquisitors.

Heresy prosecutions were unevenly distributed across Toulouse's most active phase. Although 1552 and 1553 seem busy years, with seventy prisoners judged for heresy during the twenty months for which we possess usable records, over 60 percent of them were released without punishment, and only four were sentenced to death. But this court had been unusually active during the years on either side. In 1551 the Parlement of Toulouse judged three dozen accused heretics in nine months; from September through December, immediately after the court registered Henry II's Edict of Chateaubriand, eight heretics were executed. However, all previous records were eclipsed during 1554, when the Par-

Table 4.   Paris and Toulouse heresy cases, 1545–1554

Years	% of *arrêts* preserved	Cases per month	Death sentences
1545–1549			
Paris	75	12.5	93
Toulouse	73	1.7	16
1550–1554			
Paris	95	2.0	11
Toulouse	83	4.3	31

Sources: AN, X2a 97–116, X2b 10, 14–15; ADHG, B 3373–3406.

Note: Figures for Paris omit death sentences known from Crespin's martyrology but not preserved among the surviving *arrêts*. Mentzer does not measure changes across time in the relative severity of the Toulouse Parlement's pursuit of heretics. Figures for Toulouse reflect damage to surviving *arrêts* (especially those from 1538–1546) caused by an arsonist in 1994. In both cases, averages of heretics judged per month are based upon the number of months still available in usable condition.

lement of Toulouse judged seventy-two accused heretics in eleven months, including at least thirteen whom it sentenced to death. This is the highest one-year total of heresy executions currently preserved from any French provincial parlement.

What best explains the remarkable campaign against heresy by the Parlement of Toulouse in 1554? No new royal edicts encouraged them, and recent punishments had been sporadic. The most convincing explanation for their behavior comes from an enormous scandal that erupted late in 1553 when one of its judges, Antoine de Lautrec, suddenly fled to Geneva, accompanied by his wife and a niece who had fled from her nunnery. He had been a much-respected colleague, whom one even finds as rapporteur on a few heresy trials in 1552, when persecution began to slacken. Lautrec was formally condemned in absentia on 6 February 1554 and burned in effigy the next day, a Shrove Tuesday.[58] This scandal was truly unprecedented. It was a more or less open secret that several judges at various French parlements, including Paris, were extremely sympathetic toward defendants accused of heresy; it was even whispered that a few of them secretly read heretical books and may even have known about clandestine meetings of Protestants; but Antoine de Lautrec was the first sitting judge from any French parlement to disappear suddenly from his post and to resurface in Calvin's Geneva. The embarrassment of his former colleagues at Toulouse, particularly those who had been his closest friends, provides much of the explanation for the unusual severity with which this court pursued accused heretics throughout 1554. At Toulouse they were ably abetted by the unusual zeal of one of the 1554 municipal *capitouls,* whose diligence was directly responsible for the capture and conviction of three men belonging to the "detestable sect of heretics and Genevan Lutherans."[59]

Since this year holds the record for preserved heresy executions by any French provincial parlement, let us examine the types of defendant whom the Parlement of Toulouse saw fit to burn in 1554, at perhaps the final moment when one can still speak of a Protestant movement rather than a clustering of Reformed churches in France. Nearly everyone who was condemned to death that year by the Parlement of Languedoc can be fitted into one of three categories. The largest group was still composed of former monks, apparently all natives of this region, who had to be put through the lengthy and cumbersome process of formal defrocking *(dégradation)* before being handed over to the secular arm. Between April and November we find a friar from the diocese of Castres, an Augustinian from Gimont, a Franciscan from Limoux, a Jacobin from Narbonne, and a monk from the convent of St. Léger de Bigorre in the diocese of Tarbes, all of whom endured defrocking and burning on charges of formal heresy.[60] One also finds information about three priests who were formally defrocked for heresy by the Languedoc episcopate between October 1553 and February 1555, although none of them was executed by order of the Parlement of Toulouse. One priest had the luck to escape after being defrocked; another, who had married a former nun, was "handed to the secular arm" early in 1555 but ultimately sentenced to perpetual imprisonment instead;[61] the third was executed early in 1554, although not by direct order of the Parlement.[62]

Alongside this collection of defrocked monks and priests, one finds a few laymen who were not natives of Languedoc. In this group belong a man from Issoire in upper Auvergne, then residing in Béziers; a shoemaker from Dauphiné, then living at Narbonne; a student from Guyenne, arrested at Toulouse; and possibly a cloth-dyer from Orléans, living at Montpellier.[63] One might add the bizarre figure who called himself "John the Evangelist" (the Parlement never learned his real name), who must be classified as a bogus cleric but a real immigrant. In 1553 he had been arrested by the Parlement of Bordeaux, who expelled him from their district after clipping his long beard and shearing his hair. He wandered into Languedoc, becoming an unwanted guest at the Dominican convent of Toulouse. In October 1553 the Dominicans handed him over to the Parlement, who ordered him imprisoned in a tiny private cell of the royal prison because of his "rash, execrable, and scandalous speech." Exactly a year later he tried to set fire to the prison, provoking a huge disturbance; one day after this incident, the "prophet" who had played with fire was condemned to be burned at the stake, with the additional proviso that his tongue would be cut out to minimize his blasphemies.[64]

Finally, a few prominent men were executed for heresy. To this category belong Estienne de Rouyeres, *seigneur* of Montgrand, burned on heresy charges at Le Puy, condemned primarily in connection with the escape of a defrocked priest; *Maître* La Failhe, licentiate in laws, burned with a less distinguished companion; and perhaps *Maître* André, a professional scribe.[65] The entire list of heretics executed by order of the Parlement of Toulouse in 1554 falls into one of these three categories: clerics or immigrants (the large majority), supplemented by a few local notables. Local artisans and merchants, who formed the core of Protestant church membership in Languedoc after 1560, are absent from the list of martyrs in the mid-1550s.

How thorough was the reach of the Parlement of Toulouse across its large district? Raymond Mentzer discovered that the repressive activities of the Languedoc parlement were not only intermittent but also unevenly distributed. "The Rhône–Cévennes–Lower Languedoc triangle . . . dominated the religious emigration to Geneva, but not the geographic pattern of heresy accusations."[66] The largest clusters of accusations came from the western half of the district, the parts closest to the court at Toulouse, rather than its eastern half, which produced most of the emigrants to Geneva and where most of the early Reformed churches were founded. Yet when one examines who was being arrested and punished in 1554, this east-west distinction blurs. Only two executions were carried out west of Toulouse, one monk dying at Gimont and another at Auch. Many more heretics were burned east of Toulouse—at Carcassonne, along the eastern littoral at Béziers, Montpellier, and Nîmes, and in the northeastern capital of Le Puy.

Public executions, of course, are only part of the story. In order to provide better depth, let us examine how the repressive mechanism of the Parlement of Toulouse worked in a few important towns of Langue-doc in 1554, when heresy trials reached their recorded maximum. The major heretical groups prosecuted in 1554 lived in the north, at Ville-franche-en-Rouergue; at the future Protestant stronghold of Castres, east of Toulouse; and at some of the largest cities near the Mediterranean, especially Narbonne and Montpellier. In most places, the parlementary crackdown of 1554 failed to inhibit the growth of a vigorous and dy-namic Reformed church by 1561; generally, its punishments seem futile. At Castres, where the Parlement convicted and executed a monk in April 1554, its effects may have been counterproductive. Before dying, the monk accused only an illiterate baker, who possessed some compromis-ing papers and songs. He escaped with a warning, although a cabinet-maker was required to make an *amende honorable* at the cathedral of Castres, whipped, and banished. Two months later, a bookseller also performed an *amende honorable* at Castres while his books burned; a canon from Castres was imprisoned for heresy at Toulouse, but ulti-mately realeased on bail.[67] The paper trail left behind at Castres by a heretical monk seems relatively short, and the monk's steadfast behav-ior at his execution reportedly encouraged the movement's subsequent growth.[68]

In the mountainous north at Villefranche-en-Rouergue, an investiga-tion of the muncipal college led to the arrests of several students, peda-gogues, a few women, and a bookseller. The school's regent was released; by summer the Parlement ordered three prisoners tortured (one of them subsequently died in jail at Toulouse). The bookseller and his assistant had "bound and offered for sale . . . forbidden books printed at Geneva." The Parlement ordered a special procession at Villefranche, before the bookseller performed an *amende honorable* on a scaffold in front of the cathedral. His books were burned together with the effigies of five sus-pects who had escaped during this investigation. He and two others were banished from the district for a few years; another student attended the ceremony but was allowed to stay in Villefranche; two more arrests were ordered, and all booksellers underwent a special inspection.[69] The 1554 repression at Villefranche-en-Rouergue thus exhibited the same kinds of suspects found since the 1530s—booksellers, students, pedagogues, a few artisans. It did not reach into the town's professional and mercantile elite, the kind of people who led the well-organized and politically active Protestant church at Villefranche by 1559.[70]

On the Mediterranean littoral, repression seems sharper in 1554, as it had been in the early 1540s. At its southern end, Narbonne, the Parlement of Toulouse intervened vigorously against a sizable group of heretics. Two men were hanged and burned; the local clerical leader was defrocked and executed at Toulouse, after naming many of his associates; an immigrant shoemaker living in Narbonne was also executed at Toulouse. But unlike the situation at Villefranche-de-Rouergue or Castres, the 1554 repression at Narbonne reached far up the social ladder. Here local officials burned effigies of no fewer than thirteen fugitives, all convicted in absentia; they included such notables as a merchant, a notary, a lawyer, a physician, and two noblemen. It was the largest such conflagration ever carried out in Languedoc. Several other Narbonne notables were imprisoned and tried, including Jacques Cogenbus, bachelor of law, finally released for insufficient evidence; an apothecary; a student; another merchant, who was tortured and required to make a formal abjuration in court; two prominent widows, who were kept imprisoned for a long time but ultimately released in 1555; the king's "Manager of the Warehouse" at Narbonne, released for insufficient evidence; the local Salt Warehouse watchman, who escaped with a fine of 200 livres; another merchant and another apothecary, both released because of insufficient evidence.[71] At Narbonne—the exception that confirms the rule about Languedoc repression in 1554—the Parlement of Toulouse frightened the sort of people who soon organized Reformed churches in other Languedoc cities. Here the judges intimidated many local notables in addition to the usual suspects, thereby inhibiting the growth of clandestine Protestant congregations; in 1562 Narbonne was the largest city in Languedoc with no organized Reformed church.

Further northeast, at Montpellier and Nîmes, the Parlement of Toulouse simply did not control the repression of heresy in 1554. Montpellier had long been the great insitutional rival of Toulouse within Languedoc; it too boasted a famous university and served as the traditional capital of lower Languedoc, the place where the provincial Estates were most likely to meet. It is not accidental that Montpellier was the one city that produced at least twice as many residents of Geneva as officially accused heretics during the 1550s.[72] Very few heresy appeals ever moved from Montpellier to Toulouse. The most dramatic illustration came in December 1553, when the Parlement refused to hear the appeals from four accused heretics imprisoned at Montpellier, "in view of the danger that they will escape." This decision and its explanation (which was never used for any other part of Languedoc, including places like Le Puy or Annonay, which were much more remote from Toulouse) is reminiscent of the Paris Parlement's dealings with the five students imprisoned at Lyon earlier that same year. We know that two of those four prisoners were publicly executed for heresy at Montpellier in January 1554. Guillaume d'Alençon, whom Felix Platter watched being defrocked in October 1553, was described in the Parlement's ruling of early December as a "bookseller from Geneva."[73] He was therefore the only man who fits both major categories among Languedoc's 1554 heresy executions: a renegade cleric, and an immigrant bookseller. But, at a moment when they were digesting the news of Lautrec's scandalous flight to Geneva, the Parlement of Toulouse avoided a test of institutional wills with the governor of Montpellier over d'Alençon and his three companions. Like Lyon, Montpellier was effectively autonomous in pursuing and executing heretics during the 1550s; and like Lyon, Montpellier fell under Huguenot control during the first religious war.

The legal situation at Nîmes, the other important city in lower Languedoc, resembled that at Montpellier. Early in 1554, one finds a prisoner from Nîmes condemned to be strangled and burned at Toulouse while the official *arrêt* of his condemnation was read at the cathedral of Nîmes (it is not specified that his crime was heresy). During the rest of the year only two minor heresy cases from the other capital of lower Languedoc and future Protestant stronghold reached the Parlement; one was dismissed for insufficient evidence, while a woman was ordered to perform an *amende honorable* in her parish church.[74] However, we know that a defendant was tried and narrowly avoided being sentenced to death at Nîmes late in 1553 by the new presidial court, which was highly self-conscious about its capacity to judge heresy cases without any possibility of appeal to the Parlement. (A shoemaker was reportedly burned for heresy by the same court in 1554.)[75] At Nîmes or Montpellier, as at Lyon, local officials now operated largely independently of parlements; although these municipalities were still willing to burn stubborn Protestants in the mid-1550s, their attempts at repression could not prevent the formation of unusually strong Reformed churches in these places by 1561.

After its record severity in 1554, the Parlement of Toulouse confronted the first official emissary ever sent to them by the Republic of Geneva on 4 July 1555.[76] An irritated and perplexed presiding judge dictated a report: "there came to the palace an unknown man wearing a two-colored gown with a coat-of-arms on the shoulder, calling himself a herald from the city of Geneva." He publicly presented the First President with a sealed letter addressed to the court, concerning "those who are separated from the obedience and union of the Catholic church." The president asked his colleagues if it was "tolerable . . . that such apostates, schismatics, and heretics send heralds and letters to courts of Parlement, without express permission." Duly consulted, his colleagues ordered the president to open and read the letter (whose contents are not described)[77] while the herald was escorted outside and interrogated by two judges.

On the following day the Toulouse Parlement composed its official answer. It began by declaiming against the "enterprises and practices to seduce His Majesty's subjects . . . from the integrity of the faith and to induce them into the apostasy . . . and congregation of Geneva." These nefarious practices were done

> both through the means of the mad, false, and sensual liberty of the said city, and the easy access, traffic, and favorable reception in it, being a neighbor and close to the said Kingdom; and to the freedom and immunity which all schismatics and heretics obtain in the said congregation, as has been known and verified through the indubitable experience of trials held in this court, against several preachers and dogmatizers coming from the said city of Geneva, carrying prohibited books to distribute among His Majesty's subjects.

Nor was this all. "Even today," continued the Toulouse judges, we respond to these problems "through the judgments made against a schoolteacher and a bookseller, born in Auvergne, who coming from said Geneva have been captured with several books and small treatises which they were carrying, full of blasphemies and abominations against our holy faith. Such is the frequency and astuteness of the representatives and commerce of Geneva; in brief, if such license and liberty is not reproved by authority of His Majesty, some irreparable evil is to be feared."[78]

The Creation of Calvinist Martyrology

French parlements, especially Toulouse, tried to counter the successful propaganda of Calvin and his French refugee associates in the early

1550s. They could supplement words with deeds, answering the Genevan herald by sentencing two Genevan booksellers to death in their next piece of official business. But the Genevan propaganda machine, undisturbed by the paper tigers of French censorship outlined in the vehement but futile Edict of Chateaubriand, created a remarkably original response to the persistence of heresy executions. Deeply frustrated by their inability to save five French students of Protestant theology from the authorities at Lyon in 1553 despite their intense efforts and Swiss diplomatic pressure, Calvin and the French refugee community in Geneva devised an innovative and extremely effective propaganda tactic. The imprisoned students' frequent correspondence with the Reformers of Geneva during their year-long captivity became the longest and richest section of Jean Crespin's celebrated martyrology. Their story fills one-third of the first edition, published at Geneva in 1554.

With this book Crespin attempted to turn the existing French judicial system on its head, transforming its rituals of public atonement and bonfires of heretical bodies and heretical writings into present-day symbols of an ongoing apostolic tradition, hitherto largely confined to the most radical or Anabaptist wing of the Reformation. In one respect, Crespin's project was simply the Genevan version of an idea whose time had fully arrived; 1554 was also the year when John Foxe produced the first Latin edition of his martyrology, and when Ludwig Rabus produced his Lutheran compilation of Christian martyrs. All three Protestant authors worked from the same premise, that there was a fundamental continuity between ancient martyrs for the truth of the gospel and some of their medieval predecessors, which continued to the present day. Furthermore, all three martyrologists shared St. Augustine's dictum that "not the punishment but the cause makes a martyr" and therefore excluded all Anabaptists, who (as they probably knew) accounted for the vast majority of Protestants executed for heresy in Reformation Europe. Crespin's work, however, differed from those of his German and English peers in some significant ways. First, it was composed and published in the vernacular, being translated into Latin (not by the author) only after three printings in French and a pirated French version had already appeared. Moreover, the author was also the printer and the publisher; one cannot imagine a more completely personal book. Finally, Crespin frequently updated his compilation of testimony about Calvinist martyrs. An augmented and revised version appeared in 1555, followed by a third set of additions in 1557 and a fourth set in 1561, while further supplements were added after the first French religious war.[78]

Crespin's project was sufficiently novel to generate some confusion before it achieved a more orderly shape. On the one hand, Genevan censors had objected to Crespin's use of the words "saint" and "martyr," finding the former superstitious and the latter provocative. The response of the author/printer was disingenuous; bibliographers note that the very first Calvinist martyrology appeared under two different titles in 1554, one boldly calling itself the *Book of Martyrs* and the other using the more politically correct circumlocution *Collection of several people who have constantly endured death for the name of Our Lord Jesus Christ.*[79] The author intended not to provide a complete list of every evangelical executed by French parlements or other European authorities, but rather to provide a series of examples (he called it a *patron et exemplaire*) full of essential primary sources such as confessions of faith, letters, or extracts from legal testimony that would enable his readers to understand the principles for which these people had died.

Himself a subject of Charles V, Crespin did not confine himself to French martyrs, although they provided both the original pretext for his work and the bulk of his entries.[80] Through his contacts in the Low Countries, Crespin had acquired information about the very first Lutheran martyrs of Antwerp and a handful of others; in fact only two of the ten Protestant martyrs he knew about from the 1520s had died in France. For the 1530s, however, the proportions are reversed: Crespin knew something about six people executed at Paris in the wake of the Affair of the Placards and added six other French martyrs, while reporting only three non-French martyrs, including one from his home town of Arras. From the 1540s, Crespin similarly identified only a handful of Protestants dying at Rome or in the Low Countries, including the one who had provoked Crespin's own arrest and condemnation. However, he knew two major French stories—the Meaux martyrs of 1546, identifiable through a printed pamphlet; and the 1545 persecution of the Waldensians of Provence, the subject of a recent cause célèbre at Paris—and he added two dozen other French examples (eleven of them from Langres), including a young man whose execution he had witnessed at Paris in 1541. Among the martyrs since 1550, Crespin again mentioned barely a half-dozen from the Low Countries or Rome to set alongside a story dominated by the persecutions at Lyon, to which he added fifteen other recent French examples. Together, they offered him enough material to fill more than eight hundred very small pages, or half as many in Baduel's elegant octavo Latin version.

In one sense, Crespin's martyrology was a logical complement to Calvin's writings against Nicodemism a decade before. Flight was not the only possible alternative for the convinced Calvinist; if punishment was a constant risk, there was also the possibility of suffering steadfastly for one's faith, witnessing, giving glorious testimony. If diplomatic methods could not rescue the French students from Lausanne captured at Lyon, then let them be commemorated, along with those who had gone before and those who were still following them. But exile and martyrdom were not the only possible alternatives for the sincere Calvinist who remained in France. It was possible to grow beyond the small, secret gatherings and create one's own properly governed church, free from idolatry and superstition. By 1555 Calvin and the other Genevan pastors (all of them refugees from France) were ready to offer properly trained personnel to those groups among their French audience who were willing to risk this alternative.

6

From Confessionalization to Decriminalization, 1555–1560

But, unfortunately, most of the senior judges of the Parlement . . . became intoxicated and poisoned by this Lutheran and Calvinist heresy.

—*Claude Haton*, Mémoires *(1556)*

Historians of the French Reformation uniformly agree that genuinely well-ordered Reformed churches began to replace the undisciplined and poorly organized secret congregations after the mid-1550s. In 1580 the semiofficial *Ecclesiastical History of the French Reformed Church* described the phenomenon. "In the reign of Henry II," it asserted, "there was not yet any church properly organized [*dressée*] in all of France." The faithful were only "instructed sometimes through special exhortations, without any ordinary administration of the Word or the Sacraments, nor established Consistories; they consoled each other as best they could, gathering to pray together whenever the opportunity presented itself, without having any proper preachers other than the Martyrs." However, the account concluded, "in the years 1555, 1556, and following, the heritage of the Lord began to be properly arranged and ordered": real churches were formed.[1]

Once begun, this process spread with extraordinary rapidity. Within a few years, hundreds (its leaders said thousands) of organized Reformed churches were established, scattered across the kingdom of France. The *Ecclesiastical History,* which up to this point had devoted most of its space to recounting histories of persecution, now concentrated on the personnel and deeds of these fledgling Reformed churches. Ever since Robert Kingdon's work more than forty years ago, historians have recognized that this sudden growth was so far as possible directed from Calvin's Geneva, whose Venerable Company of Pastors sent nearly a hundred well-trained ministers to serve these newly created French churches from 1555 through 1562.[2] This process of ecclesiastical organization attained full maturity when the underground French Reformed church held a three-day national synod in Paris during May 1559, in order to hammer out a standard confession of faith to which all its members would adhere. To recapitulate: the creation of Reformed churches in France developed rapidly after 1555, displayed a remarkable degree of self-awareness in its early organization, and approved an official doctrinal platform by 1559.

The rapid growth and disciplined organization of France's Reformed churches during the late 1550s constitutes a textbook example of what German Reformation scholars have labeled as the process of confessionalization.[3] It offers an unusually important illustration of this process, since it occurred in Europe's largest state under difficult circumstances. Though happening around 1560, the chronological center identified by German scholars, the confessionalization of the French Reformed church diverged radically from other contemporary examples. The Lutheran instances that preceded it in many territories within the Holy Roman Empire and the Zwinglian churches of the Swiss confederation had without exception been imposed by local rulers. Large monarchies acted no differently: Tridentine reforms were imposed in Philip II's Spain and the Thirty-nine Articles in Elizabethan England under direct pressure from their respective royal governments. However, French Reformed confessionalization took place in defiance of state authority rather than under state patronage. It was completely illegal; all these developments constituted criminal actions under French law. Furthermore, they occurred in Europe's largest proto-absolutist monarchy not during a royal minority or other period of weak government, but several years into the reign of a monarch who had committed himself to unwavering opposition toward all forms of heresy. The point of French confessional "exceptionalism" needs to be stressed in order to highlight the confused and confusing reactions to it by Henry II and by royal judges.

The first collision between the nascent Genevan confessional movement and the French parlementary system became a major tragedy.[4] In the late spring of 1555, a French religious refugee named Jean Vernou returned to Geneva from his reconnaissance mission to the Waldensian valleys of Piedmont. Calvin's Company of Pastors sent him back early in June, accompanied by two other well-trained men and an additional escort, to serve as regular pastors among the Alpine Waldensians. It was the first such special commission ever undertaken with the official blessing of the Genevan Reformed church, the precursor of more than a hundred others in the next few years. While crossing a mountain pass barely sixty kilometers from Geneva, all six men were captured in an ambush by a French official, a *prévot des maréchaux,* who had accidentally learned something of their business during a recent trip to Geneva.[5] As he confiscated their books, including a copy of Calvin's *Institutes,* and rushed his prisoners to the Savoyard capital at Chambéry, the Genevans rushed couriers to their Bernese allies in order to put diplomatic pressure on French officials. Bern, whose theologians were then locked in a dispute with Calvin, failed to pry these missionaries loose from a Savoyard Parlement that had previously executed other Frenchmen residing in Geneva. However, the Bernese did manage to have their judgments deferred until after a Swiss Protestant envoy had approached the king.

After this maneuver had failed, the Parlement of Chambéry ordered these cases to be decided within three days. On 17 August the inquisitors of Tarentaise and Grenoble, following a five-hour disputation with Vernou, declared all six to be formal heretics and handed them to the secular arm. Four days later the local court of the *vibailli* of Chambéry (perhaps as a gesture toward the Bernese) refused to pronounce any death sentences. It sentenced the three men whom it correctly identified as leaders to perpetual service in the galleys, while their companions got ten years apiece. The prisoners raised no protest, but the royal prosecutor immediately appealed *a minima* to the Parlement. After some further questioning, the court increased their punishments on 30 August: all five who refused to abjure were now ordered to be burned. The Republic of Geneva, at Calvin's instigation, made one final but futile official effort to save their preachers by sending a special herald to Chambéry in early September.[6] A final flurry of letters exchanged between the prisoners and Geneva enriched Crespin's subsequent account but did not alter the result. On 12 October Bèze mourned the burning at Chambéry of "five of our best brothers, of whom two were of remarkable piety and uncommon learning."[7] A sixth man, the only Piedmontese in this group, finally abjured and was permanently banished after performing an *amende honorable.* Their official sentence offers a savory description of one of

Calvin's letters, dated 10 June but with no indication to whom it was sent, proving that one of these men had previously preached his "false doctrine" to other subjects of the French king, adding that "he had been sent again by the said Calvin with two others, which project the said Calvin had approved and had long planned to do."[8] The Savoyard *parlementaires* were not duped. They were reasonably sure that Vernou had previously "dogmatized" on French soil, and they even had a correct idea of where he had done it. The Genevan missionaries lied their way out of this dilemma in late July, as they admitted in a letter sent to Calvin under diplomatic cover.[9]

The "Chambéry five" quickly joined the "Lyon five" whose deaths had triggered the first edition of Crespin's martyrology. This episode filled ninety pages of Crespin's next supplement; it probably constituted an even worse setback for the professional elite of the nascent Reformed church than the executions of the French students at Lyon. But its consequences reached well beyond such considerations. Although the fate of Vernou and his companions tightened the secrecy with which Calvin and his colleagues worked, it did not slow the missionary drive of their Reformed church to the Piedmontese valleys. A Frenchman named Estienne Noel, who had been recruited by a Waldensian *barbe* to serve as minister in Piedmont, wrote to Calvin early in 1556 about Waldensian affairs. Between June and November 1556, Calvin's Company of Pastors despatched at least three more pastors, including Vernou's companion from the reconnaissance mission of 1555, to the Piedmontese Waldensians.[10] All arrived safely. In 1557 they sent an Italian-speaking former monk to join Noel as pastor at Angrogna, and apparently approved two other French refugees into these valleys.[11] Nothing better reveals their determination than their reaction after the Italian-speaking ex-monk had been martyred in 1558: the Company of Pastors immediately despatched Scipione Lentolo, then pastor of the Italian church in Geneva, to succeed him at Angrogna. The Waldensians also inhabited some upper Alpine valleys in the passes west of Piedmont, regions that formed part of Dauphiné. Vernou had also visited them and preached there early in 1555, as the Dauphiné judges suspected after learning about the arrests at Chambéry. This region was apparently a lower priority than Piedmont, but the Genevan Company of Pastors also began despatching French refugees as pastors to Val Chisone in January 1557; by mid-1558 they apparently had three men serving in this region.[12]

Meanwhile Henry II's parlementary system had not been idle. Vernou and his companions had been captured, tried, and executed by the Parlement of Chambéry, whose district surrounded Geneva but contained no Alpine Waldensians. Before being executed, the prisoners revealed just enough about their mission to cause the Chambéry court to alert its two neighbors in whose Alpine districts these heretics lived. The Parlement of Turin held jurisdiction over the Piedmontese valleys to which Vernou and his companions had been sent; the Parlement of Grenoble held jurisdiction over the western Val Chisone, where Vernou had preached early in 1555. During Vernou's trial, Grenoble briefly arrested two village officers of Fenestrelle in the Val Chisone, but released them on bail.[13] One of the Chambéry judges was the son of the First President at Grenoble, so the collaboration between these courts was unusually close. Both Turin and Grenoble reacted to the news from Chambéry in October 1555 by ordering special investigations. By March 1556 the Parlement of Grenoble had ordered the village officials of Fenestrelle to erect a special stone cross at the meadow where the heretical service had been held the previous Easter, and required them to swear a special oath to invite no outside preachers before they could take office.[14]

At Turin the problem was more serious and the reaction more vigorous. Two special commissioners, including one of the Parlement's two presidents, traveled to the Waldensian valleys in March 1556 in a futile attempt to compel its inhabitants to attend Catholic services and hand over their *barbes*. Henry II, informed of their failure, ordered the persecution enforced in November 1556; he then ordered forty-three local notables to Turin in March 1557 in an attempt to compel them to surrender their ministers. The Waldensians appealed to their old friends in the north. Guillaume Farel and Bèze persuaded the Bernese, supported by some leading German Lutherans, to intervene once more at the French court. Henry answered the resulting special embassy ambiguously, but apparently suspended direct legal action against these communities. However, one of the new pastors sent from Geneva was captured late in 1557, brought to Turin, and finally executed there in March 1558.[15] The differences between the Parlements of Turin and Grenoble in their severity toward heretics emerge clearly from the parallel histories of two Genevan book-peddlers who had once worked in partnership. One, from Poitou, was caught with his supplies of heretical books in the Piedmontese Alps early in 1556; he was handed to the special commissioners, subsequently brought to Turin, and publicly executed there in June. Afterward another French *colporteur* was caught in the Val Chisone with his full supply of heretical books; at Grenoble he was merely sentenced to the galleys for five years after performing an *amende honorable* in 1558.[16]

By this time the French had suffered crushing military defeats in Italy and the Low Countries, and their grip on the possessions of the duke of Savoy had already begun to weaken. The French parlements of Chambéry and Turin, proud creations of Francis I, were rapidly dismantled in the early summer of 1559, and their records left behind. Persecution of the Piedmontese Waldensians accelerated under the restored Savoyard authorities, with further executions for heresy at Turin in 1559 and 1560 and military action in the Waldensian valleys in 1560 and 1561—but it is no longer part of our story. The Parlement of Grenoble, aware that Genevan-trained pastors were working among the Waldensians in its Alpine valleys, could not lay hands on them. In October 1558 they offered a reward of 300 livres for the capture of two of them, ordered some houses where they had preached to be demolished, ordered another commemorative cross erected, and made one prominent villager perform two *amendes honorables* for having his infant daughter baptized by such heretics.[17] Further scandals resulting from the activities of the same preacher erupted in the Val Chisone during the summer of 1559, followed by further arrests in August. Another round of fines and a few more *amendes honorables* followed, but the Genevan-trained pastor remained safely beyond their reach.[18]

The Decline of Persecution, 1555–1558

After the Chambéry disaster of 1555, only one of the ten Genevan-trained pastors known to have been sent to the Alpine Waldensians of Piedmont and Dauphiné during the next few years was ever caught, tried, and martyred by a French parlement. Yet Euan Cameron is correct in asserting that "in the later 1550s, the mission to Piedmont was one of the most dangerous of all postings for a Protestant minister," because apparently none of the sixty men sent from Geneva to serve nascent Reformed churches elsewhere in Henry II's domains was captured and executed until the spring of 1560.[19] This phenomenon requires a moment's reflection. The first three men specifically sent on mission by

Calvin's Company of Pastors were almost immediately caught and executed. But only one of the next seventy (who was also the only Italian in this group) suffered a similar fate. Increased security surely provides part of the answer, but only part. Success on this scale in eluding capture must also owe something to reluctance by a great many well-placed people to carry out their duties. Royal officials throughout France were aware of these new Reformed preachers, and many of them knew when and where they held their services. The thick official silence surrounding clandestine pastoral activity on this scale speaks eloquently to the profound unwillingness of public authorities in many different regions of France to enforce royal edicts against heresy. But because it is composed of hundreds of individual silences adding up to a collective nonevent, it cannot be directly documented. We will never know how much of this inactivity was due to active collaboration with the new churches by local royal officials, how much to reluctance to enforce laws against people who did not seem dangerous, and how much to sheer incompetence. Whatever the mixture of motives, the result was that every clandestine Reformed pastor sent to France worked safely until 1560.

In 1555—the year Pope Paul IV accelerated the prosecution of heretics in Italy and Mary Tudor began to execute heretics in England—the Parlement of Paris executed nobody for heresy. Its criminal *arrêts* from 1555 are complete, but they contain only one death sentence that even included charges of heresy. Antoine de Genes, who had been arrested at Tours in August 1554 on minor charges of heresy ("heretical and erroneous speech against the Catholic faith, together with execrable blasphemies against the honor of God") and major charges of sedition (he and two companions had replanted the town gibbet in front of the prosecutor's house and had posted defamatory placards on three churches), was finally ordered hanged and burned, despite his petition to Parlement in October 1554.[20]

Meanwhile the Parlement of Paris reduced six capital punishments for heresy decreed by lower courts, and released sixteen of its twenty-six prisoners charged with heresy. Perhaps most tellingly, it reprimanded three royal officials for using illegal methods against Pierre Lormeau, who had been condemned by the *lieutenant criminel* of Blois to perform an *amende honorable* at his parish church, have his tongue pierced with a hot iron, then be whipped and banished from the kingdom. The Parlement ruled his case "badly judged" charged the royal officials at Blois twenty-four livres toward the costs of a new trial, and summoned the judge and the royal prosecutor to lecture them about their "fault, which is evident and visible to the naked eye . . . such that it cannot be excused" in Lormeau's trial. The officials denied any "malice on their part," protesting that they operated very quickly "in business which concerns religion, in order to extirpate the heresies that flourish in our province," and promised that "henceforth they will work more carefully." President de Thou gave them an elaborate warning about the need to follow procedural rules carefully, "even with things that concern matters of religion," and threatened them with suspension and worse should they repeat such blunders.[21]

Parlementary activity against accused heretics slackened everywhere in the mid-1550s. Even the Parlement of Toulouse, which had set records for provincial severity against heretics in 1554, began to back off from imposing death sentences early in 1555. In February it overturned the capital punishments decreed by city officials in Toulouse against four university students who had visited Calvin's Geneva, commuting them to only six months of imprisonment after they performed *amendes honorables* at the cathedral. The same day, it also avoided executing a runaway priest and nun who had gotten married. The judges of Toulouse subsequently ordered death sentences against two Auvergnats who had been caught with large quantities of heretical books, "given their pertinacity and arrogance."[22] The Parlement of Bordeaux, whose criminal *arrêts* from 1555 are virtually complete, released seven of its ten prisoners charged with heresy, although they did execute a schoolteacher.[23] The Parlement of Rouen (whose surviving criminal *arrêts* cover only seven months in 1555) ordered one man strangled and burned at Rouen with a placard identifying him as a *hereticque sacramentaire*.[24] As we have seen, the Parlement of Grenoble released its only prisoners charged with heresy in 1555. We have no criminal *arrêts* from the Parlement of Aix in 1555, the year President Maynier d'Oppède was finally allowed to resume his post, but it seems improbable that they dared to execute anyone for heresy that year. Thus the Parlement of Chambéry probably burned as many heretics on one day in 1555 as other French parlements did during the entire year.

Over the next few years, as Genevan-led churches began to form across the kingdom, only one determined attempt was made to destroy any of them. A judge from Provence, Remy Ambroise, became a special commissioner armed with exceptional powers (his decisions could not be appealed to Paris). Accompanied by the principal inquisitor for northern France, Ambroise instituted a reign of terror at Angers in the summer of 1556. With strong local support, they dismantled an evangelical conventicle, burning six men and effigies of more than thirty others who had escaped their grasp.[25] Except under such unusual circumstances, French heresy executions remained relatively infrequent in the mid-1550s.

From January 1556 through September 1557, the Paris Parlement condemned five people to death for heresy, including one who escaped before he could be executed.[26] But it reduced several other death sentences during this period. Few of its cases were as dramatic as that of Marcel Granier, originally tried by the *bailli* of Etampes in July 1554 for "several execrable words against the Sacrament of the Altar and other speech against the Christian religion." As Granier's case slowly wound its way to the Parlement of Paris two years later, it had acquired two perplexing dimensions. First, Granier claimed to have been ordained by the bishop of Mende in the Lenten season of 1538; second, he claimed an insanity defense, including episodes of "madness and dementia" preceding his arrest. Two judges were ordered to investigate, one taking each claim. In January 1557, equipped with adequate information from physicians and from the bishop of Mende, President de Thou dismissed the accusations and sent Granier to the bishop of Tulle "to be nourished, nursed, medicated, treated charitably, admonished, and consoled for as long as the said Granier shall live," at an annual cost of forty livres, to be paid by the bishop of Tulle.[27] From January 1556 through September 1557, the Parlement of Paris released without punishment fifty-three of its ninety-two prisoners accused of heresy.

The Parlement of Toulouse maintained a steady quota of burning one heretic per year between 1556 and 1560.[28] However, they progressively reduced the physical punishments inflicted on accused heretics. From 1556 through 1558, they ordered fifteen of their forty prisoners charged with heresy to be whipped, banished, or sent to the galleys after performing public abjurations; from 1559 until April 1561, when they reluctantly registered a royal pardon, the Toulouse judges imposed only four such penalties while releasing thirty-three prisoners charged with heresy. Over the protest of the archbishop of Narbonne, they also registered the official pardon of a lawyer who had been arrested for heresy in 1554.[29]

Perhaps the most revealing episode occurred in the autumn of 1558, after the bishop of Pamiers petitioned them to send a special investigator to his city to press charges against a group of nearly fifty suspected heretics, led by two renegade Franciscan friars. After the Parlement's *huissier* filed his report from Pamiers, he was charged with "negligence and failure to do his duty" because all the important suspects had escaped, and ordered arrested on his return.[30]

Although they too released most of their recorded prisoners charged with heresy, the Parlement of Bordeaux executed a few heretics in 1556–1557, including the leader of a clandestine congregation.[31] Philibert Hamelin, a former priest convicted of heresy at Bordeaux in 1546, moved to Geneva after his abjuration and took up printing. He returned to Guyenne by 1553 and soon established a tiny church on the island of Arvent. After he dared to baptize a child in public, Hamelin was captured. Details from other sources illustrate the sort of pressures his judges faced after his arrest. At Saintes, the famous Huguenot potter Bernard Palissy lobbied six judges in their homes, urging them not to convict a genuinely holy man whom he had known personally for eleven years. The prisoner reportedly refused several plans for his escape proposed by his friends. Once inside the Parlement's prison at Bordeaux, Hamelin was consoled "in the presence of the jailer and all the other prisoners" by a well-known heretic who had fled the city a year earlier after two other heresy executions. Times were changing rapidly, but Hamelin was nonetheless put to death at Bordeaux in April 1557; trumpeters, we are told, played constantly in order to prevent him from speaking before he could be strangled.[32] This man who refused to break jail became the only known Reformed preacher executed in France in the late 1550s.

In 1556 the Parlement of Rouen uncovered a network of Protestants at Le Havre who had not yet formed a properly organized church. A special commissioner eventually arrested at least eighteen people at Le Havre, while twelve others escaped. The Norman Parlement executed two ringleaders, both recidivists. A schoolteacher had been caught in possession of a "letter from Geneva titled 'to my brothers and good friends at Havre de Grace,' and a great number of prohibited books by Bucer, Calvin, Melanchthon, Luther, and others." He died at Rouen in the summer of 1556, followed by another prisoner, who had previously been whipped and banished from the kingdom by the Parlement of Paris on heresy charges.[33] Afterward the Parlement of Rouen ordered no further known heresy executions until 1559.

After their humiliations in Paris the Parlement of Aix seemed reluctant to impose severe punishments on accused heretics. This court made great shows of activity against absentees in 1556, once condemning almost a hundred of them for heresy in a single *arrêt*.[34] It also arrested another sixteen people from Mérindol, including the curé, although the Maynard clan escaped once again. One defendant, who had been carrying several prohibited books when he was arrested, claimed that the incriminating evidence had been planted on him by servants of the absentee lord of Mérindol, who engineered the entire episode after quarreling with the village headman. The Parlement dismissed everybody, including the man with the forbidden books, on grounds of insufficient evidence.[35]

Presented with a schoolteacher who had been caught after being condemned to death in absentia, the Parlement of Aix waited a full month before ordering a completely new trial for him. They delayed seven more months before ordering him to present witnesses in his defense. Four more months passed before they decided to spend their own money in order to take testimony at Toulouse from one of his defense witnesses. Two months later there were further procedural delays. Since their *arrêts* for the next nine months are unreadable, we never learn what they finally did with the schoolteacher; but they evidently did everything possible to delay a decision for at least fourteen months, and bent every resource to help a poor man defend himself.[36] Apart from one execution reported by Crespin,[37] their most heavily accused heresy prisoner in these years was probably Jean Gay, a resident of Ste. Tulle charged with heresy and sedition in November 1553 and finally jailed at Aix by December 1556. Seventeen witnesses were brought from as far away as Sisteron to testify against him. Four months later Gay was sentenced to perform an *amende honorable* at the cathedral of Aix, have the two heretical books in his possession burned, then "the tip of his tongue to be cut off," and perpetual service in the galleys. His rapporteur had been one of the three special commissioners of 1545 later put on trial in Paris, and Gay's condemnation was as close as this court came to recording a death sentence after Maynier and his colleagues returned to Provence.[38]

The Parlement of Dauphiné continued to treat accused Protestants gently. When confronted in the summer of 1559 with an obstinate young man from Normandy captured in an Alpine valley full of Waldensians, the Grenoble court avoided inflicting serious physical punishment. Florent Godard was convicted and "handed to the secular arm" on 9 August; but nothing further happened until a Grenoble monk reported on 25 October that Godard had finally decided to repent. He abjured in private to the episcopal judge at Grenoble; on 29 November the court discharged him and allowed him to recover his personal property.[39] The same judges had ordered the son of a local notary to the galleys in January 1559 for misbehavior that had nothing to do with religion. While in their prison, he wrote an admiring letter to Calvin at about the same time as his father frantically arranged a royal pardon for his son from Henry II.[40] We have no evidence that the young man ever became a committed Protestant or that his father ever knew about the letter to Calvin; but the episode says as much about the Parlement's prison in Grenoble as their treatment of Florent Godard says about its judges. In the late 1550s, French parlements ordinarily used their arbitrary discretion to avoid imposing severe punishments against accused Protestants.

Protestant Obstruction of Heresy Prosecution

Across Henry II's domains, the rhythm of heresy prosecution slowed in the mid-1550s, just as the process of "confessionalization" described by the *Ecclesiastical History* got underway. Even including the burnings at Angers in 1556 and the arrest of an extremely large congregation in Paris late in 1557 (to which we shall soon turn), French parlements averaged only thirteen public executions for heresy per year during 1555–1558, a drop from sixteen executions per year during 1550–1554. Although Henry II followed his severe Edict of Chateaubriand in 1551 with his draconian Edict of Compiègne in 1557, threatening ever-greater punishments for heretics, his decrees had little practical effect in the royal appellate courts. Of course, one does not gain this impression from reading Crespin's martyrology, principally because Crespin became far better informed about French heresy executions after Reformed churches proliferated across France in the later 1550s. Although both Protestant sources and royal edicts suggest that judicial prosecution of French Protestants increased in the later 1550s, it actually declined, even though the number of French Protestants was increasing rapidly and illegal Reformed churches were being formed.

It is possible to understand, but difficult to document, why heresy prosecutions ebbed as the Reformed churches organized themselves. The single most important reason, the failure of royal courts to enforce royal wishes about the detection and punishment of heretics, almost never appears directly in sources produced by that court system. It is extraordinarily rare to detect judicial obstruction of justice at work. One can occasionally see officials conducting heresy investigations in such a way as to cover up any real delinquency; a clear example can be found at Montélimar in Dauphiné early in 1557, when a parlementary commissioner was promised full cooperation by local officials but managed to record only a few scraps of insignificant evidence against local Protestants.[41] In several other places with active Protestant movements in the mid-1550s, there were no recorded investigations. For example, no heresy cases ever reached Normandy's parlement from Alençon, a town where heresy had been a serious problem since 1533. The explanation was suddenly revealed in December 1554, when the Rouen court sentenced the *lieutenant criminel* for the district of Alençon for abuses and misconduct, particularly in connection with a death sentence he had handed down in May 1553. The royal official in question was none other than the poet Charles de Sainte-Marthe, twice convicted of heresy in other provinces and banished from Dauphiné in 1543. The patronage of Marguerite of Navarre, duchess of Alençon, explains why he settled comfortably into an important royal office there. This time, however, Sainte-Marthe was convicted of judicial misconduct, required to make an official apology to the Parlement, stripped of office, fined 1,200 livres, and banished from the kingdom.[42]

In March 1554 Sainte-Marthe had sent an attestation to the Rouen Parlement about his deputy *(lieutenant particulier)*, certifying that Jean Le Pelletier was a good Christian who had been charged with nothing worse than eating meat during Lent. In fact Le Pelletier had been banished from the kingdom for heresy by the Parlement of Paris in September 1534, a detail that did not prevent him from holding royal office in the same town shortly afterward. Despite Sainte-Marthe's attempt to protect him, Le Pelletier was ordered arrested in May 1554. Once again, he managed to avoid capture, although the king's privy council pronounced defaults against him that autumn and the Parlement of Rouen finally declared his property confiscated in 1555. Despite his "banishment" of 1554, Sainte-Marthe soon resurfaced at Alençon as a judge on the new presidial court organized in 1558, alongside at least one other known Protestant; by 1562 the court had a Protestant majority.[43]

If it was difficult to remove royal officials with previous major convictions for heresy, it was impossible to remove those who had only been accused of helping heretics, as we saw with the careers of Claude d'Angleur and Hugues Poutard at La Rochelle. Perhaps such situations usually occurred in places where an evangelical movement was already well entrenched by 1540. But even in a town where Protestantism was not widely accepted among the local notables, it was impossible in the 1550s for local Catholic zealots to convict and remove a royal official who was almost certainly a Protestant. Consider the example of Baptiste Perrochet, lieutenant of the regional seneschal at Forcalquier in Provence. Although he had been investigated for heresy in September 1549, October 1552, August 1555, and November 1558, Perrochet was formally tried for heresy by the Parlement of Aix only in February 1559. Apparently a local cleric became infuriated because Perrochet prohibited the people of Forcalquier from singing a "song against the Lutherans." Although fifteen witnesses were summoned to testify against him, Perrochet was released on bond in a month, and formally absolved in two months. Eleven years later, during the third war of religion, the Parlement of Aix decreed a blanket condemnation of the leading Huguenot rebels at Forcalquier. At the very top of their list, preceding even the two local Reformed ministers, stood Baptiste Perrochet, still lieutenant of the regional seneschal.[44] Unless they grievously offended some other local notable, royal officials like Perrochet slept soundly at their posts.

The conventions of arbitrary sentencing in French criminal cases make it impossible to determine how often royal judges actively colluded with people whom their king wished to exterminate. We do know that in these years, trials were often avoided. If they could not be avoided, the judges generally refused to convict. If the evidence was so strong that conviction became unavoidable (such as heretical books found in the prisoner's possession), extremely mild punishments were imposed. Appeals cost a lot of public money if made *a minima* by the prosecution rather than by the defendant. Even zealous Catholics hesitated to push such appeals before parlementary judges who they suspected were no more likely to impose serious punishments than local judges. Least of all would a royal official denounce a colleague for heresy. Claude Haton, the priest-chronicler of Provins, explained why heretics were rarely punished late in Henry II's reign. "Whenever one of them fell into the hands of the courts," he claimed with only slight exaggeration in 1558, "he didn't stay there, being encouraged and supported by his brothers in this so-called religion, and more of them escaped from the hands of justice than were punished." Haton added that "the judges, above all the court of the Paris Parlement, dabbled in the said heresy," and even those "who abhorred that heresy and its followers could not perform rigorous justice according to the royal edicts," because various influential personages intervened on their behalf.[45]

Such reasons inhibited heresy trials at all levels of the French legal system by the late 1550s. It is not really surprising that a dozen people were being executed for heresy each year in a kingdom as large as France at a time when Protestants were establishing dozens of illegal churches every year. Perhaps it is stranger that so many were still being burned in public, because judicial reluctance to convict (and risk finding one's prisoner celebrated as a martyr) was only one obstacle inhibiting a successful policy of repression. The French legal system confronted a second and more direct challenge in the late 1550s, coincident with the sudden growth in numbers and organization of French Protestants. Members of Reformed congregations now began to organize rescues of prisoners who had been convicted of heresy.

We have little direct evidence about the extent of this phenomenon, for several reasons. Parlementary sources seldom mention rescues, because most of them occurred when a heretic who appealed his conviction was being taken to a regional parlement. In such instances, the legal responsibility to find the culprits belonged to the local court that had conducted the original trial—and their records have disappeared. We generally learn about rescues made after a parlement had sentenced a heretic, since the responsibility for locating the culprits then devolved upon the appellate court. Because parlements could not ignore such insults to their authority, a successful rescue created a paper trail. But if parlements tried to minimize the publicity surrounding these rescues, so did Reformed spokesmen, perhaps for even better reasons. Crespin discusses such incidents only when he cannot avoid doing so, in those rare contexts in which someone was sentenced to death for heresy twice and actually executed the second time.[46] At a time when the Reformed churches wished to demonstrate that they were fundamentally law-abiding even though their organizations were illegal, rescuing convicted prisoners constituted a flagrant challenge to public authority. In the end, the

Reformed churches of France condoned a practice that they could not prevent. Moreover, every successful rescue constituted a threat that further inhibited judges from condemning their members to death.

The problem of rescues was most acute for the parlements with the largest districts. The Parlement of Paris short-circuited appeals from heresy prisoners at Lyon in 1553 because of potential rescues; the Parlement of Toulouse behaved similarly with respect to Montpellier later that year. It is only because of Crespin's need to relate a subsequent martyrdom that we learn of successful rescues en route from Lyon to the Parlement of Paris early in 1553 and en route from Tulle to the Parlement of Bordeaux in 1554. Such incidents seem to have become more common as Reformed churches organized, particularly at Paris. Nicolas Balon, a peddler of heretical books and resident of Geneva, en route to be executed for heresy at Poitiers, was rescued in March 1557 just beyond Etampes, not very far from Paris, by "men who were armed, covered, and masked." A priest who was being taken to Poitiers with Balon was promptly recaptured and taken back to Paris, where he provided enough information for the Parlement to issue arrest warrants against eight men associated with the rescue team. At least one man was prosecuted in August 1557 for arranging this rescue. Unfazed by his adventure, Balon returned to Geneva, but soon went back to work peddling forbidden literature under a pseudonym. He was rearrested in Champagne. The Parlement of Paris discovered his real identity and before his final execution ordered Balon to be tortured "moderately" about the circumstances of his earlier escape. The final postscript to this event came in August 1559, when the unlucky *conducteur des prisonniers* was legally discharged for his negligence in letting Balon escape thirty months previously.[47]

Rescues of accused heretics also spread to other parlementary districts in 1558 and 1559. Deep in Provence, at Arles, an immigrant tailor named Antoine Cavalis was condemned to be burned for heresy by joint sentence of the archbishop of Lyon and the seneschal of Arles. We learn about their decision only because the Parlement of Aix issued arrest warrants in February 1559 for eight people suspected of organizing Cavalis's escape near St. Martin de Crau on the previous 20 September, while he was being transported to Aix after appealing to the Parlement.[48] At the other end of France, one finds two priests, Germain Philippe and Jean LeFebvre, successfully appealing their heresy convictions from the court of the bishop of Bayeux to the Parlement of Rouen in May 1559. Six days after the Parlement approved their request, it was sending orders to arrest two men from Caen in connection with the rescue of these two priests while en route from Bayeux to Rouen. One understands the reactions of the Parlement of Rouen after two confessed "sacramentarians" appealed to them later that month from Vire, which lay even farther away than Bayeux in lower Normandy. The local prosecutor requested that the royal governor of Normandy provide a special guard to bring these two to Rouen and avoid rescues "as has been done recently to several others." Specifying that they were trying to avoid setting any precedents ("pour ceste foys et sans tirer a consequence"), the Rouen judges ordered the court at Vire to ignore any appeals from these prisoners until after their trials had been completed; only if the prosecutor appealed *a minima* would the governor provide an armed escort for the prisoners. Meanwhile a woman convicted of infanticide at the same time by the same court at Vire was transported to Rouen without incident.[49]

Rescues of condemned heretics en route to either their appeals or their executions once again embarrassed the Parlement of Paris in 1559. On 16 May the local royal court at Châlons began investigating the rescue of Etienne Millaut, who was being taken to Paris after appealing his death sentence for heresy. They arrested two men in connection with Millaut's rescue in September; another man whom they arrested was ultimately released by the Parlement of Paris next April on grounds of insufficient evidence.[50] Far more embarrassing to the Parlement were the rescues of a weaver and his wife, both of whom they had sentenced to death for heresy on 7 August. Though captured in the duchy of Valois, they had been ordered back to their home town, Meaux, a traditional center of heresy only fifty kilometers from the Parlement's prison, for their executions. The court granted a two-day extension for orthodox theologians to convert them and avoid their being burned alive, but other people also took advantage of the delay. The Parlement, taking notice of the "almost daily rescues and despoilings of prisoners sent back for the crime of heresy, to the great scandal of Christian religion and of justice," ordered a convicted heretic from Sens to be burned in the city of Paris on 31 August "in order to avoid rescues." In this ruling, the Parlement cited the recent rescues of the weaver from Meaux and his wife;[51] otherwise, we would not understand why they never appear among Crespin's list of martyrs. The Parlement never ordered anyone arrested in connection with their deliverance, although this modest couple could not have escaped from their armed escort during the short trip to Meaux without considerable aid.

The problem of rescues persisted during the next few months. In late September, President de Saint-André ordered an accused heretic from near Melun to be executed "in this city of Paris, in order to avoid any rescue of the person of said prisoner, given the inconveniences which have already happened and often happen to *conducteurs* of prisoners accused of the said crimes in returning them to the judges from whom they have appealed."[52] But most rescues happened while prisoners were being taken to Paris rather than from it. In December 1559 two men were released on bail after an investigation into the rescue, "near Laon, of certain prisoners accused of heresy." A richer account of an exploit by a group that deserves to be known as the Huguenot Commando of Paris nests among the Parlement's *arrêts* two weeks earlier. An unlucky *conducteur* from Troyes, leading a prisoner named Girard Corlieu who had been condemned to be burned, was ambushed "near this city of Paris" by a group of eighteen or twenty masked men. They not only rescued his prisoner, but also stole the official copy of Corlieu's trial, disarmed the *conducteur* and his escort, taking their horses, swords, daggers, and clubs; the raiders even stole their uniforms and insignia, doubtless for use in their next escapade.[53]

Late in 1559, we also learn of the partial rescue of several prisoners from Poitiers who had appealed their convictions for heresy. Like the earlier rescue of Nicolas Balon, it was probably organized at Poitiers rather than Paris. In early January 1560 one suspect in this rescue was released on grounds of insufficient evidence; in an apparently unrelated *arrêt* decreed the following day, a man from Poitou was ordered arrested on heresy charges. One month later this man, Simon Boisson, was sentenced by the Paris Parlement, "after lengthy interrogations," to be hanged and his body burned at Paris as an "obstinate and pertinacious sacramentarian heretic," with a parallel ceremony to be carried out in effigy at Poitiers. Boisson's most serious crime, however, was participation in the rescues "at the village of Bourg la Reyne, of several prisoners accused of heresy [*du faict de la religion*]," including Boisson's wife. Like Balon, Simon Boisson was tortured "moderately" about the rescue before being strangled. Not everyone got away: two "sacramentarian" heretics from Poitiers had been burned at Paris just a few days before Boisson's arrest warrant was issued.[54]

By now the successful transportation of a convicted heretic to Paris from some distant location constituted an exploit. Crespin mockingly describes how a prisoner of humble background, Pierre Arondeau, was taken from La Rochelle to Paris late in 1559. "One fine day, before dawn, led out by a secret exit and taken by his guards along every byway, unused path, and oblique road, from fear of rescues," his escort finally arrived at Paris "after great effort and a long journey" to throw him into the Parlement's prison. A few months later, royal officials at Auxonne faced the formidable task of taking a convicted heretic named Nicolas Dupont, who led the Parlement's list of suspected "sacramentarians" in their city, all the way to Paris in order to have his appeal judged. On 25 January 1560 the royal messenger of Auxonne finally undertook the assignment, "insofar as no one else would do it, because of the danger in conducting such prisoners." Germain Sixdeniers pocketed forty livres in advance, hired seven armed men and a boat captain, and brought Dupont safely to Paris. Because he had also spent a "large sum of money" beyond his advance, the Parlement ordered him paid in full at Auxonne.[55]

Serious as the problem of rescues had become for the Parlement of Paris, at least they experienced no problems in actually executing condemned heretics within the city, apart from restraining overzealous spectators who tried to lynch them before public officials could perform their responsibilities. However, another Parlement suffered the indignity of having a condemned heretic rescued while being led to execution within their city walls. The episode occurred at Rouen, when a tailor from the Cotentin peninsula of lower Normandy was being taken to his execution on 29 January 1560. One day later the court ordered the city's gates kept closed and offered a huge reward of a hundred écus for information on his whereabouts or a full pardon to any of the culprits who turned the tailor over to them. These tactics worked: their prisoner was recaptured almost immediately, and this time his sentence was carried out. Within two weeks, ten suspected conspirators had been arrested, although all of them were released a month later.[56] The whole episode offered devastating evidence of just how fragile parlementary control over accused heretics had actually become by the winter of 1559–60. The Reformed were literally taking the law into their own hands.

The Final Surge of Heresy Persecution, 1557–1559

Despite the difficulties resulting on the one hand from the increasing reluctance of royal judges to prosecute and condemn heretics and on the other from the eagerness of fellow Protestants to rescue those who did get condemned, the machinery of royal justice lumbered along. Between the autumn of 1557 and the winter of 1559–60, the Parlement of Paris undertook one last major burst of activity against Protestants. Both the beginning and the climactic finish of this cycle originated within the capital city itself. It began in September 1557, in the wake of news about France's disastrous defeat at St. Quentin, when a Parisian mob broke up a large meeting of the Reformed church on the rue St. Jacques; the police imprisoned more than a hundred people, many of them women, who had been unwilling or unable to escape. It ended with the execution of Anne du Bourg, a judge of the Parlement of Paris, just before Christmas 1559. Between these events, the Parlement of Paris ordered more than thirty executions for heresy, surpassing the combined totals for the entire kingdom between January 1555 and September 1557. A continuous thread connects the "affair of the rue St.-Jacques" to du Bourg's martyrdom and enables us to treat the entire Parisian cycle as one continuous dialectical process, the concluding episode of the Valois dynasty's twenty-year war against domestic "Lutheranism" waged primarily through its appellate court system.

Many historians have described the "affair of the Rue St.-Jacques," and diligent scholarship has even unearthed in the archives of Zurich a list of the 130 prisoners who were captured, but the Parlement of Paris apparently destroyed virtually all of its records describing how they were judged.[57] Although most of the lacunae in its preserved *arrêts* during the age of heresy prosecutions seem fortuitous, the complete disappearance of all criminal decisions of the Paris Parlement between September 1557 and March 1558 arouses suspicion.[58] However, precisely because the "affair of the rue St.-Jacques" belongs to the age of nascent confessionalism, we can fill in the general outlines of the Parlement's responses to this record influx of accused heretics from well-informed local Protestant sources. Antoine de la Roche Chandieu, one of the Reformed pastors serving the young Paris church, published a pamphlet at Lyon in 1563 that furnishes much information about the legal and political consequences of this "affair," including a complete list of the martyrdoms that resulted from it between the autumn of 1557 and the summer of 1558.[59]

Contemporary Catholic apologists like Claude Haton claimed that virtually all these prisoners, especially the women, were treated with remarkable mildness. However, Protestant sources show that the Paris Parlement responded exactly as one would expect, by creating a special commission of two presidents and sixteen judges to handle the huge volume and to make a few bloody examples. Three convicted heretics who had been sitting in the Parlement's prison for some time were now returned to their home towns to be executed. Three presumed leaders of the Paris church were quickly condemned and burned with great fanfare: a pedagogue from Guyenne (previously burned in effigy by the Parlement of Bordeaux), whom the judges mistakenly supposed to be a preacher; a lawyer practicing before the Parlement, who had provided the residence in which the assembly met; and a recently widowed wealthy young noblewoman, whose child had been baptized secretly and whose husband (an elder of this fledgling church) had been buried secretly.[60] Two others followed them five days later: a visiting physician from Normandy (whose brother had recently been executed for heresy at Dijon) and a low-ranking member of the Parisian legal profession.

Repression slowed during the first week of October. A noblewoman objected to some of her judges; a German prisoner, whose godfather was the Elector of Brandenburg, was released; and the king ordered that henceforth only pertinacious "sacramentarians" could be executed with his approval. Two Parisian students from southwestern France met these criteria and were accordingly burned in late October. But at this time, with a dozen more cases prepared for sentencing, another imprisoned noblewoman raised conflict-of-interest objections against her judges, German and Swiss ambassadors arrived to put more diplomatic pressure on the king, and the judges stopped pronouncing death sentences. As La Roche Chandieu put it, "God, satisfied for the moment with the number of these seven martyrs, found another way to restrain the rage of His enemies until the following July."[61] The only further victims he could find among the prisoners captured on the Rue St.-Jacques were two men who died unrepentant in the Parlement's prison that winter.

Chandieu explained what happened to all the other prisoners, many of them women and students. After the Protestant ambassadors arrived, many prisoners were released. Students were usually sent to monasteries to get a proper Christian education. Most of them

> were sent to the Official [the episcopal judge] to make their confession of faith, or rather their abjuration, and receive absolution. The judges, seeing their hands tied from sending them to the stake, used this means to get rid of them, hoping that they would at least make them disavow the holy doctrine of our Lord Jesus Christ. And many unscrupulous

cowards worried very little about obeying that; others used ambiguous language in their confessions. Whatever one says, many people proved to be very disloyal.[62]

Our only preserved *arrêt* reveals two such people, a nobleman and his wife, who avoided the confiscation of their estates by making formal abjurations before the Official of Paris on the final day of 1557.[63] By April 1558 only three prisoners remained from the huge crowd captured on the Rue St.-Jacques. One of them, a young man from Normandy, was subsequently executed in July 1558 after refusing to perform the *amende honorable* that the Official had required of him three months previously.[64]

Meanwhile other prisoners charged with heresy trickled into the Parlement's prison. By March 1559, President Séguier decided to wrap up the trial of the final unconverted "sacramentarian" prisoner captured nineteen months before on the Rue St.-Jacques,[65] connecting it with the cases of three recently convicted heretics (a student and a baker captured in Paris, and an artisan from Reims), all of whom were appealing death sentences. Séguier's idea evolved into a most unusual ruling on 7 April 1559, which had unforeseen consequences. Even from a purely formal and legal point of view, the resulting document was unprecedented. No other sixteenth-century Parisian parlementary *arrêt* combined four separate appeals that had already been assigned to four separate rapporteurs; but both the copy in the Parlement's official register and the draft version in the *plumitifs* carry five signatures, headed by that of Séguier.[66]

The substance of this joint decision was no less remarkable. Although all four men persisted in upholding their doctrinal errors, none of them was to be executed. All four were ordered to quit Paris within three days and to leave the kingdom within a fortnight, perpetually banished with their property confiscated to benefit the poor. But none died or was even sentenced to the galleys, usually the first step below death for a convicted felon. Séguier's ruling also bent customary court procedure. For example, the language of the official *arrêt* (in which two passages have been crossed out) makes no reference to the royal prosecutor, who was routinely mentioned even when his advice was not followed. Irregularities also abound in its second version, inserted in correct chronological order among the Parlement's collection of *plumitifs*. But unlike every other entry in this series, it records no actual interrogations of any of the four prisoners concerned. (Protestant sources claim that efforts were made to reach some compromise with the prisoners over eucharistic theology that would justify overturning their death sentences, but insist that the arrangement failed at the last moment.) Despite its numerous irregularities, President Séguier's ruling was implemented immediately, with the proviso that it did not constitute a precedent.

Séguier's solution slightly disappointed Protestant zealots; Chandieu observed that "this exception still contained some unjust rigor," adding immediately, "but it was nothing compared with the cruelty that had been hitherto exercised."[67] But this decision infuriated Catholic zealots and caused a huge scandal within the Parlement. The royal prosecutors, so conspicuously missing from the formal *arrêt* copied into the register, had immediately protested that Séguier's criminal court ruling reversed established procedures in the court's senior branch, the Grande Chambre. They requested and obtained a plenary session of the entire court, held only on Wednesdays and therefore known as a *mercuriale,* in order to resolve this schism between the court's main branches. Shortly before it met, the Grande Chambre sharpened the conflict by upholding a death sentence against a poor winegrower from the region around Meaux who qualified as a "sacramentarian."[68] When the *mercuriale* finally began, a lengthy and acrid but inconclusive debate revealed considerable support for reducing the general severity of punishments to somewhere near the level of Séguier's recent ruling. But the senior president of the Grande Chambre, Claude le Maistre, Lizet's successor since 1550 as the "hammer of heretics," accompanied by a few prominent like-minded colleagues, approached the king in order to trump their opponents with royal support. Their strategy succeeded, but with different consequences than they expected.

On 10 June, King Henry II, accompanied by many senior advisers and an especially large delegation of senior clerics including three cardinals, entered the plenary session of Parlement and announced that he wished to hear their debates on religious questions in person. The royal presence did not intimidate many judges who sympathized to a greater or lesser degree with the "Lutherans." Following his gracious instructions, they continued to discuss these issues with the same candor as they had in his absence, while king and courtiers listened silently: a *mercuriale* was totally unlike a *lit de justice.* Henry II and the cardinals heard several bold speeches opposing abuses in the church and even favoring innovations going well beyond conciliarism. One in particular, from a relatively obscure judge, insolently argued that the cause of the "Lutherans" was really the cause of Jesus Christ. Before striding out of the session, an infuriated Henry II ordered his Scots Guards to seize him and one other speaker. After conferring with his advisers, he ordered six more judges arrested. Five parlementary judges were quickly put in the Bastille; three others escaped.

Henry II had just then made peace with Spain, sacrificing nearly all of his Italian possessions and eliminating two parlements in the process. He needed to whittle down his war debts. But he also sent a circular letter to every province claiming that he had made a disadvantageous peace principally in order to be able to combat heresy more effectively, if necessary by armed force, and urging all his courts to redouble their efforts against heretics. Henry's noisy campaign had some effect on the Parlement of Bordeaux, which ordered the execution of four heretics within six weeks in the summer of 1559, along with two deaths for extreme blasphemy against the Virgin Mary. However, this outburst of severity ended after another judge replaced the zealot Roffignac as president in August. Overall, Montaigne's colleagues released more than half of their thirty prisoners charged with heresy in 1559, while the provincial governor turned a blind eye to the rapidly multiplying Reformed churches in Guyenne and Saintonge.[69]

Crespin's report of renewed severity by the Parlement of Rouen in the summer of 1559 is misleading. Although these judges upheld death sentences against a fanatical iconoclast who had thrown a crucifix into the prison latrine and against a nobleman from Guyenne, charged with pillage and assault as well as heretical speech,[70] their behavior after receiving the new king's order of 29 August to appoint three special commissioners to combat heresy in specified regions of Normandy reveals either reluctance or inability to prosecute the well-organized Reformed congregations in their district. The first commissioner went to the most distant region of Normandy, the Cotentin. Our only direct trace of his activities, however, is a receipt for 400 livres paid to him and his special prosecutor on 18 November.[71] A second commissioner went to Caen, the capital of lower Normandy, where he was insulted, harassed, and even besieged in his room; he soon returned, having accomplished nothing. The third commissioner wriggled out of his assignment to the Pays de Caux four weeks later by pleading illness; the Parlement named a substitute, who then presented a different set of excuses three weeks afterward; a second substitute was chosen, but three weeks later he too refused this assignment. After much crossing out of names, a fourth man was appointed for Caux on 20 November, although we have no evidence that he ever left Rouen.[72] Perhaps these Rouen judges were simply being realistic; the next time they tried to execute a convicted heretic, he was rescued within their city walls.

If Henry II's extremely bloodthirsty Edict of Ecouen in 1559—his final attempt to spur his parlements into vigorous action against Protestants—had serious consequences at Paris, it produced only temporary results at Bordeaux, muted results at Rouen, and had no effect anywhere else. In three other provincial parlements with surviving criminal *arrêts* from 1559 (Toulouse, Aix, and Grenoble), almost fifty accused heretics were judged in person. Forty of them were released without public punishments; three men were banished for relatively short periods; five performed *amendes honorables* but were not whipped or banished; and only one man, who had made a full confession under torture, was executed at Toulouse in early December.[73]

The force of Henry II's final assault on heresy was therefore felt only at the Parlement of Paris, but its effects outlasted Henry's sudden death exactly one month after attending the *mercuriale*. The story of how the young Francis II quickly fell under the influence of his wife's zealously Catholic Guise cousins has been told often and well.[74] The cycle of death sentences against heretics pronounced by this Parlement continued across the next several months, accelerating after Francis II became king on 10 July. Chandieu's account and the parlement's *arrêts,* sources that overlap but are not quite identical,[75] show them confirming three death sentences for heresy in July (two of them after the king's death), four more in August (two of whom escaped), one in September, five in October, five in December, and four more in January 1560—numbers exceeding those of Lizet's Chambre Ardente, on which some of these judges had sat. During the first six months of Francis II's reign, the Parlement of Paris released only about a dozen prisoners accused of heresy, many fewer than it put to death.

Significantly, President Séguier did not dare to reduce another death sentence for heresy until December 1559. A minor official of the royal treasury *(clerc suyvant les finances)*, imprisoned for several months, was then released in the custody of his cousin, a merchant of Chinon, and told to be properly confessed, to hear Mass regularly, and to avoid scandals in future.[76] The next month Séguier sharply reduced two more death sentences. One defendant flatly denied the charges; the other, a blacksmith who had appealed his condemnation as a *sacramentaire* in mid-September, finally broke down under the "special admonitions" of two theologians and his rapporteur and "confessed that he had failed in his duties." In both cases Séguier merely ordered the prisoner to bring a signed copy of his profession of faith and formal absolution from his local episcopal court. In a significant decision three days afterward, Séguier's conservative rival, President le Maistre, signed an *arrêt* reducing the death sentence of a young recidivist to a whipping and five years' imprisonment in the episcopal prison of Paris; he would be released if he performed "acts of a good Christian" during that time.[77]

One of these trials and executions overshadowed all the others during the Guise ascendancy in the first half of Francis II's brief reign. Just before Christmas 1559, Anne du Bourg became the most famous martyr of the French Reformation. He was the first sitting judge of a French Parlement to be executed as a pertinacious Protestant in over thirty years. Antoine de Lautrec had been burned in effigy at Toulouse more than five years before; four of du Bourg's 120 Parisian colleagues were imprisoned with him in the Bastille in 1559; whispers circulated about the heretical opinions of various judges in several parlements. A few other sitting judges would subsequently be hanged during the religious wars or lynched during the St. Bartholomew's massacres, but only du Bourg was strangled and burned at the stake during the confessional era.

The manner of Anne du Bourg's trial was almost as remarkable as its outcome. Unlike his imprisoned colleagues, this young judge (he was only thirty-seven in 1559) admitted at his third interrogation that he had not only heard Reformed sermons but had even taken communion at their recent Easter service. He insisted that he was the only *conseillier* or judge who had done so. His interrogators were particularly scandalized because du Bourg (like Berquin) was a *conseillier-clerc*, a post open only to men who had been ordained as deacons. Upon hearing these disclosures, the bishop of Paris promptly ordered du Bourg defrocked on 30 June, the same day that Henry II, who had sworn to see du Bourg burn, suffered his fatal accident while jousting. As Henry lay dying, du Bourg began a series of escalating legal appeals. Crespin explains that he employed these tactics "not just to gain time and prolong his life by subterfuges, but in order to remove any suspicion of being precipitous and being the cause of his own death too soon [*avant le temps*] by forgetting some thing that might serve for his justification."[78] By these means du Bourg managed to remain alive for exactly six months after making a full confession of his "sacramentarian" beliefs and practices.

On 7 July, the Parlement's Grand Chambre rejected du Bourg's first appeal from the decision of the bishop of Paris, so the prisoner turned to the bishop's immediate superior, the archbishop of Sens. After being rejected a second time, du Bourg appealed *comme d'abus* to his colleagues, who heard his case at the beginning of August. At first the defendant tried to remove all six presidents on grounds of prejudice and partiality, along with three of the most notorious zealots, led by Louis Gayant; this was a tactic to prevent anyone from presiding at his hearings, and it did not work. Four days later, du Bourg lifted his objections to three presidents, including Séguier, and the Parlement overrode his objections to two others. His trial then proceeded, lasting three full weeks before his appeal was denied on 30 August. However, du Bourg had not yet exhausted his legal rights; he immediately appealed from Parlement to the "primate of the Gauls," the archbishop of Lyon. Cardinal Tournon had been on vacation, but took the time to reject du Bourg once again on 28 September. His decision reached the Paris Parlement on 10 October, accompanied by yet another appeal *comme d'abus* from du Bourg. Another month-long cycle of hearings followed until du Bourg was once again denied on 18 November. Only now, on 20 November, could the bishop of Paris actually carry out his June sentence of formal defrocking and thereby strip du Bourg of his official status as *conseillier-clerc* before handing him over to the secular arm. Now a layman, Anne du Bourg made one last appeal *comme d'abus* to the Parlement. This was, finally, legal checkmate. Last-minute efforts to avoid the scandal of his public execution sought to find an ambiguously phrased confession of faith that would be acceptable both to du Bourg and to his moderate ex-colleagues, and adequate to justify a punishment less than death for a repentant offender. On 13 December, before a ruling had been made on his final appeal, he signed such a document. At the same time (12 December), the youngest parlementary president, a hard-line zealot, was shot to death on the streets of Paris by assassins who were never identified. This remarkable provocation, mentioned only briefly in contemporary sources (Protestants were too embarrassed and Catholics too frightened) probably sealed du Bourg's fate. Six days later, under pressure from the Reformed pastorate, du Bourg formally repudiated his compromise confession of faith. Under such circumstances the Parlement had no choice but to carry through their ex-colleague's execution, which they did on 23 December.

Did the Paris Protestants, who organized several rescues in 1559 in the open countryside and were capable of murdering a senior judge on the streets of Paris, also try to rescue their most prominent church member from the Parlement's prison? In October Catholics intercepted a letter in code from du Bourg that, when deciphered, proposed an escape plan. One piece of previously overlooked evidence, Robert Stuart's second horse, suggests that a second attempt to rescue him was made in December and very nearly succeeded. Catholic sources report that an armed man, claiming to be the queen's relative, was arrested in the Parlement's prison shortly before du Bourg's execution. Three eyewitnesses testified against him; he was tortured, but admitted nothing. En route to his death, Anne du Bourg was vainly questioned twice by his official escort about his dealings with a mysterious Scot named Stuart. In late February 1560, Robert Stuart was transferred from Vincennes to Blois and soon escaped. The mystery clarifies a bit in March and April 1560, when a Paris innkeeper received the Parlement's permission to sell two horses that had been confiscated from "a Scotsman named Stuart, formerly prisoner in the Parlement's jail and then ordered before the king by special command." This innkeeper had been feeding Robert Stuart's horses since 17 December.[79] The pieces fit: why did this Scottish adventurer need two horses? We also have one important clue to explain why Robert Stuart failed to rescue Anne du Bourg on 17 December. While du Bourg made appeal after appeal to different ecclesiastical courts, he remained a *conseillier-clerc;* the Parlement therefore used his salary in order to pay his prison expenses. By December, with his salary gone and his final conviction highly probable, they hired full-time guards (subsequently paid from du Bourg's confiscated estate) in order to watch their illustrious prisoner.[80] These special guards probably arrested Robert Stuart and became the eyewitnesses who testified against him; their watchfulness probably foiled his mission.

The final cycle of French parlementary executions for heresy intersected the process of confessionalization by the French Reformed church at both ends. The "Chambéry five" personified the beginnings of the missionary pastors in the mid-1550s; Anne du Bourg's Paris church hosted the clandestine national synod of 1559 that hammered out both a confession of faith and a church organization for the entire kingdom. Both the "Chambéry five" and du Bourg were unusually important prisoners, fully cognizant of their position and anxious for recognition as representatives of a legitimate and responsible community of believers. Far from being embarrassed by Servetus' execution for heresy at Geneva in 1553, both the missionaries of 1555 and the parlementary judge agreed that it was justified. In his defiant final confession of faith, du Bourg claimed that magistrates should "chastise and punish false prophets who . . . and instead of the gospel, preach and teach fables and human traditions."[81] Clearly, the most prominent representatives of the new Reformed churches believed that Geneva's demonstrated willingness to execute a heretic was a strong point in their favor.

Catherine de Médicis Decriminalizes Heresy in 1560

One seldom sees a sharper change in major policy than Francis II's about-face on heresy prosecutions during the late winter of 1559–60, approximately in the middle of his eighteen-month reign. The Guise ascendancy suddenly began to totter; the influence of the king's wife and her cousins was slowly replaced by the growing influence of his mother. On both a literal and a figurative level, the fires of French heresy persecutions were extinguished early in 1560. At Paris, public burnings for heresy ceased abruptly after the first week of 1560, except for one man, executed primarily for his role in rescuing prisoners. For that matter, heresy executions slowed to a virtual halt throughout France. After Le Monnier's death at Rouen one day after his temporary rescue and Boisson's death at Paris in early February, only two other cases are known in the whole kingdom during 1560. At Toulouse, Jean David *alias* Massip, who had been sought on heresy charges for several years, was burned together with his books on 10 April.[82] At Rouen, Jean Cottin was burned alive on 27 March, and two of his associates were hanged. However, a Protestant diarist tells us that this libertine hedge-preacher had infuriated Rouen's recently arrived Genevan-trained pastors by denying the existence of the Last Judgment; they persuaded the elders of their Reformed congregation to put a price of a hundred écus on Cottin's head. Their reward exactly matched the sum that the Parlement had offered two months previously for capturing Le Monnier's rescuers, and it got similar results: Cottin was captured the following day, along with two men who had collected money at his sermons.[83] Only an exceptional degree of collaboration between normally hostile organizations, the Reformed church and the Rouen Parlement, produced the final public executions for heresy in Normandy. The only man burned alive for heresy in France in 1560 can be seen as a victim of Calvinist, as much as of Catholic, persecution.

A careful search reveals signs of Catherine de Médicis' growing influence in softening punishments for heresy early in 1560. For example, the other parlementary judges imprisoned in the Bastille with du Bourg returned quietly to their places on the bench not long after his execution. Three of them had to perform humiliating ceremonies of public apology before their reinstatements. However, Antoine Fumée, long suspected of being strongly sympathetic to the Reformed cause (in fact he had written to Calvin as early as 1544), was reinstated on 23 February without any form of public punishment, apparently through the influence of a favorite of the queen mother.[84] A more dramatic sign followed within two weeks. When the Guises first revealed the dangerous conspiracy of Amboise to Francis II, his mother apparently persuaded the young king not to step up persecution, but instead to offer Protestants their first general pardon in twenty-five years. It was decreed at Amboise in early March 1560—the exact time and place where dissidents organized by Protestant noblemen mounted an unsuccessful conspiracy to kidnap the young king. As the Protestants' general pardon was being printed and sold in Paris, more than a hundred conspirators were being hanged on the walls of the castle of Amboise.[85]

The person behind this general pardon was undeniably the king's mother, Catherine de Médicis, whose responsibility is explicitly recognized in its text. Its preamble began by repeating the now-traditional royal explanations, blaming the recent spread of heresy on "preachers coming from Geneva, mostly common people with no knowledge of letters" accompanied by a "malicious dispersion of books" from Geneva that had "infected part of the ordinary people of our kingdom." As the decree candidly acknowledged, so many subjects were now "infected" that the existing corpus of antiheresy legislation had become unworkable. "If," continued the preamble, "we punished [all heretics] with the full rigor of the law under our ordinances, there would be a remarkable effusion of blood of people of all ages and sexes" who had transgressed them from a mixture of reasons: malice, ignorance, sheer curiosity. "If this happened, it would turn to our perpetual regret and displeasure, not being suitable to our nature or our age." The sentiments and the language were coming less from the king than from his mother, as Francis II acknowledged. "We have often discussed these matters with our most honored Mother, and finally, following her advice, have put this matter in deliberation in our Council, at which were present our most honored Mother" and the queen, in addition to the usual councillors.

Catherine's proposed remedy involved the complete abolition of her late husband's now unworkable antiheresy legislation. "Not wishing that the first year of our reign should be remembered by posterity as bloody and full of executions," Francis and his mother declared a complete moratorium on punishments regarding "all incidents whatsoever concerning matters of faith and religion," offering "pardon, remission, and general abolition for all past matters for all our subjects" on condition that they live henceforth as conforming Catholics. They exempted only three groups: heretical preachers; conspirators against persons of the royal family (who were at that very moment descending in droves on the castle of Amboise, where this document was drafted); and those who had, "by force and violence, rescued prisoners from the hands of justice" (twenty years later, the semiofficial history of the French Reformed churches admitted that "the last point concerning the rescue of some prisoners was true, to the great regret of the ministers").[86] This pardon provides the first clear sign of Catherine de Médicis' influence on French policy toward heretics since Henry II had created the special Queen's Chamber court in 1548.

The pardon of Amboise had different effects in different places. At Bordeaux, the Parlement registered it on 22 March; a week later, they released six men and a woman who had been imprisoned on heresy charges.[87] At Rouen, whose judges were burning a heretic handed to them by the local Reformed church, there were apparently no suitable prisoners available to be released; however, the new pardon encouraged the Reformed churches of St.-Lô, Caen, and Dieppe to conduct their services in public, although the Parlement compelled the large church at Rouen to operate in formal clandestinity.[88] At Toulouse, which had executed Massip in April, the Parlement grudgingly acknowledged the pardon in early June, but quietly resumed a few heresy prosecutions in October.[89] At Paris, it was registered on 11 March but not put into effect, probably because of the conspiracy of Amboise. A Guisard parlementary judge noted that many of his colleagues found it "very strange," but their perplexity merely delayed its application for several months.[90] Catherine de Médicis' pardon probably saved the life of Nicolas Dupont, leader of the Reformed congregation at Auxerre, who had been brought to the Parlement's prison in Paris in late February 1560 by a large armed guard. On 27 May President de Harlay finally released Dupont, together with five other men and three women imprisoned on heresy charges, citing the pardon of 11 March for "every kind of case . . . concerning issues of faith and religion . . . for all times past and for all his subjects," after they all took a vague oath to live as good Christians and to commit no public scandals.[91]

The wind of heresy persecution stirred up by Henry II in his final month had now been stilled by his widow. By late May the queen mother's protégé Michel de L'Hôpital had been installed as chancellor, and another edict in midsummer 1560 returned all heresy cases to episcopal courts. These two pieces of legislation, the Edict of Amboise and the Edict of Romorantin, effectively decriminalized the newly confessionalized Reformed churches of France. Only a few heretics would be punished in the following months, and none would be burned anywhere in France until after the outbreak of civil war.[92] In the autumn of 1560, Crespin noted that the jail of the Paris Parlement had once again filled with Protestant suspects, but "God so tied the judges' hands that no one was sent to death."[93] Well before the queen mother became regent for her underaged son early in 1561, she had managed to end those public burnings that had upset her at the "Joyous Entry" into Paris in 1549.

However, the end of public executions for heresy did not mean the end of official harassment for the Reformed churches. Preachers, for example, had been exempted from the general pardon; a recently arrived pastor from Geneva was arrested at Troyes in May 1560, but "the night before he was to be condemned to death," notes the Protestant church history, "he was subtly and dextrously, without any noise or breaking of doors, taken from the prison."[94] The Edict of Romorantin returned heresy trials to the church, but secular courts still judged cases of sedition. By the summer of 1560 the French legal system had shifted from convicting "sacramentarians" to repressing public disorders by members of organized but illegal churches. The simplest way to understand this change is to examine the circumstances under which the first Genevan missionary pastor suffered a public execution in France since the "Chambéry five" died in 1555. Although the Parlement of Grenoble had executed nobody for heresy since 1541, its special commissioners carried out public hangings of two Reformed ministers and three laymen at Valence in May 1560. One of them, Lancelot d'Albeau, had been despatched to Valence by Geneva's Company of Pastors. But whereas Vernou and his companions had been burned for heresy, less than five years later d'Albeau and his colleague were hanged for sedition.

Why had the notoriously lenient Parlement of Grenoble intervened so violently at Valence in the late spring of 1560? Basically because a mob had driven the local Franciscans out of their convent shortly before Easter, occupied it, and conducted Protestant services in their new meeting-place. This provocation to public authority outraged the duke of Guise, titular governor of Dauphiné, and scandalized even the Parlement of Grenoble. Guise named a new deputy and despatched veteran soldiers, accompanied by no fewer than seven parlementary judges, to restore order in Valence and to punish the ringleaders. To rub in the message that what was being punished was not heresy but sedition, the special commissioners ordered that both pastors were to be hanged with signs around their necks reading "Here are the chief rebels." They also ordered a layman's home demolished, except for one wall on which a sign proclaimed: "This was the house of the seditious people's secretary."[95] Heretics got commemorative chapels erected on the sites of their meetings; seditious rebels had plaques erected to perpetuate their infamy. By mid-May 1560, times had changed: hangings instead of burnings, plaques instead of chapels, well-organized churches instead of inchoate assemblies. And soon came civil war instead of domestic tranquillity.

7

Martyrology and Jurisprudence

It's not a matter of laurel wreaths . . . but of a new way to conquer after being condemned, and to triumph over every placard, decree, and edict of emperors and kings.

—*Simon Goulart (1582)*

In 1554 three Protestant authors began reshaping the early Christian genre of compiling histories of martyrs for the edification and fortification of the faithful, now disseminating them through printed books. Whereas both his Lutheran colleague Ludwig Rabus and his Anglican colleague John Foxe concentrated on ancient and late medieval martyrs, Jean Crespin's collection featured recent Protestant martyrs.[1] Crespin's work constituted a genuine breakthrough, one of the more original ways in which Protestant authors adapted early Christian examples to their own times. Lay judges carried out public punishments for condemned heretics in the sixteenth century much as their lay predecessors had in ancient Rome or during the Middle Ages. However, their victims had hitherto been commemorated only through historians like Eusebius, who wrote after Christianity's triumph in fourth-century Rome. Because medieval heretics did not triumph, we know their doctrines primarily through the agencies that repressed them. Crespin's sixteenth-centuy Reformed martyrology, published in order to aid a cause that had not yet triumphed, was new, *engagé,* and undeniably effective. At the same time, Crespin completely changed the rules for interpreting a public execution for heresy—at least when the victim's beliefs generally resembled those of Calvin. Rarely do historians encounter a situation in which contemporaries read the same event in such utterly contradictory ways as did the martyrologist and the appellate judge in Valois France.[2] When the *parle-*

mentaire and the propagandist for the Reformed faith each tried to explain how the public execution of heretics fitted God's inscrutable plan, their assumptions were so far apart that they rarely used the same vocabulary. Even when they did, their words did not convey the same meanings.[3]

Crespin's martyrology offered a radically new challenge to French legal authorities by affirming unambiguously in the preface to its first edition that the existence of martyrs constituted "one of the principal marks of the true Church."[4] It also explained how martyrs testified to the power of a living God and obtained "glorious victories" exactly at the moment when they seemed most completely defeated. The power of Crespin's martyrs lies almost entirely in their words, rather than in their heroic actions; not even Michel Foucault can surpass Crespin's paeans to the value and power of discourse. God is always present for faithful martyrs, Crespin insisted, and his first act of grace is to "open their mouths." The testimony of God's martyrs in this century had been so great "that even the reprobates and sworn enemies of the truth have been constrained to shut their mouths" from astonishment at God's marvels. Describing how martyrs should be commemorated, Crespin asserted that one must not venerate the physical remains of their courage in the face of death, their bones and ashes: this was a mistake constantly made by idolaters. Instead, what must be preserved and remembered were their words: "their sayings and writings, their answers [to the judges' questions], their confessions of faith, their final words and exhortations." Two recent innovations of the French judiciary especially aroused Crespin's wrath. Judges, he noted, had adopted the peculiar barbarity of cutting out the tongues of uncooperative prisoners in order to prevent them from making speeches on the scaffold. And they sometimes burned a copy of the trial together with the prisoner, a tactic that not only "extinguished the good cause of these innocents" but also concealed the barbarous iniquity of the judges. Both tactics suppressed the martyrs' spoken and written words, which he strove so valiantly to record.

Words mattered so much to Crespin because they provided the surest way of distinguishing genuine martyrs from the "stooges of Satan" who cluttered the mid-sixteenth century public stage. The devil, using Catholic judges, "has put so many men's minds to sleep and dazzled so many people's eyes, that without discernment they have judged to be heretics those who have spoken truthfully, as well as those whose false doctrines have corrupted the truth." Crespin enumerated these odious trouble-makers—Anabaptists, libertines, Atheists, Epicureans, Servetians—and bemoaned that "the poor Christians, who have commonly been called Lutherans in these times, have carried all this garbage and infection on their shoulders." But finally "the God of all consolation has begun to send his true messengers to pluck out such scandals from his kingdom; for the most part, he has undone the enemies of his Son by the breath of his mouth."

Crespin therefore collected the words of his martyrs "as faithfully and simply as has been possible." Like Calvin trying to expound scripture, Crespin aimed at verbal transparency. Rhetoric was unhelpful; an authorial voice could only interfere with the infinitely more valuable discourse of the martyrs themselves. It probably helped that Crespin had been well trained in law before becoming a publisher in Calvin's Geneva: he understood how legal testimony needed to be presented to be effective. And he was in position to harvest a great many words from his martyrs. Sometimes we have no trouble understanding how Crespin obtained the material he printed. Sixteenth-century prisoners were ordinarily supplied with materials for both reading and writing; Admiral Coligny found the time to read Calvin's *Institutes* while a prisoner of the Spaniards after the battle of St. Quentin. Many of Crespin's martyrs had friends or family in Geneva, who kept anxious track of them when they fell afoul of French law. Pastors and theological students produced a remarkably rich verbal harvest: almost one-fourth of Crespin's first edition came from the five students executed at Lyon in 1553. Crespin's schema, however, did not confine him to documents emanating from his friends. He also had enough informants in the French judiciary to provide him with authentic copies of several parlementary sentences, which he included among his collections of texts. Crespin never knowingly altered a Catholic legal text, although he glossed them carefully in order to guide his readers.

Until now, historians have been unable to measure exactly how much Crespin actually knew about French heresy executions. Scholars have been able to examine only a few specific instances of how he probably obtained his information and how accurate it was.[5] With the evidence now at our disposal about the distribution of heresy executions in Reformation France, it is an informative exercise to compare the picture of executions for "Lutheranism" obtained from the surviving *arrêts* of various French parlements with the picture of martyrdoms presented by Crespin. (See Table 5.) He seems relatively well informed about the earliest handful of "Lutherans" burned by order of the Paris Parlement in the 1520s, where his account can be corroborated from Paris chronicles, but for which no court decisions survive. If Crespin omitted the hermit of 1523 who was deliberately mislabeled as "Lutheran," he reported the three clearest cases of genuine Protestants executed between 1526 and 1529, never misdating an episode by more than one year. Although Crespin correctly identified the first two men executed for heresy at Paris in the early 1530s (one of them came from nearby Savoy, and the other had been arrested after meeting with Guillaume Farel), his information about the affair of the placards in 1534–35 seems woefully inadequate. The martyrologist identified only six of the two dozen "sacramentarians" burned at Paris during the resulting repression, and modern scholarship has established that he never found an authentic copy of one of these famous placards.

However, after criminal *arrêts* from the Paris Parlement first become available in late 1535, Crespin ignored all of their earliest recorded heresy executions. In other parts of France, where recorded heresy executions began in the 1530s, Crespin's grasp seems similarly feeble, unless the victim had been well known to Farel. Significantly, there is no instance between spring 1535 and the death of Claude le Peintre at Paris in 1541 in which Crespin's martyrology and French parlementary *arrêts* agree on the circumstances of any executions for heresy. Although Crespin provides evidence about a few authentic Protestant martyrs who cannot be found in parlementary records, such as the barber from Sancerre who was burned by the Paris Parlement during its autumn session at Angers in 1539,[6] he apparently missed most French heresy executions during the 1530s and provided misleading information about those he did record. Wherever some *arrêts* survive (Paris, Toulouse, Rouen, or Aix), we find scattered heresy executions that remained unknown to sixteenth-century Genevans. Whenever Crespin names someone executed for heresy who can be located in surviving parlementary documentation of the late 1530s, the martyrologist either misdated the event by several years (sometimes by a full decade)[7] or else badly garbled the official charges against the defendant.[8] Although Crespin described five provincial French martyrs correctly in the late 1530s, he provided misleading information about five others, meanwhile overlooking

Table 5.　Crespin and French heresy executions, 1540–1560

Period	Crespin alone	Crespin + *arrêts*	*Arrêts* alone	Crespin total (as %)
1/1540–3/1547	5	9[a]	91	14/110 (13%)
4/1547–12/1554	28	30	86	58/144 (40%)
1/1555–12/1559	38	21	18	59/77 (77%)

Sources: AN, X2a 89–121, X2b 6–8; ADHG, 3368–3430; ADBR, B 5443–59; ADI, B 2023–30; ADG, 1B 210–225; ADS, B 48–60; ADSM, 1B 3004, 3122–52; AN, U 1084; and Romier; all compared with Crespin.

a. I have omitted five instances in which Crespin made errors of five years or more in dating heresy executions: three at Paris, one at Rouen, and one at Toulouse.

at least eighteen more heresy executions mentioned in fragmentarily preserved parlementary archives.

From 1540 until Francis I's death in 1547, Crespin's information about French heresy executions remained grossly inadequate. However, in the early years of Henry II's reign, after he himself had settled in Geneva, his information became significantly better both at Paris and in the provinces. Although he said nothing about the enormous majority of French heresy executions in the early 1540s and made some serious mistakes about those he did mention, Crespin profited from a much better flow of relevant information after 1548, when numerous refugees brought accurate news about several recent executions to him in Geneva. After he published his martyrology in 1554, and especially after Reformed churches arose in France and maintained regular contacts with Geneva, Crespin's information about French heresy executions improved remarkably. Crespin's supplements include over three-fourths of all known French heresy executions after 1555.

Although it would be absurd to suggest that Crespin deliberately misled his readers about the chronology of French heresy prosecutions, his uneven grasp of his material has misled all modern scholars on the French Reformation into assuming that repression of heresy accelerated under Henry II. Given the remarkable growth of the French Protestant movement in the 1550s and its transformation into a well-organized church, this assumption has always seemed perfectly plausible. Crespin's data, easily accessible and widely read for centuries, have powerfully reinforced this impression: the entries in his martyrology average only about three executions per year in the second half of Francis I's reign, but quickly rise to almost ten per year under Henry II as the numbers of French Protestants mushroomed. However, as we now know, the intensity of French parlementary persecution varied *inversely*, not *directly*, with the size and seriousness of the Protestant movement. Crespin and the French parlementary judges moved in religious worlds that were diametrically opposed. Both their respective methods of operation and the respective stories that each had to tell about the dynamics of repression are also diametrically opposed.

Public Abjurations and Social Privilege

Reversing Crespin's attempts at transparency, parlementary judges tried to conceal their motives when judging heretics "arbitrarily." Reconstructing their logic is therefore a much more difficult matter. However, because they left a great deal of indirect evidence, one can make inferences about their priorities in the punishment of heretics. The principal purpose of the judges was less to punish prisoners than to provide an exemplary lesson for the general public, showing royal justice at work chastising unworthy subjects. The most important aspect of punishment was to carry it out in public, with particular variations according to the particular crime. Parlements knew very well that the courts rarely caught more than a small fraction of all offenders, sometimes an infinitesimal fraction (for example, blasphemers). Their priority was therefore to perform "acts of justice" that would impress the largest possible number of people.[9]

If heresy was a novel category of crime for *parlementaires*, it bore some resemblance to other categories with which they were thoroughly familiar. In punishing serious cases of heresy, therefore, they acted much as they had previously when punishing such related crimes as blasphemy against the virginity of Mary or sacrilege exacerbated by selling objects used in worship. As we have seen, such people were hanged and their corpses burned. For that matter, the custom of burning a copy of the trial together with the corpse of the prisoner, which so irritated Crespin in his 1554 preface, had been employed previously with blasphemers and was even customary for a few categories of such "enormous" crimes as bestiality. Less extreme forms of heresy were treated exactly like less severe blasphemy or sacrilege that did not involve desecration of venerated objects. But they too were to be punished in a manner to provide maximum public edification.

Given these priorities, French royal judges adopted another customary feature as the keystone of their public punishments for heresy. Crespin avoids mentioning it except at junctures where it is unavoidable, but it was normally the very first element of any official *arrêt* in which a prisoner had been convicted of relatively serious heresy. It was the shaming-and-atonement ritual called the *amende honorable*. One finds it already in the sentence of the unlucky hermit on 8 August 1523, to be performed in the cathedral of Notre-Dame before Berquin's books were burned outside in the courtyard. One finds it again in a sentence of the Paris Parlement during the first war of religion, to be performed by a repentant Huguenot in the parish church of Montlhéry,[10] and at hundreds of points in between. Exactly how it was performed is difficult to discover, although we know that an *amende honorable* usually preceded a Sunday High Mass in the prisoner's home parish. Judges were extremely explicit about what kind of minimal clothing one was required to wear (no shoes or hats), and about the exact size of the burning expiatory candle that the condemned person was expected to carry during the ceremony. They sometimes insisted that the apology be spoken "in a clear and loud voice." An *amende honorable* for heresy was equivalent to a formal abjuration under canon law. As its name implies, it was a "dishonoring" ceremony, carrying what lawyers called a *note d'infamie*. As social historians have reminded us, "honor" was not a concept confined to the upper classes in the sixteenth century, so the *amende honorable* was a serious matter indeed for someone caught in a trial for heresy. It offered no opportunity to debate or to display the courage of one's religious convictions, which suffices to explain why Crespin avoided mentioning it.

We almost never possess the exact text that the condemned heretic was expected to recite; the two exceptions come from a court (Aix) that rarely imposed this penalty. The first man had been ordered to

confess that stupidly, boldly and indiscreetly I said in the square of Pellissane that "I was a Lutheran and wanted to be one, and that I wished to live and die in Luther's faith. And that there had been a time when I and my companions hadn't dared speak out for fear of being burned, but that now we were maintained and sustained by God through prayer." I now repent having said this and demand pardon of God, the Virgin Mary, and all the saints in paradise, and also of the king and the court.

However, because he refused to perform the ceremony as ordered, this prisoner was then whipped, made a formal apology to the court on his knees, and was sent to the galleys for his disobedience.[11] The second prisoner, a local innkeeper, behaved better. Nine months later he abjured six specific errors at the same cathedral:

that Purgatory did not exist and was never mentioned in Holy Scripture; that one should not pray to any saint in paradise; the images in church are good only after their arms, legs and heads have been cut off to make shoe frames; that one shouldn't go to Mass; that the precious body of Jesus Christ is not in the Holy Sacrament of the Altar and the sacred Host; and of having mocked holy days and Lent by eating prohibited food, and speaking ill of holy relics.

A note reports that he performed the ceremony the following day and paid a fine of fifty livres.[12] He got off lightly, considering that his fifth error made him a *sacramentaire* who qualified for the death penalty. Unfortunately, however, these are the only two instances in which we know exactly what scripts the judges wrote for their prisoners to recite.

Under what circumstances did parlementary justice order its prisoners in heresy cases to perform some form of *amende honorable*? With a convicted heretic, the judges might demand an *amende honorable* before execution in exchange for a less painful or less demeaning death. However, most *amendes honorables* were imposed on convicted heretics who had not been condemned to death. They might be accompanied by various forms of physical punishment: banishment, whipping, further imprisonment, even sometimes, at the parlements of Aix and Toulouse in the 1540s, by a term in the galleys. But very often, the *amende honorable* was itself the principal punishment for a prisoner's heresy. Samples from the two largest parlements suggest that these public *amendes* were far more common than death sentences. (See Table 6.) In every period and at both major courts, parlementary judges ordered more than twice as many *amendes honorables* as death sentences for heresy. After 1550 the congruence in this respect between Paris and Toulouse is remarkable. Despite the lacunae in our sources, we have information on almost six hundred instances of parlements ordering the *amende honorable* for her-

Table 6. *Amendes honorables* for heresy, Paris and Toulouse, 1540–1559

Location and years	Heresy deaths	*Amendes* + physical	*Amendes* alone
Paris (1540–1544)	25	35	45
Paris (1545–1549)	79	86	110
Toulouse (1542–1549)	18	31	21
Paris (1550–1559)	35	27	42
Toulouse (1550–1555)	33	29	40

Sources: AN, X2a 79–117, X2b 10–15; ADHG, B 3368–3406.

esy. After 1552 presidial courts presumably behaved no differently from parlements. Since we know that well over four hundred people were publically executed for heresy in Valois France before 1560, it is probable that approximately a thousand people were ordered to perform public abjurations for heresy during those years. The novelty that one can notice at the Parlement of Bordeaux in 1538, when the judges marched in procession during Holy Week to attend a ceremony featuring eleven public abjurations "for the crime of heresy" on a scaffold placed in front of the local cathedral,[13] must have worn off rapidly, but the procedure continued to be applied with relentless regularity. The Bordeaux tribunal pronounced only ten death sentences for heresy during the 1550s, but ordered thirty-eight *amendes honorables*.[14] Regardless of its effects on the beliefs and behavior of the person performing the *amende,* this spectacle continued to make good public theater. It was much less gory than a public execution. Above all, it was impossible for a prisoner to appear heroic or defiant while performing this ritual.

Although the *amende honorable* was an extremely widespread sanction, a few categories of prisoners charged with heresy almost never performed it. Foreigners, for example, were normally exempted. It was an easy and obvious solution for the judges to expel them from France, but it seemed unnecessary to require them to abjure their heretical doctrines before departing. The fact that most foreigners who were arrested for heresy and eventually judged by parlements were German Lutherans, and thus political allies of Francis I and Henry II, helps explain why they rarely received this particular form of punishment. Of course, the judges might keep them imprisoned for a long time, as happened to Andreas

Melanchthon at Bordeaux. If there were aggravating circumstances such as heretical writings composed by the prisoner himself, they might even make him do an *amende* and burn his confiscated books.[15] However, judges rarely encountered foreigners among their heresy prisoners and generally treated them rather mildly. Ordinarily it made little sense to order such a shaming ritual for people with no roots in a French parish.

Foreigners also presented procedural problems. Confronted with a stubborn Frisian Protestant arrested at Nogent-sur-Seine, Parisian judges relied to a great extent on written reports from the Faculty of Theology and noted that German diplomats had interceded on his behalf. They had to interrogate him in Latin; judging from the amount of text crossed out and emended in their record, the exercise strained the competence of their clerk and perhaps of the judges as well, although in the end they concluded that the witnesses who had accused him of "sacramentarianism" were even less competent Latinists. They released him with a solemn warning (also delivered in Latin) to avoid "scandalous speech" while in France.[16] At the same time, the Paris Parlement interrogated another Frisian and the nobleman from Poitou who employed him. This Frisian servant had been taught French by an employer who presumably knew some German, since he owned a copy of Luther's translation of the New Testament, along with psalters by Marot and Bèze and a Calvinist catechism. The nobleman, who possessed a couple of abbeys, first denied that he was in holy orders but later admitted that he had become a subdeacon more than twenty years before. He admitted visiting Germany and once saying that he wished to live as the Germans did. The servant claimed he had never been taught about transubstantiation or the practice of confession. The court released him but upheld the nobleman's original sentence; like the German law student at Toulouse, he performed an *amende honorable* (now at the cathedral of Notre-Dame in Paris), watched his books burn, and received a solemn warning about "frequenting countries and people who have been separated from the holy Catholic faith and from union with the Roman church." Because he had been ordained, the Poitevin nobleman was then handed to ecclesiastical justice.[17]

Almost without exception, whenever one encounters a nobleman among these heresy defendants, one can observe "class justice" in operation. Noblemen very rarely underwent the indignities of a public *amende honorable*. By testing the forbearance of President Séguier, Charles du Berger became an exception. This prisoner owned too many prohibited books, was too ostentatiously Germanophilic, lied about his clerical status, and wrote out his own translations of some favorite Lutheran texts from the New Testament. But even du Berger performed his *amende* far from his native region, among a crowd of strangers in the capital. The solution that Raymond Mentzer noted among several upper-class heresy defendants in Languedoc was probably more customary. Their monetary fines were sometimes heavy (one prisoner was assessed the huge sum of 2,000 livres), but their public humiliations were softened as much as possible. For example, two university-trained physicians performed their abjurations in a judge's chambers in order to avoid the *note d'infamie,* and a nobleman did likewise.[18]

Noblemen and their kin were treated in much the same way by other parlements. The fate of a Norman gentleman and his family, arrested in 1547 for harboring a notorious heretical preacher in their home for ten or twelve days and listening to his sermons, seems representative of how royal justice treated the second estate. The *seigneur* was fined the hefty sum of 400 livres, plus a 20-livre donation to a Rouen nunnery. He was further ordered to subsidize two special sermons in his village church refuting the heretical propositions that had been spelled out in his trial, using a preacher named by his local bishop and with a royal official present to ensure compliance. Although the parlement's sentence also included a stiff warning, its principal operative clause was that the compensatory exercise—orthodox sermons obliterating the heretical ones made in his own household—entailed no *note d'infamie.* Honor was saved for himself, his wife, and his sister.[19]

Erasing the heretical stains made by noblemen could even be quite literal. At the end of 1545 the seneschal of Maine arrested a squire (*écuyer*) on charges of heretical speech, compounded by the unusual offense of defacing the interior of his parish church with heretical writings. The official sentence describes in extremely precise detail the locations of both offensive scripts inside the church, including their exact height from the floor: one was four feet up, the other four and a half, one being near the bench where the squire and his wife habitually sat. But, exactly reversing the martyrologist's perspective, it says absolutely nothing about what words had been written on the church walls. No punishment was imposed on the squire beyond the obligation to prove that he had effaced his writings within six weeks, and this prisoner was released on his own recognizance.[20]

If social considerations enabled noblemen to avoid performing an "infamous" *amende honorable* in front of people who knew them, similar considerations operated even more strongly in favor of upper-class women. For example, four *demoiselles* were judged by the Parlement of Bordeaux. The first, charged with "scandalous propositions" against the traditions of the Church, walked away after receiving a warning and paying a fine of only ten livres. The next, who may have been related to the notorious La Rochelle judge Claude d'Angleur, defended herself vigorously by producing additional witnesses, but still had to pay a sizable fine of 100 livres. The other two *demoiselles* were released because of insufficient evidence.[21] Four nuns arrested by the Parlement of Toulouse suffered even less. The first to be investigated was a prioress in Lauragais, who employed a crypto-Protestant business manager. Her family connections got her case and that of her three male managers evoked to the royal privy council, where their indictments were quickly quashed.[22] The other three had fled their convents but were soon captured.[23] They were quickly handed over to ecclesiastical justice, doubtless in order to reduce scandal, while the men who had helped them escape received very stiff penalties: one was executed, while another narrowly escaped burning.[24] Upper-class women could also use their considerable resources to strike back at accusers. When a *demoiselle* was convicted of heresy at Le Mans in 1554, sentenced to perform two *amendes honorables* and fined 200 livres, the deputy prosecutor appealed *a minima* to the Paris Parlement. But he made a huge mistake, because the high court subsequently investigated her countercharges of perjured testimony. Nineteen months after her original conviction, she was released with the right to countersue her principal accusers for trial costs and defamation.[25]

If noblewomen got off lightly in heresy cases, so did their humbler sisters. At Bordeaux, for example, women performed only two of the thirty-eight *amendes honorables* decreed in heresy trials during the 1550s; one of them had confessed during torture that she had avoided both confession and communion at Easter.[26] Things were not very different in Languedoc. Although a woman was deeply involved in the scandal at Ganges in 1542 and received a three-year banishment for "scandalous and reprobate speech" in addition to her *amende honorable,* one finds only three more women among the next hundred public *amendes* ordered by the Toulouse Parlement in heresy cases.[27] It says much about the legal and social status of women in the Midi that two wives, whose households had hosted clandestine sermons by a heretical preacher, were ordered to attend the *amendes honorables* performed by their husbands, but not to speak themselves.[28] Northern France was not greatly different. One finds a half-dozen women among the eighty people performing *amendes honorables* for heresy by order of the Paris Parlement between 1540 and 1544, but only the last instance also involved serious physical punishment (perpetual banishment from the kingdom).[29] They were matched by another half-dozen women who atoned for their heresies by appearing at special Masses with expiatory candles but without making public apologies.[30] In a subsequent sample from Paris in the 1550s, one finds three women among seventy *amendes honorables* for heresy.[31] Two of them had originally been sentenced to death. Another woman who had been sentenced to death ended up under house arrest without public punishment after her brother appealed.[32]

Both noblemen and women of all classes were poorly represented among French heresy prisoners and therefore among Protestant martyrs. Even the exceptions are revealing. As we have seen, a couple of noblemen from Normandy were put to death for heresy in the 1540s, but both died outside their native province. A squire from the Beauce, Mathurin de Boisguyon, wound up being beheaded at Paris in 1545 despite letters of pardon. The summary of his offenses notes that he and his son "had said and repeated that one should not pray to the Virgin Mary and the saints, because they had no power," and both had committed "several insolences in their parish church." However, it seems evident that the lord of la Rosaye lost his head not for his heresies but for "having struck the effigy and representation of the king."[33] Women similarly lost their lives on heresy charges only under unusual circumstances. One finds three women among thirteen Waldensians executed for heresy during Jean de Roma's campaign in Provence in the early 1530s, because there Waldensianism was a deeply-rooted tradition among many intermarried clans. Since early French Protestantism was not family or clan oriented, few women emerged as major suspects.

Crespin noted female martyrs whenever he could, because he was concerned to find examples of theologically correct heroism among persons of all nations, ages, and sexes. He commemorated the Parisian schoolmistress known as *la Catelle,* the only woman burned in the aftermath of the Placards Affair. He knew about the wives of two leaders, caught in the roundup of "Lutherans" at Langres and executed in 1548, and about a widow martyred at Orléans the following year. But Crespin omitted four other women executed for heresy between 1544 and 1549 by order of the Paris Parlement;[34] he also missed the two women executed for heresy in 1546 and 1547 by order of the Parlement of Toulouse,[35] and a Frenchwoman martyred at Rouen after fleeing from Mary Tudor's recatholicized England. However, being very well informed in the late 1550s, Crespin noted the final two women to be martyred at Paris, including the wealthy young widow executed in the aftermath of the Rue St.-Jacques affair. Despite his eagerness to discover women who could provide examples of steadfast courge for his female readers, Crespin's collection includes fewer than half of the female martyrs in Reformation France. Their total, however, is quite small. Overall, women accounted for less than 5 percent of all French martyrs before 1560— about the same as their ratio of *amendes honorables* for heresy. Except for a few autonomous women in unusual situations, early "Lutheranism" was overwhelmingly a man's crime.

The *Auto-da-fé* in France

In order to be effective, repression sometimes required far more than a simple *amende honorable* before Sunday Mass at the local church. The most elaborate spectacle ever undertaken by French royal justice in pursuit of heresy during the Reformation era was staged at Meaux in October 1546. It deserves to be called an *auto-da-fé,* because the Spanish label fits the French circumstances almost perfectly. Ironically, the Spaniards themselves were not greatly worried about Protestants at this time, although the Aragonese Holy Office complained in 1546 about the religious dangers coming from French immigrants. Spain did not stage a specifically anti-"Lutheran" *auto-da-fé* until August 1559. Thirteen years previously, however, the French had serendipitously adapted the essential features of this Spanish ceremony, hitherto used exclusively against descendants of Jewish *conversos,* and employed it against Protestants.

Meaux had been a trouble spot for conservative Catholics ever since the days of Bishop Briçonnet and Lefevre d'Etaples, but what happened there on 8 September 1546 was unprecedented, and it provoked an unprecedented official response. A large clandestine congregation was captured during its worship service by a handful of royal officials.[36] Ironically, our first documented glimpse of the existence and operations of a Protestant church on French soil is provided by the attempt to eradicate it. Sixty-two prisoners were immediately taken to Paris and dumped into the Parlement's prison. They were interrogated and judged with all deliberate speed by the court's Chambre des Vacances, which sat during the traditional vacation months of September and October. In just four weeks, all of them were ready for sentencing. The court thereupon assembled an arsenal of ingredients in order to stage the most theatrical set of punishments ever inflicted during the French Reformation. Decreed on 4 October, these events took place at Meaux on 7 and 8 October.

The Parisian judges identified fourteen men as the ringleaders of this congregation and condemned them to death by fire. Four more, somewhat less deeply involved, were ordered to perform an *amende honorable* with nooses around their necks before being whipped and banished from France for five years. Eighteen other rank-and-file members, including five women, were also ordered to perform *amendes honorables* at the local cathedral of St. Etienne. Another nine men and three women participated in the special commemorative procession, but suffered no further public indignities. Five women were released after solemn warnings about staying away from suspicious gatherings; six more were released outright. A most unsual punishment was devised for a lad whom they judged too young to be burned, but too stubborn to be spared. Louis Picquery was to be strung up by his armpits, facing the fourteen men being executed, then taken down, whipped, and placed in a monastery. The prisoners were then returned to Meaux in two carts, with the fourteen men who had been condemned to death riding separately. The prisoners were accompanied by two Sorbonne theologians, who attempted to persuade the fourteen to recant in exchange for a gentler death. The Parisian public executioner also accompanied them, since killing fourteen people at one time far surpassed the local resources. As soon as everyone arrived at Meaux, the executioner set to work torturing the fourteen in order to extract any names of additional suspects, but he apparently had no better luck than the theologians.

On 7 October the spectacle opened with the public executions of all fourteen men, burned in a large circle in the center of the main market of Meaux, facing the site of their secret church. Those sentenced to death had the choice between showing signs of repentance (it was enough to whisper a few words of contrition into the ears of one of the numerous clerics present) or remaining steadfast. Those who repented would be strangled before their corpses were burned; those who did not would have their tongues cut out before being burned, in order to avoid the "blasphemy" of defiant last words. Two sources from opposing religious camps describe what transpired next; Crespin claimed that eight men repented and six lost their tongues, while a local Catholic counted seven in each group.[37] Our sources describe a musical cacaphony during the executions. Crespin reports that the victims, those who still had some use of their tongues, sang Marot's Psalms in their agony. But the Catholic source reports that young Piquery, hanging in front of them under the watchful eye of the two theologians, helped the priests sing such Catholic hymns as the *Salve Regina* and particularly, since this congregation had celebrated its own communion services, *O Salutatis Hosta.* The executions at this French *auto-da-fé* included two details of particular barbarity that were completely unknown to the Spanish Inquisition. The Spaniards, who almost never burned people alive, never pulled out anyone's tongue and never tortured an adolescent in public. Barbarism, however, can be effective. The Catholic chronicler tells us that young Piquery became a zealous convert who was employed by the monastery after his sentence had expired, and was buried there.

One day after the executions came the religious festival. Crespin's account drips with sarcasm. "The adversaries," he says, "ordered a magnificant general procession, where they displayed their Host, accompanied by innumerable torches and candles in full daylight. When all this pomp reached the site of the executions, where the fires had not yet stopped burning, they put down their so-called Host [*ladite oublie*]. Then Doctor Picard mounted his platform, beneath a pavilion made of cloth of gold, to shield him from the sun, and began to rage against those who had been executed." The Catholic source offers more detail about the procession. It was headed by the schoolchildren of Meaux, followed by three thousand adults, then the clergy, then the Host. Immediately behind the Host marched, two by two, the prisoners condemned to make *amendes honorables;* behind them came various local notables carrying torches. While Doctor Picard was preaching in the marketplace, the barefoot prisoners huddled together on a separate platform facing the crowd, just as in a Spanish *auto.* Afterward, they crossed the river to the cathedral, where all thirty-four, each carrying a two-pound candle, knelt before the principal door and repeated in a loud voice that "stupidly, boldly, and indiscreetly they had attended the meetings in Etienne Mangin's house in order to hear Pierre le Clerc's sermons, for which they ask pardon of God, the king, and the judges." Then everyone crowded inside to hear Mass.

One day before the executions, 6 October, Etienne Mangin's house on the marketplace, the site of the church and of the arrests, had been demolished by special command of the Paris Parlement. They further ordered that a chapel, dedicated to the Holy Sacrament of the Altar, be erected on the site, where a High Mass should be celebrated every Thursday morning at seven in honor of the Eucharist. Its cost would be covered by profits from selling the confiscated property of the fourteen men who were executed. However, this expiatory chapel was never built. The Catholic chronicler explained that the cost of building the special equipment for the executions and the procession ate up nearly all the income from confiscations. Parlement had foreseen this possibility; it ordered the bishop of Meaux, whose pastoral negligence had enabled this heresy to flourish, to make up any additional costs for constructing the chapel. He quietly ignored their ruling. Meanwhile Protestantism continued to flourish at Meaux, especially in the neighborhood where Mangin had lived. Thirteen years after the *auto-da-fé*, sixteen additional local Protestants were executed at the main market of Meaux by order of the Paris Parlement—but this time only in effigy, because they had fled to Calvin's Geneva. Perhaps more significantly, the Meaux clergy cancelled their annual procession in honor of St. Simon and St. Jude that summer "because of insults from heretics."[38]

The great *auto-da-fé* of Meaux failed as propaganda. Two months later, the Parlement of Paris burned a man named Jacques Fayol together with "the apology and defense, written and signed in his own hand . . . for the excuse and defense of the unhappy and pestiferous heretics recently condemned and executed in the city of Meaux." It was, they said, a book "containing a real form of both divine and human *lèse-majesté*," and they made strenuous efforts at both Paris and Meaux to discover if any additional copies could be found.[39] They succeeded so well that we have no idea what Fayol actually wrote. However, the French government approved the printing of its parlementary *arrêt* against the congregation of Meaux, evidently believing it made effective propaganda.[40]

Within two years after capturing the Protestant congregation at Meaux, Catholic authorities uncovered a much smaller congregation at Langres. Starting when two peddlers of Protestant literature denounced their customers, the authorities finally caught an itinerant preacher who had employed at least two aliases.[41] Under torture he apparently revealed the names of his principal contacts at Langres. Several arrests followed, although some key suspects managed to escape. The Parlement condemned four principal prisoners to be executed together at Paris in August 1548, the preacher being placed on a scaffold slightly higher than the others. A month later, a smaller-scale *auto-da-fé* was staged at the main market of Langres. This time the religious festivities (High Mass, special sermon expounding the doctrine of transubstantiation, denunciations of secret assemblies and of pernicious books in French, *amendes honorables* by two women kneeling in the cathedral) preceded the public executions. Eight people, three of them women, perished together with a large quantity of heretical books. All were strangled first. One woman who had made her *amende* was compelled to watch the executions "kneeling on a scaffold . . . erected in a highly visible spot near the place of execution by fire." Crespin's account is unusually brief; "through the malice of the judges," he complained, "the rest of their deeds cannot be recounted." Once again the house in which this congregation had met was demolished. But this time the bishop of Langres actually built the commemorative chapel, as ordered, on the site of the clandestine church, where it stood until 1825. In 1549 he also founded a confraternity of the Holy Sacrament at Langres. Though less durable than the chapel, it may have contributed even more to keeping Langres a safely Catholic city after 1560. Here, with a smaller congregation and a shallower local tradition of religious innovation, repression through public rituals seemed to work.

After 1550 there is no evidence that a French parlement arranged anything resembling an *auto-da-fé* on those rare occasions when they judged groups of convicted Protestants. In fact the surviving documentation suggests that they deliberately avoided staging such spectacles. In the summer of 1555, for example, the Paris Parlement had to judge such a group from the town of Aurillac, located deep in the Auvergne in the furthest reaches of its huge district.[42] There were sixteen defendants in all, only six of whom had been taken to Paris. Four of them had been sentenced to death by fire, as had ten others (including their leader) who had escaped from jail in Aurillac. Because this group had held a communion service, the local court had ordered a full-dress ceremony, replete with a bonfire of heretical books seized from the defendants, a procession involving every schoolboy over the age of seven, and a special sermon in honor of the Eucharist and the Virgin Mary. Following the precedents of Meaux and Langres, they had also ordered that the place where this blasphemous ritual had been performed be destroyed and replaced by a commemorative chapel.

The Parlement, however, doused the flames of persecution, "having regard to the contrition and repentance" of the four main prisoners. Although they never said so, they were doubtless also inclined to mercy on account of the defendants' youth. All four were students, and their communion service, presided over by their regent, had been held in a room of the municipal *collège*. The Parisian court therefore upheld several provisions of the original sentence—burning the books, giving a special sermon on the Eucharist after High Mass, even maintaining the provision that every schoolboy over seven march in the special procession, attend the Mass and hear the sermon, and later have his schoolbooks inspected at the local royal court. But no one was to die. The four main prisoners marched in the procession with ropes around their necks, made *amendes honorables,* and further "revoked and abjured" their errors to a representative of their diocesan bishop. But none got so much as a public whipping afterward. The oldest boy was sent to a monastery for five years; two others were sent to monasteries for two years, while the fourth was released after the ceremony. The two remaining defendants in Paris were released "into the custody of their relatives, if any can be found in these parts." In a sense, the person who lost this court case was the bishop of St. Flour. Not only was he required to pay the cost of lodging and feeding the three boys sent to live in monasteries, but he also had to pay 240 livres for subsidizing a Sorbonne theologian, who would take a one-year tour of duty preaching throughout his mountainous diocese, trying to counter the heretics who were already preaching there.

The judges' consideration for youthful prisoners charged with heresy, demonstrated in Auvergne, reappeared two years later in Savoy. A youth from the environs of Geneva named Balthasar Sacqueponeur had been arrested for creating a serious scandal at Chambéry; his three associates escaped.[43] The local parlement ordered him, "without regard to the youth and tender age of said Balthasar" (but in fact for exactly that reason), to perform an *amende honorable* with a noose around his neck at his parish church. Afterward he was to be hanged by his armpits for half an hour, as young Picquery had been at Meaux, but with a significant difference. At the boy's feet would be a "fire of faggots," which was to be lit "in such a way that nevertheless said Sacqueponeur would not be personally damaged in any way." The public executioner of this provincial capital was therefore expected to carry out a bogus execution, using real fire and a real person. The court also forbade anyone in Savoy from taking servants or apprentices "coming from Geneva or other places suspect in the faith," ordering this decree to be read throughout the province but especially in the districts closest to Geneva.

When the Parlement of Paris received well over a hundred prisoners in the aftermath of the Rue St. Jacques affair in 1557, they carried out several executions, but never in groups of more than two or three. Unlike their behavior at Meaux or Langres a decade previously, they now avoided any major auxiliary commemorations; the brief age of the French *auto-da-fé* had definitively ended. During the early 1550s French *parlementaires* changed their habits of punishing convicted heretics in other ways, which effectively imposed silence on their unrepentant victims and thereby frustrated Crespin's desire to commemorate their final words. Crespin's preface expressed his irritation at the recent custom of gagging unrepentant heretics being led to execution, but this was simply a less barbarous method of preventing unsuitable speech by someone being executed than the previous alternative of cutting out the tongue—and easier for the public executioner to perform beforehand.

After 1550 French parlements also made increasing use of effigies in order to inflict symbolic public punishment on notorious heretics. Prisoners were passive in *amendes honorables* and speechless if gagged, but wreaking havoc on a piece of cardboard with someone's name on it was the ultimate form through which early modern Europe turned people into objects. It was often a legal preliminary to confiscating a fugitive's property; moreover, circumstances sometimes demanded some kind of exemplary punishments for heretics who were safely beyond the court's reach. Though done occasionally in the late 1540s,[44] it became more common after 1550, when many Protestants had fled to Geneva or other foreign destinations. We know of a few instances (for example, at Noyon in 1552 or Narbonne in 1554) in which parlementary judges arranged spectacles involving large groups of absentees executed in effigy. Although many of these absentees were wealthy men, it is highly unlikely that their effigies were burned for fiscal reasons. Financial motives are all but invisible in the history of French heresy prosecutions; at least before the religious wars, effigy executions were not routine gestures permitting public officials to seize the known property of a suspected heretic. Moreover, the provision about confiscating the property of convicted heretics was sloppily enforced. Although the French crown frequently awarded confiscated assets of convicted heretics to various petitioners,[45] most important movable assets—including offices in church and state—eluded its grasp. Laurent de Normandie, for example, sold his royal office before moving to Geneva. His successor played naïve when interrogated by the Paris Parlement and was briefly suspended, but soon resumed enjoying the fruits of his investment. Much the same thing happened to the man who bought Theodore de Bèze's benefice.

Dialogues between Judges and Prisoners

In the 1550s, French judges can be glimpsed engaging in discussions with their heresy prisoners, thanks to the fortuitous survival of a few interrogations, or *plumitifs*, regarding these prisoners at Paris and Rouen. Most of these cases involve lay judges asking relatively straightforward religious questions to lay prisoners, with neither side trying to develop the elaborate theological positions that fill so many pages of Crespin's collection. But the impression these documents give is quite different from either the laconic *arrêts* of Lizet's Chambre Ardente or from the copious discourses published by Crespin. These theologically untrained judges attempted to establish degrees of guilt among their heresy prisoners—their primary concern in a system of arbitrary justice which gave them enormous latitude in passing sentence. Under interrogation, most prisoners displayed some degree of repentance, evasiveness, or both, so that calibrating the extent of their guilt was no easy matter.

Four prisoners charged with heresy sat in the prison of the Rouen Parlement in the spring of 1552.[46] Three of them had arrived together in April, using the same lawyer to make an appeal *comme d'abus* from the judge of the archbishop of Rouen, who had declared that all three had "fallen into manifest heresy" and should be handed to the secular arm.[47] With two prisoners, establishing sufficient cause for imposing a death penalty was a relatively simple matter. One, imprisoned since August 1551, had been caught carrying heretical books and suspicious correspondence from Geneva to England. He claimed to have been born in Switzerland, but the judges believed that he was actually a French subject from Guyenne.[48] What really decided his case, however, was his flat refusal to make a confession or to accept communion at Easter. More-over, he had encouraged other prisoners to act the same way, saying that Catholic communion was a "stupid abuse" and making similar talk "full of scandalous words and teaching evil doctrines." Proselytizing within prison was dangerous and, in his case, fatal. One of the three who arrived at Easter was also sentenced to death relatively quickly. He was a recidivist, a barber from Rouen condemned for heresy less than four years earlier.[49] He admitted having lived in England, Naples, and Geneva, but was evasive about everything from his age to the nature of the previous charges against him, and unconvincing about his religious behavior at Geneva. Memory lapses never impress judges, so they upheld his death sentence from the archbishop's court.

The other two who had appealed jointly with him in April proved far harder to judge. The younger man, Jean Hyllard, appealed his condemnation to perform an *amende honorable;* he had been charged with associating with notorious heretics, asserting that a sermon was better than a Mass, and denying the existence of purgatory. He explained that "a sermon was given in French, which was easier to understand than the Mass," and denied saying that souls go directly either to heaven or to hell. Hyllard concluded his first interrogation by asking God's pardon and "said that he wished to live and die according to the commandments of God and the Church." Meanwhile he got into serious trouble by blaspheming at a meal brought to him in prison by the woman for whom he worked. At his first interrogation, his judges asked him why he had "renounced God, saying that he had no more power than a dog" and had affirmed something "in spite of God and his old whore of a mother." Hyllard "had no memory of having said those words" and may have been drunk on the wine his mistress brought him, but the judges did not believe his excuses.

Mandin le Roy, a local clothier in his late fifties with wife and family, claimed he had been falsely accused by his enemies, although he admitted fraternizing with people who denied the divinity of Christ. He dodged the major question about the Eucharist by saying "that it's not his business to talk or dispute about it" and responded to a follow-up question about Christ's body by remarking that "he believed what St. John wrote in his Gospel." When asked exactly what St. John had said, he waffled an answer "that he is no cleric, but believes what the Church says about it." He answered a question about pilgrimages in terms close to

Luther's ("it was better that people stayed in their homes"), knowing that this was a minor doctrinal issue.

On 29 April each defendant was given a different attorney, and on 10 May the Parlement dismissed their appeals *comme d'abus*. All remained in prison. In July Hyllard was tried by the *bailli* of Rouen on charges of blasphemy and sentenced to be burned; he again appealed to Parlement on the grounds that the witnesses against him were unreliable. Meanwhile the clothier still refused to answer any questions about the Eucharist, denied even knowing where Geneva was, gave orthodox opinions about the perpetual virginity of Mary, and persisted in his views about pilgrimages. In mid-July the Parlement deadlocked on Hyllard's case and postponed both men's final sentences. We learn nothing more about their fate until January 1553, when Hyllard's rapporteur obtained a majority in favor of upholding the *bailli's* death sentence for blasphemy plus heresy.[50] Meanwhile a further interrogation of Le Roy on 17 January continued to be indecisive. He denied making "sacramentarian" remarks about the Eucharist, but again gave inconclusive answers during detailed questioning on the uniqueness of Christ's Passion. Asked about Hyllard, he replied that "this was a horrible man, whom he didn't wish to discuss." Once again, his sentence was postponed. There is no record of any further questioning, but on 13 March the judges finally voted to release him, after approximately a year spent in prison.[51] The evidence against le Roy remained inconclusive. No matter how often the judges questioned him, he would not give satisfactory answers to their main questions. Their logic must be inferred; but they did not wish to torture him, had ample precedent for counting imprisonment as a type of punishment, and presumably concluded that he had suffered enough for his faults.

The *plumitifs* not only shed light on the way judges assessed degrees of guilt and thus determined levels of punishment for prisoners charged with heresy, but they also complement some of Crespin's accounts of martyrdoms by presenting a different side of the story. In particular, the interrogations of two men, Jean Filleul and Julien Lesveillé, both sentenced to death after appealing to the Paris Parlement and finally executed in January 1555, provide invaluable evidence about the ways in which Crespin fashioned his martyrs. His account of their martyrdom, which appeared soon afterward in his 1556 edition, seems absolutely typical.[52] Crespin knew a fair amount about them, because both men had lived in Geneva and were taking their families to live there when they were captured.

Crespin's account bristles with drama and Reformed theology. It opens with a cautionary tale revealing "the ruses that *prévots des maréchaux* employ to trap the poor faithful," explaining how the officers of Bourbonnais tricked Filleul and Lesveillé into admitting that they were taking a boy and girl with them to Geneva. He immediately questioned them about the Eucharist, and then touched such other major theological issues as the Mass, purgatory, and confession; Crespin summarized their duly signed answers at length. The *prévot* thereupon turned them and their confessions of faith over to the nearest royal court. The presiding judge questioned them on the same topics and heard the same answers. As required, he then consulted a panel of lawyers to advise him in passing sentence. Crespin informs us that their opinions were sharply divided, most apparently preferring to sentence them to perpetual banishment from France with confiscation of their property, "if any could be found." But the presiding *lieutenant criminel* ruled that both should be burned alive after performing *amendes honorables*. Filleul and Lesveillé promptly appealed his sentence to the Paris Parlement. Crespin tells us about the sudden death of the *prévot des maréchaux* who had trapped them, which occurred while both prisoners were en route to Paris.

However, his account passes very quickly over what happened to them at the Parlement of Paris. He says only that "however closely they were examined" at Paris, "God gave them invincible power and constancy. For whatever favors their friends did, whatever letters they obtained by which the king ordered that the whole trial be done over afresh, paying no heed to the sentence, still they in no way varied from the truth, but always persisted in their confessions." Then he passes directly to what happened after they returned to St. Pierre le Moûtier on 15 January 1555. His narrative emphasizes only their treacherous capture and unjust condemnation, the death of the trickster who entrapped them, and their heroic end. The most remarkable part of the martyrologist's tale is its assertion that "the Lord manifestly revealed to all those who were present at the execution, that he did not attach the power of speech to the member of the tongue. Because after theirs had been cut off, God gave them the power of speech." And Crespin records the last words of these martyrs, heard as they were being attached to be burned: "Farewell, sin, flesh, world, and devil; nevermore can they hold us." Here is a Calvinist miracle, the power of discourse given to two men whose tongues had just been cut off.[53] The Parlement of Paris remains the silent party in this transaction, although they held the power of life and death for Filleul and Lesveillé.

The *plumitifs* of December 1554 offer an unusually rich account of what transpired between Filleul and Lesveillé's arrival and first interrogations in early December and their final sentence on 18 December.[54] The judges wasted no time, interrogating Filleul on 4 December and Lesveillé the following day. Filleul explained that he came from Berry, had been married eight years before, and had lived for three years in Geneva. He insisted he was no cleric and had never been tonsured, although he had attended school. Asked about his religious beliefs, he answered that "he believed in God and the saints, and in the Old and New Testaments." But their next question raised the burning issue: "Did he believe that Our Lord is in the Host?" He answered that "he didn't know and didn't understand the question." Prodded again, he said "that he didn't know what to say, except what God had said about it." Asked whether confession was a good thing, he answered "that he confessed every day." At this point the session apparently ended, and the royal prosecutor requested that they proceed with his trial and investigate the issue of his ordination.

On 5 December came Lesveillé's turn. He first explained that he had gone to Geneva with his family for their spritual health, "because they no longer swear or blaspheme there." They asked him about Christ's presence in the Eucharist, but he too evaded giving a direct answer: "says he knows nothing about how to answer." He explained to his judges how he had been tricked by the *prévot des maréchaux* into believing that he would not be punished for admitting that he was going to Geneva. His judges, however, repeated their questions about the Host two or three times, but again received the same nonanswer. He similarly refused to answer their question about the necessity of confession before communion. They briefly changed to a noncontroversial subject and asked his occupation; Lesveillé answered that he was a needlemaker (*esguilletier*) and his companion was a cabinetmaker (*menuisier*). Asked how long it had been since he had taken communion, he refused to answer, other than to admit that "he had been at Geneva for a long time and they didn't do an elaborate Easter." Their final question sounded ominous: "the faith that he had learned at Geneva, did he want to leave it or not?" But

Lesveillé dodged it the same way that he avoided any other major issue: "he didn't wish to say anything more."

The judges then summoned Filleul and again put him under oath. "Had he thought over what he had been reproached about, and would he uphold the faith of Jesus Christ and his church?" This was obviously a far easier formula for a Calvinist to accept, so he responded that "he believed in the faith of Christ Jesus and in the holy scriptures." He repeated that he was not a priest. The judges then read from his confessions made to the *prévot des maréchaux,* but he responded that "he had not said that, and that he followed what God and the holy scriptures had ordered." The judges then returned to another lengthy cat-and-mouse game over the Eucharist and the practice of auricular confession, once again without obtaining anything satisfactory. The session closed with the summoning of the royal prosecutor, whom the judges questioned about the procedural irregularities in their trial at St. Pierre le Moûtier. It transpired that the diversity of opinions among the lawyers had not been resolved, and that one had been so irritated by the judge's high-handedness that he refused to sign the official record. At this point the Parisian judges, led by President Séguier, voted eight to two to postpone their sentence in order to resolve the problem of faulty procedure, a favorite concern of theirs.

On 7 December the royal prosecutor petitioned to finish their trial. Four days later the matter came up again, and many different opinions were recorded. One judge, DuDrac, wanted to throw out the whole trial and begin a new one, although he believed that the defendants should probably be strangled and burned. Another judge, de la Rosiere, spoke in favor of a lesser penalty than death. The two presidents, speaking last, preferred the death penalty, but added that they should seek advice at court about the procedural problems before passing any sentence. This resolution was duly passed. The same resolution is repeated in a brief entry on the following day, 12 December. Three days later, after reading the report of the royal prosecutor, President Séguier again insisted on approaching the king before resolving the case, and two judges (DuDrac and the rapporteur, Maulevert) were chosen for this mission. We do not know exactly what they learned. Our next entry in the *plumitifs,* three days later (18 December), once again consists of interrogations of both Filleul and Lesveillé. It was apparently fairly brief, once again pivoting on the Eucharist and the practice of confession. The last entry on Filleul is tantalizing: "he was admonished that he said he had no great knowledge or letters and nevertheless he said . . . [the rest is blank]." Lesveillé's recorded answers offer a perfect example of stonewalling: "said he wouldn't answer that"; "said he wouldn't say anything more"; "said he had nothing to say about it and wouldn't answer it"; "said he had nothing to say." The judges (who never contemplated using torture in cases like these) could not coax even the slightest semblance of discourse out of either defendant.

They then dismissed both prisoners and proceeded to vote their sentence. The rapporteur, as always, spoke first, proposing to "burn them and attach them to a pole and strangle them first." DuDrac, who voted next, supported this opinion, as did seven other judges including both presidents, Séguier and Baillet. However, one judge (Bouette) voted to "send them to a doctor [of theology] to admonish and convert them." Another voted for banishment. But nine to two was a decisive majority, so President Séguier began summing up their official sentence: "send them to the country, burn them on a post, and strangle them." At this point Bouette intervened to propose an amendment, knowing that their property would be confiscated: "make provision from their goods to instruct their children, if they have any," and President Séguier immediately supported the idea. The rapporteur then proposed inserting the customary clause that both men be tortured before their executions in order to acquire additional information about their acquaintances; it received general assent. Someone then added another ordinary precaution for such cases: "additionally, to cut off their tongues before the execution if they keep making scandalous remarks." From their confiscated property, forty livres would be reserved to help provide their children with a proper Christian education. When this sentence was entered into the official register that same day, however, it carried one further postscript: the *bailli* of St. Pierre le Moûtier was ordered to appear in person before them at Paris in order to answer questions about his unusual procedural methods.

The pieces of this particular puzzle fit together quite well. Filleul and Lesveillé were indeed martyred in the Nivernais in January 1555. We will never know what they said, or tried to say, after the hangman cut out their tongues, or tried to cut them out. But we have persuasive evidence of what they said (mostly, what they refused to say) on the famous interrogation stool used by the Parlement of Paris. We can understand why the judges behaved as they did, why President Séguier, soon to emerge as a leader of the moderate faction in the Parlement, delayed the prisoners' fate. We can see the process by which eleven appellate-court judges cobbled together a final ruling that punished both prisoners for their obstinacy, but also condemned their first judge for his arrogance. Since nothing in Crespin's account contradicts anything in the *plumitifs*, or vice versa, the general reliability of source materials provided by both opposing camps is enhanced, while their respective silences are often filled in. In different ways, both Protestant and Catholic accounts provide reliable information about the shortcomings of French justice, such as the unethical manner in which Filleul and Lesveillé were captured by the *prévot des maréchaux* or their flawed trial before the royal judge of St. Pierre le Moûtier, who made an embarrassing midwinter trip to Paris at his own expense in consequence.

Seldom can one find such a neat fit as with Filleul and Lesveillé. Sometimes even when we are fortunate enough to possess a *plumitif* to complement the entry in Crespin, as with Guillaume Néel, another Genevan courier executed by the Parlement of Rouen in 1553, the court's account adds relatively little.[55] We also possess a few *plumitifs* of prisoners who clearly belong in Crespin's collection, such as the Genevan courier executed at Rouen in 1552 for refusing to take Catholic communion at Easter, or Jean Ponthieu, executed at Clermont-Ferrand in August 1556 after several futile attempts by Sorbonne theologians to persuade him to recant;[56] but the martyrologist never learned about them. The most fascinating problems, however, come at the very end of the 1550s. The Parisian judges had now become aware both of Crespin's achievement and of the growth of Reformed confessionalism, and responded by trying to avoid martyrdoms. Their cautious behavior after the capture of huge numbers of prisoners on the rue St.-Jacques in September 1557 emerges clearly even through the Protestant pamphlets, which provide our only useful information at a time when the official court records have entirely disappeared. After they had made a few exemplary executions to quench the Parisian public's thirst for revenge, and then coaxed recantations from most of the women and men who had been captured, the *parlementaires* engaged in prolonged theological negotiations with their more stubborn prisoners.

One of the very last people whom they failed to convert, Geoffroy Guerin, was finally executed at Paris in the summer of 1558. La Roche

Chandieu's account of his martyrdom offers vivid glimpses of the negotiating tactics employed by the judges.[57] During his captivity, Guerin wrote long letters to a Protestant minister. Following a futile exchange of views with the episcopal judge, Guerin described a stormy interview with an unnamed parlementary judge "sent in order to find some way to make us change our minds; which he did for three consecutive days, soliciting us by every means imaginable, but in vain." Finally, the judge resorted to threats of burning this "unlettered cabinetmaker who nevertheless kept talking back," and stormed out after forbbidding him to talk further. Two Sorbonne theologians were then sent to argue with him, but in vain. Then, "because it was not customary for an *arrêt* to be delayed for such a long time, there was a rumor that the king was displeased." Two judges, including President Minard, were sent to court to excuse their behavior, but were ordered to hurry things up. In his next letter Guerin described (a rarity in Protestant sources) his interview of 4 June on the *sellette* before the parlement's Grande Chambre. Under these circumstances, Protestant discourse was extremely difficult. "They questioned me about certain articles," he reported, "which I answered only with great difficulty. My lips, with every remark I made, were closed together."[58] Next day he underwent further sessions with two Sorbonne theologians, who returned two days later on the same errand, and then reported back to Parlement. Further delays followed. Finally, on 1 July, the judges could stall no longer, so President Minard, accompanied this time by four theologians, held one last argument with their prisoner. Another judge who was present also intervened. At last the public executioner lost patience and took Guerin away, putting the customary gag in his mouth upon leaving the prison. The account of his "final words" reads oddly, because we are told of two remarks by Guerin, before and after an episode when the executioner removed Guerin's gag in order to ask him to say 'Jesus Maria!' so that he could be strangled before being burned (the martyr, of course, refused to speak at such a moment).[59]

The judges' frustration with prisoners like Guerin and a few others soon led to the more remarkable strategy devised by President Séguier. He actually tried to negotiate some key theological issues, particularly eucharistic doctrine, with them. Séguier first employed this tactic with four Protestant "irreductibles" who were on his criminal docket in the early spring of 1559. The process by which he and several colleagues converted four death sentences into perpetual banishments from France quickly became a cause célèbre; as we have seen, it led directly to the fateful *mercuriale* in April. We know about these negotiations only through a somewhat embarrassed Protestant version. Like the successful escape of a condemned prisoner, the episode was mentioned only because the author had to explain some otherwise inexplicable event that flowed directly from it. In a genuine negotiation, neither side really controls the agenda; moreover, if it succeeds, neither side has great interest in recording the process, since neither can draw propaganda value from the results. Séguier's tactic effectively brought the judges down to the level of their prisoners. Therefore, their preserved *plumitifs* read very oddly, because they contain no trace of the actual interrogations, but include a draft of the compromise decision.

Chandieu's account, however, is less coy.[60] He descibes how two moderate presidents, whom he names, "not ignoring the good rights of the cause," finally undertook a responsibility that they had long evaded, because it placed them between royal edicts and their consciences. They first tried to persuade their prisoners to dissimulate, but this attempt failed. Then they decided to attack the problem of the Eucharist in such a way as to avoid the issues of transubstantiation and the physical presence of Christ in the Host, "hoping by this means to absolve them of the crime of being *sacramentaires,* on which the death sentences were customarily based." The tactic worked. But their more conservative judges then demanded that the prisoners be questioned about the Mass, "which could not be avoided without contravening the ordinary style of interrogations." Here their prisoners refused to compromise, so the judges asked them exactly what they opposed about the Mass. "Some judges," reported Chandieu, "were constrained to say out loud that in truth there were abuses"; but the judges were not in fact very far from the opinions of the cardinal of Lorraine, since they only favored communion in both kinds and the use of vernaculars instead of Latin. Chandieu remarked that "one would never have thought that such a frank confession would have been received in such a place, where all those who had previously made similar confessions had been condemned to death." Séguier and his colleagues lurched ahead, reducing all four death sentences to banishments, and soon watched the storm break over their heads.

His policy of negotiation with stubborn heretics was not quite dead, even after Henry II had broken up the second *mercuriale* and ordered several judges arrested. The almost-surrealistic situation in which the court found itself six months later, after one of their colleagues had revealed that he was a fully confessionalized Protestant, provoked a brief attempt to revive it. After Anne du Bourg had exhausted his long cycle of ecclesiastical appeals and had been defrocked, some of his former colleagues ("temporizing people," said Chandieu, who does not name any of them) made one final attempt to avoid the embarrassment of sentencing him to death.[61] They urged him to compose a kind of Nicodemite confession of faith, "not directly contrary to the true doctrine, but ambiguous and presented in such a way as to satisfy his judges." Du Bourg agreed, and the tactic might well have spared his life, if not his career. His conservative colleague and fellow *conseillier-clerc*, Nicolas Brulart, grumbled in his memoirs that on 13 December Du Bourg presented a manuscript confession and abjuration to his judges, who immediately sent a copy to the king, although "it was doubtful whether it was pretended or real."[62] Protestant sources claim that a crestfallen minister rushed to see du Bourg in prison and persuaded him to recant his recantations. Brulart's dilemma was solved six days later when du Bourg presented a second handwritten confession of faith, this one in total agreement with the recently approved national synod of the Reformed church. There is no known copy of du Bourg's first confession of faith, but his second was soon published at Geneva in 1560, at an unknown locality in 1561, and again at Lyon during the Huguenot occupation of 1562.

Du Bourg's execution not only gave Crespin and the French Reformed church their most prominent martyr; it also made some Catholic observers uneasy. We know that the young Florimond de Raemond, later a *parlementaire* at Bordeaux and chronicler of the rise and decline of Protestantism, retained vivid memories of du Bourg's courage; like most of his fellow students at the time, who debated the subject with great passion, he sympathized with the victim. He was no less impressed by the ordinary people who endured death for their convictions. "These sad and constant spectacles caused some trouble, not only in the minds of ordinary people but also the great of the land, most of whom could not help being persuaded that these people were right, seeing that, at the price of their lives, they maintained [their beliefs] with such firmness and resolution."[63] The system of heresy prosecutions was then dismantled in 1560 and 1561, a process capped by the Edict of Toleration in January 1562. There would be no more stakes, no more tongues ripped out or gags stuffed in, to prevent the wrong kind of last words from people about to die.

When the Wars of Religion began, French parlements adapted by changing the basic religious crime from *lèse-majesté divine* to *lèse-majesté humaine,* from heresy to sedition. This shift had the advantage of frustrating Crespin's design even better than gagging prisoners, because people being hanged as rebels could not offer the exemplary courage and dignity of people being burned to death for their beliefs. But it also had the disadvantage of frustrating Catholic audiences, above all at Paris, who were out for the heretics' blood. One legal practice of the 1550s increased greatly during the religious wars: the use of effigies to wreak symbolic punishment on absent Protestant leaders. For example, the Parlement of Bordeaux, which had seldom commissioned effigies of condemned heretics before 1560, paid for four pictures of Huguenot fugitives to be "executed" for sedition and *lèse-majesté* in August 1562, shortly after the failure of the Protestant coup against their city. A month later they paid their hangman for executing effigies of twenty-two noblemen, the principal captains of the Huguenot army.[64] The Parlement of Toulouse similarly reserved its use of effigies for major political enemies, especially seven local magistrates who they believed had engineered a Huguenot coup at Toulouse in 1562. The names of these seven were also engraved in marble in the city hall, so that their descendants could never hold office or claim nobility; an eighth magistrate, a Catholic who had remained in Toulouse, was ceremonially stripped of his robe of office at the city hall before being beheaded—a clear analogy to defrocking a priest who had been convicted of heresy.[65]

Overt confessionalism affected both the language and style with which the Paris Parlement interrogated its prisoners in the 1560s. Barbara Diefendorf, the only contemporary scholar to have read the *plumitifs* of Huguenot prisoners in the 1560s, observes that "judges questioned suspects on their actions—what religious assemblies they had attended, where their children had been baptized, and whether they had ever participated in a Protestant rite of the Lord's Supper—and not on their fundamental beliefs."[66] Even the handful of prisoners who were sentenced to death for heresy in 1569 were questioned in this dry manner, always about external forms of worship and never about their theological content. The judges even used the neutral-sounding euphemism *nouvelle opinion* instead of "heresy" in many of their most private entries.[67] The language of interrogations had changed drastically in ten years. Practicing the *religion pretendue réformée* was once again illegal, but Parisian judges now treated it as a religion.

After the Day of the Barricades in 1588, the Holy League controlled Paris, intimidated the Parlement, and inaugurated a final brief cycle of public burnings for heresy. Two aspects of their anachronistic enterprise stand out sharply against the background of traditional heresy trials and interrogations. The first is that all four people burned for heresy by the Paris Parlement between June 1588 and June 1589 were women. Their share of Protestant martyrdoms in the Parisian *ressort* thus rose from 5 percent before 1560 to 100 percent under the Holy League. The second remarkable aspect is the private language the judges now employed in their *plumitifs*. What their predecessors had called "Lutheranism" in Lizet's and le Maistre's day, what conservatives of the 1560s like Nicolas Brulart had called the "damnable Calvinist sect," what moderates like Séguier or de Thou had officially referred to as the "new opinion," was simply noted under the Holy League as "the new religion" (*la religion nouvelle*), abbreviated as "la Religion."[68] Even when they were finding ways to justify burning these unlucky women for the crime of heresy, the *parlementaires* had fully internalized the idea that French Protestantism may have been a mistaken religion, but it was undoubtedly a religion.

A few interesting exchanges dot these final heresy *plumitifs* from sixteenth-century France. The judges usually began by asking prisoners "for *la Religion*" whether they believed in the "Roman religion" or the "Roman Catholic church." The prisoners would answer that they belonged to the "catholic, apostolic, and universal religion" or "the Church universal." One, asked whether she was a prisoner for "the new religion," snapped back "that she didn't say new religion, but ancient religion."[69] By May 1589, one even finds a widow being questioned on details of eucharistic theology. Asked "if the bread is transubstantiated," she answered in the negative. When the judges then asked her about penance, she responded "that she has always received discipline from the church of God." Then her judges turned ugly, asking her "if she has been seduced by the devil" (reminding us that witch trials were then more common than heresy trials); she simply answered "that she remained with Christ Jesus." On that note, the judges dismissed her, then voted to uphold her condemnation to be burned alive, amending it slightly to have her strangled after having smelled the fire.[70] She was the last Protestant ever burned at Paris.

8

From Heresy to Sedition: The Eclipse of Parlements, 1560–1590

Previously, the faithful have been put to death on charges of heresy;
now, they have been crushed under the pretext of rebellion.
—*Simon Goulart (1582)*

When Catherine de Médicis persuaded her young son to decree a general pardon for accused heretics in March 1560, and when the Parlement of Paris reluctantly began to implement it a few months later, few believed that this was more than a very temporary tactic; Calvin himself thought it was a ruse. However, a variety of causes combined to make the Edict of Amboise into a watershed, marking the point beyond which heresy was never durably recriminalized and judged in French royal courts, despite a few ephemeral expedients in the late 1560s and 1580s. Until the spring of 1560 the French parlementary system had made strenuous but increasingly futile attempts to suppress the Reformation movement by organized repression of public affirmations of heretical belief and behavior, but had been unable to prevent its rapid growth. The queen mother was the first prominent person at court to understand that legal prosecution of heresy had become dysfunctional, and to suspect that the power of the new Reformed church was sharply increasing. Her response was simply to discontinue judicial repression, and thus to marginalize the role of French parlements in the history of the French Reformation.

Religious and political factors essentially explain why this expedient inaugurated a long-term policy shift. The mushrooming numbers of Reformed churches, now accepting an official confession of faith, played a major role, while the sudden growth of noble leadership in the Reformed movement greatly increased its political clout. Catherine de Médicis, searching for allies against the Guises, heard and appreciated Admiral Coligny's boast that more than a thousand Reformed churches stood behind him. Accidents also played a part. In May 1560 the Guise faction accepted the installation of a new chancellor, Michel de L'Hôpital, who soon proved to be a resolute enemy of religious persecution. An even more important accident occurred a few months later. Francis II's early death in December 1560 enabled Catherine to acquire control of the government during a critical period marked by remarkable turmoil. She and L'Hôpital tinkered repeatedly with religious policy until the Wars of Religion broke out, but they never attempted to return heresy trials to royal courts.

Barely two years separated the failed coup and concurrent royal pardon of Amboise from the outbreak of overt religious warfare in 1562. During this tumultuous period, some important features of the French situation emerged, features that persisted throughout the dreary cycles of religious warfare lasting far into the 1590s. First, simple repression of French Protestants became impossible. Their numbers had become so huge between 1560 and 1562, and their organization so formidable, that traditionalists were understandably terrified. Even after those numbers had been seriously reduced between 1562 and 1572 by massacre and military defeat, French Protestants remained ineradicable, a viable minority somewhere close to 10 percent of French subjects, entrenched in several well-defended areas and possessing an unbreakable organization. Second, after Catherine and L'Hôpital spent virtually the entire year 1561 in futile attempts to arrange some kind of Gallican religious accommodation, it became apparent that religious compromise was also impossible. Third, as both the conspiracy of Amboise and Condé's revolt of 1562 illustrated, French Protestants were never able to gain control of the French state and carry through their religious reformation. Thus, Catholics could not eliminate Protestantism, Protestants could not control the French state, and no workable compromise between them could be found.

Royal Toleration and the Marginalization of Parlements

The conciliatory measures of 1560, the pardon of Amboise and the Edict of Romorantin, were taken from fear; Catherine de Médicis understood that Protestantism had become dangerous. The clandestine political organization of French Protestants, the close interaction between a net-work of churches and a parallel network of noble leadership, seems remarkably precocious. The crown knew little about the meeting at Nan-tes in February 1560, attended by nobles, clergymen, and officials from various parts of France, which planned the ill-fated Amboise coup. It knew even less about the second national synod of the Reformed church, held at Poitiers a month later, which provided its twelve political depu-ties, a still-unidentified secret "pressure group" at court, with copies of their confession of faith to be shown to the monarch or high officials.[1] The year 1560 was filled with Protestant coups, even after their dramatic failure in March: there were Maligny's attempt on Lyon in September and Montbrun's activities in Provence and Dauphiné that autumn; a Parisian cathedral canon and parlementary judge noted in November 1560 that a nobleman, married to the niece of a cardinal, had sacked Nîmes and looted the royal treasury's receipts "on pretext of I know not what relig-ion."[2] By the summer of 1560 law and order had already broken down in Normandy. After two prolonged bursts of religious rioting in Rouen, the crown sent Marshal Vielleville to restore order in August. He first hanged eighteen plebeian rioters "of the one and the other religion" together at Rouen and then proceeded to Dieppe, where his troops spent three days demolishing the sumptuous neoclassical Reformed church that Admiral Coligny had built in this major port. When the Rouen Parlement finally condemned two Catholics to be hanged for instigating the summer riot-ing, Rouen's Catholic mob rescued the first prisoner; the other had to be hanged within the walls of their prison.[3]

Meanwhile, after summoning an Assembly of Notables in August and arranging to hold an Estates-General, Francis II made one final attempt to check Protestant rashness by arresting the prince of Condé, the "silent chief" behind the Amboise plot. The young king's sudden death, how-ever, effectively ended this attempt at repression. From Francis' death until Condé's revolt sixteen months later, the crown tried strenuously but unsuccessfully to resolve the kingdom's religious disputes through mediation and legislation. Some remarkable efforts were undertaken with the full blessing of the French monarchy, which spent most of 1561 arranging the Colloquy of Poissy.[4] That year saw no major Protestant coups and no executions for heresy, but no successful compromise could be reached. Beyond designing the Colloquy of Poissy, Catherine and L'Hôpital crafted at least four major pieces of legislation during 1561 in a futile attempt to arbitrate between the religious factions.[5] Despite rapid and frequent changes in detail about how rules should be applied, some important common features emerge. Heresy trials remained confined to church courts, with no greater punishment than banishment. "Illicit assemblies" held in public by Protestants, especially if participants carried weapons, remained punishable and could be judged by presidial courts as well as by parlements. By Easter 1561, iconoclasm became a capital crime. Past offenses were amnestied twice within seven months. But, as the preamble to the fourth royal edict of 1561 (the second issued at St. Germain) admitted with patent frustration, neither justice nor clemency had resolved the issues surrounding the form and content of Protestant worship.

An official attitude of moderation encouraged extremists on both sides. As their numbers grew, Protestant self-confidence accelerated, while Catholic fears escalated in direct proportion. Royal parlements, and even the royal government, lost control of punishing disorders resulting from the unstable French religious situation. For a conservative clerical judge like Nicolas Brulart, the year 1561 offered an unrelieved cycle of frightening scandals. In April he noted ugly riots in Paris and Beauvais; in June, the prince of Condé was formally absolved of all charges stemming from the conspiracy of Amboise; by July the Parlement had to order out the local militias in the Ile-de-France to control rioting "on pretext of religion"; in November came an even worse riot at Montpellier, where eight cathedral canons were killed and the bishop had to flee in disguise; December saw an iconoclastic outrage at a Paris church, with several people killed.[6] Another clerical chronicler unleashed a memorable diatribe against the "audacity, presumption, and pride" of the Huguenots in that same year of 1561. Throughout the kingdom, he complained, "there was neither judge nor justice against them," no way to put them in prison, let alone punish them for their effrontery.[7]

Such conservative Catholics understood very well that the most popular alternative to legal repression of Protestantism was not the policies of compromise or toleration promoted by Chancellor L'Hôpital; it was illegal repression. Long before the outbreak of overt warfare in April 1562, France suffered from a phenomenon described in now-classic form as the "rites of violence," although this recent addition to conventional wisdom about post-1560 France might well be renamed "rituals of popular justice."[8] Both factions increasingly operated outside the court system. French Protestants engaged in extralegal behavior because they never gained control of the central state apparatus or of the royal court system to sanction their policies. On the other side, French Catholic leadership lost faith in the royal judiciary. Although committed Protestants never constituted a majority in any French parlement, they sat in every parlement and every presidial court by 1560; in Languedoc they controlled several presidial courts. Their sympathizers, at least to a pessimistic conservative magistrate like Brulart, outnumbered the committed Catholics. One of the most important but little-recognized casualties of escalating French religious conflict was the eclipse of the kingdom's famous and generally well-run court system. It was caught between a growing, self-confident, fully confessionalized Protestant "cause" and an increasingly angry and mobilized majority loyal to the traditional faith, goaded by provocative Protestant actions.

Catholic rioters worked outisde the court system but sometimes imitated legally sanctioned acts of violence. Burning the corpse of a convicted heretic had been the climax of the official public execution ceremony, enacted hundreds of times across Valois France before 1560 but now officially forbidden. This practice was relatively difficult; anyone could drown or stab an enemy, but only trained experts would normally try to burn a corpse. The first recorded extrajudicial burning occurred at Beauvais in April 1561. When news spread that the local bishop (Cardinal Odet de Chatillon, one of eight French prelates later tried for heresy by the Roman Inquisition) had taken Easter communion in both kinds at a private chapel, a mob of youths and clothworkers rioted through the city, capturing a priest who had been teaching Calvin's catechism and prayers to children. "After killing him," reported the son of a president of the Paris Parlement, "they dragged him to the public square where executions are held, intending to burn him. Hearing the noise, the public executioner came running; he forbade the public to do anything, as if someone had given him the order. He then took the cadaver of this unfortunate priest, and, amidst the acclamations of a furious crowd, he burned it, as though he had been legitimately condemned." The spectators then ran to the well-fortified episcopal palace, where Odet de Chatillon, dressed in his cardinal's regalia, finally appeared at a window and dispersed the crowd as night fell. The king sent Marshal Montmorency (the bishop's seond cousin) to restore order, accompanied by some royal judges from nearby Senlis; they eventually put two men on trial, including the hangman, who was punished for acting without orders.[9]

J.-A. de Thou, whose father became First President of the Paris Parlement in January 1563, chronicled the eclipse of parlementary justice by mob actions during 1561, blaming both sides. He admitted that "there were popular riots in various places . . . and genuine seditions arose at Amiens and Pontoise." Nor was Paris immune. "After many riots," noted de Thou, "there was finally a genuine sedition in the capital during the final days" of 1561 at the Paris church of St. Medard.[10] Meanwhile Protestant apologists said relatively little about the events of 1561. Crespin slides rapidly past a year that "gave some tranquillity and rest to the churches" and produced no martyrs through the court system.[11] Although Claude Haton claimed that no judge dared to condemn Huguenots in 1561, it seems more accurate to say that when they tried, the results were embarrassing. In December 1561, Rouen's Huguenot crowd rescued a convicted iconoclast, the only person condemned to death by this parlement for religious rioting.[12] Powerless to try heretics and disoriented by constantly shifting rules for dealing with forms of religious dissent, the parlements were no longer part of the solution to resolving such conflicts; they were becoming irrelevant in the all-important business of regulating public religious behavior throughout France.

Before the prince of Condé began the Wars of Religion in April 1562, the French judicial system had begun to crack in many places under the strain of trying to implement L'Hôpital's vision of an even-handed religious toleration. Crespin described three bloody incidents from northern and western Languedoc in November and December 1561, while Catholic diarists mentioned Huguenot atrocities in Languedoc and Guyenne between November 1561 and January 1562; none of them resulted in legal actions.[13] Neither side mentioned an incident at Lectoure, on the western edge of the Toulouse *ressort,* in June 1561, when local Protestants captured three parlementary judges and a deputy prosecutor sent to investigate them, holding them hostage until the Parlement released the Lectoure Protestants imprisoned at Toulouse.[14] Even the august Parlement of Paris experienced institutional strain trying to implement L'Hôpital's rules during the winter of 1561–62, following the rioting and iconoclasm at St. Medard. Under pressure from the crown, the Parlement named two senior judges to investigate the incident: one was a notorious

Protestant who had been arrested by Henry II in 1559; the other was an ultrazealous Catholic. Each judge interrogated witnesses separately, but the Catholic judge learned that all the Protestant judge's witnesses had actively participated in the rioting, and promptly ordered them imprisoned on charges of iconoclasm. Most of these prisoners were ultimately released through the intervention of the king of Navarre, although the Huguenots, "following their unfortunate custom," also nailed up published justifications of their actions across the city.[15]

After the failure at the Colloquy of Poissy, L'Hôpital attempted to solve the judicial impasse by summoning two representatives from every French parlement to meet the royal court at St. Germain in January 1562. With religious compromise impossible, the chancellor saw religious toleration as the only viable alternative. Through intensive lobbying, L'Hôpital finally succeeded in squeezing out a plurality (but not a majority) of votes in favor of his proposed solution "to appease the troubles and seditions on account of religion," the famous Edict of January, or Edict of Toleration. Although its first article upheld the death penalty for iconoclasm, its most significant clause, explained as "tolerating this scandal in order to avoid a greater one," officially permitted public worship almost everywhere in the kingdom by congregations of the "new opinion," provided they were held outside of towns, in daylight, and without weapons. After the failure of the Colloquy of Poissy to promote agreement, concerns of public order took precedence over theology. Other clauses prescribed punishments for seditious propaganda (recidivists could be hanged for distributing such treatises) and especially for armed disobedience, including raising money for enrolling soldiers. Conservatives were outraged by the major concession of public worship. At Paris, *conseillier* Brulart called it "so pernicious for the republic and public order, that it would be impossible to do worse," and believed it amounted to "a summary approbation of this unhappy Calvinist sect." It required a supplementary declaration stipulating that the edict was provisional and that "we do not intend to approve two religions in our kingdom" and two official attempts at royal coercion to get the edict registered by the Parlement of Paris in March 1562.[16] In late winter, the chancellor dispatched pairs of traveling judges (one notoriously sympathetic to Protestants, the other more moderate) to provincial parlements in order to persuade them to ratify and implement these new rules. Their arrival, and ratification of this important edict, effectively coincided with the outbreak of religious war. By a curious paradox, therefore, Protestant worship was legally permitted throughout France during the first war of religion.

Throughout the quarter-century when Catherine de Médicis exercised considerable influence on royal policy, the juridical situation of French Protestants remained relatively constant. Between 1560 and 1590, French parlements rarely executed anyone for the crime of heresy, even during wartime. The Parlement of Paris, whose district covered half of the kingdom, ordered barely a dozen public executions for simple heresy throughout the entire period of religious wars. When they hanged the *lieutenant* of Pontoise in July 1562 for actively promoting public worship by Protestants, a Parisian parish priest noted that he was "the first person executed at Paris as a Huguenot since Francis II's pardon of Amboise."[17] When a university student was hanged in May 1569 "for having taught Huguenotery to children, without any other crime," the same priest added that "he was the first executed for heresy since the troubles began" almost two years previously. Now an old man, he noted that the Foucault sisters, daughters of a lawyer at the Parlement, died in 1588 for "simple heresy, without being accused of any other crime."[18] He noted these details precisely because such public executions were so rare in the capital, perhaps the most zealously Catholic city in France. With rare and temporary exceptions, royal courts now condemned even such nonbelligerents as preachers and women for "sedition" rather than for religious offenses, as Simon Goulart noted with considerable irritation when preparing an updated 1582 edition of Crespin's martyrology.

The public practice of Reformed Protestantism, now described in official language as the *religion prétendue réformée* and in popular slang as Huguenot, was permitted in France between 1562 and 1585, except for a few months between October 1568 and mid-1570. During the first war of religion, the Edict of Toleration of January 1562 technically remained in force; after the St. Bartholomew's massacres a decade later, Protestant worship was never outlawed. Each episode of warfare ended with a settlement that redefined the conditions for Protestant worship and pardoned past behavior. Thus, from a strictly legal point of view, the French Wars of Religion consisted of long periods when the public practice of Protestantism was perfectly legal, broken by a few brief cycles of temporary wartime illegality. Throughout the prolonged French religious crisis, the court system remained marginalized.

Parlements in the First Religious War, 1562–1563

The outbreak of war in 1562 presented problems to French parlements. While the monarchy negotiated over their heads with Huguenot grandees, Catholic rioters infringed or even ignored their claims. But the courts also mattered, because they could demonstrate the hollowness of Condé's legal claims and erode his political justification. And they could still punish Huguenots even under L'Hôpital's Edict of January. Although they could no longer condemn them as heretics, they could now sentence them as rebels, and they could also inflict capital punishment on iconoclasts—if they caught them before the Catholic lynch mobs did. The structure of the first Huguenot revolt also put most major French parlements in the spotlight. It basically consisted of an unstable alliance between several noble clientages loyal to the prince of Condé and a cluster of urban revolts affecting several important French cities; one of them, Orléans, served as Condé's capital. Although there was no Protestant rising in Paris, the other three largest parlementary cities—Toulouse, Rouen, and Bordeaux—were directly affected by attempted Huguenot coups in 1562. The results, and the legal consequences, were remarkably different in each. One smaller parlement imitated the behavior of Toulouse, while another shared the fate of Rouen.

At Bordeaux, an attempt to capture the local fortress on 26 June was easily foiled, and many suspected ringleaders were soon captured. Between mid-July and early October, the Parlement of Bordeaux carried out approximately twenty executions for sedition, including a gentleman (the only one beheaded), three Huguenot pastors, and three men charged principally with iconoclasm or sacrilege. A minor officer of the Parlement escaped with banishment and an *amende honorable,* while many of the principal conspirators who escaped were solemnly condemned and hanged in effigy.[19] There was less public disorder during the legal repression carried out by Montaigne's colleagues at Bordeaux than in the capital, where no Huguenots had attempted a military coup.

At Toulouse, the four municipal consuls led a Huguenot rising that seized the city hall in early May 1562. It was suppressed only after four days of bloody street fighting. Here, the Parlement (more precisely, the Catholic-zealot majority headed by its First President) immediately took the initiative and led the counterattack against the insurgent municipal officials. They succeeded in defeating their opponents even before a

Catholic relief force reached the beleaguered capital of Languedoc. At no other time or place in French history did an appellate court take direct responsibility for the military as well as political aspects of counterinsurgency. This unique achievement enabled royal institutions to retain some authority across Languedoc in 1562, given Huguenot successes in such other major cities as Nîmes, Montpellier, and Montauban. The Parlement's role was commemorated by a book printed locally the following year, titled *History of the Troubles Occurring in the city of Toulouse in 1562*. By then, following through on its military triumph, the Parlement of Toulouse had completed the most thorough religious purge ever performed by a sixteenth-century French appellate court. "Nothing was overlooked by the court of Parlement or the clergy," remarked Crespin, "in order that everything be exterminated."[20] A local Catholic, writing under Louis XIV, admitted that "the executions of justice that the Parlement decreed afterward were nearly as bloody as those of the war that had just ended."[21]

From the end of the rioting until a royal amnesty reached Toulouse at the end of September, using public *monitoires* from their local clergy and employing house-to-house searches, often working full-time on this purge to the exclusion of all other criminal business, the second Parlement of France (whose active membership had been drastically reduced) identified a total of 1,128 suspected *séditieulx* residing in Toulouse. In a city of fewer than nine thousand households, they represented a sizable share of the adult population. Although many suspects had fled or had already died in the fighting, the Parlement of Toulouse and its subordinate local tribunals executed more than a hundred of the most compromised among them in little more than four months.[22] By contrast, Raymond Mentzer's meticulous investigation of pre-1561 heresy trials in Languedoc shows that in forty years, across a very large district, this parlement had investigated just over a thousand suspected heretics and publicly executed about sixty of them.[23] This thorough search of the city of Toulouse had therefore generated a slightly larger number of religious suspects from one place in four months than previously from an entire province in sixty years; moreover, it provoked many more public executions for religiously motivated sedition than all of Languedoc had seen for heresy in the previous forty years. It was truly repression on an unprecedented scale.

Let us examine the principal victims of this enormous parliamentary purge. Not all of them had been involved in the street fighting, and many of those who were had fled to safety in various Huguenot strongholds. As at Bordeaux, the Parlement's wrath fell heavily on the insurgents' political leadership, and one can identify a few of the same kinds of primary victims at both cities: officers of the new Reformed churches, some minor royal officials, and members of the legal profession. Although ordinary artisans and soldiers accounted for most of the *séditieulx* at Toulouse, clerical training and church office were also well represented. Six deacons of Reformed churches were hanged, along with seven former priests or monks (one of whom had become a deacon). Among the civil officials, one finds five lesser municipal magistrates of Toulouse, three recent or current *capitouls,* and two *viguiers.* Heading the legal contingent were a judge at the local presidial court and a former episcopal judge at Montauban. Nine lawyers outnumbered the seven professional booksellers and one printer. The occupational categories of these victims fit closely with much recent information about the social composition of Reformed churches in southern France around 1560.

These Toulouse executions of 1562 included a handful of victims who do not fit into the category of armed rebels. Protestant sources claimed that a lad of only sixteen, "an excellent painter for his age . . . had his tongue pierced, was strangled and burned."[24] In exceptional circumstances, the Parlement of Toulouse was prepared to approve the traditional recipe of purging heresy, particularly by clergymen, with fire.[25] The other distinctive feature of this repression is that at least one woman was executed for sedition, and she apparently died under exceptionally ugly circumstances: "the people," said Crespin, "seeing that she would not consent to perform any act of the Roman religion, broke the noose; and being still alive, after being hit with many stones, [she] was burned."[26] (Three Augustinian nuns who refused to return to their convent, on the other hand, were simply whipped and imprisoned.) It seems more than coincidence that this parlement also upheld three death sentences for witchcraft against Catholic women—probably the first such instances in sixteenth-century France—during the same months that it ordered women executed for Protestant sedition.[27] The accused witches came from the diocese of Couserans, whose bishop had just raised a militia among his solidly Catholic flock and came in full armor to the aid of beleaguered Toulouse.

Another remarkable aspect of the Parlement's reaction to the failed

Huguenot coup at Toulouse is the extreme severity with which they treated their colleagues who had shown less than enthusiastic support of the majority during the emergency. At Rouen, five parlementary judges had been suspended from office on suspicion of overt Protestantism as early as 1554, while Henry II had imprisoned several Parisian judges in 1559. But the scale of the Toulouse purge of 1562 was unprecedented. A court that included about eighty sitting judges in 1559 proceeded to suspend thirty of them shortly after defeating the Huguenots.[28] Although Catherine de Médicis imposed a moratorium on public executions by the end of October 1562, she was unable to persuade the Parlement of Toulouse to reintegrate their suspended colleagues. However, not even the judges most notoriously sympathetic to Protestantism were put on trial for active sedition during the months of repression. But not until several months after the peace of Amboise in March 1563 did this court return to its normal size.

East of Toulouse, the Parlement of Aix participated with equal zeal in exterminating local Huguenots, though without the glory of repressing an attempted coup. By late May 1562, a large Catholic army boasted of having cleansed most of Provence of Huguenots, and they soon crushed those who tried to fortify and hold Sisteron. The butchery, symbolized by the decoration of a large tree in Aix with Huguenot corpses, was extensive and remarkably nasty. During the war this court abandoned its recent relative restraint against accused Protestants, and in July 1562 Aix became the first French parlement to hang one of its own judges for "sedition."[29] After the war ended, the conduct of this "cavern of brigands, abusing the name of Parlement," was sufficently scandalous for Chancellor L'Hôpital to abolish it temporarily. At the opposite extreme from Aix stands the Parlement of Dijon, equally Catholic and undisturbed by attempted Huguenot coups in 1562, but unwilling to engage in gratuitous cruelties toward local Protestants. After the war ended, Protestant martyrologists noted that this court had captured almost 160 local prisoners, but apparently put only one girl to death.[30]

In the seat of the third parlement of France, located in the kingdom's third largest city, a municipal Huguenot coup actually succeeded in April 1562, only a few weeks before their narrow failure at Toulouse. Rouen remained in Protestant hands until a royal army stormed it in late October. The history of the Parlement of Normandy during the first war of religion is therefore almost the exact reverse of the history of the Parlement of Toulouse. What happened to a royal parlement in a city under Huguenot rule? It was certainly not allowed to conduct business as usual. At no time did Huguenot sympathizers constitute a majority of sitting parlementary judges, regardless of what Catholic critics said; the attitude of the triumphant Rouen rebels toward their local sovereign court offers eloquent testimony to the contrary. The Parlement was too important for them to ignore and too unreliable to co-opt. Acutely aware that iconoclasm was a capital offense, they did their best to ignore its existence as they set about destroying every "graven image" in Rouen's churches. In May the king received a letter, recorded by a shocked judge Brulart in Paris, to the effect that "your Parlement of Normandy which has been, is no longer."[31] It was one thing for a king to dissolve a parlement, as Henry II had done at Bordeaux in 1548; they were after all royal creations. But it was an entirely different matter for subjects to dismantle a sovereign court. Since the records of the Rouen Parlement stop abruptly after mid-April 1562, one can assume that the rebels had shut it down.[32]

The crown could not accept this situation. Powerless for the moment to do anything in Rouen, Charles IX permitted his Parlement to remove itself to another town in Normandy. But the confusion and disorder were such that it was not until 22 July that a new locale was agreed upon, at Louviers. The Parlement of Normandy finally reopened on 8 August; five days later, only twenty-six of its seventy judges and officers were present at Louviers to take an oath of loyalty to the crown and the Catholic religion. By late August the Louviers Parlement promulgated an edict on religious policy, later censured by de Thou as "overly rigorous," which began by giving a detailed history of Normandy's problems since the death of Henry II and proposed automatic death sentences for all married priests and iconoclasts. One of the most curious and revealing legal episodes of the first war of religion shortly followed. Upon learning the news, Huguenot authorities in Rouen drew up a legal protest, or *relief d'appel*, sealed it, and sent it to Louviers with their official messenger.[33]

The exiled court at Louviers responded by devoting itself exclusively to judging cases of *lèse-majesté*, which in practice meant hanging every captured Huguenot it could find. Although none of its criminal decisions survives, the Spanish ambassador reported in early October that he had seen sixty people hanged at Louviers, including a Huguenot preacher and a pirate captain. The chancellor and the queen mother had to send a special emissary to calm the Louviers judges before Rouen was recaptured on 26 October. The Norman Parlement returned to its gothic palace in the still-smoldering city only two days later. By 29 October they were busily interrogating the four most important captured rebels, including their longtime colleague du Bosc d'Emandreville. Together with two of Rouen's *échevins* and its principal pastor, d'Emandreville was promptly sentenced to death and beheaded (the other three were hanged) on 30 October.[34] Augustin Marlorat, officially described as "convicted of being one of the authors of the great assemblies that have caused the rebellion and civil war," became the only Genevan-trained missionary pastor to be executed by parlementary order during the first war of religion. The restored Parlement of Rouen decreed several exceptions to the general pardon decreed by Chancellor L'Hôpital, which they registered only with the stipulation that some "unworthy" rebels could be added to the ten names on the original list. Five rebel captains and an elder of the Reformed church were executed on 31 October, although the judges were unable to hang the notary who had brought the official protest of the Rouen rebels to Louviers because he obtained a royal pardon.

Like Rouen, one of the smaller parlements also dissolved soon after the outbreak of religious war. When Huguenots under the notorious baron des Adrets occupied Grenoble and sacked its churches, most of its parlementary judges, including the chief justice, fled north across the border into Savoy.[35] Des Adrets named a Protestant parlementary judge, Ponat, as governor and military commander, with a venerable missionary pastor relocating from the Piedmontese Alps to provide spiritual leadership. Though besieged twice by Catholic armies, Grenoble remained under Huguenot control until the Edict of Pacification. The crown finally reestablished the Parlement of Dauphiné in August 1563, and Ponat reclaimed his seat without incident.[36] Had Rouen been less important and farther from Paris, its parlement might have imitated the trajectory of Grenoble in 1562–1563.

Legal Consequences of the First Religious War

The prince of Condé and his Huguenot advisers struggled constantly with the problem of legitimizing his revolt. Their futile exchange of lengthy letters with the Parlement of Paris in the spring and summer of

1562 illustrates the difficulties they faced in attempting to create any sort of counterlegitimacy to the Catholic "Triumvirate" that they feared and despised. The crown, royal authority itself, escaped them; Condé and the Huguenots controlled neither the monarch nor the regent. Nor did they seriously attempt to control the kingdom's capital city, seat of the most important legitimizing agency beneath the crown, the Parlement of Paris. They had their own capital at Orléans, and they occupied the kingdom's second-largest city, Lyon. But neither place held any notable political institutions capable of making it a viable alternative to Paris. Although they also controlled two cities with sovereign courts, Rouen and Grenoble, the Huguenots simply dispersed the judges; they never co-opted a parlement through which they could speak or legislate. Consequently, Condé and the Huguenots, who included sizable numbers of royal judicial officials in their ranks, suffered from what we might call a "legitimacy gap."

Their awkward legal situation worsened significantly a few months into the revolt, after their military discipline slackened and uncontrolled iconoclasm burst out in nearly every city controlled by the Huguenots. When Condé sent his first letter to the Paris Parlement, he had to apologize for the outbreaks of iconoclasm at Blois and Tours (the very first article of the January 1562 Edict of Toleration punished iconoclasm with death), but argued that there had been none at Orléans, which he personally controlled. A month later he expressed shock over the extensive iconoclasm at Lyon and Rouen. Shortly thereafter an embarrassed Condé could not prevent a serious episode of iconoclasm at Orléans cathedral, where he had placed special guards. Meanwhile the profanation of noble tombs at Vendôme proved so scandalous that even a Protestant apologist reported that "it was found extremely bad [tres-mauvais], and for good reasons."[37] The Huguenots lost considerable momentum in the first war of religion. In addition to military setbacks (losing control of most of the cities they had seized) and human setbacks (they were far more often the victims of massacres than the perpetrators), by looting churches and even tombs they were losing the propaganda war as well. A Catholic theologian, Claude de Sainctes, had begun collecting materials for a kind of antimartyrology chronicling the full range of Huguenot atrocities, which he soon published.

The Huguenots' legal situation in 1562, possessing considerable de facto authority but without controlling any established upper-level courts, required them to take steps toward creating their own jurisprudence. One significant precedent was the public execution of a priest in the Huguenot capital of Orléans for saying clandestine Masses; he was sentenced to death by the new municipal officials installed by Condé. Subsequently, after the fall of Rouen and public executions of its captured leadership, the magistrates of Orléans executed a judge of the Paris Parlement and an abbot on 11 November. Odet de Selve, the royal ambassador to Spain, captured together with them, was spared not because of his official position, but because his brother fought for Condé. As de Thou remarked, it was a matter of "reprisals, but with less justification [*droit*]."[38] An equally revealing episode of the Huguenots' "legitimacy gap" occurred near the end of the war, after Huguenot leaders in Dauphiné had arrested their leader, the baron des Adrets, on suspicion of treason. It was no simple matter to put him on trial. He was first interrogated by the seneschal of Montelimar, Felix Bourjac, a veteran royal official and an overt Protestant for more than a decade. Des Adrets was then taken to Nîmes, where he was imprisoned and questioned by four judges of the local presidial court; but the prisoner rejected them as incompetent, since he had no connection with Languedoc. This troublesome prisoner was never judged, but simply released at war's end.[39]

Late in 1562, the most important instance of Huguenot counterlegitimacy occurred in lower Languedoc, far from Condé's capital. A rump session of Huguenot notables from various towns calling itself the Estates of Languedoc met at Nîmes, rearranged their province into new "governments or dioceses," and offered the title of royal governor to the Huguenot count of Crussol. He accepted, and even made an official entry into Nîmes on 13 December.[40] In wartime Languedoc, Huguenot legal *bricolage* was matched by a Catholic riposte. On 2 March 1563, with a peaceful settlement imminent, a "Confederacy" of notables petitioned the Parlement of Toulouse to authorize a paramilitary organization to govern the province; the court approved it, although its *procureur-général* inserted a clause saying the Confederacy would operate "pending royal ratification."[41] Under the strains of civil war, new, ad hoc sources of public authority began to emerge around established institutions.

Finally, with Condé captured and the duke of Guise assassinated, the war ended through an Edict of Pacification. Released on parole, Condé consulted the fifty Huguenot pastors clustered in Orléans, but ignored many of their stipulations when agreeing to terms. The crown was also eager to end the fighting. It is a trite but valid saying that no one truly wins a war, and there were many losers in the first French war of religion. The Huguenots lost not only battles, but also credibility and members. The Catholic church fared little better; it suffered enormous physical and financial damage, while Gallicanism prevented it from adopting any reforms decreed by the just-closing Council of Trent. Sitting uneasily atop both the established church and the insurgent Protestants, the French monarchy and its court system lost prestige by attempting to uphold unenforceable policies of mediation between religious factions. Under the strain of war, its parlements wrestled with a situation in which social realities overpowered statutory law. Two of them simply disappeared, one for the duration of the war; another became a quasi-military organization and conducted a Spanish-style inquisition after winning its local battle.

The Paris Parlement apparently weathered this storm relatively well. Headed by President le Maistre (who died in December 1562, exactly one year after returning from a four-month suspension), it reacted cautiously at first to news of Condé's revolt, spending much time in April and May fencing verbally with the prince. By summer it multiplied its attacks against suspected Huguenots. In June le Maistre ordered house-by-house searches in Paris and imposed an oath of Catholic orthodoxy to unmask a few dozen crypto-Protestants among its vast pool of judges and lesser officials.[42] Two huge conflagrations of Protestant literature quickly followed, and Huguenot bodies soon followed their books. The son of le Maistre's successor condemned the Paris Parlement's *arrêts* of 30 June and 13 July, imposing the punishments for *lèse-majesté* on all armed Huguenots and ordering all *Religion Pretendue Réformée* ministers and deacons killed, as needlessly bloodthirsty and encouraging illegal and unofficial acts of violence.[43] He had a point. Judge Brulart, recording the first public execution of a Huguenot official on 20 July, immediately added that "in this month, several Huguenots were drowned and killed by the common people in the city of Paris." The royal chronicler, a staunch Catholic, concurred that many ordinary people had been killed at Paris in June and July, adding that "no one was ever punished for them."[44] Such infringements of the rule of law set Parisian precedents that would be eagerly followed a decade later.

Unable to punish Protestant worshippers under the Edict of Toleration, the Paris Parlement managed to condemn a few Huguenots under the rubric of sedition. It also hanged four of the St. Medard iconoclasts from the previous December, and burned their corpses on the site of a Reformed temple. The officer in charge of the municipal watch, who had done nothing to stop the rioters, died as a Catholic; but Catholic sources lament that the "insolence of the people" desecrated his body as well as those of the heretics.[45] The Parisian high court also hanged a Huguenot official in August and a foreign preacher in November; both corpses were desecrated by Parisian mobs.[46] Elsewhere in its huge district, public executions of Huguenots became equally disorderly. President le Maistre's final death warrant for heresy ordered a woolcarder, previously freed by the general pardon of January 1561 but recaptured, to be hanged and his corpse burned at Senlis. Crespin informs us that "mutineers" pressured the hangman to cut the rope early and sent the half-dead man into the flames in December 1562.[47] The careful compilations of Huguenot martyrologists suggest that only in a very few towns of western France (principally Le Mans, Tours, and Angers) were more Huguenots executed after trials than were lynched. In emergency situations, a court system may condone or even encourage lynch justice, but it is difficult to regain respect for its judgments afterward and to restore the rule of law.

De Thou illustrated this point nicely with respect to the Parlement of Toulouse. The second-ranking French appellate court apparently emerged from the crucible of religious conflict in 1562 with its reputation enhanced, and its behavior radiated self-assurance. It had ratified an ultra-Catholic Confederacy to govern Languedoc in March 1563, and it behaved with remarkable stubbornness in its bitter opposition to the Edict of Pacification. Chancellor L'Hôpital required three months and four attempts before the Parlement finally agreed to reinstate two notorious Huguenot judges. For good measure, the royal council also declared the municipality's 1562 magistrates legally rehabilitated (one of them posthumously), censured the laudatory pamphlet authorized by the Parlement of Toulouse, and revoked their proclamation of an annual holiday to commemorate their deeds of 10 May 1562. Beyond such acts of high policy, de Thou also discussed a petty incident in February 1563 when a Toulouse mob almost lynched an architect for trying to wall up an opening in the Parlement's main building. "The Parlement could bluster away as much as it wanted with impressive-sounding edicts," he said, but "the people, whom the Parlement itself had accustomed to so much license by authorizing their enterprises against the Protestants, no longer wished to listen to their voice nor submit themselves to their edicts."[48]

If even a triumphant and self-confident parlement like Toulouse could be humbled in this manner, imagine the situation at Rouen, its Parlement risen phoenixlike after a temporary dissolution, or Grenoble, whose court had to be restored by royal fiat months after the war's end. In the spring of 1563, Catherine de Médicis and her chancellor gave some badly needed prestige to the Parlement of Rouen by choosing it as the theater in which to proclaim Charles IX's legal majority, thereby greatly insulting the Parlement of Paris, which had delayed registration of their Edict of Pacification.[49] Problems with implementing the Edict of Amboise led to the royal council's suspending the Parlement of Aix in November 1563; it did not officially reopen for two years.[50] Even more problematic than restoring the prestige of French parlements was restoring their membership. Every parlement and every presidial court contained some overtly Huguenot judges, who had either fled or been deposed during the conflict, and now had to be reintegrated to serve alongside a radically hostile Catholic majority. At Paris, for example, where 31 of 160 judges had not taken the oath of Catholicism during the war, all but 9 had reclaimed their seats by July 1563; the remainder, who had either held Protestant services in their homes or served with Condé's army, did not reclaim their seats until the winter of 1563–64.[51] In a variety of ways, whatever their behavior had been throughout almost a year of civil war, French appellate courts needed time to mend their eroded prestige after it ended.

From War to Massacre, 1567–1572

They had little more than four years of respite before a second cycle of religious wars broke out in autumn 1567. Although it officially ended in summer 1570, its aftereffects directly influenced the notorious wave of massacres from August to October 1572. If one looks beyond the fighting to the problems of peacemaking, especially those affecting French appellate courts, one can characterize these five years as a second phase of ongoing erosion in parlementary authority. Under the strain of war, popular justice once again submerged courts of law. The unfortunate lessons from 1562 were remembered and applied, though not in the same ways or at the same places. For one thing, massacres were less common because there were now fewer Huguenots available to be lynched in many places, and the survivors had refined their techniques of camouflage or flight. Huguenots now perpetrated few outrages against church property, partly because almost every vulnerable church had already been stripped during the first war. Nevertheless, Catholics capped this five-year cycle with massive popular riots in several parts of France during the second half of 1572. This was the ultimate form of religious violence—not only because of its unprecedented scale, but even more because it was now solemnly approved by the crown, rather than done in defiance of royal authority.

Other governmental innovations marked this second cycle of warfare. In October 1568 the crown made Protestant worship illegal, thereby making heresy executions possible until the summer of 1570. However, parlements took little advantage of this opportunity, while popular violence by both sides once again bypassed the court system. Condé's former capital of Orléans, now under Catholic rule, suffered from mob violence in 1569, after the triumphant faction had quarantined the city's Huguenots in three separate strongholds. One of them was burned down and another was stormed, with a combined loss of more than a hundred lives.[52] Huguenots also perpetrated a few massacres during this cycle of violence. Shortly before the brief second war of religion began in 1567, the Protestants of Nîmes slaughtered twenty Catholic notables; shortly before it ended, the Huguenots of La Rochelle killed two dozen priests.[53]

The courts' role during this cycle of warfare began in Languedoc when the Parlement of Toulouse executed Martin Tachard in July 1567. He was the first Genevan-trained missionary pastor hanged since October 1562, and the first executed in peacetime in more than seven years. Tachard's problems began with a bloody riot at Pamiers in the summer of 1566, probably the worst episode of French religious violence between the first and second wars. Many Catholics were killed, but the local Huguenots had to flee after troops restored order. Follow-up operations included an investigation by seven commissioners from the Parlement of Toulouse, headed by its First President. Pastor Tachard, then minister at Pamiers, was captured along with several other fugitives by a large posse deputized by these commissioners in May 1567. Brought to Toulouse, he was tried by the full Parlement and hanged for "*excès*, conspiracy, sedition, enterprises, and infringements of royal edicts and ordinances," with letters and papers found in his possession used as primary evidence. His execution, Protestant sources tell us, was orderly.[54] Tachard was apparently the last Reformed pastor to be publicly executed by parlementary decision, although several of them perished in the 1572 massacres.

During these conflicts the Parlement of Toulouse continued to show unusual severity against Huguenots. In March 1568 they beheaded the prince of Condé's official, duly equipped with a royal safe-conduct, for bringing the news that the second war of religion had ended with another edict of pacification.[55] Afterward it required four official orders from the crown before this parlement ratified the second peace; even then, they inserted several modifications and reservations into their secret registers. Further confirmation of their exceptional zeal came soon, at the outset of the third war, when the Toulouse Parlement approved the formation of a "Crusade for the extirpation of heretics and rebels of the new sect and so-called religion."[56] Upon learning that the Edict of St. Maur had outlawed the "so-called Reformed religion," the Parlement of Toulouse promptly hanged seven local Huguenots in October 1568.[57] Others soon followed, including the former presiding judge of the presidial of Montpellier and nine unlucky prisoners from the troubles at Pamiers;[58] sporadic executions continued throughout 1569, although the Toulouse judges seldom ordered corpses to be burned.[59] After the Parlement had again expelled its suspected Protestant members, the Huguenots created their own high court for Languedoc late in 1568. Sitting on it were eight judges from Toulouse, whom the prince of Condé had invested with full judicial powers. They did not dare call themselves a Parlement, merely a *Chambre de justice*.[60]

The Parlement of Paris provided the principal showcase for legal reactions to this second phase of overt religious conflict. Upon learning that the Edict of January 1562 had been repealed and Protestantism once again outlawed, President de Thou immediately sent a special messenger to reclaim the great seal from the disgraced Chancellor L'Hôpital, who fell simultaneously with his Edict of Toleration.[61] By the winter of 1568–69 a blizzard of harassing edicts descended upon the Huguenots who remained in Paris, circumscribing their movements and their property, filling the Conciergerie with hundreds of prisoners labeled "heretics," but rarely threatening their lives.[62] Only the discovery of compromising letters and satirical verses caused the death of Charles IX's former writing teacher, hanged in March despite his royal safe-conduct.[63] Public pressure moved these judges to condemn a Huguenot schoolteacher to death in April 1569. Two months later, popular intervention became even more blatant. On 25 June 1569, Paris militia commanders led a crowd to the court to demand the executions of three local Huguenot merchants for heresy, threatening the judges' lives if justice was not done. "Although no direct connection can be shown," Barbara Diefendorf argues, all three men "were executed (after six months' imprisonment) within the week."[64] One week later the judges beheaded their ex-colleague Guillaume de la Chesnaye, whom Brulart called "one of the most factious Huguenots," a man who had sold three abbeys and then married a noblewoman, despite being ordained as subdeacon.[65] Two pedagogues were hanged in November 1569 after eight months of imprisonment; a professional singer, jailed for almost eleven months, was hanged in February 1570.[66] Only nine Huguenots were executed for heresy at Paris during the second cycle of religious warfare. Meanwhile, many prominent Huguenot prisoners were either fined or released, while many others remained unsentenced when the war ended.

Two significant innovations marked the 1569 anti-Huguenot campaign of the Paris Parlement. First, the condemnations of Croquet and the two Gastines, who had hosted Huguenot assemblies where communion was given, included a provision that their house should be completely demolished. Afterwards "the wood and ironwork resulting from the demolition [should] be sold and the proceeds used to construct a stone cross, beneath which shall be a copper plate engraved with the reasons why this said house has been demolished and razed." The site of the Gastines house on Rue St. Denis was to remain perpetually public property, and in fact it remained vacant until the Third Republic. As *conseillier-clerc* Brulart smugly noted, this ruling "astonished the brethren,"[67] and it had significant consequences after the war. The other important parlementary innovation during the second half of 1569 involved hanging an effigy of Admiral Coligny, printing their official sentence against him, and offering a huge reward for his capture, 10,000 écus if alive and 2,000 if dead. Hitherto French appellate courts had never offered cash bounties for capturing prominent Huguenots. Afterward, pressure from the crown prevented the Paris Parlement from conducting formal trials of the queen of Navarre and her son in November 1569, but not from executing effigies of some other Huguenot notables.[68]

Meanwhile the kingdom's third parlement, Rouen, suffered further insults to its dignity. When news of the agreement ending the brief second war reached Rouen in April 1568, a mob invaded the Parlement building, causing extensive damage and scattering the judges, then breaking into its prison and ransoming prisoners accused of religious offenses. No one died, but an armed guard surrounded the court six days later when peace was officially proclaimed. Two years later another ultra-Catholic mob again disrupted this court, with a vigilante demagogue haranguing the judges and jostling its First President; "since no one will do us justice," claimed the demagogue, "we wish to do it ourselves." The Rouen Parlement released all prisoners arrested by Catholic vigilantes as soon as it dared.[69] Between these two episodes, the Parlement of Normandy distinguished itself during 1569 by its efficient handling of two unsuccessful Huguenot conspiracies to capture port towns. Along with many soldiers, artisans, and a few lawyers, two Protestant ministers were hanged at Rouen after being tortured on charges of sedition and conspiracy, while an ex-priest involved in one conspiracy received a life sentence to the galleys.[70] As at Toulouse in 1562, several trials for witchcraft were judged at Rouen while these Huguenot conspiracies were being judicially liquidated, although the Norman court imposed no death sentences against sorcerers.

The Parlement of Bordeaux, from which Montaigne resigned in 1571, maintained a relatively discreet profile during the second and third wars of religion, despite (or rather because of) its location near much of the fighting. As at Paris, this court engaged in numerous forms of legal harassment of local Protestants, starting with economic measures in October 1567. Like other parlements, Bordeaux eagerly compiled lists of absent rebels whose property they could confiscate. By April 1569 they had conflated fifteen separate investigations into a list of 579 people whom they sentenced to death; eleven months later they had assembled a second harvest of 563 more.[71] Only a few received effigy executions; however, their ex-colleague Joseph Valier got a straw dummy, replete with a fine red robe, white hat, and special scaffold.[72] Although this parlement hanged very few unarmed rebels, its victims included a minister from Normandy and a woman whose corpse was ordered burned for "execrable blasphemy, public scandal, sacrilege, and infringement of royal edicts."[73] The relative prudence of these judges stemmed from their unusually awkward situation. Throughout most of the third war, Bordeaux was effectively blockaded after Huguenots seized the stronghold of Blaye and cut off commerce on the Gironde. Worse still, four Catholic parlementary judges, including a president, had been captured by Huguenots who held them hostage at Blaye. At the end of 1569 the desperate judges in Bordeaux ordered their quarantined English and Scottish merchants to pay 500 livres toward ransoming these colleagues, and noted that there were currently ten vacancies on their bench. The stakes escalated steadily until May 1570, when the municipality paid 25,000 livres to end the blockade and the Parlement raised another 16,000 livres to ransom their four colleagues.[74] Repercussions from this nasty episode dragged on long after the Parlement had promptly registered the royal edict of pacification in August.

The end of the long and bitterly fought third war entailed two highly embarrassing problems for French parlements. Both derived from the restored legitimacy of Protestant worship stipulated by the Peace of St. Germain in the summer of 1570. First, this edict of pacification specifically repealed all wartime decisions taken against the Huguenots. In effect, this clause annulled at one stroke a large share of the criminal business transacted by most parlements since October 1568.[75] Its consequences are still visible in their surviving series of criminal *arrêts* from 1569 and 1570, which contain page after page of barred-out decisions condemning Huguenots for "infringement of royal edicts" and confiscating their property. As we have seen, over 1,100 sentences were thereby nullified at Bordeaux alone, and other parlements reveal comparable consequences. The Parlement of Paris quietly withdrew its huge "dead-or-alive" reward for capturing Admiral Coligny, who was once again invited to the royal court.

The peace of 1570 also restored Huguenot officials, including parlementary judges, to their posts. There were many such people. Diefendorf's analysis of heresy prisoners detained by the Parlement of Paris from 1566–1570 included more than twenty royal officers at or above the level of *lieutenant du bailli,* and even more of them in minor positions.[76] Therefore, in addition to trashing eighteen months of legal decisions, the 1570 pacification also brought back Huguenot ex-colleagues who had been prominent targets of that aborted jurisprudence. Such reintegration had proved extremely difficult to impose seven years earlier at the Parlement of Toulouse. After the bitter third war and the avalanche of legislation, it created extraordinarily awkward situations everywhere—though least at Paris, where, noted de Thou, the 1568 prohibition against admitting Huguenots remained unrepealed for thirty years.[77] Elsewhere, frictions persisted. At Rouen, for instance, there was frequent bickering between the First President and the most vociferous Huguenot judge, occasionally reaching crisis levels.[78]

Apparently minor symbolic legal concessions to Huguenots in 1570 could have serious consequences. One such casualty was the "cross of Gastines," the commemorative monument erected on Paris' Rue St.-Denis by order of the Parlement in 1569.[79] Although the peace treaty specified that all monuments to the persecution of Protestants were to be demolished, this provision proved to be unenforceable in the kingdom's capital. Pressure on the crown by Huguenots accomplished nothing until December 1571. When the city's magistrates finally attempted to remove this cross to a cemetery, major rioting broke out. After delaying a week, they removed it furtively, whereupon an even worse riot ensued. The legal aftermath dragged on into 1572. One hapless rioter was caught, selected as a scapegoat, and eventually hanged by order of Parlement. Later in 1572, on the second day of the St. Bartholomew's massacres, the cemetery to which the cross had been moved became the scene of a highly publicized botanical miracle (a "sterile" tree burst into bloom)—and the place where the Gastines house had stood remained vacant. Justice, whether popular or professional, remained elusive.

The next public disturbance in Paris erupted only eight months after the "cross of Gastines" riots. The St. Bartholomew's massacre began with the botched assassination of Admiral Coligny on orders from the duke of Guise. The enormous bloodbath that followed in Paris during the last week of August 1572 constitutes by far the largest outbreak of religiously motivated popular violence in sixteenth-century Europe; de Thou claimed that "in all of ancient history there was no nation whose annals offered any example of similar cruelty."[80] Everyone agrees that because of its scale and the status of the principal victims, it was a traumatic event even during an age of chronic religious warfare and frequent bloody "seditions." We need not enter the labyrinth where historians continue to assign primary responsibility for thousands of murders;[81] our principal concern is its relationship to the ongoing erosion of respect for French justice and parlementary authority. At a *lit de justice* held in the Paris Parlement on 26 August, after three days of uncontrolled rioting, Charles IX dramatically took full responsibility for Coligny's murder and the ensuing massacre, claiming they were necessary in order to forestall a Huguenot plot against the crown.[82] An official declaration was sent to all royal authorities two days later, whereby "His Majesty declared that what has happened has been by his express commandment" in order to foil the admiral's plot. At the same time, it emphasized that the 1570 edict of pacification remained in effect. The Parlement therefore promptly launched an investigation—not of the massacre but of the conspiracy, interrogating two prominent Huguenots who had been captured as the rioting finally ended.

Official justice usually worked deliberately. The Parlement did not sentence either the nobleman who had helped negotiate the 1570 pacification, or the Languedoc parlementary judge, now a *maître des requêtes* in Paris, until a month after the king's dramatic appearance in their court. Both were hanged; young de Thou, an eyewitness, noted that the Parisian mob mutilated their corpses "in an unworthy manner." But their fate was only a sideshow to the official condemnation of the master-mind behind the Huguenot conspiracy, the long-dead Coligny. One hears a few echoes of the sentencing of the Gastines for heresy three years earlier, but this decision was embellished with refinements befitting Coligny's status. As with the Gastines, a stone column with an engraved copper plaque would commemorate their decision. It would be placed at the admiral's ancestral castle of Chatillon-sur-Loing, which would be dismantled down to the last stone, with its trees sawed off at a height of exactly four feet. Last but not least, there would be an annual holiday procession in Paris on 24 August to commemorate his murder.[83]

These heaped-up judicial indignities pale beside the story of Admiral Coligny's physical corpse. Sources as diverse as Haton and de Thou agree that it became everyone's plaything, especially after the head, genitals, and limbs had been torn off. Haton tells how Parisian children held a mock trial of the dead admiral in order to determine if his corpse should be drowned, but "finally it was burned over a slow fire as a heretic and Huguenot" before being thrown in the river. He then describes how official justice literally fished the corpse's trunk from the Seine and tied it with chains to the gibbet, where it remained for over two weeks. For Haton, Coligny's posthumous desecration offered a model to be copied. He reported that boys of ten to twelve did the same thing with a Hugue-not's corpse in his home town not long afterward, and commented on the legal sophistication of the arguments employed.[84] Both chroniclers, the priest and the *parlementaire,* agree that children acted like judges in 1572. The wording of the Parlement's *arrêt,* ordering such grotesque punishments against someone whom they had never arrested, suggests that judges were starting to act like children. Meanwhile, the murders of one of the Parlement's presidents and of another judge (who was no Huguenot) during the riots were never investigated by the high court. "The few parlementary records that have survived for these events," notes Diefendorf, "relate to incidents of pillaging and not to accusations of murder."[85] The best argument that can be alleged in the judges' defense is that they could scarcely be expected to disavow their monarch, who claimed direct responsibility for mass murder on the excuse of repressing an imaginary conspiracy.

The Parisian massacre of St. Bartholomew was soon imitated on a lesser scale in several cities of the large district regulated by its Parlement. When the king's official declaration reached the three most important provincial parlementary cities, each staged its own variant of St. Bartholomew: Rouen on 17 and 20 September, Bordeaux on 3 October, and Toulouse on the following day.[86] There are certain family resemblances among these events. At both Rouen and Toulouse, the massacres occurred after the city's known Huguenots had been rounded up and interned in the parlement's prison. After a period of confusion they were summoned for release one at a time, but were slaughtered by armed thugs as soon as they were out of earshot of their fellow prisoners. At Bordeaux, the local governor authorized the massacre by a team of killers wearing red hats. At Toulouse and Bordeaux, the Huguenot parlementary judges restored in 1570 seem to have been principal targets. The very first victims of the Bordeaux rioters were two Huguenot judges; a third was saved by a Jesuit, who promptly converted him. At Toulouse, three imprisoned judges were killed with other prisoners, but their corpses were decorated with formal red robes and hanged on an elm tree in front of the Parlement building. Although none of the restored Huguenot judges was imprisoned or harmed at Rouen, all four were expelled shortly after the rioting.

Descent into the Nadir, 1588–1591

By the autumn of 1570 the French parlementary system had experienced the temporary dissolution of two courts by rebels (Rouen and Grenoble, 1562), the suspension of another by the crown (Aix, 1563–1565), hangings of parlementary judges by their colleagues (Aix and Rouen, 1562;

Paris, 1569) or by lesser authorities (Orléans, 1562), and the kidnapping of four others (Bordeaux, 1569–70). It had endured two religious wars during which Protestant worship was technically legal, when towns throughout France had experienced popular rioting and lynchings of "heretics" who could no longer be prosecuted for heresy. If the rule of law became problematic, so did court personnel. In 1562 Paris and Toulouse had purged their Huguenot membership. Everyone did so after October 1568; but the Protestant judges from Toulouse thereupon formed their own tribunal in retaliation, and everyone who had been expelled in 1568 was reinstated in August 1570. In 1572, sitting parlementary judges were lynched at Paris, Bordeaux, and Toulouse, and their colleagues never even bothered to investigate. Could things get worse for the major French courts?

They could, and they did. The best English-language history of Valois France describes the period between the St. Bartholomew's massacre and the triumph of the Holy League in the late 1580s as a gradual slide into chaos. "One civil war followed another in an aimless procession," says J. H. M. Salmon, "that demonstrated the decline of royal authority. Famine and peasant revolts followed the path of marauding armies." Though highly intelligent, Henry III lacked the will to control his upper nobility, while his "erratic and willful self-indulgence . . . alienated the loyalty of his subjects."[87] By the late 1580s the ultra-Catholic Holy League had seized virtual control of his kingdom. The League was often suspicious of the great parlements, especially Paris, as bastions of royal authority but not of Catholic zeal. There were no President Lizets or Le Maistres around to reassure them. For that matter, the Paris Parlement was equally bereft of resolute moderates like President Séguier, who had died in 1580, or Christophe de Thou, who had followed him in 1582. Consequently, during the Holy League's ascendancy the prestige of French parlements deteriorated further, until they finally reached their collective nadir around 1590.[88]

In three particular areas, parlementary judges encountered fresh difficulties in the late 1580s. First, Henry III's decree of July 1585 outlawing Protestant worship eventually led to an anachronistic revival of heresy trials in the aftermath of the League takeover at Paris and elsewhere. After a quarter-century of confessional polemics, it had become impossible to return to the practices of Henry II's day and to question prisoners closely about their theological deviations from Catholic orthodoxy. Second, instead of ignoring court decisions, mob violence was now directed against the judges themselves. The kingdom's leading court was physically imprisoned by a petty official, and the chief magistrates of its two major parlements were lynched by Holy League zealots. Finally, the monarchy lost so much of its control over its appellate courts that Henry III ordered them to reassemble in new locations in order to restore a measure of royal authority over their decisions. The resulting schism lasted about five years in most court districts, with royalist and *ligueur* parlements nullifying each other's decisions to their mutual discredit.

The last heresy trials at Paris have been well described by a member of the parlementary milieu, Pierre de l'Estoile. Although Henry III had aimed his 1585 ban on Protestant worship against the Huguenots' property rather than their lives, their situation changed suddenly after Paris fell under control of the *ligueurs* in May 1588. On midsummer eve, the new city authorities built a large dummy labeled "Heresy," hanged it on a tree, and burned it. Live executions rapidly followed this carnivalesque effigy. Five days later, the Parlement sentenced the two daughters of a parlementary lawyer, who had been imprisoned eight months before and subsequently interrogated in the king's presence, to be gagged, hanged, and their corpses burned. One of them, we are told, was burned alive "by the fury of the mob, who cut the rope before she could be strangled and cast her into the fire."[89] Within three weeks, the Parlement ordered hanging and burning for a different kind of heretic, classified as "abominable" rather than pertinacious. Instead of local Huguenots, this prisoner was a "real atheist" from Anjou. Essentially repeating the heresy of the Norman hermit whom the Parlement had burned in 1523, he "even denied that Jesus Christ was the son of God," and one source indicates that he too was roasted alive by the Paris mob.[90] Although records of the Parlement's prison show that other people, including the famous potter Bernard Palissy, were appealing death sentences for heresy in 1588, there is no evidence of other heresy executions until the spring of 1589, after many judges had been traumatized by their own arrests and incarcerations in the Bastille. Two Huguenot widows were then sentenced to death, one of whom was burned alive at Paris.[91] They are the last known executions for heresy by the greatest French appellate court.

Although records are spotty, we know that Paris was not the only parlement to resume executions for heresy after the Holy League took control of their cities. At Rouen, for example, the Parlement hanged a writing-master "of the new opinion" shortly after they learned about the Paris barricades in 1588.[92] They condemned another local man to be hanged in January 1589; next month, an apostate priest was hanged and his corpse burned after he was caught with two prohibited books. Although some other death sentences were reduced, a nobleman was condemned to be hanged and burned in June "for the crime of heresy, and for not leaving the kingdom," while another Huguenot, who remained "pertinacious in his opinion," was hanged in October.[93] Public executions for heresy, especially those that included burning, can be directly attributed to intense pressure on the judges by zealots of the Holy League. At Rouen, for example, the final execution involving burning followed shortly after the court had been threatened by a *ligueur* governor, who suspended one judge for two months.[94] But his type of intimidation seems benign compared with the state of affairs at Paris, where a onetime minor court official, promoted by the duke of Guise, proceeded to arrest several dozen parlementary judges in January 1589. L'Estoile, who was himself arrested later that year, described how the "first court of Europe" was invaded by two dozen armed thugs commanded by one of its lowest officials. When he began reading off the names of those to be arrested, the First President (who headed the list) appealed to collegial solidarity, and they "voluntarily marched out, to the number of fifty or sixty judges from all branches of parlement, including many who had not been named." Watched by jeering crowds, "arrested like criminals by a nobody and led through the streets as if in triumph," they followed their captors across town to the Bastille. Those not on the list were quickly released, but the other judges remained imprisoned for months. Meanwhile the *ligueurs* purged the court's membership and named a new First President, who immediately took the remarkable step of drawing up a notarized document certifying that he assumed his new office under duress.[95]

Soon after the "first court of Europe" underwent this humiliation, the kingdom's second parlement (and the king himself) suffered an even greater indignity. After the duke of Guise was murdered, the bishop of Comminges escaped from Henry III's custody, galloped to Toulouse, and, in alliance with one of the Parlement's presidents, was named commander of the rebellious city. After heated debate on 27 January, the Parlement could not find a majority either for supporting Henry III or for repudiating him. When the royalist leader and First President, Duranti, tried to flee the meeting, he was placed under arrest in the Dominican convent. On 10 February he was lynched by a mob, together with the king's attorney Daffis (brother of the First President at the still-loyal Parlement of Bordeaux), whose letters appealing for help had been intercepted. President Duranti's corpse was hung on a gallows facing a portrait of the king, similarly in a noose. A third judge, a *conseillier-clerc* who later became bishop of Montpellier, was condemned to death in absentia by his colleagues. Nor was this the end of the 1589 disturbances at Toulouse. In August, after Henry III's assasination, this parlement ordered an annual celebration of the event. In October the bellicose bishop of Comminges returned triumphantly after a brief exile decreed by the Parlement, governing Toulouse with the help of an armed monk and one of the court's fully armed presidents. The defeated faction, led by Duranti's successor as First President, followed the royalist governor into exile at Carcassonne.[96]

Henry III was aware that his parlements, nearly all located in cities controlled by the Holy League, were slipping away from his control early in 1589. After the assassination of the duke of Guise, their chief magistrates lived in peril of their lives unless they repudiated the king. The First President of the Parlement of Normandy fled from Rouen, while his counterpart at the Parlement of Brittany was captured but eventually ransomed. Both were more fortunate than the loyal chief magistrates at Paris, who remained imprisoned much longer, or at Toulouse. Shortly before his assassination, the last Valois ruler legally transferred the seats of many appellate courts to smaller but still-loyal cities in their district. The largest one, Paris, was ordered to reassemble at Tours, and opened its doors in April 1589; the historian de Thou, whose uncle was still jailed in the Bastille, sat among its new judges. The Parlement of Normandy was to reassemble at Caen; the Parlements of Grenoble and Aix, at Pertuis. It was a desperate gamble, because these new creations were both unprecedented and understaffed in 1589. At first their writ did not run very far, but after Henry III's assassination that summer they had one significant advantage over their rivals: they agreed about who was now the legal king of France.[97]

The *ligueur* courts, which remained in their traditional locations, kept a majority of the judges and retained much of their prestige throughout the tumultuous year of 1589, but could not decide which king they served. After Henry III's death, the Parlement of Paris solemnly proclaimed the cardinal of Bourbon as Charles X in November 1589, and most *ligueur* parlements followed suit. But the Parlement of Bordeaux, under a royalist governor who had expelled the Jesuits, continued to make its proclamations in the name of the dead king until late in 1590.[98] A situation in which schismatic parlements anathematized each other's decisions in the names of rival kings of France persisted well beyond 1589. The zealots of Paris continued to discredit their famous court, whose rival at Tours lacked prestige. L'Estoile records more threats in the summer of 1590, when several judges paid ransoms. Next year, the First President who had been installed in 1589 and two of his colleagues were captured by their own clerks, who immediately strangled them. Three days later, a parish priest proposed recreating a special court to judge heretics, composed equally of royal officials and theologians.[99] Just as the errors of the pseudo-"Lutheran" hermit of 1523 had been rediscovered and their propagator had once again been burned alive in 1588, so the ill-fated "delegated judges" of 1525 were about to be reinvented in 1591. In *ligueur* Paris, both the heresies being punished and the ideal system for punishing them had very nearly come full circle back to the days of Noel Béda—but that was the standard way that sixteenth-century "revolutionaries" operated.

Within a few years, Henry IV had untangled the ugly impasse between the royal parlements and the Reformed church created by his predecessor. Two keys unlocked all the barriers: the king's second conversion to Catholicism in 1593 and his conquest of the kingdom's capital a year later. As Paris, along with such lesser parlementary seats as Rouen or Dijon, finally recognized the Bourbon claimant, he acknowledged the legitimacy of the traditional appellate courts by officially restoring them, while obliging them to accept judges from the new tribunals created in 1589. His royalist parlements had quickly repealed Henry III's heresy legislation; *ligueur* judges accepted this *fait accompli* in exchange for being confirmed in office. In the mid-1590s Henry IV required the Parlement of Paris and his other reconstituted appellate courts to accept a few known Huguenots as judges. Several years before officially resolving the Protestant issue through his "perpetual" Edict of Nantes in 1598 and creating mixed tribunals to settle disputes between Protestants and Catholics, the first Bourbon king of France had already brought the juridical side of the French Wars of Religion to a satisfactory conclusion.

Retrospective

What had the long sixteenth-century confrontation between Europe's most prestigious judicial system and Europe's best-organized unofficial Protestant confession demonstrated? Primarily, it had shown that neither was capable of overcoming the other. The story of French heresy trials during the Protestant Reformation is richly ironic. France was both the largest monarchy in Europe and the only major state that never encountered any form of Anabaptism, the most radical Protestant doctrine. Nevertheless, in the 1520s and 1530s the French judicial system itself developed one of Europe's most successful antiheresy campaigns. And once the French state took control of heresy prosecution, it conducted the most severe repression anywhere in Europe during the mid-1540s. However, the relative severity of French punishments failed to retard the growth of Protestantism in France. And the sudden decriminalization of heresy in 1560 did not prevent the French Reformed church from plunging into the adventure of civil war shortly afterward.

During the 1530s and 1540s, the French judicial system dominated the history of early Protestant movements, but could not destroy them. During the 1550s, as French Reformed Protestantism grew rapidly and greatly strengthened its organization, it began to exercise some indirect influence over the French court system, but could not control it. Because the survival of French parlements was never in doubt, it is the endurance of the French Protestant movement, despite its inability to control the levers of power in Europe's largest kingdom, that requires explanation. How did it survive waves of legal persecution?

The history of sixteenth-century French Protestantism reverses the history of its repression. Judicial prosecution of French "Lutheranism" was most successful in the early decades, the 1520s and 1530s, when it destroyed Briçonnet's evangelical experiment at Meaux, burned the only "Lutheran" with a judicial office, disrupted programs of Christian humanism at leading universities, and responded rapidly to the most daring organized religious provocation, the 1534 "sacramentarian" placards, with a savage campaign of executions. Parlementary initiatives drove a program of repression that accomplished many of its intended purposes, frightening French religious dissenters into conformity or flight. During the 1540s, as French heresy trials and executions reached their apogee under increasing monarchical direction, repression continued to produce some of its intended effects. Under duress, French Protestants remained divided in both doctrine and behavior. The artisans of Meaux, attempting to organize an alternative church, were captured en masse with relative ease and punished in a display of surpassing cruelty. A few other clandestine Protestant groups were uncovered and examples were made; in at least one case (Langres) the movement never recovered. However, the worst excesses of heresy prosecution under Francis I—the crusade of 1545 against the Waldensians of Provence and the *auto-da-fé* staged at Meaux in 1546—provoked significant protests from his nonheretical subjects. Although the despoiled landlords of Provence received no material benefits from the special court of Queen's Chamber in 1548, and even though Jacques Fayol perished along with his manuscript criticizing the Meaux bonfires, they were understood at the summit of the French judiciary: such mistakes were never repeated.

Governmental persecution peaked many years before the diverse movements of early French Protestantism coalesced into organized churches following Genevan doctrines. The number of executions and public abjurations imposed by royal judges fell slowly but steadily after Francis I died. Henry II's series of increasingly draconian edicts against "Lutheran" and "sacramentarian" heretics in the 1550s had no more effect on parlementary judges than the endlessly repeated royal edicts condemning blasphemy. The most important (but unintended) consequence of the intensive French heresy prosecutions of the 1540s and the anti-Protestant edicts of the 1550s was to stimulate many Protestant sympathizers into following Calvin's advice and emigrating to Geneva.

French Protestantism grew so rapidly in the 1550s partly because of the ineffective manner in which it was prosecuted. A major paradox surrounding the history of French heresy trials began to develop: the more that Genevan-based propaganda screamed against the atrocities of Catholic persecution, the fewer the number of atrocities that actually occurred. French judges rarely articulated what they were doing. The deliberate laconism of parlementary legal *arrêts* masks the judges' motivations, regardless of whether they decided cases with lenience or severity, while the gags that they stuffed into the mouths of prisoners being led off to be executed for heresy literally muffled their opponents. If the prisoners could not speak, a flood of printed Protestant propaganda, which government authorities were completely unable to control, spoke for them.

Realizing how powerless French authorities were against the tide of printed propaganda from Geneva helps us understand why the courts were unable to punish any of the Genevan-trained preachers serving several key French Reformed churches after 1555. Even the fortuitous capture of three of their earliest missionaries in Savoy and their execution at Chambéry served only to increase the Genevans' precautions while giving them a prestigious set of martyrs. As the French Reformed church developed in the later 1550s, heresy prosecution continued to slacken. Catholic observers complained that French parlements could not or would not enforce Henry II's stringent laws against heretics; Protestant sympathizers within the court system ensured that many suspects were never arrested, or else not prosecuted vigorously after they were caught. At the same time, the Protestants' will to resist these laws increased. Although neither the Calvinists nor the judges advertised these events, successful rescues of convicted prisoners multiplied dramatically in the late 1550s.

The crisis and resolution of parlementary prosecutions for heresy occurred between the Paris *mercuriale* of April 1559 and the better-known Edict of January in 1562. An outraged Henry II had thrown several parlementary judges into the Bastille in 1559 and sworn to see one of them burned—which he ultimately was, during a final burst of severity at the Paris Parlement. However, barely thirty months after Henry's outburst, his widow and her chancellor pressured handpicked pairs of judges from each French parlement into approving the daring innovation of permitting public worship by Protestants. The interval had been extraordinarily tumultuous. Fear of a movement that had grown beyond the government's power to control it led Catherine de Médicis first to appease it through royal pardons and then to accommodate it through some type of theological compromise that would preserve the essential features of the Gallican church. But the pardons served mainly to confuse and irritate loyal Catholics, while the attempts at compromise (begun at the Parlement of Paris before the fateful 1559 *mercuriale*) ultimately shattered against the rock of irreconcilable eucharistic differences. Toleration then became the alternative official policy—but could it work?

Most of the essential provisions of Catherine's Edict of January remained in effect throughout the long and dreary Wars of Religion, which filled the final third of sixteenth-century French history. Except for brief periods in the late 1560s and after 1585, heresy was no longer a criminal offense in France. The government and the judges implicitly acknowledged the legal reality of the Reformed church, using such politic euphemisms as the "new opinion." Protestsant opposition escalated into civil war but remained caught in an insoluble dilemma. The "so-called Reformed religion," as it was now officially called, suffered from a legitimacy gap. The Huguenots could not overthrow the established French church, because they could never gain control of the monarch or of his court system. At the same time, their tight-knit organization and strong noble leadership could mobilize a vital minority of the kingdom's human resources. During the first religious war, everyone suffered from the ensuing stalemate. With heresy decriminalized, French parlements generally played only marginal roles during an age of chronic warfare. One exception confirms this rule: after the Parlement of Toulouse successfully directed their local war effort in 1562, they harvested a French record for executing "seditious" Huguenots.

By the 1590s, France's religious wars had wreaked enormous damage on the kingdom's appellate court system. In the 1560s, several parlements had suffered indignities from Protestants, who dismantled two of them, and who later kidnapped judges at a third court. However, French parlements suffered even worse insults to their authority during the Wars of Religion from Catholic zealots, who began these wars by lynching masses of Huguenots. In the 1560s a few parlementary judges were hanged by their colleagues, but by 1572 Catholic mobs were lynching Protestant judges from three different parlements. At the apogee of religious warfare in the late 1580s and early 1590s, it was not the Protestants but the zealots of the Holy League who terrorized the chief justices of several parlements, all of whom were Catholics. They lynched the head of France's second-ranking court, then imprisoned many judges and even hanged the chief justice whom they had themselves installed at what had been and would be again Europe's premier law court, the Parlement of Paris. Only the compromises of Henry IV rescued French royal parlements from virtual chaos in the mid-1590s; within a decade after the last Protestant was burned for heresy at Paris, this king imposed solutions that enabled both the parlements and the French Reformed church to coexist peacefully throughout most of the seventeenth century.

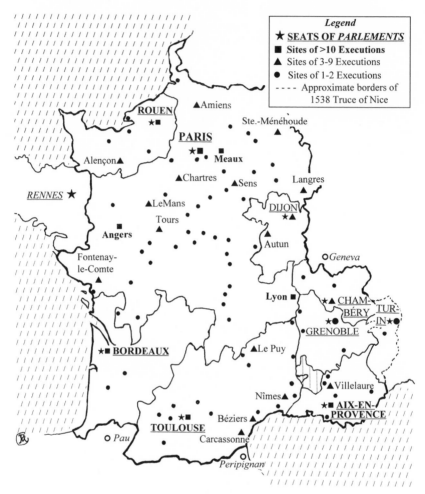

ROUEN
★■

▲Amiens

Ste.-Ménéhoude

PARIS
★■
●Meaux

Alençon▲

▲Chartres ▲Sens Langres

RENNES ★

▲LeMans

Tours

■
Angers

Fontenay-
le-Comte
▲

DIJON
★▲

Autun

○_Geneva_

Lyon ■ ★▲ **CHAM-
BÉRY** TUR-
★● IN★●
★★
●**GRENOBLE**

★■ **BORDEAUX**

▲Le Puy

▲Villelaure

Nîmes▲

**AIX-EN-
PROVENCE**
★■

★■
TOULOUSE Béziers ▲

○ _Pau_ Carcassonne

○
Peripignan

Locations of Heresy Executions in France
1523–1560

Appendix: Heresy Executions Ordered in France, 1523–1560

Dates are given in European style (day/month/year). Entries in italics were never appealed to a Parlement. (W) = Waldensians; (I) = iconoclasts.

Date	Parlement	Name	Occupation	Place arrested	Place executed	Reference
8/8/1523	Paris	Jean Valliere	hermit	?	Paris	Versoris, 127–128
28/8/1526	Paris	Jacques Pavanes	student	Paris	Paris	Crespin, I, 263–264
26/10/1527	Paris	Monsieur de la Tour	gentleman	Paris	Paris	*JBP*, 326–327
15/12/1528	Paris	Denis Rieux	boatman	Meaux	Paris	Crespin, I, 272
26/4/1529	Paris	Louis de Berquin	gentleman-author	Paris	Paris	*JBP*, 378–381
?/?/1530	Grenoble	*Etienne Renier*	monk (Aug.)	Annonay	Vienne	Crespin, I, 283
6/5/1532	Toulouse	Jean de Caturce	law professor	Toulouse	Toulouse	ADHG, B 3355, fol. 67
17/2/1533	Aix (W)	Jean Roux	farmer	?	Aix (corpse)	ADBR, B 4488
"	Aix (W)	Guillaume Serre	farmer	?	Aix	"
"	Aix (W)	Jean Balmas	farmer	?	Aix	"
"	Aix (W)	Jeanne Bosque	?	?	Aix	"
"	Aix (W)	Marguerite Gros	housewife	?	?	"
"	Aix (W)	Pierre Bouchard	farmer	?	?	"
"	Aix (W)	Thomas Martin	farmer	?	?	"
11/12/1533	Rouen	Etienne Le Court	priest	Alençon	Rouen	ADSM, G 2154
?/3/1534	Paris	Jean Pointet	surgeon	Paris	Paris	Crespin, I, 287
17/6/1534	Paris	Laurent Canu	monk (Fran.)	Lyon	Paris	Crespin, I, 285–287
7/9/1534	Paris (I)	Nicolas Briolay	?	Alençon	Alençon	AN, X2a 83
9/9/1534	Paris (I)	Jean Ruel	?	Alençon	Alençon	"
12/9/1534	Paris (I)	Etienne Taignel	?	Paris	Alençon	"

Date	Parlement	Name	Occupation	Place arrested	Place executed	Reference
12/9/1534	Paris (I)	Jean Coumyn	?	Paris	Alençon	AN, X2a 83
15/9/1534	Paris (I)	Jean LeBrun	?	Alençon	Alençon	"
10/11/1534	Paris	Barthelemy Mollon	? (crippled)	Paris	Paris	JBP, 444
"	Paris	Jean DuBourg	merchant	Paris	Paris	"
"	Paris	unnamed	printer	Paris	Paris	"
18/11/1534	Paris	unnamed	weaver	Paris	Paris	BSHPF 11 (1862)
19/11/1534	Paris	unnamed	bookbinder	Paris	Paris	"
"	Paris	Henri Poille	stonemason	Meaux	Paris	"
4/12/1534	Paris	Hugues Nissier	servant of cleric	Paris	Paris	"
5/12/1534	Paris	unnamed	illustrator	Paris	Paris	JBP, 446
23/12/1534	Rouen	Richard Le Blond	priest	Rouen	Rouen	ADSM, 1B 3117
24/12/1534	Paris	Antoine Augereau	printer	Paris	Paris	BSHPF 11 (1862)
21/1/1535	Paris	Jean Lenfant	fruit wholesaler	Paris	Paris	"
"	Paris	Nicolas L'Huillier	law-court scribe	Paris	Paris	"
"	Paris	Nicolas Valeton	tax-collector	Paris	Paris	JBP, 447
"	Paris	unnamed	cabinetmaker	Paris	Paris	BSHPF 11 (1862)
"	Paris	Simon Foubet	king's singer	Amboise	Paris	JBP, 449
"	Paris	unnamed	basketmaker	Paris	Paris	BSHPF 11 (1862)
22/1/1535	Paris	"La Catelle"	school teacher	Paris	Paris	"
15/2/1535	Aix (W)	Catherine Bertina	?	Villelaure	Villelaure	ADBR, B 4491
"	Aix (W)	Estienne Vilhot	innkeeper	Pertuis	Pertuis	"
"	Aix (W)	Jean Vincens	farmer	Lourmarin	Lourmarin	"
"	Aix (W)	Jean Blanc	farmer	Villelaure	Villelaure	"
"	Aix (W)	Jean Roux	farmer	Lourmarin	Lourmarin	"
"	Aix (W)	Michel Coures	farmer	Villelaure	Villelaure	"

Date	Parlement	Name	Occupation	Place arrested	Place executed	Reference
16/2/1535	Paris	Etienne de la Forge	merchant	Paris	Paris	JBP, 447
26/2/1535	Paris	Louis de Medici	dry-goods merchant	Paris	Paris	JBP, 448
"	Paris	unnamed	university student	Paris	Paris	
5/5/1535	Paris	Estienne Bénard	attorney	Paris	Paris	AN, X2b 2
"	Paris	Jean Fouan-dit-Tournay	shoemaker	Paris	Paris	"
"	Paris	Martin du Val	tailor	Paris	Paris	"
10/5/1535	Paris	Jean Aubin	?	Chartres	Chartres	"
30/8/1535	Rouen	Guillaume Huchon	apothecary	Dieppe	Rouen	ADSM, 1B 3118
18/9/1535	Paris	unnamed	ribbonmaker	Paris	Paris	JBP, 452
"	Paris	unnamed	ribbonmaker	Paris	Paris	"
22/12/1535	Paris	Guillaume Carteri	?	Ste. Mene-hould	Ste. Mene-hould	AN, X2a 86
25/4/1536	Grenoble	Martin Gonin	printer-preacher	Dauphiné	Grenoble	Crespin, I, 317–320
11/7/1537	Toulouse	*unnamed*	?	*Nîmes*	*Nîmes*	Herminjard, IV, 315–321
"	*Toulouse*	*unnamed*	?	*Nîmes*	*Nîmes*	"
12/4/1538	Paris	Etienne Sabray	student	Paris	Paris	AN, X2b 5
15/4/1538	Paris	Jean de la Garde	bookseller	Paris	Paris	"
27/4/1538	Paris	Jean Salmon	?	Paris	Paris	"
10/9/1538	Toulouse	Louis de Rocheta	monk (Dom.)	Toulouse	Toulouse	ADHG, B 3360
12/12/1538	Toulouse	Gabriel Amalin	?	Carcassonne	Carcassonne	ADHG, B 3361
4/2/1539	Bordeaux	Jerome Vendocin	schoolmaster	Agen	Agen	Crespin, I, 342
26/2/1539	Aix	Jean Bailliet	?	?	Aix	ADBR, B 4496
19/4/1539	Chambéry	*Loys Curtet*	*attorney*	Annecy	Annecy	Crespin, I, 328
26/4/1539	Chambéry	Jean Lambert	?	Chambéry	Chambéry	Herminjard, V, 281

Date	Parlement	Name	Occupation	Place arrested	Place executed	Reference
10/5/1539	Toulouse	Etienne Margeti	priest	Montauban	Toulouse	ADHG, B 3362, fol 412
?/9/1539	Paris	Denis Brion	barber	Sancerre	Angers	Crespin, I, 341
28/11/1539	Paris	Jacques de Neuvilliers	?	Sézanne	Sézanne	AN, X2a 89A
13/12/1539	Paris	Jean Michel	monk	Bourges	Bourges	"
5/2/1540	Paris	Jean Boursault	?	Montargis	Montargis	"
17/2/1540	Paris	Nicolas Le Moine	wool-carder	Meaux	Meaux	"
"	Paris	Toussaint Brochet	fuller	Meaux	Meaux	"
17/6/1540	Dijon (I)	unnamed	?	Autun	Autun	AN, U 1084
"	Dijon (I)	unnamed	?	Autun	Autun	
27/6/1540	Toulouse	Prosper Reboul	?	Viviers	Viviers	ADHG, B 3363
?/6/1540	Grenoble	Etienne Brun	farmer	Gap	Gap	Crespin, I, 335–336
16/10/1540	Aix (W)	Colin Pellenq	farmer	Apt	Aix	ADBR, B 5443
"	Aix	Noé Tabuys	barrelmaker	St. Vincent	Aix	"
18/11/1540	Aix (W)	Jacques Pellenq	miller	Apt	Aix	"
?/2/1541	Paris	Denis Saureau	?	Angers	Angers	Crespin, I, 526
"	Paris	François Fradeau	?	Angers	Angers	"
"	Paris	Guillaume de Rey	?	Angers	Angers	"
"	Paris	Jean de la Vignole	?	Angers	Angers	"
"	Paris	Simon Le Royer	?	Angers	Angers	"
31/3/1541	Grenoble	Jean Rosteng	?	Romans	Romans	ADI, B 3023
30/6/1541	Aix (I)	Vincent Tabuys	barrelmaker	Peypin d'Aygues	Aix	ADBR, B 5443
17/11/1541	Paris	Claude Le Peinctre	?	Paris	Paris	AN, X2a 92
17/5/1542	Paris	Geoffroy Le Blanc	?	Paris	Paris	AN, X2a 93

Date	Parlement	Name	Occupation	Place arrested	Place executed	Reference
8/7/1542	Paris	Jean Dubec	priest	Troyes	Troyes	AN, X2a 93
10/7/1542	Paris	Damien du Ruel	nobleman	Normandy?	Paris	"
18/7/1542	Paris	Gabriel Barre	forester	Paris	Paris	"
26/7/1542	Bordeaux	Jean Joyau	?	?	Bordeaux	Patry, 14–15
"	Bordeaux	Pierre Faguet	?	?	Bordeaux	"
8/8/1542	Bordeaux	Guillaume Boyer	priest	?	Bordeaux	Patry, 17–18
26/8/1542	Bordeaux	Aymon de la Voye	schoolmaster	Ste. Foy	Bordeaux	Patry, 19–20
7/10/1542	Bordeaux	Paul d'Enserville	nobleman	Normandy?	Bordeaux	Patry, 28–29
14/11/1542	Paris	Jacques Ryau	?	Angers	Angers	AN, X2a 94
1/3/1543	Paris	Jean Burgeat	lawyer	Vassy	(escaped)	"
3/3/1543	Paris	Gilles d'Angers	executioner	Meaux	Paris	"
16/3/1543	Paris	Jacques Segné	barber-surgeon	Dun-le-Roi	Dun-le-Roi	"
10/4/1543	Toulouse	Antoine Sabatier	?	Beaucaire	Toulouse	ADHG, B 3368
"	Toulouse	Antoine Armandes	?	Beaucaire	?	
4/2/1544	Paris	Jean Besme	shoemaker	Clermont-Ferrand	Clermont-Ferrand	AN, X2a 96
5/3/1544	Aix	Denis Aumenge	?	?	Aix	ADBR, B 5446
27/3/1544	Paris	Antoine de la Vau	student	Bourges	Bourges	AN, X2a 96
2/4/1544	Aix (W)	Thomas Pellenq	farmer	Apt	Apt	ADBR, B 5446
29/4/1544	Paris	Jean du Chasteau	barber-surgeon	Laval	Laval	AN, X2a 96
30/4/1544	Paris	Loys Villat	?	Issoudun	Issoudun	
30/5/1544	Toulouse	Pierre de la Serre	schoolmaster	?	Toulouse	BSHPF 24 (1875), 550–551
2/9/1544	Paris	Charles Anthoine	?	La Rochelle	La Rochelle	AN, X2b 6
"	Paris	Jacques Morin	?	Cognac	Cognac	"

Date	Parlement	Name	Occupation	Place arrested	Place executed	Reference
2/9/1544	Paris	Marie Gabaride	?	Fontenay-le-Comte	Fontenay-le-Comte	AN, X2b 6
"	Paris	Pierre Vallet	?	La Rochelle	Paris	"
12/11/1544	Paris	Adam Le Maistre	clothmaker	Amiens	Amiens	AN, X2a 97
15/12/1544	Rouen	Richard Ponchet	?	Montrevillier	Rouen	ADSM, 1B 3127
"	Rouen	Vincent Périer	?	Montrevillier	Rouen	"
2/1/1545	Paris	Olivier Le Noir	?	Reims	Reims	AN, X2a 97
8/1/1545	Paris	François Bribart	royal secretary	Chaumont-en-Bassigny	Paris	"
4/2/1545	Paris	Simon Courtemaiche	wool-carder	Meaux	Meaux	"
11/3/1545	Paris	Mathurin de Boisguyon	nobleman	Chartres	Paris	"
17/3/1545	Aix	Jean de la Croix	?	?	Aix	ADBR, B 5448
20/3/1545	Paris	Mathurin Blondeau	?	Tours	Tours	AN, X2a 97
13/4/1545	Paris	François Fremon	weaver	Chatellerault	Chatellerault	"
23/5/1545	Aix	Anthoine Guerin	apothecary	Marseille	Marseille	ADBR, B 5448
"	Aix	Gaspard Boulart	montanes	Marseille	Marseille	"
15/6/1545	Aix	Laurens Gay	?	Ste. Tulle	Aix	"
"	Aix (W)	Peyron Dupuy	farmer	Cabrières d'Avignon	Aix	"
16/6/1545	Aix	Denis Gaultier	?	Digne	Aix	"
"	Aix	Jean Baussar	?	?	Aix	"
"	Aix (W)	Michel Maynard	farmer	Mérindol	Aix	"
19/6/1545	Paris	Arnauld Galdras	?	Angouleme	Angouleme	AN, X2a 99
"	Paris	Jean Dongeon	?	La Rochelle	Fontenay-le-Comte	"

Date	Parlement	Name	Occupation	Place arrested	Place executed	Reference
19/6/1545	Paris	Pierre Achard	?	Angouleme	Angouleme	AN, X2a 99
22/6/1545	Paris	Jean Fevre	?	La Rochelle	Fontenay-le-Comte	"
15/7/1545	Paris	Antoine Georges	ran salt warehouse	Chinon	Chinon	"
29/7/1545	Aix (W)	François Dupuy	?	Cabrières d'Avignon	Aix	ADBR, B 5448
1/8/1545	Paris	Liette Gibier	wife of Gilles Foulard (18/3/1546)	Niort	Niort	AN, X2a 99
24/9/1545	Paris	Olivier Guillebault	furrier	Poitiers	Le Mans	"
"	Paris	Pierre Fallodin	?	Le Mans	Le Mans	"
28/9/1545	Paris	Olivier Prieur	goldsmith	Loudun	Loudun	"
8/10/1545	Paris	Nicolas Marchant	draper	Chaumont-en-Bassigny	Chaumont-en-Bassigny	"
15/12/1545	Paris	Gillet Pierre	?	Nevers	Nevers	AN, X2a 100
23/12/1545	Paris	Noel Dubois	monk	Meaux	Paris	"
16/1/1546	Toulouse	Marsal Guersin	?	Béziers	Béziers	ADHG, B 3379
17/3/1546	Toulouse	Jean Garde	?	?	Toulouse	ADHG, B 3375
18/3/1546	Paris	Gilles Foulard	weaver	Niort	Niort	AN, X2a 100
26/3/1546	Toulouse	Jean Moquet	?	Marmejols	Marmejols	ADHG, B 3375
30/3/1546	Rouen	Victor Duboys	?	?	Rouen	ADSM, 1B 3129
5/4/1546	Bordeaux	Jean Bernede	teacher	Agen	Agen	Patry, 48–49
30/4/1546	Toulouse	Philibert Noveau	?	?	Toulouse	ADHG, B 3376
?/4/1546	Bordeaux	Simon Paillard	bookseller	Périgueux	Bordeaux	AN, X2a 98
1/5/1546	Paris (I)	Jean Guintel	?	Varennes	Varennes	"
"	Paris (I)	Antoine Saclier	?	Varennes	Varennes	"

Date	Parlement	Name	Occupation	Place arrested	Place executed	Reference
5/5/1546	Paris	Robert Dupont	?	Angers	Angers	AN, X2a 98
17/7/1546	Paris	Me Pierre Chapot	?	?	Paris	"
"	Paris	Nicolas Gobillon	carpenter	?	Paris	"
2/8/1546	Paris	Etienne Dolet	publisher	Lyon	Paris	"
19/8/1546	Paris	Michel Vincent	printer	?	Paris	"
27/8/1546	Paris	Olivier Rousset	?	St. Pierre-le-Moustier	Seze	"
10/9/1546	Paris	Antoine Le Sot	printer	?	Paris	"
13/9/1546	Paris	Pierre Questeau	?	?	Paris	"
27/9/1546	Paris	Guillaume Aubert	?	Angouleme	(escaped)	AN, X2a 108, fol. 27v
2/10/1546	Paris	Etienne Mangin	wool-carder	Meaux	Meaux	AN, X2a 98
"	Paris	François Leclerc	?	Meaux	Meaux	"
"	Paris	Henri Hutinot	?	Meaux	Meaux	"
"	Paris	Jacques Bouchebec	?	Meaux	Meaux	"
"	Paris	Jean Baudouin	?	Meaux	Meaux	"
"	Paris	Jean Flesche	?	Meaux	Meaux	"
"	Paris	Jean Piquery	?	Meaux	Meaux	"
"	Paris	Jean Matelon	?	Meaux	Meaux	"
"	Paris	Jean Brisebarre	?	Meaux	Meaux	"
"	Paris	Michel Caillou	?	Meaux	Meaux	"
"	Paris	Philippe Petit	?	Meaux	Meaux	"
"	Paris	Pierre Leclerc	?	Meaux	Meaux	"
"	Paris	Pierre Piquery	?	Meaux	Meaux	"
"	Paris	Thomas Honoré	?	Meaux	Meaux	"
5/10/1546	Paris	Macé Moreau	?	Troyes	Troyes	"

Date	Parlement	Name	Occupation	Place arrested	Place executed	Reference
13/10/1546	Paris	Jean Volant	?	Blois	Blois	AN, X2a 98
14/10/1546	Toulouse	Jeanne Sendresse	?	Montauban	Toulouse	ADHG, B 3378
15/10/1546	Paris	Jean Bataille	?	Le Mans	Le Mans	AN, X2a 98
21/10/1546	Paris	Guillaume Saulnier	?	Poitiers	Poitiers	"
6/12/1546	Toulouse	Simon de Macris	monk	Castres	Toulouse	ADHG, B 3379
15/12/1546	Paris	Philippe Adenet	?	Vitry-le-François	Vitry-le-François	AN, X2a 102
22/12/1546	Paris	Jacques Fayol	author	Paris	Paris	"
5/1/1547	Paris	François Malot	?	Aubigny	Aubigny	"
"	Paris	Pierre Baulgence	?	Aubigny	Aubigny	"
"	Paris	Pierre Bonpain	?	Aubigny	Paris	"
7/1/1547	Paris	Jean Lefevre	?	Meaux	Meaux	"
10/1/1547	Paris	Etienne Bellault	?	Beaugency	Beaugency	"
17/1/1547	Paris	Denis Brochard	?	Paris	Paris	"
18/1/1547	Paris	Etienne Polliot	?	Chateau-Thierry	Paris	"
19/1/1547	Paris	Jean Pibrasse	?	Poitiers	Paris	"
21/1/1547	Paris	Antoine Balarin	?	Lyon	Lyon	"
22/1/1547	Paris	Me Jean Langlois	lawyer	Sens	Sens	"
27/1/1547	Paris	Guillaume Alix	candlemaker	Tours	Tours	"
10/3/1547	Toulouse	Astorgue Baillete	?	Charnac	Mende	ADHG, B 3380
22/4/1547	Rouen	Jean Labbey	blacksmith	Pontlevesque	Pontlevesque	ADSM, 1B 3131
6/5/1547	Bordeaux	Jean Moreau	?	Barcilhac	Bordeaux	ADG, 1B 89, fol. 27v
7/6/1547	Toulouse	Pierre Sapientis	monk	Lodeve	Toulouse	ADHG, B 3380
16/7/1547	Chambéry	Nicolas de la Motte	embroiderer	Chambéry	Chambéry	ADS, B 51, fol. 137v

Date	Parlement	Name	Occupation	Place arrested	Place executed	Reference
12/8/1547	Toulouse	Claude Dimenche	?	Carcassonne	Carcassonne	ADHG, B 3381
10/9/1547	Paris	Benoît Ravasset	tailor	Lyon	Paris	AN, X2a 103
21/10/1547	Rouen	Loys Marant	?	St. Lo	Rouen	ADSM, 1B 3132
27/1/1548	Toulouse	Arnauld Escullier	?	Montech	Montech	ADHG, B 3382
"	Toulouse	Me Pierre Delamans	?	Montech	Toulouse	"
7/2/1548	Rouen	Loys Payet	?	Pontlevesque	Pontlevesque	ADSM, 1B 3133
3/3/1548	Paris	Jean Brugere	?	Clermont-Ferrand	Issoire	Crespin, I, 520–525
19/4/1548	Toulouse	Antoine Treille	priest	Beaucaire	Toulouse	ADHG, B 3383
18/5/1548	Rouen	Jean du Rozel	monk	Bayeux	Caen	ADSM, 1B 3134
26/5/1548	Paris	Pierre Guyon	?	Auxerre	Paris	Weiss, no. 23
2/6/1548	Paris	Pierre Ravon	?	Paris	Paris	Weiss, no. 28
23/7/1548	Paris	Jean Chalamond	?	?	Riom	Weiss, no. 93
"	Paris	Pierre Grant'homme	?	Sézanne	Sézanne	Weiss, no. 94
1/8/1548	Paris	Jean Thuillier	musician	Langres	Paris	Weiss, no. 101
"	Paris	Jean Le Camus	swordmaker	Langres	Paris	"
"	Paris	Michel Mareschal	?	Langres	Paris	"
"	Paris	Robert Le Lievre	preacher	Langres	Paris	"
3/9/1548	Paris	Catherine Cremer	?	Langres	Langres	Weiss, no. 119
"	Paris	Guillaume Michau	goldsmith	Langres	Langres	"
"	Paris	Jacques Boullerot	polisher	Langres	Langres	"
"	Paris	Jacques Royer	tinsmith	Langres	Langres	"
"	Paris	Jean Taffignon	?	Langres	Langres	"
"	Paris	Jeanne Baillye	wife of Taffignon	Langres	Langres	"
"	Paris	Marguerite Sejournant	wife of Michau	Langres	Langres	"

Date	Parlement	Name	Occupation	Place arrested	Place executed	Reference
3/9/1548	Paris	Simon Mareschal	shoemaker	Langres	Langres	Weiss, no. 119
4/9/1548	Toulouse	Etienne Issoire	?	?	Le Puy	ADHG, B92J, fol. 10
18/9/1548	Toulouse	Vidal Badoc	?	Marvejols	Le Puy	ADHG, B92J, fol. 63
2/10/1548	Paris	Blaise Chappière	?	Auxerre	Auxerre	Weiss, no. 140
3/10/1548	Paris	Leonard Dupré	?	Bar-sur-Seine	Paris	Weiss, no. 142
4/10/1548	Paris	Antoine Sebilleau	?	Chinon	Paris	Weiss, no. 143
24/10/1548	Paris	Jeanne Philippe	wife of Verdel	Vitry-le-François	Vitry-le-François	Weiss, no. 166
25/10/1548	Paris	Pierre Jarlatte	?	Vierzon	Vierzon	Weiss, no. 169
26/10/1548	Paris	Nicolas Huart	?	Hesdin	Hesdin	Weiss, no. 172
4/12/1548	Aix	Pierre de l'Ecluse	monk (Aug.)	Arles	Aix	ADBR, B 5449
10/12/1548	Paris	Sanctin Lyvet	?	Meaux	Paris	AN, X2a 106
14/12/1548	Paris	Pantaleon Hebert	?	Lagny	Lagny	"
6/3/1549	Paris	Jean Bluteau	?	Ste. Menehould	Ste. Menehould	"
"	Paris	Perrette Bouillon	?	Ste. Menehould	Ste. Menehould	"
8/3/1549	Paris	Jean Bourgeois	?	Noyon	Paris	"
9/3/1549	Paris	Pierre Le Maçon	?	La Ferté-Bernard	La Ferté-Bernard	"
21/3/1549	Paris	Jean Desars	clothmaker	Amiens	Amiens	"
"	Paris	Mathieu Glenard	?	Amiens	Amiens	"
?/3/1549	Dijon	Hubert Chériet	apprentice	Dijon	Dijon	Crespin, I, 537
8/4/1549	Paris	Loys Jolippon	?	Etampes	Paris	AN, X2a 106
?/5/1549	Paris	Octavian Blondel	merchant	Lyon	Paris	Crespin, I, 528

Date	Parlement	Name	Occupation	Place arrested	Place executed	Reference
9/7/1549	Paris	unnamed	tailor	?	Paris	Crespin, I, 538
"	Paris	Florent Venot	?	Brie	Paris	Crespin, I, 540
"	Paris	Me Leonard Galimar	priest	Blois	Paris	"
19/7/1549	Aix	Etienne Moucheron	apothecary	?	Aix	ADBR, B 5451
20/7/1549	Toulouse	Jean Gairouste	?	Villefranche-en-Rouergue	Villefranche-en-Rouergue	ADHG, B 3386
?/7/1549	Paris	Etienne Peloquin	?	Blois	Paris	Crespin, I, 537
28/9/1549	Paris	Anne Audibert	widow	Orléans	Orléans	Crespin, I, 541
"	Paris	Claude Thierry	apothecary	Orléans	Orléans	Crespin, I, 541
7/10/1549	Bordeaux	Me Thomas de la Fontaine	?	Tulle	Bordeaux	Patry, 56–57
21/11/1549	Paris	Jean Cochet	?	Beaugency	Beaugency	AN, X2a 107
28/11/1549	Bordeaux	Me Jean Seguin	schoolmaster	Bergerac	Bordeaux	Patry, 62–63
4/12/1549	Paris	Jacques Duval	tailor	Soissons	Paris	AN, X2a 107
4/1/1550	Bordeaux	Peyrothon Anchier	priest	Agen	Bordeaux	Patry, 63–65
13/1/1550	Toulouse	Jean Banguil	monk (Dom.)	Montauban	Toulouse	ADHG, B 3387
13/3/1550	Toulouse	Jean Morelet	?	Beaucaire	Beaucaire	ADHG, B 3388
27/3/1550	Chambéry	Jean Godeau	?	Chambéry	Chambéry	ADS, B 54, fol. 18
29/3/1550	Chambéry	Gabriel Beraudin	?	Chambéry	Chambéry	" fol. 28
8/5/1550	Toulouse	Guillaume Forjo	shoemaker	Cassagnies de Begones	Cassagnies de Begones	ADHG, B 3388
20/5/1550	Toulouse	Charles Emond	monk (Fran.)	Rodez	Toulouse	"
23/5/1550	Rouen	Jean Filleul	?	Rouen	Rouen	ADSM, 1B 3138
"	Rouen	Pierre Mailloux	?	Rouen	Rouen	"
10/6/1550	Bordeaux	Jean Dumoulin	locksmith	Mont-de-Marsan	Mont-de-Marsan	Patry, 83–84

Date	Parlement	Name	Occupation	Place arrested	Place executed	Reference
10/6/1550	Bordeaux	Me Pierre Dandejoux	priest	Mont-de-Marsan	Mont-de-Marsan	Patry, 83–84
17/10/1550	Toulouse	Laurens Leuze	?	Montpellier	Béziers	ADHG, B92L/ f. 146
26/11/1550	Bordeaux	Etienne de la Vigne	priest	?	Bordeaux	Methivier, 516–524
11/12/1550	Paris (I)	Jean Thuars	?	Paris	Paris	AN, X2a 109
23/12/1550	Turin	Paul de la Rive	monk (Fran.)	Pignerol	Pignerol	Romier, 201–202
14/8/1551	Toulouse	Michel Chateaumolin	?	Pézenas	Pézenas	ADHG, B 3392
17/8/1551	Toulouse	Jean Pech (alias Medici)	?	Uzès	Uzès	"
27/8/1551	Toulouse	Jean Duran	?	Béziers	Toulouse	"
2/9/1551	Toulouse	Pierre Farget	?	Carcassonne	Toulouse	ADHG, B 3393
19/9/1551	Paris	*Thomas de St. Paul*	*merchant*	*Soissons*	*Paris*	Crespin, I, 558–560
25/9/1551	Toulouse	Jean Juery	?	Mende	Toulouse	ADHG, B 3393
"	Toulouse	Jean Blansenne	?	Mende	Toulouse	"
16/10/1551	Bordeaux	Guillaume de Beaulieu	?	Tulle	Bordeaux	Patry, 100–101
26/10/1551	Paris	Claude Monier	tutor	Lyon	Lyon	Crespin, I, 552–555
29/10/1551	Toulouse	Jacques Formé	cabinetmaker	Lectoure	Toulouse	ADHG, B 3393
7/11/1551	Aix	Jean Guichard	?	Draguignan	Aix	ADBR, B 5452
23/12/1551	Toulouse	Etienne Angelin	?	Nîmes	Nîmes	ADHG, B 3394
?/1/1552	Chambéry	*Hugues Gravier*	*schoolmaster*	*Baugé*	*Bourg-en-Bresse*	Crespin, I, 681–682
22/3/1552	Toulouse	André Chambon	?	Baignols-les-Bains	Baignols-les-Bains	ADHG, B 3396
26/4/1552	Rouen	Michel Pol	courier	?	Rouen	ADSM, 1B 3004
13/7/1552	Rouen	Fouquet Thorel	barber	Rouen	Rouen	"
30/7/1552	Toulouse	François d'Augi	tanner	Annonay	Annonay	ADHG, B 3398

Date	Parlement	Name	Occupation	Place arrested	Place executed	Reference
4/11/1552	Rouen	Jean Hubert	parish pantryman	Rouen	Rouen	ADSM, 1B 3141
?/?/1552	Paris	René Poyet	shoemaker	Saumur	Saumur	Crespin, I, 682–683
16/1/1553	Rouen	Jean Hyllard	?	Rouen	Rouen	ADSM, 1B 3141
3/2/1553	Toulouse	Jean Affoc	?	?	Toulouse	ADHG, B 3400
21/3/1553	Toulouse	Pierre Serres	priest	Couserans	Toulouse	"
?/3/1553	Paris	Nicolas Nail	shoemaker	Paris	Paris	Crespin, II, 12
?/4/1553	Paris	*Pierre Bergier*	*pastrymaker*	*Lyon*	*Lyon*	Crespin, I, 674–678
15/5/1553	Rouen	Guillaume Neel	monk (Aug.)	Evreux	Evreux	ADSM, 1B 3004
16/5/1553	Paris	Bernard Seguin	student	Lyon	Lyon	Crespin, I, 614–618
"	Paris	Charles Favre	student	Lyon	Lyon	Crespin, I, 652–655
"	Paris	Martial Alba	student	Lyon	Lyon	Crespin, I, 587–595
"	Paris	Pierre Escrivain	student	Lyon	Lyon	Crespin, I, 598–615
"	Paris	Pierre Naviheres	student	Lyon	Lyon	Crespin, I, 635–650
15/6/1553	Paris	Nicolas Dubois	?	Noyon	Noyon	AN, X2a'114
?/6/1553	Paris	Etienne Le Roi	notary	Chartres	Chartres	Crespin, II, 26–30
"	Paris	Pierre Denocheau	clerk	Chartres	Chartres	"
7/7/1553	Paris	Antoine Magne	?	Bourges	Paris	AN, X2a 114
?/7/1553	Paris	Mathieu Dymonet	?	Lyon	Lyon	Crespin, I, 712–715
31/8/1553	Paris	*Etienne Gravot*	?	*Lyon*	*Lyon*	Crespin, I, 716–718
31/8/1553	Paris	*Loys de Marsac*	*gentleman*	*Lyon*	*Lyon*	Crespin, I, 725–730
5/9/1553	Paris	*Denis Peloquin*	?	*Lyon*	*Lyon*	Crespin, I, 683–686
21/11/1553	Dijon	Simon Laloé	made glasses	Dijon	Dijon	Crespin, II, 25–26
7/12/1553	Aix	Etienne Michel	priest	Aix	Aix	ADBR, B 5454
7/1/1554	Toulouse	Guillaume d'Alençon	priest-bookseller	Montpellier	Montpellier	Crespin, II, 34; also ADHG, B 3402

Date	Parlement	Name	Occupation	Place arrested	Place executed	Reference
15/1/1554	Paris	Vincent Patruges	?	Dun-le-Roi	Dun-le-Roi	AN, X2a 115
?/1/1554	Toulouse	François Malot	cloth-trimmer	Montpellier	Montpellier	Crespin, II, 34
6/3/1554	Toulouse	Claude Brochier	?	Nîmes	Nîmes	ADHG, B 3403
20/3/1554	Paris	Jean Bourdin	?	Montfort l'Amaury	Montfort l'Amaury	AN, X2a 115
18/4/1554	Toulouse	Antoine Berjade	?	Béziers	Béziers	ADHG, B 3403
21/4/1554	Toulouse	Etienne Martin	monk (Fran.)	Montauban	Toulouse	"
4/5/1554	Bordeaux	Guillaume de Pierre	monk (Aug.)	Bordeaux	Bordeaux	Patry, 173–174
9/6/1554	Toulouse	Antoine Barriere	monk (Aug.)	Lombes	Gimont	ADHG, B 3404
23/6/1554	Bordeaux	Bertrand de Borda	monk (Fran.)	Agen	Bordeaux	Patry, 182–183
6/7/1554	Toulouse	Jean Escullier	monk (Fran.)	Limes	Toulouse	ADHG, B 3404
7/7/1554	Paris	Richard Le Fevre	goldsmith	Grenoble	Lyon	Crespin, II, 37–59
1/8/1554	Toulouse	Etienne de Royeres	nobleman	Le Puy	Le Puy	ADHG, B 3405
9/8/1554	Rouen	Denis Le Vair	priest-peddler	Coutances	Rouen	Crespin, II, 88–90
6/9/1554	Toulouse	Girauld Bonet	?	Toulouse	Toulouse	ADHG, B 3405
	Toulouse	Me Pierre La Failhe	jurist	Toulouse	Toulouse	"
12/10/1554	Toulouse	Regnier Badarossi	monk (Fran.)	Narbonne	Toulouse	"
13/10/1554	Toulouse	Roget Fabre	shoemaker	Narbonne	Toulouse	"
16/10/1554	Toulouse	François Linhac	student	Toulouse	Toulouse	"
23/10/1554	Toulouse	"Jean l'Evangeliste"	hermit	Toulouse	Toulouse	"
29/10/1554	Toulouse	Barthelemy André	scribe	Le Puy	Carcassonne	"
16/11/1554	Toulouse	Pierre de Honoribus	monk (Ben.)	Tarbes	Auch	ADHG, B 3406
18/12/1554	Paris	Jean Filleul	cabinetmaker	St. Pierre-le-Moustier	St. Pierre-le-Moustier	AN, X2a 116

Date	Parlement	Name	Occupation	Place arrested	Place executed	Reference
18/12/1554	Paris	Julien Lesveillé	needlemaker	St. Pierre-le-Moustier	St. Pierre-le-Moustier	AN, X2a 116
19/2/1555	Paris	Antoine de Genes	?	Tours	Tours	"
4/5/1555	*Bordeaux*	*Guillaume Dongnon*	*priest*	*Limoges*	*Limoges*	Crespin, II, 151–154
14/5/1555	Bordeaux	Jerome Casabonne	schoolmaster	Monflanquin	Bordeaux	BSHPF 51 (1902), 245–248
5/7/1555	Toulouse	Jean Fenure	book-peddler	Le Puy	Le Puy	ADHG, B 3409
"	Toulouse	Pierre Barbat	schoolmaster	Le Puy	Le Puy	"
1/10/1555	Rouen	Jacques Lemercier	*mesguich*	Rouen	Rouen	ADSM, 1B 3143
12/10/1555	Chambéry	Antoine Laborie	royal judge	Chambéry	Chambéry	ADS, B 59/f. 183v
"	Chambéry	Bertrand Bataille	student	Chambéry	Chambéry	"
"	Chambéry	Girod Thoran	dry-goods merchant	Chambéry	Chambéry	"
"	Chambéry	Jean Vernou	jurist	Chambéry	Chambéry	"
"	Chambéry	Jean Trigallet	jurist	Chambéry	Chambéry	"
1/2/1556	*Paris*	*Claude Canesière*	*musician*	*Lyon*	*Lyon*	Crespin, II, 315–317
22/2/1556	Toulouse	Jacques del Cayre	stockingmaker	Castres	Toulouse	ADHG, B 3412
24/4/1556	Paris	Jean Rabec	monk (Fran.)	Angers	Angers	Crespin, II, 364–366
6/5/1556	Bordeaux	Arnauld Monnier	?	Bordeaux	Bordeaux	Crespin, II, 428–430
"	Bordeaux	Jean de Cazes	?	Bordeaux	Bordeaux	"
11/5/1556	Paris	Jean Bertrand	forester	Blois	Blois	AN, X2a 118
19/5/1556	Rouen	Guillaume Blondel	barber-surgeon	Arques	Rouen	ADSM, 1B 3144
22/5/1556	Paris	Pierre du Rousseau	priest	Angers	Angers	Crespin, II, 377–380
19/6/1556	Turin	Barthelemy Hector	peddler	Pignerol	Turin	Crespin, II, 437–440
18/8/1556	Paris	Jean Ponthieu	?	Clermont-Ferrand	Clermont-Ferrand	AN, X2a 120

Date	Parlement	Name	Occupation	Place arrested	Place executed	Reference
20/8/1556	Rouen	Me Pierre Le Françoys	schoolmaster	Le Havre	Rouen	ADSM, 1B 3144
?/8/1556	Paris	Louis Le Moine	?	Angers	Angers	HE, 61
"	Paris	Imbert Bernard	?	Angers	Angers	"
"	Paris	Richard Yette	?	Angers	Angers	"
"	Paris	Claude Donas	?	Angers	Angers	"
"	Paris	Guillaume Boystanné	?	Angers	Angers	"
15/10/1556	Dijon	Andoche Minard	priest	Autun	Autun	Crespin, II, 466
9/11/1556	Rouen	Antoine Le Tellette	?	Le Havre	Le Havre	ADSM, 1B 3145
18/1/1557	Bordeaux	Mathurin Escuyer	cook	?	Bordeaux	Patry, 224
?/2/1557	Toulouse	Jean Calmet	nobleman	?	Toulouse	ADHG, B 3418
16/3/1557	Paris	Nicolas Balon	peddler	Poitiers	(escaped)	AN, X2a 119
12/4/1557	Bordeaux	Philibert Hamelin	priest	Saintes	Bordeaux	Patry, 234
?/4/1557	Dijon	Jacques ?	apothecary	?	Dijon	Crespin, II, 478–480
"	Dijon	Philippe Cène	apothecary	?	Dijon	"
?/5/1557	Dijon	Archambault Seraphon	dry-goods merchant	Aussonne	Dijon	Crespin, II, 471–473
12/6/1557	Paris	Lazare Bonorey	schoolmaster	Troyes	Paris	AN, X2a 119
16/6/1557	Aix	Benoit Romyen	dry-goods merchant	Draguignan	Draguignan	Crespin, II, 529–531
16/7/1557	Paris	Jean Buron	?	Craon	Craon	Crespin, II, 484–486
27/9/1557	Paris	Nicolas Clinet	schoolmaster	Paris	Paris	Crespin, II, 563
"	Paris	Philippa de Luns	widow	Paris	Paris	"
"	Paris	Taurin Gravelle	attorney	Paris	Paris	"
8/10/1557	Paris	Nicolas Le Cène	physician	Paris	Paris	Crespin, II, 568
"	Paris	Pierre Gabart	solicitor	Paris	Paris	"
26/10/1557	Paris	François Rebezies	student	Paris	Paris	Crespin, II, 571
"	Paris	Frédéric Damville	student	Paris	Paris	"

Date	Parlement	Name	Occupation	Place arrested	Place executed	Reference
?/?/1557	Dijon	feu Nicolas du Rousseau	lawyer	Aussonne	Dijon (corpse)	Crespin, II, 481–483
"	*Toulouse*	*Claude Rozier*	*monk (Fran.)*	*Nîmes*	*Nîmes*	Menard, IV, 79
?/2/1558	Paris	Georges Tardif	?	Paris	Sens	Crespin, II, 561
"	Paris	Jean Caillou	?	Paris	Tours	Crespin, II, 562
"	Paris	Nicolas Guyotet	?	Paris	Sens	"
"	Paris	Nicolas de Joinville	?	Paris	Joinville	"
29/3/1558	Turin	Geoffrey Varaglia	monk (Fran.)	Angrogna	Turin	Crespin, II, 519–521
1/7/1558	Paris	Geoffroy Guerin	cabinetmaker	Paris	Paris	AN, X2a 121
22/12/1558	Toulouse	François Mercier	priest	Fréjac	Toulouse	ADHG, B 3423
27/2/1559	Paris	Jean Morel	pastor's servant	Paris	Paris	AN, X2a 122
6/3/1559	Paris	Jean Barbeville	?	Paris	Paris	"
26/4/1559	Paris	Pierre Chevet	winegrower	?	Paris	"
31/5/1559	Bordeaux	Pierre Faugière	merchant	Bordeaux	Bordeaux	ADG, 1B 202, no. 20
14/6/1559	Bordeaux	Jacques Mesnade	?	St. Jean d'Angely	Bordeaux (corpse)	" no. 171
16/6/1559	Paris	Nicolas Balon (alias duBreuil) (16/3/1557)		Reims	Paris	AN, X2a 122
28/6/1559	Bordeaux	Jean Maury	shoemaker	Agen	Bordeaux	ADG, 1B 202, no. 345
6/7/1559	Bordeaux	François Garnier	?	Bordeaux	Bordeaux	ADG, 1B 203, no. 70
12/7/1559	Paris	Nicolas Collot	employed by Balon	Reims	Paris	AN, X2a 122
"	Paris	Nicolas Oudin	tailor	Reims	Paris	AN, X2a 123
19/7/1559	Rouen	Denis Huet	?	Caen	Caen	ADSM, 1B 3150
2/8/1559	Paris	Marin Marie	book peddler	?	Paris	AN, X2a 124
7/8/1559	Paris	Florimond Didolet	weaver	Meaux	(escaped)	"

Date	Parlement	Name	Occupation	Place arrested	Place executed	Reference
7/8/1559	Paris	Guilmette Aussart	wife of Didolet	Meaux	(escaped)	AN, X2a 124
19/8/1559	Paris	Marguerite Le Riche	wife of bookseller	Paris	Paris	"
31/8/1559	Paris	Nicolas Moret	carpenter	Sens	Paris	"
19/9/1559	Paris	Pierre Richard	winegrower	Melun	Melun	Crespin, II, 669
23/10/1559	Paris	Adrien d'Avise	dry-goods merchant	Paris	Paris	Crespin, II, 669
24/10/1559	Paris	Gilles Le Court	student	Lyon	Paris	Crespin, II, 670
"	Paris	Marin Rousseau	goldsmith	?	Paris	"
"	Paris	Philippe Parmentier	shoemaker	Paris	Paris	"
26/10/1559	Paris	Pierre Millet	merchant	Paris	Paris	Crespin, II, 671
6/12/1559	Toulouse	Jean des Bordes	?	?	Toulouse	ADHG, B 3428
7/12/1559	Paris	Jean Beffroy	locksmith	Paris	Paris	AN, X2a 125
23/12/1559	Paris	Anne du Bourg	Parlement judge	Paris	Paris	"
29/12/1559	Paris	André Coiffier	?	Dommartin	Dommartin	"
30/12/1559	Paris	Jean Ysabeau	?	Tours	Paris	Crespin, II, 706
31/12/1559	Paris	Jean Judet	bookseller	Paris	Paris	AN, X2a 125
2/1/1560	Paris	Pierre Gidier	?	Poitiers	Paris	"
4/1/1560	Paris	Michel Gens	tailor	Poitiers	Paris	"
5/1/1560	Paris	Pierre Girard	tailor	Paris	Paris	"
6/1/1560	Paris	Pierre Arondeau	dry goods merchant	La Rochelle	Paris	ADSM, 1B 3151
29/1/1560	Rouen	François Le Monnier	tailor	Valognes	Rouen	AN, X2a 125
5/2/1560	Paris	Simon Boisson	?	?	Paris	ADSM, 1B 3151
27/3/1560	Rouen	Jean Cottin	preacher	Rouen	Rouen	"
"	Rouen	Pierre Pollet	?	Rouen	Rouen	"
"	Rouen	Thomas Pollet	?	Rouen	Rouen	"
10/4/1560	Toulouse	Jean Massip	?	Montauban	Toulouse	ADHG, B 3430

ABBREVIATIONS

Dates are given in European style (day/month/year).

Archives

AN	Archives Nationales, Paris
ADBR	Archives Departementales des Bouches du Rhône (dépot d'Aix)
ADG	Archives Departementales de la Gironde, Bordeaux
ADHG	Archives Departementales de la Haute Garonne, Toulouse
ADI	Archives Departementales de l'Isère, Grenoble
ADS	Archives Departementales de la Savoie, Chambéry
ADSM	Archives Departementales de la Seine-Maritime, Rouen
AEG	Archives d'Etat, Geneva
AMT	Archives Municipales, Toulouse

Primary Sources

Aubéry	Jacques Aubéry, *Histoire de l'exécution de Cabrières et de Mérindol,* ed. Gabriel Audisio (Mérindol, 1982)
Audisio, *P-V*	Gabriel Audisio, *Procès-verbal d'un massacre. Les vaudois du Luberon (avril 1545)* (Aix-en-Provence, 1992)
Brulart	Nicholas Brulart, "Journal . . . (1559–1569)," in *Mémoires de Condé,* ed. D.-F. Secousse, 4 vols. (London, 1743), I, 2–211
Crespin	Jean Crespin, *Histoire des martyrs persecutez et mis à mort pour la verité de l'Evangile,* ed. D. Benoît, 3 vols. (Toulouse, 1884–1887)
HE	G. Baum and E. Cunitz, eds., *Histoire Ecclésiastique des Eglises Reformées de France,* 3 vols. (Paris, 1883–1889)
Haton	Claude Haton, *Mémoires,* 2 vols. (Paris, 1857)
Herminjard	*Correspondance des Réformateurs dans les pays de langue française,* ed. A. L. Herminjard, 9 vols. (Geneva, 1886–1887)
JBP	Ludovic Lalanne, ed., *Journal d'un bourgeois de Paris sous le règne de François Ier (1515–1536)* (Paris, 1854)

LH	Paul-F. Geisendorf, ed., *Livre des habitants de Genève. Tome I (1549–1560)* (Geneva, 1957)
La Faille	Germain de la Faille, *Annales de la ville de Toulouse*, 2 vols. (Toulouse, 1695–1701)
La Fosse	Jean de la Fosse, *Journal d'un curé ligueur sous les trois derniers Valois,* ed. Barthélemy (Paris, 1866)
Metivier	Jean de Metivier, *Chronique du Parlement de Bordeaux*, 2 vols. (Bordeaux, 1886–1887)
Patry	Henri Patry, ed., *Les débuts de la Réforme protestante en Guyenne, 1523–1559. Arrêts du Parlement* (Bordeaux, 1912)
Romier	Lucien Romier, "Les vaudois et le Parlement français de Turin," *Mélanges d'archéologie et d'histoire de l'École française de Rome*, 30 (1910), 193–207
de Thou	Jacques-Auguste de Thou, *Histoire universelle depuis 1543 jusqu'en 1607*, vols. 2–8 (London, 1732–1736)
Versoris	Nicolas Versoris, "Livre de raison (1519–1530)," ed. G. Fagniez, in *Mémoires de la Société pour l'Histoire de Paris et de l'Ile-de-France,* XII (1885), 99–222
Weiss, *CA*	Nathaniel Weiss, *La Chambre ardente. Etude sur la liberté de conscience en France sous François Ier et Henri II (1540–1550), suivie d'environ 500 arrêts inédits rendus par le Parlement de Paris de mai 1547 à mars 1550* (Paris, 1889)

Secondary Sources

ARG	Archiv für Reformationsgeschichte
BSHPF	*Bulletin de la Société pour l'Histoire du Protestantisme Français*
Audisio, *Vaudois*	Gabriel Audisio, *Les vaudois du Luberon. Une minorité en Provence (1460–1560)* (Mérindol, 1984)
Cameron	Euan Cameron, *The Reformation of the Heretics: The Waldenses of the Alps 1480–1580* (Oxford, 1984)
Crouzet, *Genèse*	Denis Crouzet, *La genèse de la Réforme française, 1520–1562* (Paris, 1996)
Diefendorf	Barbara B. Diefendorf, *Beneath the Cross: Catholics and Huguenots in Sixteenth-Century Paris* (Oxford, 1991)
Farge, *Orthodoxy*	James K. Farge, *Orthodoxy and Reform in Early Reformation France: The Faculty of Theology of Paris, 1500–1543* (Leiden, 1985)
Farge, *Parti*	James K. Farge, *Le parti conservateur au XVIe siècle: Université et Parlement de Paris à l'époque de la Renaissance et de la Réforme* (Paris, 1992)
Floquet	Amable Floquet, *Histoire du Parlement de Normandie*, 7 vols. (Rouen, 1840–1842)

Heller	Henry Heller, *The Conquest of Poverty* (Leiden, 1986)
Imbart de la Tour	Pierre Imbart de la Tour, *Les origines de la Réforme,* 4 vols. (Paris, 1905–1922)
Maugis	Edouard Maugis, *Histoire du Parlement de Paris de l'avenèment des rois valois à la mort d'Henri IV,* 3 vols. (Paris, 1913)
Ménard	Léon Ménard, *Histoire civile, ecclésiastique et littéraire de la ville de Nîmes,* 7 vols. (Nîmes, 1874)
Mentzer	Raymond A. Mentzer Jr., *Heresy Proceedings in Languedoc, 1500–1560* (Philadelphia, 1984)
Olson	Jeanine Olson, *Calvin and Social Welfare* (London/Toronto; Associated University Presses, 1989)
Roelker	Nancy L. Roelker, *One King, One Faith: The Parlement of Paris and the Religious Reformations of the Sixteenth Century* (Berkeley, 1996)
Soman	Alfred Soman, *Sorcellerie et Justice Criminelle: Le Parlement de Paris (16e–18e siècles* (Hampshire, U.K., 1992)

NOTES

Introduction

1. Compare Mentzer, p. 170, with ADHG, B 3424–28. Only two men were physically punished for heresy in 1559: a physician living near Lectoure (previously sentenced in 1552 by the Parlement of Bordeaux) was condemned to a public abjuration at his local cathedral, three years of imprisonment, and perpetual banishment from France; another prisoner, who made a full confession, was burned alive at Toulouse.
2. For the story of this peculiar institution, see Amabile Floquet, *Histoire du privilège de St. Romain*, 2 vols. (Rouen, 1835). Heretics were ineligibile to benefit from this pardon.
3. See Romier for a complete critical edition of these *arrêts*.
4. A preliminary sketch of this second topic was given at a conference at Cambridge University in 1994, subsequently published as "Heresy Executions in Reformation Europe, 1520–1565," in *Tolerance and Intolerance in the European Reformation*, ed. O. P. Grell and R. Scribner (Cambridge, 1996), pp. 48–64.

1. Criminal Justice in Sixteenth-Century France

Epigraph: Jean Bodin, *Démonomanie des sorciers* (Paris, 1580), bk. IV, chap. 5 (pp. 194–195).

1. Arlette Lebigre, *La justice du roi. La vie judicaire dans l'ancienne France* (Paris, 1988), pp. 13–34.
2. Noel Valois, "Le roi très chrétien," in *La France chrétienne dans l'histoire*, ed. E. Baudrillart (Paris, 1896), pp. 319–320, as quoted by Joseph Strayer, "France: The Holy Land, the Chosen People, and the Most Christian King," in *Action and Conviction in Early Modern Europe: Essays in Memory of E. Harris Harbison*, ed. T. K. Rabb and J. E. Seigel (Princeton, 1969), p. 9.
3. It is an interesting commentary on parlementary autonomy in Valois

France that the introduction of entrance examinations at the Paris court was a response to the king's first attempts to sell judicial office (and entrance examinations coincided with the court's first investigations of "Lutheranism"); Maugis, I, 181–182.

4. See the useful sketch by Gordon Griffiths, "Jean de Selve," in *Contemporaries of Erasmus,* ed. P. Bietenholz and T. Deutscher, 3 vols. (Toronto, 1985), III, 238–240.

5. Jacques Brejon, *André Tiraqueau (1488–1558)* (Paris, 1937), pp. 28–39.

6. See Chapter 3, note 32.

7. Metivier, I, 480–502.

8. Eugène Burnier, "Le Parlement de Chambéry sous François Ier et Henri II (1536–1559)," *Mémoires et Documents publiés par la Société Savoisienne d'histoire et d'archéologie* 6 (1862), 317.

9. On the French career of Giacopo de Minuti (alias "Jacques Minut"), see Etienne Dolet, *Correspondance,* ed. Claude Longeon (Geneva, 1982), p. 40 n. 1.

10. ADHG, B 3406 (20/12/1554).

11. Normandy was the center of masculine witchcraft in western Europe; see William Monter, "Toads and Eucharists: The Male Witches of Normandy, 1564–1660," *French Historical Studies* 20 (1997), 563–595.

12. ADSM, 1B 3170 (1/4/1574: unsuccessful poisoning of professional court tennis player, but three other people died in the attempt; defendant confessed under torture).

13. ADSM, 1B 3148 (20/6/1558). Her accomplice was a priest, who managed to get transferred to episcopal jurisdiction and therefore escaped capital punishment.

14. ADSM, 1B 3118–21 (July–December 1535, March–July 1537, September 1538–July 1539). These registers include three death sentences for heresy and five for infanticide, all of which included burning as part of the punishment. All the infanticide convictions were upheld, but two of the three heresy cases were transferred to other courts.

15. ADSM, 1B 3119 (7/3 and 13/3/1537). The fact that both defendants were arrested at the same place suggests a single episode of major sacrilege performed by two men. Alençon, where a spectacular episode of sacrilege occurred in 1533, is also in Normandy—but the punishments were carried out by the Parlement of Paris, not Rouen.

16. J. Papon, *Arrests notables* (Paris, 1563), pp. 462–462v.

17. ADSM, 1B 3141 (24/11/1552: his codefendant was hanged for buying a silver cup stolen from the same church). See also 1B 3142 (20/3/1555: defendant fined 300 livres in order to endow a chapel in honor of the Eucharist, and had his hand cut off before being hanged).

18. ADSM, 1B 3231 (10/4/1598) and 1B 3236 (13/5/1600). Such scandals

persisted into the next century: an English printer was hanged and burned at Caen for "taking the chalice above the altar" at a Jesuit chapel "and trying to carry it away by force"; 1B 3296 (26/11/1621).

19. ADSM, 1B 3120 (5/10 and 8/11/1538, and 21/1/1539); 1B 3121 (19/4 and 18/6/1539).

20. ADSM, 1B 3119 (29/11/1538).

21. ADSM, 1B 3121 (18/6/1539: convicted of aggravated battery, rape, and homicide).

22. ADSM, 1B 5724 (6/7/1591).

23. Nearly all of the numerous modern accounts of La Barre's trial and execution rely heavily on Marc Chassaigne's richly documented study, *Le procès du chevalier de La Barre* (Paris, 1920). For a legal approach, see Jean Imbert, ed., *Quelques procès criminels des XVIIe et XVIIIe siècles* (Paris, 1964), pp. 166–180; for a recent apologetic account of Voltaire's intervention in the case, see René Pomeau et al., *"Ecraser l'Infâme," 1759–1770* (Oxford, 1994), pp. 293–306.

24. ADSM, 1B 5727 (27/3/1593: also tried for theft, cutting of tongue upheld); compare 1B 5729 (7/2/1594: tried for homicide, death sentence reduced, and cutting of tongue eliminated, despite appeal *a minima*). During the following decade, the Rouen Parlement threw out three of four lower-court sentences to cut or pierce blasphemers' tongues, while upholding one—against a priest, convicted of witchcraft aggravated by "execrable blasphemies" pronounced during a sermon: 1B 3259 (27/6/1607).

25. See Farge, *Parti,* pp. 62 (quotation), 63–64. For a summary of French blasphemy legislation, consult the tables in F.-A. Isambert, *Receuil général des anciennes lois françaises,* vol. XXIX (Paris, 1828–1832).

26. La Faille, II, 93 (my emphasis).

27. Isambert, *Receuil général,* vol. XVIII (Paris, 1829), 86–87 (No. 486).

28. Brejon, *Tiraqueau,* pp. 60, 395.

29. See Bernard Schnapper, *Les peines arbitraires du XIIIe au XVIIIe siècle* (Paris, 1974).

30. See ibid., pp. 44 (Maranta, who died in 1530, coined the phrase), 45 n. 263 (Carpzov on punishment of undefined crimes), and 43 n. 248 on Menochius' *De arbitrariis judicum* (Lyon, 1606).

31. See Montaigne's *Essays,* trans. M. A. Screech (London, 1991), p. 1208 n. 7 (bk. III, chap. xiii).

32. Lebigre, *Justice du roi,* pp. 138–143 (quotation, p. 140).

33. Schnapper, *Peines arbitraires,* p. 60.

34. G. B. Depping, ed., *Correspondance administrative sous le règne de Louis XIV,* II (Paris, 1851), 214.

35. Schnapper's relevant articles are reprinted in his *Voies nouvelles en his-*

toire du droit (Paris, 1991), pp. 53–105 (on Bordeaux) and 107–144 (on Paris).

36. Soman, chap. VII.

37. Schnapper, *Voies nouvelles,* p. 113.

38. Lebigre, *Justice du roi,* pp. 180–193.

39. Quoted in ibid., p. 191.

40. See Soman, chap. VII, p. 24, tableau 2. His totals include 555 defendants over a two-year span between November 1539 and October 1542; by 1572 he counted 567 defendants, which rose only to 593 defendants in 1610. Schnapper (*Voies nouvelles,* p. 109) found a total of 525 defendants as early as 1546, but they included a huge number of accused heretics; his "net total" of 353 is thus far closer to Soman's average numbers for 1539–1542 than to the 1572 or 1610 totals.

41. Schnapper, *Voies nouvelles,* p. 63.

42. Soman, chap. VII, p. 22.

43. At Bordeaux, capital punishments were upheld in more than one-third of their 82 decisions in 1523; in 1532, death sentences still accounted for 30 percent of their 87 cases. A quarter-century after Villers-Cotterets, they pronounced 34 death sentences among 278 rulings (12 percent): Schnapper, *Voies nouvelles,* p. 88.

44. Ibid., pp. 65, 112.

45. Ibid., p. 111.

46. Compare ibid., pp. 114–117, with Soman, chap. VII, pp. 39–40.

47. See Schnapper, *Voies nouvelles,* pp. 72–80, esp. 77.

48. Lebigre, *Justice du roi,* pp. 205–209 (quotation, p. 207).

49. As the prosecutor noted at La Barre's first sentencing, he had not been convicted of sacrilege, but had confessed to both blasphemy and impiety.

50. Schnapper, *Voies nouvelles,* pp. 77–79, 115.

51. Ibid., pp. 101, 113.

52. Schnapper, *Peines arbitraires,* masterfully analyzes the "Enlightened" attacks on arbitrary punishments.

2. Heresy Trials in Reformation Europe

Epigraph: T. J. van Braght, *The Bloody Theater of Martyrs' Mirror* (London, 1660), p. 410.

1. Two books commemorated the 450th anniversary of Luther's appearance before the Diet of Worms: Daniel Olivier, *Le procès Luther* (Paris, 1971; English trans., London, 1978); and James Atkinson, *The Trial of Luther* (London, 1971).

2. Bernd Moeller, "Piety in Germany around 1500," in *The Reformation in Medieval Perspective,* ed. Steven E. Ozmont (New York, 1971), p. 52 and nn. 4–5.

3. Quoted from Atkinson, *Trial of Luther,* p. 178.

4. For a brief summary, see Henri Pirenne, *Histoire de Belgique,* 3d ed., III (Brussels, 1923), 349–351; see also James Tracy, *Holland under Habsburg Rule, 1506–1566* (Berkeley, 1990), pp. 153–155.

5. On pre-1530 heresy executions in the Low Countries, see Alastair Duke, *Reformation and Revolt in the Low Countries* (London, 1990), p. 58 n. 201. On the early clandestine literature praising these "Lutherans," see the forthcoming work by Brad Gregory.

6. On the very small number of "Lutherans" executed during the 1520s, see Crespin, I, 238–278: fewer than two dozen names, including three who died at Paris. Almost one-third of his total died in the Low Countries.

7. Miriam Chrisman, *Lay Culture, Learned Culture: Books and Social Change in Strasbourg, 1480–1599* (New Haven, 1982). Thousands of *Flugschriften* poured off German presses in the early 1520s, overwhelmingly favorable to Luther's cause.

8. James Stayer, *The German Peasants' War and Anabaptist Community of Goods* (Montreal, 1991), pp. 61–92, summarizes current scholarship on the connections between Anabaptism and the 1524–1525 peasant revolt. Although these events did not touch the kingdom of France, their westernmost extension, the Alsatian *Rustauds,* were crushed in May 1525 by Duke Antoine of Lorraine. The event was immediately commemorated (in French) by Nicolas Volcyr, and the remarkably gory execution of the first French Protestant followed in late July, at Metz. See Crouzet, *Genèse,* pp. 180–185 (Volcyr), 188–191.

9. Gaismair remains the least known major figure from the "Revolution of 1525" (to adopt Blickle's term). The lone English-language biography is Walter Klaassen's useful *Michael Gaismair, Revolutionary and Reformer* (Leiden, 1978). Modern study of him began with Josef Macek, *Der Tiroler Bauernkrieg und Michael Gaismair* (Berlin, 1965), and includes the posthumous account by Jürgen Bücking, *Michael Gaismair: Reformer-Sozialrebell-Revolutionär* (Stuttgart, 1978). Long without honor in his native land, Gaismair received two Tyrolean biographies on the 450th anniversary of his death.

10. Grete Mecenseffy, ed., *Österreich,* 3 vols. (Gutersloh, 1964–1983), I, 3–11 (no. 3).

11. Stayer, *Peasants' War,* pp. 65–71.

12. Mecenseffy, *Österreich,* I, 96–97 (no. 55), and 100 (no. 61) against the "verdambten Ketzereien."

13. Ibid., pp. 91–93 (no. 52), 142 (no. 92), 166–167 (no. 105); compare Claus-Peter Clasen, *Anabaptism: A Social History, 1525–1618* (Ithaca, 1972), pp. 368, 377.

14. Mecenseffy, *Osterreich*, I, 149–160 (no. 99). Hutterite chronicles list about two dozen early martyrs from Styria, half of whom died at Brück in 1528.

15. Compare the Hutterite *grosse Geschichtsbuch*, translated as *The Chronicle of the Hutterian Brethren, Volume I* (Rifton, N.Y., 1987), pp. 218–219, with Clasen, *Anabaptism*, pp. 370, 372, 437.

16. See Mecenseffy, *Osterreich*, II, 56–60 (nos. 50, 51, 56); Tyrolean officials stiffened the resolve of local jurors to condemn Lienhart Schiemer by adding extra men.

17. See Clasen, *Anabaptism*, p. 375; texts in Mecenseffy, *Osterreich*, I, 187–189 (no. 126), 195–197 (no. 130). Ferdinand notified key officials in Vienna, Innsbruck, and Ensisheim (capital of Habsburg possessions in Alsace), with additional instructions for Tyrol; his orders were repeated on 18 May.

18. Clasen, *Anabaptism*, p. 376; text of 1544 decree printed in Mecenseffy, *Osterreich*, I, 305–307 (no. 228).

19. See Clasen, *Anabaptism*, pp. 371, 299–300, 302: "Ultimately, the success of Anabaptism in the Tyrol remains a puzzle."

20. Mecenseffy, *Osterreich*, II, contains only half as many items (109) from 1531 as from either 1528 or 1529.

21. Compare the numbers and locations given in the Hutterite *Chronicle*, p. 219, with the traces of executions scattered through Mecenseffy, *Osterreich*, II and III, pp. 1–315.

22. Useful summary in Clasen, *Anabaptism*, pp. 377–378; see also Mecenseffy, *Osterreich*, II, 20–82 (nos. 25–80), for examples of early hesitations and foot-dragging by Tyrolean officials between autumn 1527 and spring 1528, particularly their response to Ferdinand of 8 February 1528, pp. 70–77 (no. 69). For the resulting response and grace period, see pp. 84–89 (nos. 84–85).

23. On 13 May they claimed that 36 of the 106 Kitzbühel Anabaptists who had used this pardon had attended Anabaptist gatherings afterward; Mecenseffy, *Osterreich*, II, p. 134 (no. 152).

24. Ibid., p. 228 (no. 327).

25. Ibid., pp. 335–336 (no. 491).

26. Ibid., pp. 341–344 no. 501). The remark about Spaniards was an obvious insult to Ferdinand, who had been raised in Spain by his namesake and grandfather, Ferdinand of Aragon.

27. Ibid., p. 337 (no. 492B).

28. Quotation from ibid., p. 342 (no. 501).

29. See ibid., p. 438 (no. 631), for first use of "synagogue" to describe a

gathering of two dozen Anabaptists in Bolzano in December 1530; the phrase reappears in ibid., III, 92 (January 1533).

30. On Gaismair's Anabaptist follower, Friedrich Brandenburger, see ibid., III, 75–78, 109 (nos. 71–73, 115), 390 (no. 513) (quotation); and Klaassen, *Gaismair,* pp. 112–113.

31. On Hutter's capture and death, see the Hutterite *Chronicle,* pp. 142–146; Mecenseffy, *Osterreich,* III, 292–313, 316–317 (nos. 365–373, 376, 382–384, 391). Katharina Hutter's escape is noted on p. 324 (no. 401C).

32. Mecenseffy, *Osterreich,* III, 378–395 (nos. 491, 493, 498, 505–507, 511–513, 515–522).

33. Texts in C. Laurent and J. Lameere, eds., *Recueil des ordonnances des Pays-Bas sous Charles-Quint,* 2d ser., 5 vols. (Brussels, 1893–1902), II, 578–583 (14/10/1529), 583 (24/10/1529); III, 262–265 (7/10/1531). Good summary in Pirenne, *Belgique,* III, 356–358.

34. Antoine de Lusy, *Le journal d'un bourgeois de Mons 1505–1536,* ed. A. Louant (Brussels, 1969), pp. 357–358 (no. 916).

35. Ibid., p. 316 (no. 781). The remark about Lille is confirmed by M.-P. Willems-Closset, "Le protestantisme à Lille . . . (1525–1565)," in *Revue du Nord,* 52 (1970), 215: six Lutherans, the first local victims, were beheaded there in the spring and summer of 1533.

36. Laurent and Lameere, *Recueil des Ordonnances des Pays-Bas,* III, 477–478 (10/6/1535); some earlier but local edicts noted in A. F. Mellink, ed., *Documenta Anabaptistica Neerlandiae* (hereafter *DAN*), 7 vols. to date (Leiden, 1975–), I, 9–12 (Frisian *plakkaat* of 23/2/1534 with grace period decreed 31/3/1534), 14–17, 20–21, 25–26 (*plakkaats* of 1/7/1534, 3/2 and 9/3/1535).

37. Duke, *Reformation and Revolt,* pp. 71 n. 1, 99.

38. Tracy, *Holland,* p. 169.

39. For the Amsterdam raid of 1531, see ibid., pp. 160–161, and *DAN,* V, 1–4 (nos. 1–4). On Menno Simons and the Melchiorite executed at Leeuwarden, see *DAN,* I, 4 n. 2. About twenty heretics were executed in the Low Countries in 1531, the year of Charles's second *plakkaat.*

40. On this coup, see *DAN,* V, 29–40 (nos. 24–27). On the repression, see Tracy, *Holland,* p. 163; *DAN,* V, 40–41 (nos. 28–29); also *DAN,* I, 12–13 (nos. 8–10) on three Frisian Anabaptists executed at The Hague in May 1534.

41. On the Oldeklooster battle, see *DAN,* I, 29–37 (nos. 29–33, 35–37); on the subsequent repression, ibid., pp. 37–42 (nos. 38–56), with names of everyone executed 10–19 April at Leeuwarden.

42. On the 10 May coup see Tracy, *Holland,* pp. 164–165, and *DAN,* V, 123–130 (no. 105). On the repression, see ibid., pp. 140–204 (nos. 124, 139, 140, 199, 200, 219–225, 227, 237–240).

43. Batenburg's confession exists in two copies, sent to Groningen and to The Hague, each listing his known associates in those places; see *DAN*, I, 144–151 (no. 24 of Groningen).

44. For the *plakkaat* against Menno Simons, see ibid., pp. 65–67 (no. 89b); on his wife, ibid., p. 85 (no. 110).

45. See ibid., pp. 49–51, 54–58, 60 (nos. 64, 66–68, 71, 73–77, 79, 81), on Friesland. For Amsterdam, see ibid., V, 277–278 (no. 318); II, 9–10, 13, 15 (nos. 8–10, 15, 18).

46. A. L. E. Verheyden, *Le martyrologue Protestant des Pays-Bas du Sud au XVIe siècle* (Brussels, 1969), pp. 172–174 (Antwerp), 218 (Bruges), 243–244 (Ghent).

47. The careful research of Alastair Duke has confirmed numerous executions of Anabaptists in every province of the northern Netherlands except Groningen during the later 1530s and early 1540s.

48. See Jan Decavele, *De dageraad van de Reformatie in Vlanderen*, 2 vols. (Brussels, 1975), II, app. 2.

49. Guido Marnef, *Antwerp in the Age of Reformation: Underground Protestantism in a Commercial Metropolis, 1550–1577* (Baltimore, 1996), p. 36.

50. Gérard Moreau, *Histoire du Protestantisme à Tournai jusqu'à la veille de la révolution des Pays-Bas* (Paris, 1962), pp. 83–116.

51. Compare Verheyden, *Martyrologue*, pp. 219–220, with Crespin, I, 575.

52. We still lack a good modern monograph on the Roman Inquisition. The most useful introduction remains John Tedeschi, *The Prosecution of Heresy* (Binghamton, N.Y., 1991).

53. See Crespin, I, 460–461 (Jaime Enzinas, Dryander's younger brother). One of the next two Roman victims, in 1549, was French; Domenico Orano, *Liberi pensatori bruciati in Roma dal XVI al XVIII secolo* (Rome, 1904), p. 1.

54. On pre-1555 deaths of Italian heretics, compare Orano, *Liberi pensatori*, pp. xiv n. 2, 1–3, with Paul Grendler, *The Roman Inquisition and the Venetian Press, 1540–1605* (Princeton, 1977), p. 57 n. 92. Crespin (I, 541–546) describes Italian Protestants executed by the Roman Inquisition at Ferrara and Piacenza in 1550. The Sicilian Inquisition executed four Italian *Luteranos* in person and twelve in effigy in 1542–1556; see William Monter, *Frontiers of Heresy* (Cambridge, 1990), p. 39.

55. Francisco Bethencourt, *L'Inquisition à l'époque moderne: Espagne, Portugal, Italie, XVe–XIXe siècle* (Paris, 1995), pp. 94, 30, 70, 94, 229, 306, 369.

56. Heresy executions in the British Isles are best approached through John Foxe's *Acts and Monuments*, ed. J. Pratt, 8 vols. (1563; reprint, London, 1877), which includes Scotland.

57. See the careful footnote in the highly favorable biography by Jasper Ridley, *Thomas Cranmer* (Oxford, 1962), p. 253 n. 1.

58. G. R. Elton, *Policy and Police: The Enforcement of the Reformation in the Age of Thomas Cromwell* (Cambridge, 1972), pp. 383–400 (quotation, p. 391).

59. My discussion draws heavily on A. G. Dickens, *The English Reformation* (London, 1964), pp. 264–272.

60. Although few known executions for heresy took place in Holland after William of Orange became Stadhouder in 1558, an Anabaptist was burned at The Hague by order of William's provincial council as late as December 1564: see Tracy, pp. 202 n. 97, 204 n. 105. Van Braght, *Bloody Theater,* pp. 680–686, reproduces two letters by this imprisoned martyr.

61. On the publishing history of all Netherlands martyrologies, see the forthcoming comparative analysis by Brad Gregory.

62. Marnef, *Antwerp,* pp. 61–87.

63. Moreau, *Tournai,* p. 384. All three upper-class people executed for heresy were immigrants, far removed from the city's governing families; one was a wealthy Anabaptist widow. Tournai's most prominent Protestant, whose brother was a famous Calvinist pastor, was never imprisoned; ibid., pp. 149–150, 345 n. 5.

64. *DAN,* VII, ix–x.

65. See Alois Hahn, *Die Rezeption des tridentinischen Pfarrideals im westtrierische Pfarrklerus des 16. und 17. Jahrhundert* (Luxemburg, 1974).

66. Compare M.-S. Dupont-Bouchat, "La répression de l'hérésie dans le Namurois au XVIe siècle," *Annales de la Société archéologique de Namur,* 56 (1972), 179–230, with E. Brouette, "La sorcellerie dans le comté de Namur au début de l'époque moderne (1509–1646)," ibid., 47 (1954), 390–399.

67. This discussion draws heavily from my *Frontiers of Heresy,* pp. 231–252.

68. Quoted in ibid., p. 109.

69. See Emil Van der Vekene, *Bibliotheca Bibliographica Historiae Sanctae Inquisitionis,* 2 vols. (Vaduz, 1982–1983), I, p. 193 (nos. 754–756).

70. Ibid., pp. 191–193 (nos. 748, 751–753 for German, nos. 747, 749–750 for illustrated Dutch versions). The lone "Judaizer" executed at Valladolid in June 1559 has disappeared from these Protestant versions.

3. Parlementary Initiatives and Public Scandals, 1523–1539

Epigraph: Pierre Lizet, quoted in Farge, *Parti,* p. 70.

1. On relations between the Sorbonne and the Parlement, see Farge, *Orthodoxy* and *Parti.* For the period 1515–1527, see Roger Doucet, *Etude sur le gouvernement de François Ier dans ses rapports avec le Parlement de Paris,* 2 vols. (Paris and Algiers, 1921–1926).

2. R. J. Knecht, *Renaissance Warrior and Patron: The Reign of Francis I* (Cam-

bridge, 1994), p. 525; see esp. pp. 264–266 on Francis' humbling of the Paris Parlement in 1527.

3. The old and rare work by François de Larfeuil, *Etudes sur Pierre Lizet* (Clermont-Ferrand, 1856), seems inadequate.

4. AN, M 137 (15/6/1554); see Roger Doucet, *Les bibliothèques parisiens au XVIe siècle* (Paris, 1956), p. 174.

5. Lizet's Protestant enemies hated him in part "because he prided himself on [his knowledge of] theology, of which he understood nothing"; quoted by Roelker, p. 215.

6. Doucet (*Bibliothèques,* pp. 40–41) records that Lizet's library contained no religious polemics and only one title by Erasmus, "very bland"; he also notes (pp. 29–30) that Lizet owned two copies of his own *Manière de procéder* but no collections of royal edicts and only two collections of French customary law.

7. Farge, *Orthodoxy,* pp. 171–173; Knecht, *Renaissance Warrior,* pp. 162–163.

8. Versoris, pp. 127–128 (no. 119); Pierre Driart, "Chronique [1522–1535]," *Mémoires de la Société de l'Histoire de Paris et de l'Ile-de France* 22 (1895), 78–79; *JBP,* pp. 145–146. The first scholar to notice the connection between burning Berquin's writings and Vallière's *amende honorable* was Nathaniel Weiss in *BSHPF* 67 (1918), 293–294; compare M. Mousseaux in *BSHPF* 108 (1962), 18–21.

9. Doucet, *Parlement,* I, 341–342 and 342 n. 1.

10. AN, X1a 1527, fols. 216v–218v (20/3/1525), printed by Farge, *Parti,* p. 62.

11. See Roelker, pp. 196–197, who adds (p. 200) that the Parlement's judges increased their punishments for negligence in enforcing sentences against heretics in March 1526.

12. Farge, *Orthodoxy,* pp. 257–259, 263. Doucet, *Parlement,* II, 157–158, laments the disppearance of all records from the *juges delegués.*

13. Versoris, p. 181 (no. 292); *JBP,* pp. 276–277; Driart, "Chronique," p. 113. None of them named the offender. Doucet (*Parlement,* II, 173–174) identified him as the Jacques Pavanes mentioned by Crespin, I, 263–264 (who places both ceremonies one year too soon).

14. See the key legal arguments of August 1525 by two famous jurists: those of the future Chancellor Guillaume Poyet, representing the bishop of Meaux, have been published by M. Veissière in *BSHPF* 132 (1986), 547–549; those of Noel Beda and Pierre Lizet are printed by Farge, *Parti,* pp. 67–78.

15. Farge, *Orthodoxy,* p. 240 n. 105, shows that three other prelates (the archbishop of Lyon, bishop of Amiens, and archbishop of Tours) were assessed sums between 100 and 400 livres to pay for heresy trials, after

Briçonnet's fine (April 1525) but before the king's return in February 1526.

16. On Berquin's trial by the Parlement's *juges delegués* and the king's decisive intervention, see Doucet, *Parlement,* II, 210–213; Farge, *Orthodoxy,* pp. 259–260, and the king's letters to Parlement, cited by Knecht, p. 260; useful summary by Roelker, pp. 199–201.

17. Driart, "Chronique," pp. 115–116 (23/3/1526); *JBP,* pp. 277–278.

18. Versoris, p. 183 (no. 300); *JBP,* pp. 280–281.

19. Versoris, p. 182 (no. 299), who adds "je estois present"; *JBP,* pp. 250–251, reports the attempted bribe; Driart, "Chronique," pp. 114–115, claims that the prisoner died contritely, adoring the cross.

20. Versoris, p. 188 (no. 321); *JBP,* pp. 291–292; Driart, "Chronique," p. 120. Farge (*Orthodoxy,* p. 259) notes that Francis prodded the judges to severity on this case a fortnight before the execution.

21. *JBP,* p. 317; Driart, "Chronique," p. 124.

22. Session of 6/6/1528 (AN, X1a 1531, fols. 261v–266), printed by Farge, *Parti,* pp. 95–108; Lizet's speech summarized on pp. 98–104 (quotations, p. 103).

23. *JBP,* pp. 358–360, 375; Versoris, pp. 206–208 (no. 379), also reports the iconoclasm. Crespin's account (I, 272) enables us to identify the victim as Denis Rieux of Meaux.

24. *JBP,* p. 403; Driart, "Chronique," p. 142.

25. See R. Rolland, "Le dernier procès de Louis de Berquin," in *Mélanges d'archéologie et d'histoire de l'École française de Rome* 12 (1892), 314–325; *JBP,* pp. 378–384. Quotation from Versoris, p. 213 (no. 396). On crowd size, see G. Guiffrey, ed., *Cronique du Roy Francoys Premier de ce nom* (Paris, 1860), p. 76 n. 1.

26. The Parlement of Toulouse investigated a handful of "Lutherans" in 1528, convicting one of them: see ADHG, B 22, fol. 200v (22/4/1528).

27. See the brief summary by Bartolomé Bennassar, "Un siècle d'or (1460–1550)," in *Histoire de Toulouse,* ed. Philippe Wolff (Toulouse, 1974), pp. 267–270; compare Mentzer, pp. 28–29, and David Hempsall, "The Languedoc, 1520–1540: A Study of Pre-Calvinist Heresy in France," *ARG* 62 (1971), 235–243.

28. La Faille, II, 76–77, prints a lengthy extract from Boysonné's official abjuration.

29. C. Roque, ed., *Inventaire-sommaire des Archives Departementales de la Haute-Garonne, Série B no. 1-92N* (Toulouse, 1903), pp. 171–173.

30. On Jean de Caturce's execution, compare ADHG, B 26, fol. 67, with Crespin, I, 283–284, and the criticisms by La Faille, II, 78.

31. For de Badet's prosecution, see Hempsall, "Languedoc," pp. 238–243.

32. On Boysonné's subsequent career, see Etienne Dolet, *Correspondance,* ed. Claude Longeon (Geneva, 1982), p. 33 n. 1; and esp. Henri Jacoubet, *Boysonné et son temps* (Toulouse, 1930). At Chambéry, Boysonné's most significant task was to prepare an elaborate procedural code for this newly built court.

33. On Servetus' naturalization in October 1548 as "Michel de Villeneuve, residing at Vienne in Dauphiné," see *Catalogue des actes de Henri II,* vol. II (Paris, 1990), 416.

34. *HE,* I, 22. On de Nuptiis' subsequent troubles with the Paris Faculty of Theology, see James K. Farge, ed., *Registre des conclusions de la Faculté de Théologie de l'Université de Paris, II (26 novembre 1533–1 mars 1550)* (Paris, 1994), pp. 14 (no. 9B), 16 (no. 11B).

35. See Gabrielle Berthoud in *BSHPF* 82 (1933), 321–325. After a year in prison, Antoine Saunier was released through Swiss diplomatic pressure.

36. Versoris, p. 220 (no. 422).

37. On the 1533 troubles at Paris, see Farge, *Orthodoxy,* pp. 200–205; Knecht, pp. 308–312; and Pierre Jourda, *Marguerite d'Angoulême, Duchesse d'Alençon, Reine de Navarre (1492–1549),* 2 vols. (Paris, 1931), I, 172–179.

38. Driart, "Chronique," p. 134; Herminjard (III, 162 n. 16) identifies the man mentioned in a letter of Myconius on 8 April 1534 as the Jean Pointet commemorated by Crespin (I, 287).

39. Driart, "Chronique," p. 169; *Cronique du Roy Francoys,* p. 111. Crespin (I, 285–286) omits his marriage, which Paris chroniclers stressed; the cleric also claimed that the friar showed some degree of repentance, which does not enirely contradict Crespin's version.

40. See Alexis François, *Le magnifique Meigret* (Geneva, 1947); *JBP,* pp. 438–439.

41. See N. Weiss in *BSHPF* 36 (1887), 299–314; Farge, *Orthodoxy,* pp. 198–199; ADSM, G 2154 (15/4, 6/8, 7/8, and 11/12/1533); and A. Heron, ed., *Deux chroniques de Rouen* (Rouen and Paris, 1900), pp. 146–147. As at Paris, the first heretic executed in Normandy after 1520 was no "Lutheran." A Rouen merchant was strangled and burned in 1528 "for having said there was only one God, that Jesus was not the son of God, nor the Virgin Mary the mother of God." He was clearly a "Judaizer," with a Spanish *conversa* mistress. See Floquet, II, 223–224; Héron, *Chroniques,* pp. 131–132; and ADSM, G 2153.

42. Best introduction by B. Robert in *BSHPF* 85 (1936), 365–390.

43. The absent king's 1533 ruling, declaring the Alençon judges incompetent and naming Parisian parlementary commissioners to investigate the sacrilege, is in *Catalogue des Actes de François I,* (Paris, 1889), II, 467 (no.

6061). An undated letter by Marguerite, promising her cooperation with a parlementary investigation, probably concerns events at Alençon in 1533–34; see E. Jourda, *Correspondance de Marguerite d'Angoulême, Duchesse d'Alençon, Reine de Navarre (1492–1549)* (Paris, 1930), p. 128 (no. 573).

44. The commission's final report (AN, X2a 83) was carefully edited by Paul Guérin in *BSHPF* 33 (1884), 112–128, 162–175. See also Jourda, *Marguerite,* I, 183–184.

45. See Robert in *BSHPIF* 85 (1936), 375–376, 382–384: one man, condemned to be burned in 1534, reappeared as a royal official in 1545; another, banished in 1534, also regained his official post in 1545; a third, whose property was confiscated, had acquired public office by 1548.

46. The most detailed investigation is Robert Hari, "Les placards de 1534," in *Aspects de la propagande religieuse,* ed. G. Berthoud (Geneva, 1957), pp. 79–142. Best recent summary by Knecht, pp. 313–322, who includes (p. 314) a facsimile reproduction of the original placard.

47. Among contemporary chroniclers, Driart ("Chronique," pp. 173–178) and *JBP* (pp. 442–452) agree closely on names and dates, while the *Cronique du Roy Francoys* (pp. 111–113, 129–132, 136) adds useful information. Another list was printed from Ms. 189 of the Bibliothèque Municipale at Soissons in *BSHPF* 11 (1862), 253–258. Two German eyewitnesses reported on these events in December 1534 and March 1535; see Herminjard, III, 225–228 (no. 488), 266–270 (no. 499). After Henry II's attempted purge of the Paris Parlement in mid-1559, this record would be matched but not surpassed.

48. *HE,* I, 28.

49. Knecht, p. 316 n. 25.

50. On these absentees, see Gabrielle Berthoud, "Les 'ajournés' du 25 janvier 1535," *Bibliothèque d'Humanisme et Renaissance* 25 (1963), 307–324.

51. AN, X2b 2 (*arrêts* for May 1535), largely corroborated by *JBP.*

52. See ADSM, G 2154 (24/7/1534) and 1B 3117 (23/12/1534).

53. See Héron, *Chroniques,* pp. 147–148 (misdating his execution to 30 April); ADSM, 1B 3118 (*arrêt* of 30/8/1535).

54. ADSM, 1B 3118 (24/7 and 9/12/1535).

55. On Rouen's attitudes toward Lutherans, see Floquet, I, 505–522; on the king's anger toward them, see Knecht, pp. 528–530.

56. Nicola Sutherland (quoted by Knecht, p. 322). Audisio, *Vaudois,* pp. 302–303, notes the tactics of the Parlement of Aix to sabotage the Edict of Coucy, and the objections of the local archbishop.

57. On Marot's pardon, see Knecht, pp. 466–467. Another man received the Parlement's permission to annul his conviction as a "contumacious" here-

tic and thereby have his confiscated property restored; AN, X2a 86 (13/12/1535). Zacharie Bertrand, a lawyer at the Paris Parlement, charged with having "written words sounding badly against our holy faith" and banished perpetually from France in absentia on 15 May 1535, similarly had his conviction annulled on 5 February 1536, his property restored, and resumed his practice before the Parlement, "insofar as he is not one of the *sacramentaires* or recidivists" excluded from the king's pardon; compare X2b2 (15/5/1535) and X2a 86 (30/4/1536). For two more examples of royal pardons for heretics, see *BSHPF* 39 (1890), 269–271 (March 1537 pardon of widow of merchant executed during placards panic, now remarried to wealthy German Protestant merchant at Lyon) and *BSHPF* 34 (1885), 171–177 (September 1537 pardon of a nobleman from Dauphiné who had corresponded with many heretics, composed anticlerical songs, and sheltered a "sacramentarian").

58. A prisoner charged with blasphemies against "the glorious Virgin Mary and the saints of paradise" was released by Parlement under terms of the Edict of Coucy; X2a 86 (2/12/1535); another, charged with "erroneous propositions and scandalous words sounding badly about the faith," was also released (8/3/1536).

59. *JBP*, p. 452, dates their execution to 18 September; the *Cronique du Roy Francoys,* p. 139, dates it to 24 September.

60. AN, X2a 86 (22/12/1535).

61. Ibid. (4/2 and 6/10/1536).

62. Ibid. (24/12/1535: a monk). A priest and a schoolteacher from the diocese of Meaux were released on 22 September 1536, after they had abjured their "false and heretical propositions and doctrines."

63. Ibid. (19/8 and 7/9/1536).

64. This entire section closely follows Audisio, *Vaudois,* pp. 71–92; the briefer account by Cameron, pp. 148–150, is also reliable.

65. See the edited transcript of Griot's interrogations by Gabriel Audisio, *Le barbe et l'inquisiteur* (Aix, 1979).

66. De Roma's defense before the Parlement of Aix is printed by Herminjard, VII, 477–488 (quotation p. 486). In defending his investigative methods, the old inquisitor even cited the *Malleus Maleficarum* (p. 481) as his guide to dealing with heretics who made patently insincere confessions.

67. On this episode, see Cameron, pp. 49–54.

68. ADBR, B 4488, fols. 352–353.

69. Audisio, *Vaudois,* pp. 81, 83–85; see also Herminjard, VII, 465–477.

70. See his annual report to the royal treasury in December 1536, printed by G. Bourgeois in *BSHPF* 24 (1875), 547.

71. For de Rochette's investigations at Agen, see Heller, pp. 73–107.

72. Mentzer, pp. 31–33, explains the vendetta against Louis de Rochette but underplays the importance of the rapidity with which the Parlement acted. De Rochette was arrested on 27 August, dismissed from office on 6 September, degraded by ecclesiastical officials on 10 September, and promptly burned; ADHG, B 31, fols. 485v, 510, 514v.

73. De Rochette's official sentence (which never mentions sodomy) is in ADHG, B 3360; see also the criticisms of Crespin's account by LaFaille, *Annales,* pp. 108–109.

74. Ricardi's sentence in ADHG, B 3362, fol. 40. To the best of my knowledge, he was the first person punished for sodomy by the Parlement of Toulouse; the charge was legally necessary in order to justify a death sentence, since protecting heretics never constituted a capital crime, even for a deputy inquisitor.

75. For de Becanis' petition to hold the office to which he had been appointed in March 1535, see G. Bourgeois in *BSHPF* 24 (1875), 548; compare ibid., 25 (1876), 19 (his 1540 salary), 109 (fine imposed by him as inquisitor in April 1547).

76. At Paris the Parlement's criminal *arrêts* survive for only two months between October 1536 and November 1539. Even at Rouen, Aix, or Toulouse, we possess fewer than half of parlementary criminal decisions before the important procedural code of Villers-Cotterets was adopted in 1539.

77. On Martin Gonin, one of the *barbes* who had arranged the famous synod at Chanforan in 1532, see Crespin, I, 317–320. Gonin was about to be released from the Parlement's prison in Grenoble when an alert jailer noticed that he was carrying letters from Farel and other well-known heretics. Before condemning Vindocin, the Parlement of Bordeaux did nothing against heretics except watch the public abjuration and penancing of eleven barefoot "Lutherans" on a scaffold in front of the city's cathedral in April 1538; Metivier, I, 341.

78. In April 1538 Lizet presided as three prisoners unsuccessfully appealed death sentences for heresy; they implicated five other suspects, at least two of whom were then in jail. In June the more prominent of those two was sentenced. See AN, X2b 4, and Lizet's letter to Chancellor du Bourg in April 1538, printed by Herminjard, IV, 418–420 (no. 702).

79. Herminjard, IV, p. 419 n., quotes Johann Sleidan on the "Tolosanus quidam adolescens nobilis et literarum studiosus," aged about twenty, burned at Paris on the ides of April; his description fits Sabray.

80. See Alfred Cartier in *BSHPF* 38 (1889), 575–588, who ignores the final outcome of Morin's trial; see X2b 4 (17/6/1538).

81. ADBR, B 4491, fols. 18–18v (5/2/1535); Audisio, *Vaudois,* pp. 325–326.

82. Compare V.-L. Bourrilly in *BSHPF* 60 (1911), 111–112, with ADBR, B 4496 (26/2/1539, condemning the prisoner to be burned alive).

83. See ADHG, B 3359 (7/11/1537); Herminjard, IV, 315–321 (nos. 668, 669).

84. Printed by N. Weiss in *BSHPF* 38 (1889), 72–74. At the same time, Francis was warning his new Parlement at Chambéry against Genevan "dogmatizers," one of whom they imprisoned in December 1538; compare Henri Hauser in *BSHPF* 43 (1894), 594–598, with Herminjard, V, 201.

85. Doucet, *Bibliothèques,* pp. 35–37, notes the absence of anything resembling "Lutheran" literature, or even a vernacular Bible, among a sizable collection of pre-1560 Parisian private libraries (one minor parlementary official, who died in 1548, owned a copy of the Koran).

86. See the classic investigations of Henri Hauser, *Etudes sur la Réforme française* (Paris, 1909), reinforced by the more recent investigations of Heller, pp. 27–69.

87. Compare Imbart de la Tour, IV, 219–265, with Lucien Febvre, "Une question mal posée? Les origines de la Réforme française et le problème des causes de la Réforme," *Revue historique* 161 (1929), 1–73.

88. Berthoud, "Les 'ajournés' du 25 janvier 1535," found additional information about only twenty-nine of more than fifty who were condemned.

89. *HE,* I, 26–28. The use of three widely different destinies also recalls its description of the earlier fates of Farel, Martial Mazurier, and Lefèvre d'Etaples; ibid., pp. 12–13.

90. Ibid., pp. 28–30. None of them can be found on either list of names of those condemned in absentia in January 1535.

4. Royal Escalation and the Crisis of Nicodemism, 1540–1548

1. Published by N. Weiss in *BSHPF* 38 (1889), 240–243. Confusion resulted from its provisions that lay courts should add eight or nine "learned, literate, good people . . . of good conscience" when voting sentences in heresy cases, and six or seven of them when torturing heresy suspects. However, the edict stated clearly that bishops would pay the cost of heresy trials, no matter who judged them.

2. See F.-A. Isambert, *Recueil général des anciennes lois françaises,* 29 vols. (Paris, 1827–1833), XII, 600, n. 1.

3. See text in ibid., pp. 676–681 (no. 305).

4. On censorship, see the synthesis of Francis Higman, *Censorship and the Sorbonne: A Bibliographical Study of Books in French Censured by the Faculty of Theology of the University of Paris, 1520–1551* (Geneva, 1979). See Farge, *Orthodoxy,* pp. 208–213, on the articles of faith, which contain between twenty-five and twenty-nine articles in different versions.

5. Soman, chap. VII, p. 24, tabulates 555 defendants judged over a span of twenty-four months between 1539 and 1542.

6. The fifty-four names listed as tried for heresy in AN, X2a 1200, were published by P. Beuzart in *BSHPF* 82 (1933), 326–330. However, this list is incomplete; for example, its very first entry (Giles Bobusse) was charged with heresy, although no marginal note to that effect accompanied his name.

7. After June 1542 the Parlement of Paris evoked heresy cases when lower royal courts had completed a trial but had not yet passed sentence.

8. AN, X2a 91, fols. 175v–176 (20/1/1541).

9. AN, X2a 95, fol. 516v (3/8/1543).

10. AN, X2a 94 (28/2/1543); the *arrêt,* published by N. Weiss in *BSHPF* 41 (1892), 525–527, is unsigned.

11. Claude Longeon, ed., *Documents d'archives sur Etienne Dolet* (Saint-Etienne, 1977), offers the most complete account of Dolet's legal problems; additional information and context in Natalie Z. Davis, *Fiction in the Archives* (Stanford, 1987), pp. 8, 151–152. The old biography by R. C. Christie, *Etienne Dolet: The Martyr of the Renaissance (1508–1546)* (London, 1899), has not been entirely replaced.

12. AN, X2a 93 (3/7/1542); X2a 94 (1/3/1543).

13. AN, X2a 94 (7/4/1543); X2a 95, fols. 298–298v (28/6/1543); X2a 96, fol. 680v (27/3/1544). X2a 1200 shows that Burgeat's relatives and in-laws were arrested and questioned about the case in 1543.

14. AN, X2b 6 (4/7/1544); X2a 1200 (14/3/1543).

15. AN, X2b 10 (1/10/1548), printed by N. Weiss in *BSHPF* 48 (1899), 600–601.

16. Olson, pp. 103–104, 255 n. 31; compare *LH,* p. 21.

17. See AN, U 1084, entries for 19/5 and 17/6/1540 (scandal at church of St. Jean de la Croix, Autun). Crespin (II, 156) misdates these events by fifteen years, his worst chronological error.

18. ADI, B 2023, fols. 46v–47, 60v–61, on "Jean Garnier dit Rostaing" (4/3, 31/3, and 16/7/1541); also fols. 64v–108 (nine entries between 15/7 and 23/12/1541).

19. *HE,* I, 81.

20. ADI, B 2024, fols. 298–299v (18/5/1543). Herminjard, V, 207 n. 19, notes German and Swiss diplomatic intervention on his behalf.

21. See ADSM, 1B 3127 (15/12/1544), for the first documented heresy executions by this court since the summer of 1535. Although we possess Rouen's criminal *arrêts* from only twenty months during the five years after 1539, no other evidence suggests any important action against heretics at this time.

22. See David Nicholls' articles, esp. "Social Change and Early Protestantism in France: Normandy, 1520–1562," *European Studies Review* 10 (1980), 279–308.

23. AN, X2a 93 (10/7/1542); du Ruel was to be tortured in order to elicit information about his "accomplices and adherents wherever they are, in Normandy, [Ile-de-] France, or elsewhere in this kingdom." Compare ADG, 1B 86, fol. 551.

24. See Patry, pp. 2–34, drawn from ADG, 1 B 86.

25. Compare Patry, p. 11 (22/6/1542), with Metivier, I, 390, 410–411, 430 (15/4/1545, after Melanchthon's debts to his jailers had finally been paid).

26. See ADHG, B 3363 (27/6/1540) and B 3369 (29/8/1543).

27. Ibid., B 3368 (*arrêt* of 10/4/1543). Compare B 3369 (*arrêt* of 18/7/1543: two jailers responsible for the escape of these prisoners were sent to the galleys for five years).

28. Ibid., B 3368 (17/3/1543); B 3372 (24/8/1545).

29. ADBR, B 5443 (1/4/1540). Audisio, *Vaudois,* pp. 350–360, provides an indispensable introduction to these issues.

30. See ADBR, B 5443 (two *arrêts* of 16/10 and 18/11/1540); quotation from Audisio, *Vaudois,* p. 356.

31. The "edict of Merindol" has been printed by Audisio, *P-V,* pp. 60–73.

32. ADBR, B 5443 (30/6/1541); B 5446 (5/3, 7/3, 17/3, and 2/4/1544): Thomas Pellenc, trying to take advantage of the 1543 pardon, was promptly jailed and soon burned at Apt.

33. Audisio has published the major sources about the "crusade" of April 1545; see his *Vaudois,* pp. 347–407, and his editions of the official *P-V* and of Aubéry.

34. Quotation from Audisio *P-V,* p. 98. Although this document reported these phrases as hearsay, they have a ring of authenticity.

35. Ibid., p. 100.

36. Ibid., pp. 88–90.

37. Aubéry, pp. 113–114.

38. Ibid., pp. 114, 189, 193, 199–200, 203–204, 214; Audisio, *P-V,* p. 49; compare Cameron, p. 155 and n. 127, on the subsequent career of Perreri (here called Poirier).

39. Aubéry, pp. 175–177, gives an excellent account. Audisio, *Vaudois,* pp. 390–397, presents confirmatory evidence from the archives at Marseilles.

40. See L. Bertrando and B. Ely in *BSHPF* 118 (1972), 349–353.

41. See Audisio's introduction to Aubéry, pp. viii–ix and n. 1.

42. The death warrant for Michel Maynard, a son of the *bayle* of Mérindol, referred specifically to the famous *arrêt* of 18/11/1540; ADBR, B 5448

(16/6/1545); the rapporteur was de Badet, one of the three commissioners. On the total number of heresy trials and executions judged by the Parlement of Aix in 1545, see Aubéry, pp. 177–179. Apart from Maynard, the only Waldensians executed by the Parlement in 1545 were two men from Cabrières d'Avignon and thus papal subjects; ADBR, B 5448 (15/6/1545: Peyron Dupuy; and 29/7/1545: François Dupuy). Gabriel Audisio verified that no other heretics executed in 1545 had surnames of known Waldensian clans.

43. Aubéry, pp. 178–179.
44. This was the official estimated total from the original investigation, carried out by the special tribunal of the Chambre de la Reine in 1548 with information supplied by landlords whose villages had been destroyed and whose tenants had been massacred; figures quoted by Aubéry, pp. 179–180.
45. Ibid., pp. 198–199.
46. Audisio, *Vaudois,* p. 443.
47. The petitions of Christofle de Pierre are in AN, X2b 6 (26/7/1544); X2a 97 (27/2/1545). In February 1545 the Parlement ordered the royal treasury to pay him 326 livres.
48. AN, X2a 97 (6/3/1545), printed by N. Weiss in *BSHPF* 44 (1895), 453. Lizet had planned on questioning d'Angleur since September 1544 (ibid., p. 450). A 1542 revolt against the salt tax preceded the flurry of heresy cases from La Rochelle tried at Fontenay in 1544; see Judith P. Meyer, *Reformation in La Rochelle* (Geneva, 1996), pp. 127–128.
49. AN, X2a 99 (19/6 and 1/10/1545).
50. See AN, X2a 100 (23/11/1545; 22/1, 1/2, 16/2, and 17/2/1546), all printed by Weiss in *BSHPF* 44 (1895), 454–456.
51. AN, X2a 102 (16/11 and 24/11/1546); X2a 104 (31/7/1548).
52. See Judith P. Meyer, "The Success of the French Reformation: The Case of La Rochelle," *ARG* 84 (1993), 261–275.
53. AN, X2a 115, fols. 52–53 (2/12/1553).
54. AN, X2a 99 (29/7/1545).
55. Ibid. (27/8/1545).
56. AN, X2a 100 (12/12/1545; 11/1, 15/1, 16/3, 24/3/1546; plus 4/3 and 26/3/1546 among the *arrêts obmis* at the end of this register).
57. AN, X2a 101, fol. 207v. The Parlement ordered the bishop of Nevers to pay forty livres to help prosecute those accused of "blasphemy and heretical speech" (ibid., 6/10/1546).
58. See AN, X2a 100 (15/12/1545); X2a 98 (1/5/1546) and fols. 643–643v (27/8/1546).
59. For his arrest, see AN, X2a 98 (15/4/1545); Dubois was not originally

charged as a *sacramentaire*. However, X2a 99, fols. 11–11v (4/5/1545), shows him making copious confessions under torture, provoking five arrests and a search for heretical books. Shortly before Christmas, the Parlement's Grand Chambre finally approved Dubois's execution, originally proposed on May 2; X2a 100 (22/12 and 23/12/1545).

60. See AN, X2a 99 (30/10/1545); X2a 100 (19/12/1545, 26/1 and 4/3/1546); X2a 98 (5/4/1546). Thomas Le Moine had indeed been executed for heresy at Meaux five years before; see AN, X2a 89A (17/2/1540).

61. AN, X2a 98, fols. 77–77v: Pierre Saullaye, a shoemaker.

62. Compare AN, X2a 97 (4/2/1545), with X2a 102 (7/1/1547).

63. See AN, X2a 97 (13/4/1545); X2a 99 (31/8/1545); X2a 100 (5/12 and 13/12/1545); X2a 98 (6/5/1546).

64. AN, X2a 98, fols. 739v–740, 742v–743 (5/10/1546: three defendants), 754–756 (13/10/1546: two defendants).

65. AN, X2a 102 (13/12 and 30/12/1546).

66. See *HE,* I, 86: Henry II's "whole reign has been nothing but perpetual persecution against religion inside [his kingdom] and perpetual war outside."

67. Compare Weiss, *CA,* with Imbart de la Tour, IV, 327. While Imbart's research was considerable, his section on legal repression was published posthumously and the relevant documentary references were missing, making it impossible to build from his research but difficult not to endorse his conclusions.

68. AN, X2a 102 and 103, give complete *arrêts* from November 1546 to October 1547; there was also one execution for non-Protestant forms of blasphemy in each period.

69. X2a 102 (10/3/1547); X2a 103, fols. 457v–458 (20/8/1547).

70. ADI, B 2024, fols. 782–782v (21/5/1547), 807v–808 (19/7/1547); B 2026, fols. 332v–333 (18/4/1550).

71. J. J. Hemardinquer, "La Réforme en Dauphiné, jusqu'aux guerres de Religion, notamment d'après les registres du Parlement de Grenoble" (D.E.S. d'Histoire, Grenoble 1950), at ADI, Ms. 2 J 7, p. 50.

72. ADHG, B 3374 (28/1/1546); B 3375 (17/3 and 26/3/1546; B 3376 (17/4 and 30/4/1546); B 3378 (14/10/1546); B 3379 (16/11, 6/12, 22/12, and 23/12/1546). See also B 3378 (24/10/1546: heirs of a carpenter imprisoned since 7/6 [see B 3377] summoned to clear his name on heresy charges, posthumously).

73. ADHG, B 3379 (7/2 and 16/2/1547: two canons burned for sodomy); B 3380 (10/3 and 7/6/1547: a woman and a monk burned for heresy); B 3381 (12/8/1547); B 3382 (16/1, 27/1, and 3/3/1548: man burned for "heresy," although his first sentence on 5/12/1547 had condemned him

only for "sodomy"); B 3383 (19/4/1548: defrocked priest burned for blasphemies plus other "crimes et maléfices"). Since B 3384 has been so badly damaged as to be unusable, we know no further criminal decisions from Toulouse in 1548, except for its special vacation session at Le Puy, where two men were strangled and burned for heresy on 4/9 and 18/9; ADHG, B92J, fols. 10–11, 63–64.

74. ADSM, 1B 3132 (21/10/1547); 1B 3134 (18/5/1548).

75. *HE*, I, 67.

76. On Colin, surely the only convicted heretic who asked the king's pardon in rhyme, see N. Weiss in *BSHPF* 40 (1891), 57–75. Five members of Colin's group were executed; although *HE* (I, 80) places them near the end of Francis I's reign, they probably died during the first half of 1541, when Parisian criminal *arrêts* have disappeared; Colin himself abjured—twice—in July 1540.

77. See the persuasive study by Maurice Causse, "Les dissimulations de Marguerite de Navarre et l'Aventure Nicodémite," *BSHPF* 132 (1986), 347–389.

78. See N. Weiss in *BSHPF* 37 (1888), 241–266, including the official text of his famous abjuration. For the remark about Roussel, see *BSHPF* 65 (1916), 215.

79. Translated in John Calvin, *Three French Treatises,* ed. Francis Higman (London, 1970), pp. 144, 145. The *HE* discussed Calvin's assault on French Nicodemites (I, 66), immediately after the Council of Trent in 1545. For the fullest bibliographical account, see Eugénie Droz, "Calvin et les Nicodémites," in her *Chemins de l'hérésie,* 4 vols. (Geneva, 1970–1976), I, 131–171.

80. Quoted in Paul-F. Geisendorf, *Théodore de Bèze* (Geneva, 1967), p. 27; and Jean-F. Gilmont, *Jean Crespin: Un éditeur réformé au XVIe siècle* (Geneva, 1981), p. 40 n. 54. Both men described serious physical illnesses that accompanied their prolonged difficulties in resolving their material circumstances in the mid-1540s; de Normandie left no recorded comments on his *crise de conscience.*

5. The Limits of Prosecution and the Challenge of Geneva, 1549–1554

Epigraph: Simon Goulart, preface to 1597 edition of Crespin.

1. *LH*, p. xi.

2. See Audisio, *Vaudois,* pp. 402–405; this special tribunal has left no surviving records.

3. *CA,* p. lxxii n. 1, notes that Henry II adopted a precedent that his father had tried to impose at Rouen in April 1545. Essentially, Weiss's text (*CA,* pp. 19–318) prints Paul Guérin's transcription of X2a 105, fols. 49–552v. See also Roelker, pp. 214–219.

4. AN, X2a 105, fols. 149 (31/8/1548), 258 (22/9/1548), overlooked by Weiss, *CA.* All four, who were tortured and executed at Paris, had been brought from Sens at considerable expense; ibid., fols. 252v–253 (19/9/1548).

5. Weiss, *CA,* pp. 340 (no. 235), 381 (no. 366), overlooks the information from Languedoc in AN, X2a 106, fol. 560v (16/3/1549). See also Imbart de la Tour, IV, 359–360.

6. Imbart de la Tour, IV, 358.

7. Bernard Schnapper, "La justice criminelle rendue par le Parlement de Paris sous le règne de François Ier," *Revue du droit historique français et étranger* 52 (1974), 252–284, seems unaware of the enormous practical impact of heresy trials on the court's collective behavior.

8. Aubéry, pp. 221–227, outlines the legal maneuvers before the Paris Parlement in the autumn of 1551.

9. Audisio, *Vaudois,* pp. 404–407, ignores the arguments used by Aubéry's principal opponent, who represented Maynier d'Oppède, although Audisio cites at least five manuscript copies of his arguments.

10. AN, X2a 106, contains 1,600 written pages.

11. Ibid., fols. 42v–43v (22/11/1548).

12. Ibid., fols. 360–360v (7/2/1549).

13. In March they passed sentence against a Renaissance musical sextet from Noyon, the "Carefree Lads" *(les enfants sans souci),* who used nicknames like Narcissus, Troilus, Leander, and Priam. Charged with immoral songs, scandalous speech, and possession of illegal books, they abjured at the cathedral of Paris; ibid., fols. 571–571v (9/3 and 17/3/1549).

14. Ibid., fols. 189–189v (2/1/1549), 529v (9/3/1549).

15. Ibid., fols. 317–318 (31/1/1549).

16. Olson, p. 49.

17. AN, X2a 106, fols. 675v (2/4/1549), 686v (5/4/1549), published by N. Weiss in *BSHPF* 37 (1888), 531–532.

18. AN, X2a 106, fols. 701–701v (6/4/1549), also published by Weiss (*BSHPF* 37 [1888], 532–533).

19. See text following reception of two noblemen in April 1549, in *LH,* p. 1.

20. Olivier Reverdin, *Quatorze Calvinistes chez les Topinambous* (Geneva, 1947), p. 26.

21. Compare *LH,* p. 4, with Patry, p. 234.

22. Compare *LH,* p. 7, and A. Covelle, ed., *Le Livre des Bourgeois de l'ancienne*

République de Genève (Geneva, 1897), p. 243, with ADBR, B 5443 (16/10/1540 and 30/6/1541).

23. After Lizet was compelled to resign in mid-1550 as a result of court intrigues, he was replaced by an equally conservative but less talented first president.

24. AN, X2a 109, fol. 78 (11/12/1550); additional information from N. Weiss in *BSHPF* 35 (1886), 97–111.

25. See AN, X2a 109, fols. 530v–531, for le Coq's second commission to Blois. For its results, see X2a 110, fols. 476v–477, and twenty-two different *arrêts* in X2a 111, scattered among fols. 111–300.

26. See P. Chaix, A. Dufour, and G. Moeckli, *Les livres imprimés à Genève de 1550 à 1600* (Geneva, 1966), p. 15.

27. Published at Rouen, also in 1550; Francis Higman, *Piety and the People: Religious Printing in French, 1511–1551* (Aldershot, 1996), p. 169, identifies this as the first French literary attack against Geneva.

28. Alain Dufour, "Le mythe de Genève au temps de Calvin," in his *Histoire politique et psychologie historique* (Geneva, 1966), pp. 85–90.

29. See Paul-F. Geisendorf, *Théodore de Bèze* (Geneva, 1967), pp. 47–51.

30. *HE*, I, 103–104.

31. ADHG, B 3392 (14/8/1551).

32. On François d'Augi, see ibid., B 3398 (30/7/1552). Crespin misdated this affair by seven years: see Mentzer, p. 121.

33. ADSM, 1B 3004 (26/4/1552).

34. Compare Crespin, II, 13–25, with ADSM, 1B 3004 (15/5 and 17/5/1553).

35. ADBR, B 5451 (20/12/1548).

36. See ADSM, 1B 3004 (13/7 and 14/7/1552).

37. AN, X2a 112, fols. 6–7v (3/5/1552), 647v–648 (7/9/1552).

38. AN, X2a 112, fols. 460v–461v (7/9/1552).

39. See Calvin's letter of 13 February 1553 to an unknown person (W. Baum, G. Cunitz, and R. Reuss, eds., *Calvini Opera,* 59 vols. [Brunswick, 1863–1900], XIV, 477): "the Parisian court showed a ridiculous fear in making no mention of me while citing Abel [Poupin] and declaring him convicted of heresy . . . the thing would seem inconceivable, if I hadn't seen with my own eyes the parchment *arrêt*, copied by some friends."

40. AN, X2a 113, fol. 402 (17/2/1553), published by N. Weiss in *BSHPF* 41 (1892), 306–308.

41. AN, X2a 113, fols. 404–405v (18/2/1553), also published by Weiss (*BSHPF* 41 [1892], 308–310).

42. AN, X2a 113, fols. 465v, 474v (6/3 and 8/3/1553).

43. AN, X2a 114, fols. 135v–136 (13/6/1553); compare Crespin, I, 713–718.

44. Crespin, II, 151–156 (spring 1555).

45. AN, X2a 110, fols. 491–491v. Compare Jean Guérard, *La chronique lyon-naise . . . 1536–1562*, ed. J. Tricou (Lyon, 1929), pp. 54–55; Natalie Z. Davis, *Society and Culture in Early Modern France* (Stanford, 1975), pp. 4–5.

46. See Crespin, I, 552–557, 585–674 (the five theology students), 674–681, 683–712, 712–718; II, 37–59.

47. See J. Roman and N. Weiss in *BSHPF* 52 (1903), 127–130: the seneschal of Montélimar, Felix Bourjac, was indeed openly Protestant by 1553.

48. See the Appendix. No criminal *arrêts* survive for 1550 from the Parlement of Aix, which recorded heresy executions in both 1549 and 1551; Greno-ble was the only French parlement with recorded criminal *arrêts* but no known heresy executions in 1550.

49. For the troubles of the Bordeaux Parlement after the revolt of August 1548, see Metivier, I, 480–502.

50. For decisions of the replacement judges, see ADG, 1B 90. Three of the next five executed heretics were former monks; Patry, pp. 83–84, 172–174, 182–183.

51. ADSM, 1B 3138 (23/5/1550). In January the court sent a commissioner to Lille to investigate the "vie, estat et conversation desdits prisonniers."

52. See Romier, pp. 201–202 (23/12/1550), 204–205 (5/9/1551); this register ends early in 1552. The first known multiple deaths for witchcraft ap-proved by any sixteenth-century French parlement occurred in occupied Italy.

53. ADS, B 55, fols. 78–78v (13/3/1551), 215v–216v (27/10/1551).

54. The response of young Michel de L'Hôpital to the duke of Guise's irrita-tion with the way the Chambéry court was handling this case falls be-tween these dates (11/10/1551); see Roman and Weiss in *BSHPF* 52 (1903), 130.

55. On this Germain Colladon, homonym and nephew of the famous Calvin-ist jurist, see E. H. Kaden, *Le juriste Germain Colladon* (Geneva, 1972), p. 39 n. 117. Roman and Weiss (*BSHPF* 52 [1903] 127–128) mention Protin's appearance in the records of Geneva's Bourse Française soon after his sentencing. In all probability both Colladon and Protin were allowed to escape. Former heresy prisoners appear often in the account books of this institution (AEG, Kg 12–15).

56. See ADS, B 57, fols. 131v, 199v (5/8 and 27/9/1553).

57. See Mentzer, pp. 50–51; the official warrant is also in AMT, II 47, *pièce* 11. For Lautrec's actions as rapporteur in heresy trials, see ADHG, B 3397 (4/6/1552: prisoner released because of illness; 9/6/1552: prisoner released for insufficient evidence; (13/6/1552: prisoner released on pa-role).

58. Quotation from AMT, BB 274, p. 163.
59. ADHG, B 3403 (15/3 and 21/4/1554); B 3404 (9/6/1554: a former Augustinian; 12/6 and 6/7/1554: a former Franciscan); B 3405 (12/10/1554: a former Jacobin); B 3406 (16/11/1554: Benedictine monk, defrocked and burned at Auch).
60. ADHG, B 3405 (1/8 and 12/9/1554). The sad tale of Jean Formals, former curé at Graissac, and a former nun from the convent of Vielmur (diocese of Castres), can be followed in ADHG, B 3403 (20/4/1554); B 3407 (15/2/1555); and B 3410 (5/9/1555).
61. Felix Platter, then a medical student at Montpellier, described d'Alençon's defrocking on 16 October 1553 in his memoirs; see Mentzer, p. 119. Early in December 1553 he and three other prisoners charged with heresy at Montpellier had appealed their condemnations to the Parlement—but the magistrates at Toulouse agreed that none of them should be extradited, "vu le danger qu'est a l'evasion"; B 3402 (exact date illegible).
62. ADHG, B 3403 (18/4/1554); B 3405 (13/10 and 16/10/1554).
63. Mentzer, p. 118.
64. ADHG, B 3405 (6/9 and 29/10/1554).
65. See Mentzer, pp. 142–150 (quotation p. 147).
66. ADHG, B 3404 (28/5 and 16/6/1554); B 3405 (20/8 and 12/9/1554). On the monk and nun, see note 60 above.
67. See the diary of a local Huguenot, begun shortly after this friar's martyrdom; Jacques Gaches, *Mémoires sur les guerres de Religion à Castres (1555–1610),* ed. C. Pradel (1879; reprint, Geneva, 1970).
68. ADHG, B 3405 (1/10 and 27/10/1554: bookseller plus several students and pedagogues; one man died in prison in September, another in October).
69. See the persuasive analysis of Protestantism at Villefranche by Nicole Lemaitre, *Le Rouergue flamboyant. Le clergé et les fidèles du diocèse de Rodez, 1417–1563* (Paris, 1988), esp. pp. 449–451. The regent of Villefranche was released in the spring of 1554 and became a leading municipal official in 1569.
70. For executions of the ex-Jacobin and the shoemaker, see above, notes 59 and 62; also ADHG, B 3404 (4/7/1554); B 3405 (12/10/1554: twelve effigies burned at Narbonne; 13/10/1554: an apothecary, a student, and another effigy; 16/10/1554: two widows, finally released in March 1556 for insufficient evidence; 13/10 and 29/10/1554: merchant tortured and fined 150 livres; 17/10/1554; 23/10/1554); B 3406 (6/12/1554: apothecary; 13/12/1554: a *garde du sel*).
71. Mentzer, p. 148 (twenty-nine *habitants* and fourteen suspects). At the other regional capitals of lower Languedoc, Nîmes and Uzès, Mentzer's

comparisons reveal that accused heretics outnumbered *habitants de Genève* (70–54 at Nîmes and 29–19 at Uzès).

72. See above, note 61. The prisoner named first in this group, ahead of d'Alençon, was an immigrant from Orléans named André Borgoing. Because the first person named was usually the most seriously accused, he was probably the unnamed cloth-cutter executed at Montpellier a few days after d'Alençon, having made an *amende honorable* and then retracted; Crespin, II, 34–35. Platter attended d'Alençon's martyrdom, noting that three recantations accompanied it.

73. ADHG, B 3403 (6/3/1554: uncertain, since heresy is not specified); B 3405 (2/8/1554); B 3404 (27/6/1554); and B 3405 (24/10/1554).

74. Albert Puech, *La Renaissance et la Réforme à Nîmes* (Nîmes, 1893), pp. 62–70, describes a heresy trial by the local presidial in October 1553; Crespin (II, 90) describes Pierre de la Vau's execution in 1554, but Puech (p. 80) offers pertinent reasons to doubt its authenticity.

75. ADHG, B 3409 (4/7/1555).

76. This mysterious letter, sent by a merchant named Pierre Ferrieres, can be read in AEG, Copies de Lettres, vol. 4, fol. 66 (20/6/1555).

77. ADHG, B 3409 (5/7/1555); the death sentences against the two Genevan *colporteurs* immediately follow this entry.

78. For an exhaustive compilation of Crespin's various revisions of his martyrology, see Jean-F. Gilmont, *Bibliographie des éditions de Jean Crespin*, 2 vols. (Verviers, 1981); a useful short list appears in idem, *Jean Crespin* (Geneva, 1981), pp. 248–260.

79. See Gilmont, *Crespin*, pp. 166–167, 169–170, 249.

80. I have compared the virtually identical entries from two 1556 versions—Claude Baduel's original Latin translation and Crespin's first pocket-sized edition (Gilmont, *Crespin*, p. 250, nos. 56/7b and 56/8)—at Chicago's Newberry Library. Crespin had not yet included any information about the Chambéry martyrs of October 1555, and he was still unaware of Foxe's work.

6. From Confessionalization to Decriminalization, 1555–1560

Epigraph: Haton, I, 27.

1. *HE*, I, 117–118.

2. R. M. Kingdon, *Geneva and the Coming of the Wars of Religion in France, 1555–1563* (Geneva, 1956), counted eighty-eight pastors sent to France from Geneva during this period, most of them in 1558 and 1559.

3. Current usage of this term dates from Ernst W. Zeeden's classic *Die Entstehung der Konfessionen* (Munich, 1965). For almost twenty years this con-

cept has been shared by Protestant and Catholic scholars in Germany; scholars of French Protestantism have been reluctant to employ it.

4. Fullest account in Crespin, II, 201–245.

5. This man, with the unusual name of Clereadus de la Noé, had himself been arrested for heresy; ADS, B 56, fols. 31v–33 (18/12/1551).

6. AEG, Reg. du Conseil, vol. 49, fol. 185v (19/9/1555): "M. Calvin a payé l'herault qui est allé à Chambéry, et qu'il n'est raisonnable que ledit ministre porte cette charge combien qu'il le veult faire."

7. Théodore de Bèze, *Correspondance,* ed. H. Meylan and A. Dufour (Geneva, 1960), I, 180.

8. Official sentence printed by Eugène Burnier, "Le Parlement de Chambéry sous François Ier et Henri II (1536–1559)," *Mémoires et documents publiés par la Société Savoisienne d'histoire et d'archéologie* 6 (1862), 399–404. It is out of proper chronological order in the series of criminal *arrêts,* placed after 30 December though carried out on 12 October; ADS, B 59, fols. 183v–186v.

9. Their letter of 25 July, printed in W. Baum, G. Cunitz, and R. Reuss, eds., *Calvini Opera,* 59 vols. (Brunswick, 1863–1900), XV, col. 696 (no. 2248), coincided with magistrate Curtet's return with optimistic news: a royal secretary had informed him that the prisoners would only be condemned to the galleys.

10. *Registres de la Compagnie des Pasteurs de Genève* (hereafter RCP), 24 vols. to date (Geneva, 1960–), II, 68–70.

11. *RCP,* II, 74, 79.

12. Good summary in Cameron, p. 159 and nn.

13. ADI, B 2028, fols. 176v–177 (12/7/1555).

14. Ibid., fols. 311–314 (28/3/1556). A special tax was to be levied on all village residents except widows and orphans in order to pay for a commemorative cross.

15. See Cameron, pp. 160–162.

16. Compare Crespin, II, 437–443, with ADI, B 2029, fols. 352v–353v (30/9/1558).

17. ADI, B 2029, fols. 363v–366, 411–411v, 412v–413, 417v, 421–421v, 423–423v (15/10, 3/12, 9/12, 12/12, and 20/12/1558). Nine men were jailed; three of them performed *amendes honorables* in their parish churches, and all were fined between fifty and five livres. Five men (including two who escaped after being arrested) were ordered burned in effigy.

18. ADI, B 2030, fols. 2v–3v, 15, 16v–17, 21v–22, 23v–24, 26v, 28v (21/7, 10/11, 13/11, 16/11, 18/11, and 24/11/1559). Twelve men from Val Chisone were arrested this time; the Parlement ordered three *amendes honorables,* fined five, and released seven with warnings.

19. Cameron, p. 161. See Kingdon, *Geneva and the Wars of Religion,* app. V,

p. 144. The first man sent to France in 1555, immediately after Vernou, was finally martyred at Lyon in the aftermath of the St. Bartholomew's masssacres. Martin Tachard, sought vainly in the Val Chisone by the Grenoble Parlement in 1558, was hanged at Pamiers in Languedoc in 1567 (see Chapter 8).

20. See AN, X2a 116–117. On Antoine de Genes, see X2a 116, fols. 340v–343 (19/2/1555).

21. On Lormeau, see ibid., fols. 451–451v, 751–752v, and 855v–856 (15/3, 28/5, and 29/6/1555). The royal prosecutor at Blois countersued Lormeau in order to postpone his summons to Paris; X2a 117, fols. 42v–43 (11/7/1555).

22. ADHG, B 3407 (9/2/1555: after abjuring, they were transferred to their close relatives); compare the account in AMT, BB 274, p. 175, which insists that they abandoned the "teachings they had received from John Calvin, heresiarch of the city of Geneva," before the Parlement, which then spared them only because of their youth. See also ADHG, B 3407 (15/2/1555); their next death sentences are in B 3409 (5/7/1555).

23. On Bordeaux, whose *arrêts* in ADG, 1B 154–162, cover all of 1555 except October, see Patry, pp. 205–216 (omitting the execution of Jerome Casaubon, which Crespin misdated to 1556).

24. ADSM, 1B 3142 (20/3/1555).

25. On this persecution, see *HE*, I, 129–130, describing it as "merveilleusement aspre." The circumstances were ideal for prosecuting a group of heretics: commissioner René Ambroys worked closely with both Inquisitor Matthieu Orry and the head of the local presidial court, with no right of appeal to Paris from their sentences. Nevertheless, a Protestant congregation formed again at Angers in 1559 and built an effective church.

26. For Parisian heresy executions in these years, see AN, X2a 118 (11/5 and 16/6/1556); X2a 120, fols. 178v–179 (18/8/1556); X2a 119 (15/2 and 12/6/1557).

27. AN, X2a 120, fols. 275–275v (22/9/1556), 496v (14/11/1556); X2a 119 (15/1/1557). On 19 June Parlement ordered the bishop of Tulle to pay their *conducteur des prisonniers* eighty livres for transporting Granier to Tulle, which they had reached on 24 February.

28. For these executions, see ADHG, B 3412 (22/2/1556); B 3418 (14/3/1557); B 3423 (22/12/1558); B 3428 (6/12/1559); B 3430 (10/4/1560).

29. ADHG, B 3414 (27/7/1556: Jacques Cogombris); on his previous arrest, see B 3404 (4/7/1554).

30. See ADHG, B 3422 (27/9 and 24/10/1558).

31. For 1556–1558, Patry's collection (which covers thirty of these thiry-six

months) shows fourteen accused heretics released, ten punished *citra mortem,* and one (Hamelin) executed. Two other executions noted by Crespin (II, 428–435, 444–446) occurred during a lacuna in the *arrêts* during April and May 1556.

32. On Hamelin's first trial, see Patry, p. 24 (26/3/1546). On his execution, ibid., p. 234 (12/4/1557); compare Crespin, II, 468–471.

33. ADSM, 1B 3145 (22/9, 5/10, 13/12, 16/12, and 23/12/1556). Fourteen prisoners were ordered to Rouen, and twelve absentees from Le Havre investigated; see also 1B 3146 (10/1/1557) on paying transportation costs. See also ADSM, 1B 3144 (20/8/1556); 1B 3145 (11/9/1556).

34. ADBR, B 5455 (27/3/1556). All of them, including thirty-seven people from Rossillon, had long since departed for Geneva.

35. ADBR, B 5455 (3/2 and 5/2/1556). Antoine de Cabassol, lord of Mérindol, charged the local curé with heresy and the local *bayle* with "negligence of justice" for failing to prosecute anyone who had beaten and killed Cabassol's employees. On 27 May the judges promulgated a twelve-page *arrêt* releasing nearly all sixteen defendants from Mérindol who had been accused by Cabassol. After his character and religious behavior were checked on 20 August, the man carrying the forbidden books was released with a warning on 7 October.

36. The remarkably slow-moving trial of Barthelemy Odoin, originally sentenced to be burned for heresy at Forcalquier in January 1554, reappeared in ADBR, B 5455 (23/10 and 23/11/1556); B 5456 (18/6, 5/10, and 3/12/1557). We do not know Odoin's fate, because B 5457 is unreadable until mid-September 1558.

37. The sentence of Benoit Romyen, a *mercier* reportedly executed at Draguignan in June 1557 (Crespin, II, 529–531), cannot be found among the fairly well-preserved *arrêts* in ADBR, B 5456.

38. ADBR, B 5455 (12/12/1556); B 5456 (8/4/1557). De Badet was his rapporteur.

39. ADI, B 2030, fols. 32–32v (29/11/1559). However, Godard was not released from prison until September 1560; B 2031, fol. 45.

40. On Pierre Girard, see ADI, B 2029, fols. 426–426v (9/1/1559), for his condemnation; B 2030, fol. 11v (5/11/1559), for registration of his pardon of June 1559. His letter to Calvin is in Geneva's Bibliothèque Publique et Universitaire, Ms. 196, fol. 152.

41. A local magistrate, who helped investigate a runaway nun in 1556, complained of stones thrown against his house (these episodes are succinctly noted by Crouzet, *Genèse,* p. 383). The seneschal of Montélimar, Felix Bourjac, was a notorious Protestant.

42. ADSM, 1B 3142 (22/12/1554).

43. Ibid. (7/1/1555). For Sainte-Marthe's later career on the bench, see B. Robert in *BSHPF* 85 (1936), 388 n. 1.

44. ADBR, B 5458 (15/2, 17/3, 12/4, and 20/4/1559); compare B 5461 (29/1/1570). The edict, barred out after the war ended later in 1570 but still legible, followed indictments against more than eighty prominent rebels in September 1569, about one-fourth of whom came from Forcalquier.

45. Haton, I, 80–81.

46. For example, see Crespin, II, 37 (rescued between Lyon and Paris in 1553), 478 (rescued between Tulle and Bordeaux in 1554), 664 (rescued between Paris and Poitiers in 1557). Only the last case appears in parlementary *arrêts,* because this prisoner was under parlementary jurisdiction when he was rescued.

47. On Balon's escape, see AN, X2a 119 (30/3 and 22/4/1557). See also AN, X2b 18 (7/8/1557): the "rescued" priest had died in the meantime. See Balon's final sentence in X2a 123 (16/6/1559); also X2a 124 (30/8/1559) on the *conducteur,* cleared of complicity in the escape by Balon's testimony under torture before he died.

48. On Cavalis's rescue, see ADBR, B 5458 (17/2/1559).

49. ADSM, 1B 3149 (6/5, 12/5, and 30/5/1559. One day later the Rouen Parlement upheld a death sentence passed at Vire for infanticide.

50. AN, X2a 123 (1/7/1559); X2a 124 (24/9 and 27/9/1559); X2b 22 (9/4/1560).

51. AN, X2 123 (7/8 and 31/8/1559).

52. Ibid. (13/9 and 26/9/1559).

53. AN, X2a 125 (5/12 and 18/12/1559).

54. On prisoners charged with participating in this rescue, see ibid. (2/1, 4/1, and 5/1/1560); on Boisson, see ibid. (6/1 and 5/2/1560).

55. Crespin, II, 674; on Dupont, see ibid. (19/3/1560) and AN X2a 124 (5/9/1559), for his arrest warrant.

56. ADSM, 1B 3151 (29/1, 30/1, 8/2, 13/3, and 19/3/1560). A Protestant diarist records that "a man from Bayeux" [*sic*] was rescued by "gens de son oppinion" but recaptured later the same day. He was burned the next day with 400 to 500 armed men present; see [Jean Berthelin], "Journal d'un bourgeois de Rouen . . . depuis l'an 1545 jusques à l'an 1564," *Revue retrospective normande,* 1837, p. 7.

57. Best introduction by N. Weiss in *BSHPF* 65 (1916), 195–235.

58. Normally its criminal *arrêts* at this period were collected into huge registers covering six-month periods. Those for the second half of 1557 and the first half of 1558 are missing (gap between X2a 119 and X2a 121). Afterward, except for October 1559, they remain unbroken until the out-

break of religious warfare. The *minutes d'arrêts* (X2b) usually fill in most of such gaps, but X2b 18 contains virtually no *minutes* after August 1557, X2b 19 is misdated (it actually covers January–March 1559, duplicating part of register X2a 122), and X2b 20 includes only *minutes* from April 1558. Thus our internal parlementary sources stop abruptly when the "affair" occurred (4/9/1557) and resume after March 1558, when almost all these prisoners had been officially judged.

59. Crespin, II, 651–683, reproduced Chandieu's pamphlet almost verbatim in its 1564 edition, as did the *HE*. See also the brief account by Diefendorf, pp. 51–52.

60. At Coligny's request, Catherine de Médicis restored the sizable estate of Philippa de Luns to her mother for the benefit of her children in January 1561; Paul Bondois in *BSHPF* 73 (1924), 118–120.

61. Quotation from Crespin, II, 582.

62. Ibid., pp. 582–583.

63. AN, X2b 18 (31/12/1557).

64. Crespin, II, 590–604; compare the *arrêt* in X2a 121 (1/7/1558).

65. Although Weiss' fine study of the Rue St.-Jacques affair (p. 229) claims not to know what became of one of the final two prisoners remaining by June 1558, "Meric Favre" is surely the "Méry Faulx" of Séguier's famous *arrêt*.

66. AN, X2a 121 (7/4/1559); compare the *plumitif* in X2a 917. Two years later, Geneva's Bourse Française still identified Nicolas Campin as "one of the four prisoners who were released in Paris by decree"; Olson, p. 232 n. 24.

67. Quotation from Crespin, II, 647.

68. Ibid., II, 646–648; AN, X2a 122 (26-4-1559).

69. ADG, 1B 197–210, covers all of 1559. President Roffignac signed death sentences for heresy on 31 May, 14 June (against the corpse of a heretic who died after confessing under torture), 28 June, and 6 July, plus two death sentences for blasphemy against the Virgin Mary on 6 July; 1B 202–203. Compare Crespin, II, 661, 706–708.

70. ADSM, 1B 3150 (19/7 and 2/8/1559).

71. ADSM, 1B 5488, dossier A. He probably prosecuted François Le Monnier at Valonges (Cotentin) and brought him to Rouen, where the Parlement finally ordered him executed in January 1560. For Francis II's orders, see 1B 3150 (16/9/1559).

72. ADSM, 1B 3150 (3/10 and 3/11/1559); 1B 3151 (20/11/1559).

73. For this execution, see ADHG, B 3428 (6/12/1559). B 3424–28 covers all of 1559 except January and shows sixteen of eighteen prisoners released. At Aix, ADBR B 5458 shows ten of twelve prisoners released in 1559. At Grenoble, ADI B 2029–30 reveals fourteen of nineteen heresy prisoners

released in 1559; none was sentenced to the galleys, and only three were banished.

74. The classic version remains Lucien Romier, *Le royaume de Catherine de Médicis. La France à la veille des guerres de religion,* 2 vols. (Paris, 1925). For the impact on the Paris Parlement, see Roelker, pp. 238–243.

75. The Parlement's *arrêts* for October are missing, but La Roche Chandieu lists five executions carried out on October 23–26. However, he omits the executions of Nicolas Collot (executed at Pons-sur-Seine on 12/7, the last heretic burned outside the city of Paris) and Nicolas Moret (condemned 29/7, but not executed until 31/8); in September Chandieu missed the execution of Pierre Richard (13/9). The *arrêts* do not contain the death sentence of Jean Judet at the very end of 1559, but they do confirm on 20 January that he had recently been executed. Finally, Chandieu places Pierre Arondeau's execution on 15 November, but the *arrêts* date it 6 January.

76. AN, X2a 125 (2/12/1559). Antoine Richard's property had been managed for him by the same cousin since early August; X2a 124 (9/8/1559). This ruling was signed by President Le Maistre.

77. See AN, X2a 125 (5/1 and 12/1/1560) for Séguier's decisions. For Le Maistre's ruling, see ibid. (15/1: same defendant recently banished for singing Marot's Psalms in public; compare X2a 123 on 12/7/1559).

78. See Matthieu Lelièvre in *BSHPF* 37 (1888), 281–295, 337–359, 506–529. Quotation from Crespin, II, 688.

79. On Robert Stuart, see Brulart (a *conseillier-clerc* at the Paris Parlement), pp. 4–5; and de Thou, II, 402–405, 504. On his horses, see AN, X2a 125 (15/3 and 7/4/1560): after both of them had been sold on 20 March, innkeeper Michel Fallaise asked six sous per day per horse for his expenses, which the court reduced to four.

80. See AN, X2a 125 (4/1/1560): on 14 October; the Parlement had used du Bourg's wages to pay 148 livres of his prison expenses; an additional bill of 72 livres for his final eighteen days included food and wages for a servant and special guards appointed by Parlement.

81. Quotation from Crespin, II, 696.

82. ADHG, B 3430 (10/4/1560). For Massip's previous arrest in 1554, see Mentzer, p. 82 and n. 5.

83. ADSM, 1B 3151 (27/3/1560); compare Berthelin, "Journal," p. 7.

84. On their reinstatements, see de Thou, II, 701–704; Maugis, II, 10.

85. The pardon was printed on 11 March; see *Edict du Roy, contenant la grace et pardon pour ceux qui par cy devant ont mal senty de la Foy* (Paris: Vincent Serrenas and Jean Dallier, 1559), copy at Newberry Library, Case F 39/.326/1560 fe. Brulart, pp. 9–11, reproduced it. A second "Edict of Am-

boise" (also copied by Brulart, pp. 11–14) followed on 17 March, urging arbitrary punishment against conspirators who failed to disperse immediately; Catherine's name is again evoked in connection with the previous pardon.

86. *HE*, I, 303.

87. ADG, 1B 212, no. 442. The commissioner who had made these arrests at Bergerac was paid in full four days before the court registered Catherine's pardon; 1B 212, no. 268 (18/3/1560).

88. Crespin, II, 762.

89. Compare ADHG, B 53, fol. 573 (8/6/1560), with B 3430–32 (*arrêts* from June–November 1560), showing heresy cases reappearing on 1/10, 7/10, 22/10, and 29/10/1560.

90. Quotation from Brulart, p. 9.

91. AN, X2a 125 (27/5: four cases, only one appealing a death sentence; 29/5: three cases; 31/5: two cases).

92. In December 1560 the Parlement of Toulouse sent François Bonnemort to the galleys for ten years for "excès et hérésie"; ADHG, B 3433 (14/12/1560).

93. Crespin, III, 70.

94. *HE*, I, 295.

95. Heller, pp. 226–233; compare Crespin, II, 763–764, and de Thou, III, 543–548.

7. Martyrology and Jurisprudence

Epigraph: Simon Goulart, preface to 1597 edition of Crespin, I, xxvi.

1. Although there is a sizable bibliography on Protestant martyrologies, Brad Gregory has made the first systematic attempt to compare Rabus' German martyrology (Strasbourg, 1554–1558) and Foxe's first Latin edition (Basel, 1554)—both containing extremely few sixteenth-century martyrs—with Crespin's first edition (Geneva, 1554).

2. This section agrees with several assertions made recently by David El Kenz in *BSHPF* 141 (1995), 27–69, such as: "Hagiography of the 1550s should not be reduced to mere counter-propaganda; it is also a discourse of confessionalization of the new church" (p. 60). Unfortunately, El Kenz, like his predecessors, remains unaware of how Crespin's discourse fitted with judicial practices in Valois France.

3. David Nicholls, "The Theatre of Martyrdom in the French Reformation," *Past and Present*, no. 121 (November 1988), 49–73, offers a valuable introduction to the assumptions underlying heresy executions in Reforma-

tion France; but apart from a brief consideration of how to read evidence about the ceremony of degradation (pp. 57–58), he often conflates evidence from Crespin with parlementary sources and thus obscures their diametric opposition. However, because Nicholls attempts to understand the judges' reasoning, his approach is preferable to those that isolate Crespin from French judicial practice. The optimal perspective is to distinguish Crespin's methods from those of the judges, and then to employ each form of "narrative" to illuminate its opposite.

4. Crespin's 1554 preface is conveniently reprinted in I, xxxiii–xxxv.
5. For a good example, see R. A. Mentzer, "Calvinist Propaganda and the Parlement of Toulouse," *ARG* 68 (1977), 268–283.
6. Crespin, I, 341–342 (Denis Brion).
7. For example, Crespin placed the execution of Marie Bécaudelle, alias Gabarite, in 1534, although she actually died in September 1544; see Nathaniel Weiss in *BSHPF* 44 (1895), 449.
8. See the case of Guillaume Huchon, an apothecary from Blois deeply involved with the seditious 1534 placards, or that of Louis de Rochette, the "liberal" inquisitor of Languedoc who was himself burned for heresy (both described in Chapter 3).
9. Nicholls, "Theatre of Martyrdom," makes this point well.
10. AN, X2a 130 (17/11/1562). The prisoner admitted taking communion at a Reformed service.
11. ADBR, B 5448 (9/1, 19/1, 21/2, and 23/2/1545).
12. Ibid. (20/11/1545).
13. Metivier, I, 341.
14. Figures drawn from Patry, supplemented by ADG for the final nine months of 1559.
15. The Parlement of Toulouse punished a German law student, Hector von Vollrath, with relative severity because he owned books with "writing in his own hand containing heretical and scandalous propositions"; ADHG, B 3400 (14/4/1553).
16. AN, X2a 913 (27/7 and 19/8/1556); see also X2a 120, fols. 83v–84, 186v–187 (21/7 and 20/8/1556).
17. AN, X2a 913 (31/8/1556), confirmed by X2a 120, fols. 208–208v (1/9/1556).
18. Mentzer, pp. 113 and nn. 5–6, 114 and n. 10.
19. ADSM, 1B 3031 (25/5/1547).
20. AN, X2a 100 (22/12/1545).
21. Patry, pp. 23–24 (9/9/1542), 195–196 (21/8/1554), 243 (25/6/1557), 270 (15/7/1558).
22. ADHG, B 3366 (10/4/1542) and B3367 (18/8/1542). The principal defen-

dants were her majordomo, an ex-Celestine monk now become a Benedictine, and his brother, both charged with *lèse-majesté divine et humaine*. The prioress protected them and herself with exemplary skill.

23. ADHG, B 3398 (30/7/1552, concerning a "scandal" at Annonay convent in May 1551); B 3407 (15/2/1555); B 3408 (24/5/1555).

24. ADHG, B 3398 (30/7/1552) and B 3410 (5/9/1555).

25. AN, X2a 118 (2/5/1556). She had been convicted 24/9/1554; her counter-charges were investigated in April 1555; her local curé made more accusations against her in March 1556. President de Thou dismissed all charges against her and summoned her judge to Paris for questioning.

26. Patry, p. 106 (11/1/1552); ADG, 1B 202, no. 235 (17/6/1559).

27. ADHG, B 3368 (17/3/1543); other instances in B 3383 (27/6/1548); B 3394 (18/3/1552); and B 3405 (24/10/1554).

28. ADHG, B 3405 (12/9/1554).

29. AN, X2a 93 (11/7/1542: a prostitute); X2a 94 (16/12/1542); X2a 94 (15/2/1543); X2a 95 (9/6/1543); X2a 96, fols. 189v–190v (17/12/1543: banished for one year); and X2a 97 (27/11/1544: banished perpetually).

30. AN, X2a 93 (12/5/1542); X2a 94 (26/1/1543); X2a 96, fols. 291v–292, 486v–487, 540v–541v (8/1, 20/2, and 3/3/1544); and X2a 97 (20/11/1544). The last two were sentenced together with their husbands.

31. AN, X2a 114, fols. 204–204v (1/7/1553), 419–419v (29/8/1553: death sentence reduced); X2a 117, fols. 287v–288 (25/9/1555). After the Parlement found that this last defendant suffered from "perturbation et alienation d'esprit," they sent a note to her preacher explaining why she had got off so lightly.

32. AN, X2a 118 (19/5/1556).

33. AN, X2a 97 (11/3/1545). The royal prosecutor appealed *a minima* after the *bailli* of Chartres had merely fined and briefly banished both men for their insolence. The Paris Parlement also raised the family's fine to 600 livres.

34. List printed in *BSHPF* 142 (1996), 218–222; Crespin omitted nos. 55, 70, 134, and 145.

35. ADHG, B 3378 (14/10/1546) and B 3380 (10/3/1547).

36. Best introduction by Herbert M. Bower, *The Fourteen of Meaux* (London, 1894), which used local Catholic chronicles of Meaux.

37. Crespin, I, 500; Bibliothèque Municipale, Meaux, Ms. 86, pp. 382–383.

38. Bibliothèque Municipale, Meaux, Ms. 87, pp. 19–20 (6/7/1559).

39. AN, X2a 102 (22/12/1546).

40. It became a three-page pamphlet, *Arrest notable donné le 4 octobre . . . contre grand nombre d'Heretiques et blasphemateurs, du grand marché de Meaulx* (Paris, 1546), the only antiheresy ruling ever published; see Fran-

cis Higman, *Piety and the People: Religious Printing in French, 1511–1551* (Aldershot, 1996), p. 50.

41. On the destruction of the Protestant *cénacle* at Langres, see Weiss, *CA*, nos. 101 and 119.

42. AN, X2a 117, fols. 140v–143 (7/8/1555).

43. ADS, B 60, fols. 38–39 (2/6/1557).

44. For example, a Norman nobleman was burned in effigy in 1548, "actendu qu'il est à present fugitif"; ADSM, 1B 3135 (4/10/1548: Louis Flambart, *seigneur* de Villiers, whose arrest had been ordered in June 1547). He became one of the earliest wealthy Protestants to claim official resident status in Geneva, on 27/11/1547; Henri Meylan, *D'Erasme à Théodore de Bèze* (Geneva, 1976), p. 95. Flambart's confiscated property was awarded to a courtier in May 1549 (*Catalogue des Actes d'Henri II*, 3 vols. to date [Paris, 1987–], III, 210–211); he was reconfirmed as a Genevan *habitant* in August 1551.

45. For examples of confiscated assets from heretics awarded to courtiers, see *Catalogue des Actes d'Henri II*, II, 98 (2/1548), 267 (6/1548), 310 (27/7/1548); vol. III, 100, 124 (2/1549), 175, 244 (6/1549).

46. These interrogations are in ADSM 1B 3004, the only register of sixteenth-century *plumitifs* surviving outside Paris. It begins in April 1552 and, with gaps, runs to the early summer of 1553. During this period our only surviving *arrêts* from Rouen's parlement (1B 3141) fall between September 1552 and January 1553.

47. ADSM, 1B 3140 (8/4/1552).

48. ADSM, 1B 3004 (26/4/1552).

49. See ADSM, 1B 3135 (15/10/1548), for Fouquet Thorel's first condemnation.

50. ADSM, 1B 3141 (16/1/1553). Hyllard performed an *amende honorable* at the cathedral, had his tongue cut out, and "smelled the fire" before being strangled.

51. ADSM, 1B 3141 (19/1/1553). Le Roy had originally been condemned to an *amende honorable* and eight days of fasting for his remarks about pilgrimages, but the prosecutor had appealed the sentence *a minima*. Since Le Roy was ultimately released, the state had to pay his prison costs.

52. Crespin, II, 65–68.

53. I wish to thank Andrew Pettegree for pointing out that this "miracle" was added by Simon Goulart, who was far more interested than Crespin in the miraculous.

54. AN, X2a 911. Compare the *arrêt* in X2a 116, fols. 162–63v.

55. Compare ADSM, 1B 3004 (15/5 and 17/5/1553), with Crespin, II, 13–25. Néel's *plumitif* reveals that his death sentence with *torture préalable* was

upheld by a single vote, whereas Crespin offers a lengthy summary of the former monk's interrogations before his episcopal judge and describes his defrocking in detail.

56. On Ponthieu, see AN, X2a 913 (*plumitifs* of 11, 15, and 18/8/1556); X2a 120 (*arrêt* of 18/8/1556); on Michel Pol, see ADSM, 1B 3004.

57. See Crespin, II, 590–604.

58. Ibid., pp. 593, 594–595.

59. Ibid., p. 603. Guerin's lengthy *arrêt* in X2a 121 (1/7/1558) confirms that he had been handed to the episcopal judge of Paris in December 1557 and had appealed his sentence to perform an *amende honorable* in March 1558.

60. Reprinted by Crespin, II, 644–645.

61. Ibid., pp. 697–698.

62. Brulart, p. 7.

63. Florimond de Raemond, *L'histoire de la naissance, progrèz, et décadence de l'hérésie de ce siècle* (Bordeaux, 1625), p. 863.

64. ADG, 1B 182, no. 247 (22/8/1562); 1B 183, no. 116 (7/9/1562: the Huguenot commander headed the list). Earlier effigy condemnations were not unknown: see Patry, pp. 111, 113 (10/5 and 1/6/1552), 207–208 (22/3/1555: two women), or 240 (23/8/1558), but only twice do we find payments recorded for making their effigies.

65. Crespin, III, 353.

66. Diefendorf, p. 174.

67. AN, X2a 934 (*plumitifs* of 1/12 and 31/12/1569). Even Richard Gastines was questioned closely about whether he had taken Protestant communion, but was never asked about his eucharistic doctrine; X2a 933 (23/6/1569).

68. See AN, X2a 956 (*plumitifs*, 1588–1590).

69. Ibid. (27/6 and 28/6/1588).

70. Ibid. (6/5/1589).

8. From Heresy to Sedition

Epigraph: Simon Goulart in the 1582 edition of Crespin, III, 640.

1. Janine Garrisson, *Les Protestants au XVIe siècle* (Paris, 1988), pp. 250, 253–254, emphasizes the strength and secrecy of these arrangements.

2. Brulart, p. 29.

3. On the unraveling of the legal system at Rouen during the summer of 1560, see Floquet, II, 310–336; compare E. Le Paquier in *BSHPF* 69 (1920), 209–226, and 70 (1921), 26–40.

4. An outstanding recent work about French moderates who mediated between religious factions in the early 1560s concentrates on theological issues: Mario Turchetti, *Concordia o tolleranza? du Moulin ed i "moyenneurs"* (Geneva, 1986).

5. Nicola Sutherland, *The Huguenot Struggle for Recognition* (London, 1980), pp. 101–133, 349–354, summarizes changes in royal legislation from May 1560 until April 1562.

6. Quotations from Brulart, pp. 29, 46–47.

7. Haton, I, 150–151.

8. Natalie Z. Davis' classic article "The Rites of Violence," first published in 1973, was revised in her *Society and Culture in Early Modern France* (Stanford, 1975), pp. 152–187; Denis Crouzet, *Les guerriers de Dieu,* 2 vols. (Paris, 1990), I, chaps. 5–10, offers a much more elaborate approach to many of the same themes. Neither author situates these extrajudicial activities within the context of the breakdown of the French judicial system.

9. De Thou, IV, 67–68. Compare Brulart, p. 27, who noted both that the bishop "was in great danger" and that the priest's body was burned at the town market by "common people." The assassinated priest does not appear in Crespin, who does note (III, 212, 213) that Catholic rioters twice singed corpses of their Huguenot victims in Languedoc in November 1561, once through a professional executioner.

10. De Thou, IV, 67, 68.

11. Crespin, III, 80.

12. See Floquet, II, 339–340, 369–370.

13. Compare Crespin, III, 194–219, with Brulart, pp. 60, 71.

14. *HE,* II, 826.

15. De Thou, IV, 131–133, reprints the Huguenot justification; see also Diefendorf, pp. 61–63.

16. On the Edict of January, compare Brulart, p. 70, with de Thou, IV, 152–161, glorifying the policies of Chancellor L'Hôpital. See also Roelker, pp. 264–270, on the painful process by which this edict was finally ratified at Paris.

17. La Fosse, p. 54, agrees closely with Brulart, pp. 89, 91, 94.

18. La Fosse, pp. 105, 107, 219.

19. See ADG, 1B 246–248, esp. 1B 247, no. 247 (22/8/1562).

20. Crespin, III, 350.

21. La Faille, II, 239.

22. For the total number of suspects, see Joan Davies, "Persecution and Protestantism: Toulouse 1562–1575," *Historical Journal* 22 (1979), 31–51. The fullest list of executions, including every notable and a few Catholics,

can be found in *HE*, III, 38–44. Copying it, Crespin (III, 351–354) under-lined incidents that recalled traditional heresy executions. The Parle-ment's criminal *arrêts* (ADHG, B 3440–42) include only about forty exe-cutions for sedition between 20 May and 27 October, but every name matches someone found in Protestant sources.

23. Mentzer, pp. 122, 142. The city of Toulouse had provided almost 150 of these previous suspects, approximately one-seventh of the total and more than twice as many as the second town of residence, Nîmes (p. 144).

24. Crespin, III, 354. This "Jean le Page" could be "Jean Faguelin," hanged alongside two other men whom Crespin identified correctly; see ADHG, B 3441 (29/8/1562).

25. Although Crespin (III, 353) claimed that "the minister of Mazeres was burned alive" at Toulouse in late June, he cannot be found in these *arrêts*. Another priest, Bernard Castilhon, rector of Asté in Bigorre, whom the Parlement ordered burned for heresy, is not included here; see Charles Durier, *Les Huguenots en Bigorre* (Paris and Auch, 1884), pp. 87–91, confirmed by ADHG, B 3441 (26/8/1562).

26. Raymonde Gelu's official sentence in ADHG, B 3441 (29/8/1562), in-cludes the stipulation that she perform an *amende honorable* beforehand.

27. See Jean-François Le Nail, "Procédures contre des sorcières de Seix en 1562," *Bulletin de la Société Ariégoise des Sciences, Lettres et Arts*, 1976, pp. 155–232. Compare ADHG, B 3440 (3/7/1562); B 3441 (18/9/1562); B 3442 (1/10 and 30/10/1562); B 3443 (17/12, 19/12 and 24/12/1562 and 11/1/1563); and B 3444 (16/2/1563).

28. On the number of judges suspended, see La Faille, II, 240; compare his *Preuves*, pp. 45–47, on the size of the court in 1559.

29. See Pierre de Paschal, *Journal de ce que s'est passée en France durant l'année 1562*, ed. M. François (Paris, 1950), pp. 40, 82; and *HE*, III, 465–466.

30. *HE*, III, 484.

31. Brulart, p. 85. The letter of 7 May is reported somewhat differently by the royal historiographer Paschal (*Journal*, p. 35) as signed by "ceux qui sou-loint tenir et ne tiennent plus vostre cour de Parlement de Rouen."

32. See E. Le Paquier in *BSHPF* 62 (1912), 27–44. After a twelve-day gap, only one routine civil *arrêt*, signed by de Civile, a noted Protestant sympa-thizer, survives from 2 May at the end of one register. The next preserved register, from the Parlement of Louviers, runs from 12 August to 27 October; many of its pages are filled by its notorious *arrêt* of 26 August 1562.

33. Floquet, II, pp. 398–402, 424–430; de Thou, IV, 236.

34. Floquet, II, 431–449; see also *Mémoires de Condé*, ed. J.-D. Secousse, 4 vols. (London, 1732–1734), IV, 59–60, on executions carried out by the

Parlement of Louviers. *HE*, III, 764–768, prints some of the interrogations and the official sentences against d'Emandreville (who had been a parlementary judge since 1544 and was then president of the Cour des Aides) and the three others, all "convaincus de crime de lese-majesté en tous les chefs."

35. See Paschal, *Journal*, pp. 39–40.

36. De Thou, IV, 290, 452–455, 502–505.

37. Ibid., pp. 196, 288; quotation from Crespin, III, 300. Bèze, the most prominent Huguenot theologian in France, was deeply embarrassed by iconoclastic excesses and the desecration of tombs; see his *Correspondance*, ed. Meylan and Dufour, IV (Geneva, 1964), 91 (letter of 23/5/1562 to Jeanne d'Albret). In general, see the illuminating study of this problem by Olivier Christin, *Une révolution symbolique. L'iconoclasme huguenot et la reconstruction catholique* (Paris, 1991).

38. De Thou, IV, 436–437; the *arrêts* condemning them were printed in *HE*, II, 231–232. Brulart, p. 100, noted the hanging of his colleague, whom he further identified as the brother-in-law of a president, but said nothing about the abbot. For the priest's public execution on 31 July, compare the brief notice in *HE*, II, 147–148, with Haton, I, 251–253.

39. See *HE*, III, 367. On Felix Bourjac, who had held the office of seneschal at Montélimar since 1550, see above, Chapter 6, note 41.

40. De Thou, IV, 451–452, refrains from labeling it "sedition."

41. Ibid., pp. 496–497. *HE*, III, 60–65, printed this subversive document in full.

42. For the Paris Parlement in 1562–1563, see Linda Taber, "Religious Dissent within the Parlement of Paris in the Mid-Sixteenth Century: A Reassessment," *French Historical Studies* 16 (1990), 687–699.

43. De Thou, IV, 221, 270.

44. Compare Brulart, p. 91, with Paschal, *Journal*, pp. 74, 80.

45. Brulart, pp. 94, 95; Paschal, *Journal*, pp. 89–90; compare De Thou, IV, 133.

46. Paschal, *Journal*, pp. 88, 98. The *plumitifs* of the Paris Parlement for 10 September–10 November, 1562 (AN, X2a 924, supplemented by the *minutes d'arrêts* in X2b 34) were published by Paul Guérin in *Mémoires de la Société pour l'histoire de Paris et de l'Ile-de-France* 40 (1913), 1–116.

47. On the execution of Jean Goujon at Senlis in December 1562, see Crespin, III, 269.

48. De Thou, IV, p. 496 (quotation); compare 532–533 on the privy council *arrêt* of 18/6/1563.

49. Ibid., pp. 548–552 and 552–556, on the protests of the Paris Parlement, which were promptly quashed; see also Roelker, pp. 294–298.

50. See ADBR, B 3653 (Registres secrets, 1564–1570). As at Bordeaux in 1548, interim judges were named, headed by a president of the Paris Parlement; the suspended judges of Aix were reinstated individually through decrees of the Parlement of Grenoble in 1565 and 1566.
51. Roelker, pp. 289–290, 293–294.
52. Crespin, III, 653–654; de Thou, V, 609–610.
53. See Janine Garrisson-Estèbe, *Protestants du Midi 1559–1598* (Paris, 1969), pp. 165–166; and Judith P. Meyer, *Reformation in La Rochelle* (Geneva, 1996), p. 103.
54. Crespin, III, 646–649; compare de Thou, IV, 538–539. Brulart, pp. 165–166, believed that 120 Catholics had been slaughtered at Pamiers, "not counting the clergy."
55. See Crespin, III, 650; and de Thou, V, 417.
56. ADHG, B 3460 (1/10/1568).
57. Ibid. (8/10 and 14/10/1568); Davies, "Persecution and Protestantism," pp. 39 n. 28, 44–45, did not realize that some of the ten death sentences were commuted.
58. ADHG, B 3460 (6/10 and 27/10/1568); B 3461 (23/12/1568).
59. For the burned corpses, see ADHG, B 3460 (22/10/1568); B 3462 (28/3/1569): B 3464 (19/11 and 22/11/1569).
60. La Faille, II, 291; reinstated in autumn 1570, half of these Huguenot judges were massacred in 1572.
61. De Thou, V, 520–521, 533–535; compare Brulart, pp. 185–187, 190, 196–197.
62. On Protestant prisoners from January and March 1569, see N. Weiss in *BSHPF* 50 (1901), 617–653, and 72 (1923), 86–97; compare Jacqueline Boucher, "Les incarcérations à la Conciergerie de Paris pour fait de religion, 1567–1570," in *Les Réformes: Enracinement socio-culturel*, ed. B. Chevalier and R. Sauzet (Tours, 1982), pp. 309–319.
63. On Pierre Hamon, compare N. Weiss in *BSHPF* 50 (1901), 649; Haton, II, 568–570; and Crespin, III, 654–655.
64. Diefendorf, pp. 167, 174 (quotation), 235 n. 88. De Thou (VI, 272–273) discussed these events only because of their consequences in 1571, obviously somewhat embarrassed by the action of a parlement then headed by his father; compare La Fosse, p. 107.
65. Brulart, p. 205.
66. See N. Weiss in *BSHPF* 72 (1923), 90 (two pedagogues hanged 10/11/1569), 92 (a *chantre* hanged 10/2/1570). Five Huguenot intellectuals were executed, along with three merchants and a judge—a tiny fraction of the 555 recorded Huguenot prisoners.
67. See Crespin, III, 656–657, esp. 657 n. 1; quotation from Brulart, p. 205.

68. Brulart, pp. 207–209, 211; de Thou, V, 626, notes that this judgment was translated into Latin, German, Italian, Spanish, and English.

69. Floquet, II, 36–41, 59–74.

70. Ibid., pp. 44–57; de Thou, V, 566–567. See sentences in ADSM, 1B 3164, including two Protestant ministers (26/2 and 17/3/1569) and a renegade priest (21/5/1569).

71. Both lists printed in *Archives historique de la Gironde* 13 (1871–72), pp. 399–420 (6/4/1569) and 429–446 (6/3/1570).

72. See ADG, 1B 318, no. 130: although Valier's "execution" cost twenty-two livres, the court finally paid only twenty (18/2/1569). Valier had previously been condemned to death for *lèse-majesté* during the second war; 1B 308, no. 188 (24/3/1568).

73. ADG, 1B 320, nos. 78–79, 120, 126 (executions on 16/4 and 23/4/1569); also 1B 328, no. 120 (a regent executed 20/12/1569).

74. ADG, 1B 328, nos. 176, 185 (both 31/12/1569); 1B 333, nos. 28, 44, 167 (5/5 and 23/5/1570); 1B 330 (11/7/1570: petition of four captured judges, copying written threats in February 1570 to drown one of them unless installments of ransom money arrive promptly); 1B 332, nos. 1bis, 81 (1/9 and 9/9/1570); 1B 333, no. 220 (25/10/1570). Not until November 1570 were the documents captured on both sides returned; 1B 334, no. 43.

75. See esp. articles 32 and 33 of the Peace of St. Germain, printed by A. Stegmann, *Edits des guerres de religion* (Paris, 1979), pp. 76–77.

76. Diefendorf, pp. 108–110.

77. De Thou, V, 535.

78. Floquet, III, 78–85. Four of the five Huguenot judges restored in 1570 were again expelled after the St. Bartholomew's massacre, on 7 October 1572 (ibid., p. 141).

79. See Diefendorf, pp. 83–88.

80. De Thou, VI, 433.

81. Major recent contributions to the study of the St. Bartholomew's massacre at Paris have come from J.-L. Bourgeon, *L'assassinat de Coligny* (Geneva, 1992) and *Charles IX devant la Saint-Barthélemy* (Geneva, 1995); and from Denis Crouzet, *La nuit de la Saint-Barthélemy* (Paris, 1994); but they may have added more heat than light to the question. I remain comfortable with the brief approach in Diefendorf, pp. 93–106, 168–177, who argues (p. 98) that it was an "unplanned—but not unforeseeable—explosion of hatred and fear touched off by the events surrounding the attempt to kill Coligny. In the end, the best explanantion for these events is the simplest one."

82. De Thou, VI, 418–420, provides the most important though self-serving

account of the 26 August *lit de justice*. Compare the critique of J.-L. Bourgeon, "La fronde parlementaire à la veille de la Saint-Barthélemy," *Bibliothèque de l'Ecole des Chartes* 148 (1990), 17–88, who misreads AN, X1a 1637, in isolation in order to make an unconvincing case for a parlementary conspiracy lurking behind the massacre of 24 August.

83. De Thou, VI, 459–461. Neither man was included in Goulart's martyrology, although de Thou, an eyewitness, tells us that the ex-judge died with courage and Protestant piety.

84. Ibid., pp. 399–400; Haton, II, 680–681, 704–706.

85. Diefendorf, pp. 107, 169, 233 n. 66 (quotation).

86. See Crespin, III, 719–733; de Thou, VI, 429–430, 468–469; J. Roman in *BSHPF* 35 (1886), 352–364; Floquet, III, 122–133, 141.

87. J. H. M. Salmon, *Society in Crisis: France in the Sixteenth Century* (London, 1975), p. 196.

88. Detailed analysis by Roelker, pp. 331–401.

89. Pierre de l'Estoile, *Mémoires-Journaux,* 12 vols. (Paris, 1875–1896), III, 120–121, 165, 166 (quotation); compare Crespin, III, 826–828, and La Fosse, p. 219.

90. Compare La Fosse, p. 219, and l'Estoile, III, 171–172. Records of the Parlement's Conciergerie indicate that this vagabond, Jean Guitel, was appealing his condemnation for banishment; Archives de la Préfecture de Police, Paris (herafter APP), Ab 10, fol. 180v (2/6/1589).

91. APP, Ab 10, fols. 172v (2/5/1588), 183v (22/6/1588), 187 (4/7/1588: Bernard Palissy, "soy disant Inventeur des Rusticques de la Royne Mere"; and a widow), 194v (23/7/1588, permitted to abjure on 28/9). For the women victims in 1589, see fols. 245v (arrived 30/3/1589, hanged on 21/6) and 247 (arrived 12/4/1589, burned 6/5). L'Estoile (III, 286) confirms that "a poor Huguenot woman, who . . . died firm and constant in her religion," was burned alive at the Place de Grève that day. Palissy perished in the Bastille in December 1590; l'Estoile, IV, 67.

92. ADSM, 1B 3212 (27/5/1588: caught with a small manuscript containing "blasphemies" against Catholicism). Two men and a woman, arrested with him, watched his execution before being whipped and banished.

93. ADSM, 1B 3215 (9/1, 10/2, 26/6, and 3/10/1589). For death sentences reduced in 1589, see ibid. (9/3, 23/3, and 18/5); compare Floquet, III, 340 nn. 2–3.

94. Floquet, III, 332–335, 342–343.

95. L'Estoile, III, 234–237; compare de Thou (who was in hiding that day, while his uncle was imprisoned in the Bastille), X, 512–516.

96. De Thou, X, 563–572; XI, 22, 40–43. The records of this royalist rump Parlement, dissolved by the *ligueurs* early in 1591, are at ADHG, B 92 b–c.

Its dispersed remnants ultimately reassembled at Béziers in 1594 (its *ar-rêts* are B 92 d). After Henry IV's conversion to Catholicism, another major schism at Toulouse created a third Parlement of Languedoc at Castelsarrasin (its *arrêts* are B 92 e–g). Not until April 1596 did a single Parlement, incorporating all three, reopen in Toulouse.

97. On loyal First Presidents, see de Thou, X, 552 (Rouen), 559 (Rennes), 561 (Bordeaux); on the Parlement of Tours, see Maugis, II, 136–178. Few *arrêts* of these temporary parlements have been preserved. An exception is ADSM, 1B 5719–29, which permits us to see how the authority of the royalist Parlement of Caen was gradually extended over much of Normandy.

98. De Thou, XI, 54 (Paris), 21–22 (Bordeaux).

99. L'Estoile, V, 44–45, 124–125, 128–129; de Thou, XI, 440–444.

INDEX